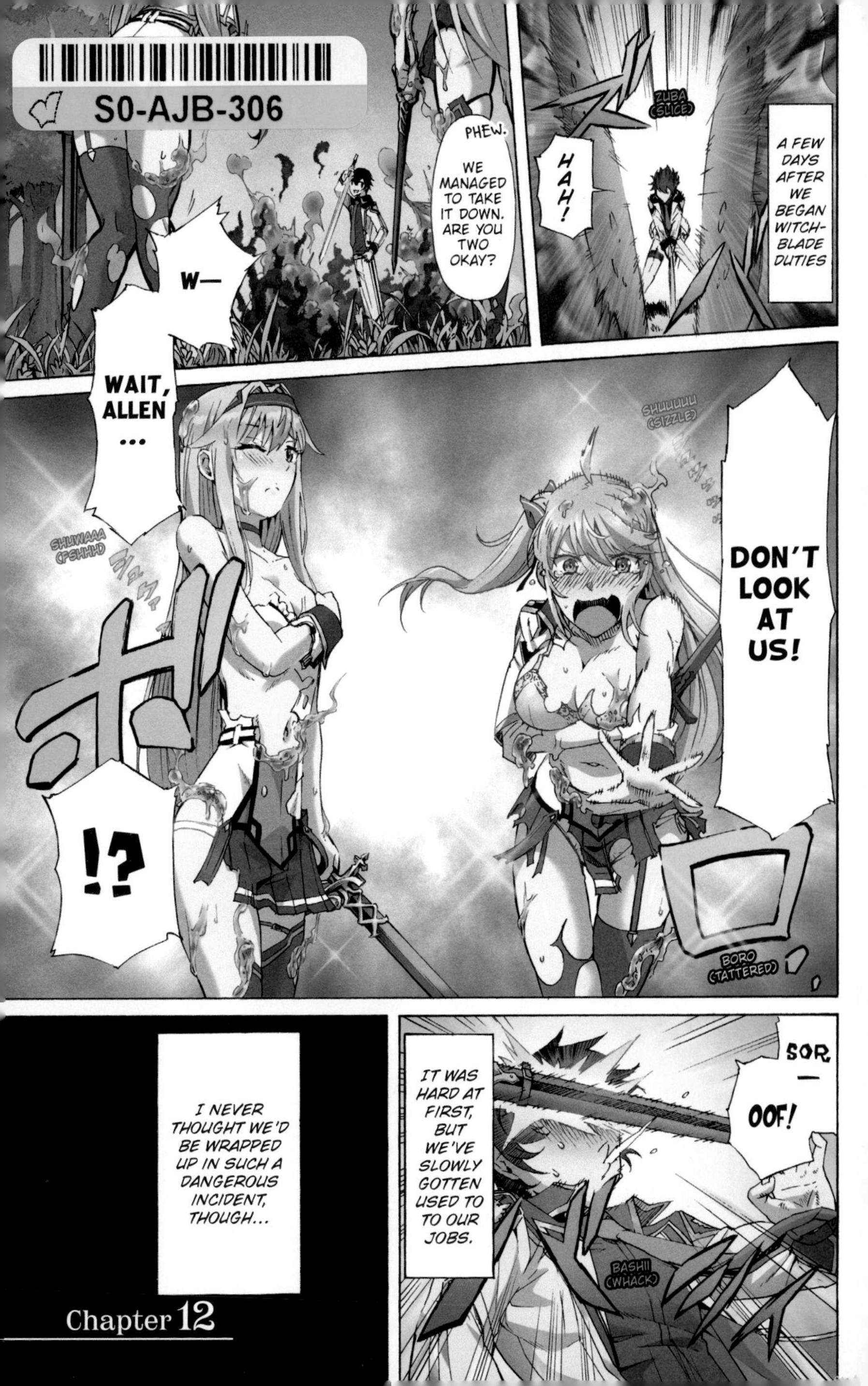
A FEW DAYS AFTER WE BEGAN WITCH-BLADE DUTIES
HAH!
ZUBA (SLICE)
PHEW.
WE MANAGED TO TAKE IT DOWN. ARE YOU TWO OKAY?
W—
DON'T LOOK AT US!
SHUUUUUU (SIZZLE)
WAIT, ALLEN...
SHUWAAA (PFSHHH)
!?
BORO (TATTERED)
SOR—
OOF!
IT WAS HARD AT FIRST, BUT WE'VE SLOWLY GOTTEN USED TO TO OUR JOBS.
BASHII (WHACK)
I NEVER THOUGHT WE'D BE WRAPPED UP IN SUCH A DANGEROUS INCIDENT, THOUGH...
Chapter 12

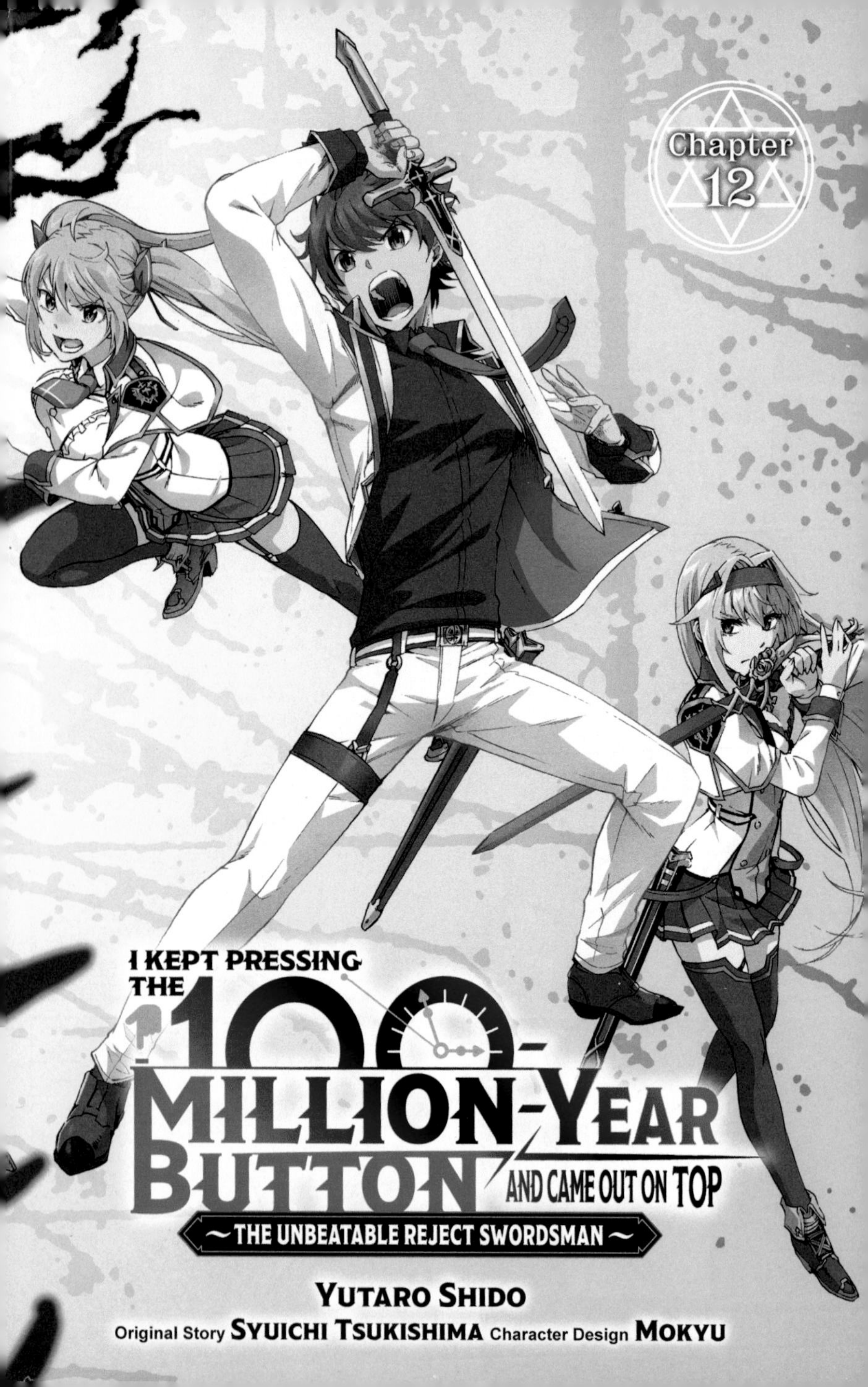
Chapter 12
I KEPT PRESSING THE 100-MILLION-YEAR BUTTON AND CAME OUT ON TOP
~THE UNBEATABLE REJECT SWORDSMAN~
YUTARO SHIDO
Original Story SYUICHI TSUKISHIMA Character Design MOKYU

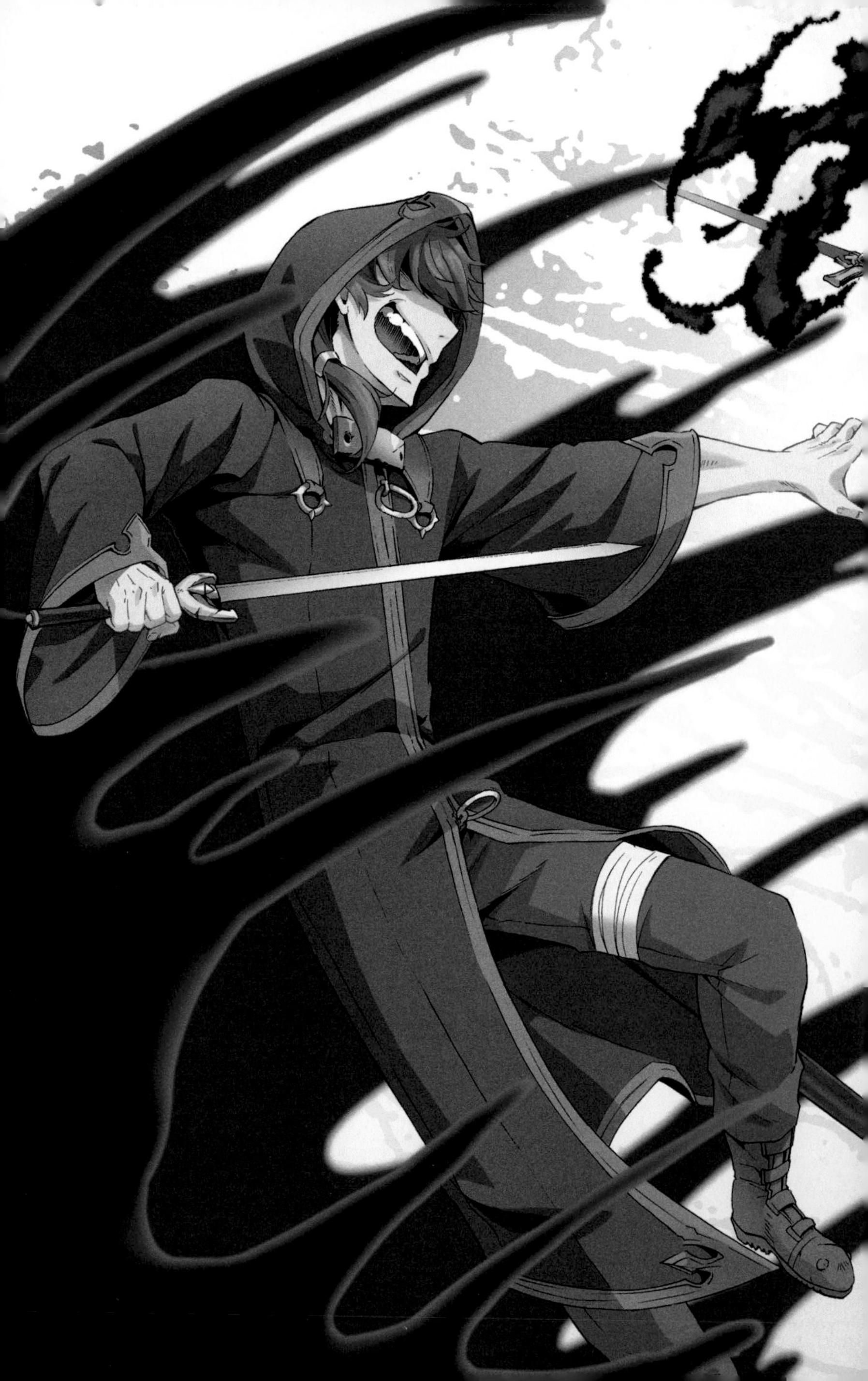

CONTENTS

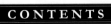

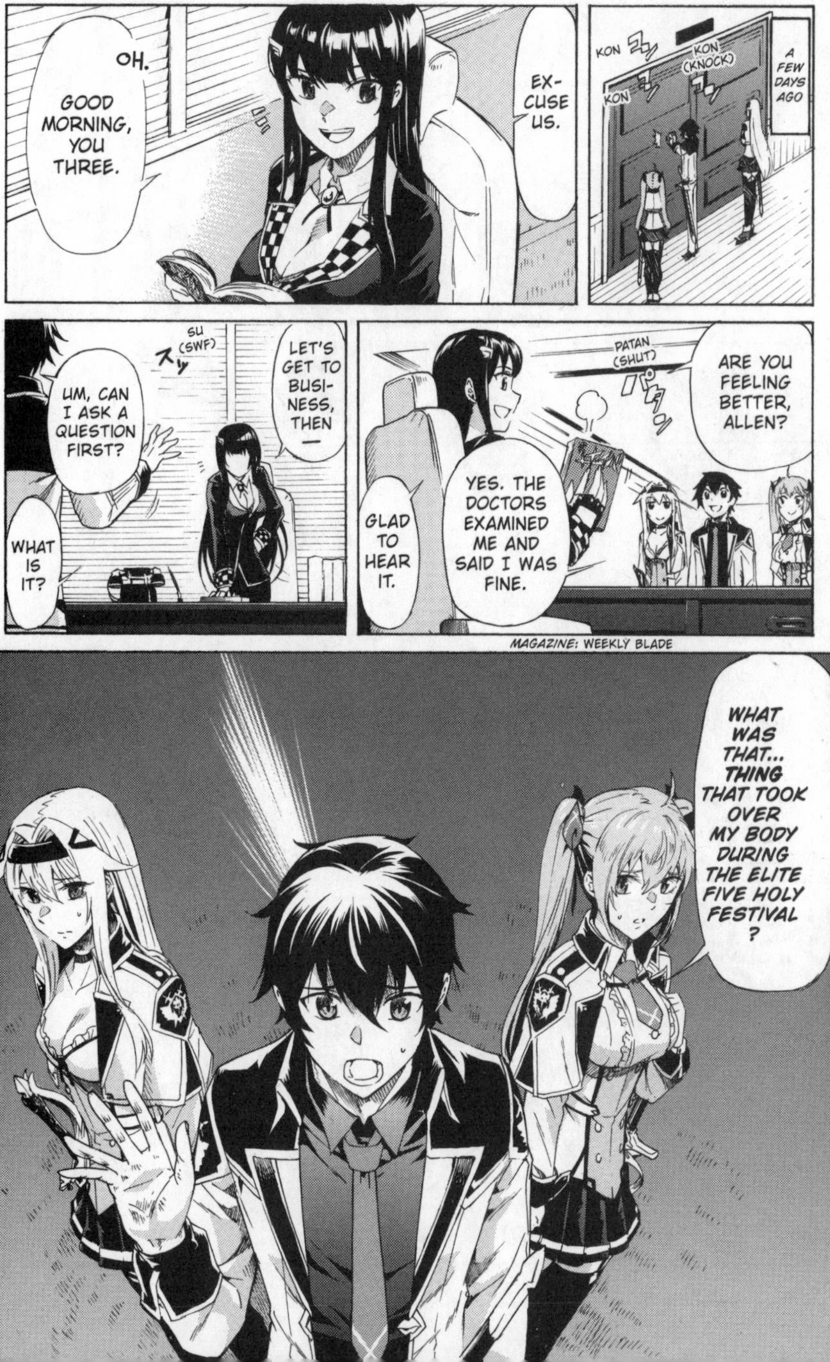
A FEW DAYS AGO
KON KON (KNOCK)
KON
KON
EX-CUSE US.
OH.
GOOD MORNING, YOU THREE.
PATAN (SHUT)
ARE YOU FEELING BETTER, ALLEN?
YES. THE DOCTORS EXAMINED ME AND SAID I WAS FINE.
GLAD TO HEAR IT.
MAGAZINE: WEEKLY BLADE
LET'S GET TO BUSI-NESS, THEN—
SU (SWF)
UM, CAN I ASK A QUESTION FIRST?
WHAT IS IT?
WHAT WAS THAT... THING THAT TOOK OVER MY BODY DURING THE ELITE FIVE HOLY FESTIVAL?

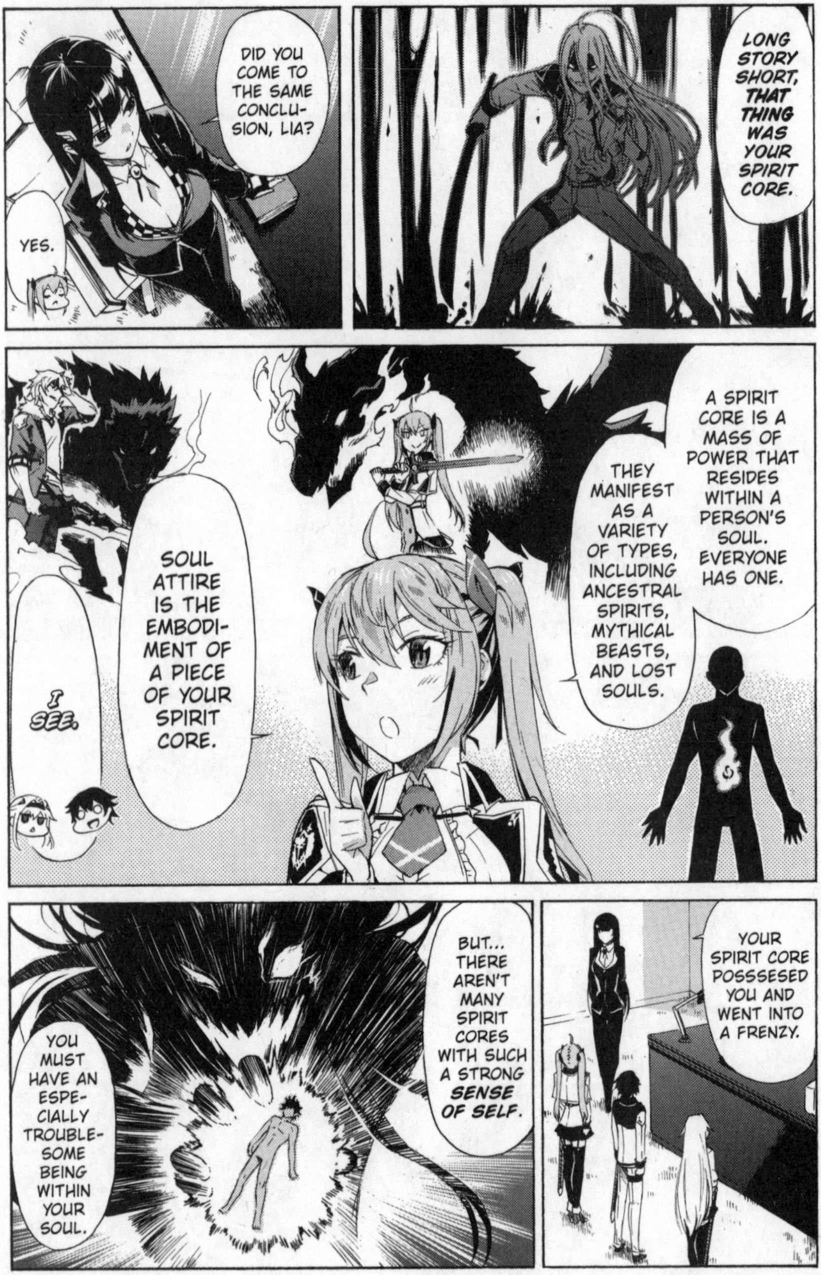
LONG STORY SHORT, THAT THING WAS YOUR SPIRIT CORE.
DID YOU COME TO THE SAME CONCLUSION, LIA?
YES.
A SPIRIT CORE IS A MASS OF POWER THAT RESIDES WITHIN A PERSON'S SOUL. EVERYONE HAS ONE.
THEY MANIFEST AS A VARIETY OF TYPES, INCLUDING ANCESTRAL SPIRITS, MYTHICAL BEASTS, AND LOST SOULS.
SOUL ATTIRE IS THE EMBODIMENT OF A PIECE OF YOUR SPIRIT CORE.
I SEE.
YOUR SPIRIT CORE POSSSESED YOU AND WENT INTO A FRENZY.
BUT... THERE AREN'T MANY SPIRIT CORES WITH SUCH A STRONG SENSE OF SELF.
YOU MUST HAVE AN ESPECIALLY TROUBLESOME BEING WITHIN YOUR SOUL.

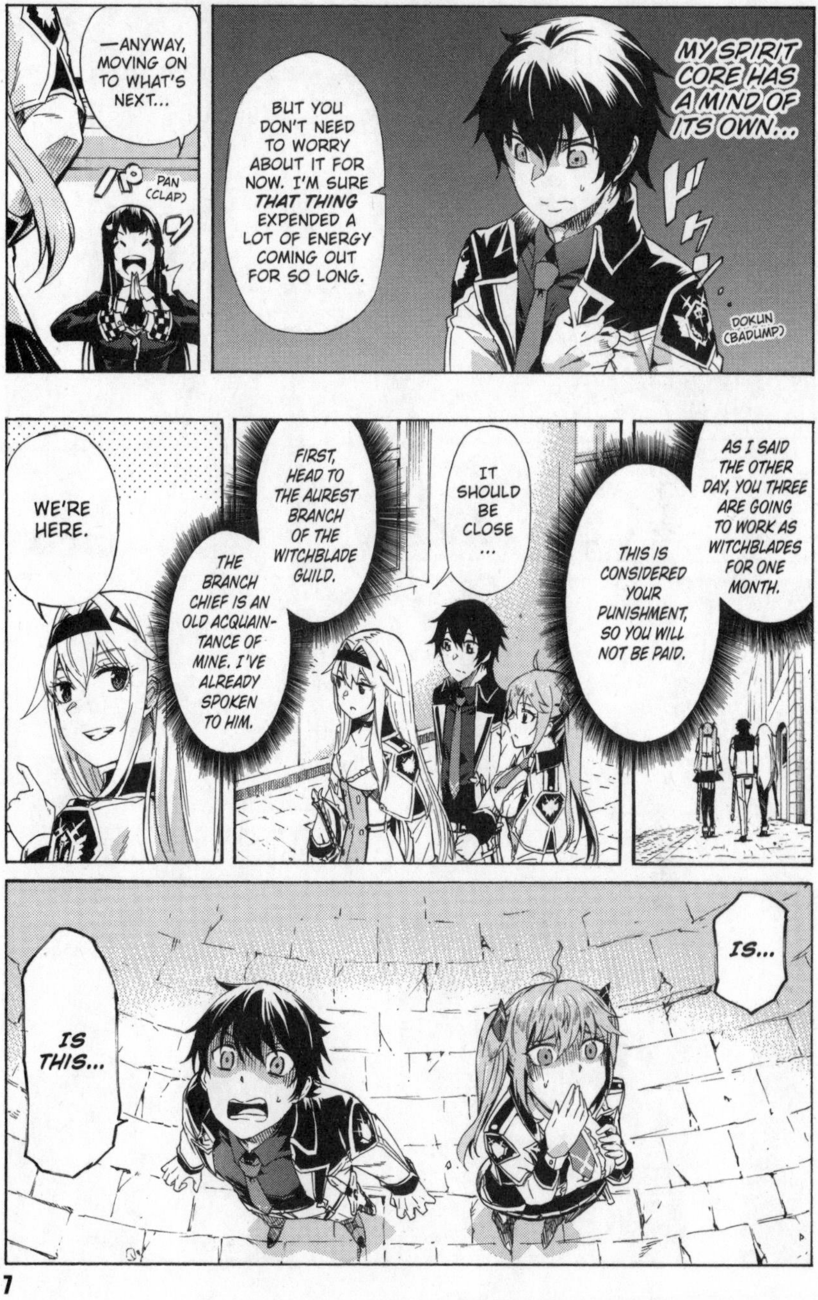
MY SPIRIT CORE HAS A MIND OF ITS OWN...
BUT YOU DON'T NEED TO WORRY ABOUT IT FOR NOW. I'M SURE *THAT THING* EXPENDED A LOT OF ENERGY COMING OUT FOR SO LONG.
DOKUN (BADUMP)
—ANYWAY, MOVING ON TO WHAT'S NEXT...
PAN (CLAP)
AS I SAID THE OTHER DAY, YOU THREE ARE GOING TO WORK AS WITCHBLADES FOR ONE MONTH.
THIS IS CONSIDERED YOUR PUNISHMENT, SO YOU WILL NOT BE PAID.
IT SHOULD BE CLOSE ...
FIRST, HEAD TO THE AUREST BRANCH OF THE WITCHBLADE GUILD.
THE BRANCH CHIEF IS AN OLD ACQUAIN-TANCE OF MINE. I'VE ALREADY SPOKEN TO HIM.
WE'RE HERE.
IS...
IS THIS...

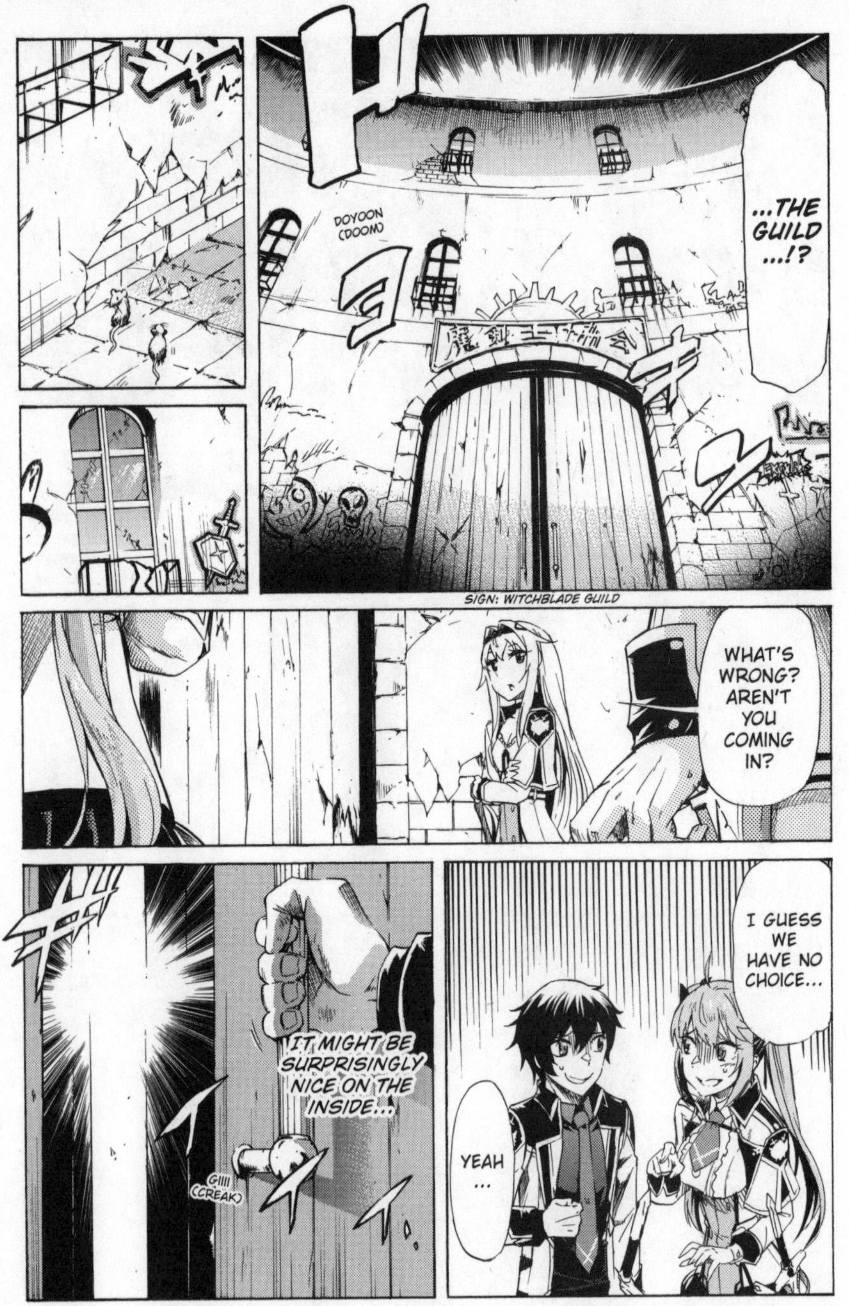
...THE GUILD ...!?
DOYOON (DOOM)
SIGN: WITCHBLADE GUILD
WHAT'S WRONG? AREN'T YOU COMING IN?
I GUESS WE HAVE NO CHOICE...
YEAH ...
IT MIGHT BE SURPRISINGLY NICE ON THE INSIDE...
GIIII (CREAK)

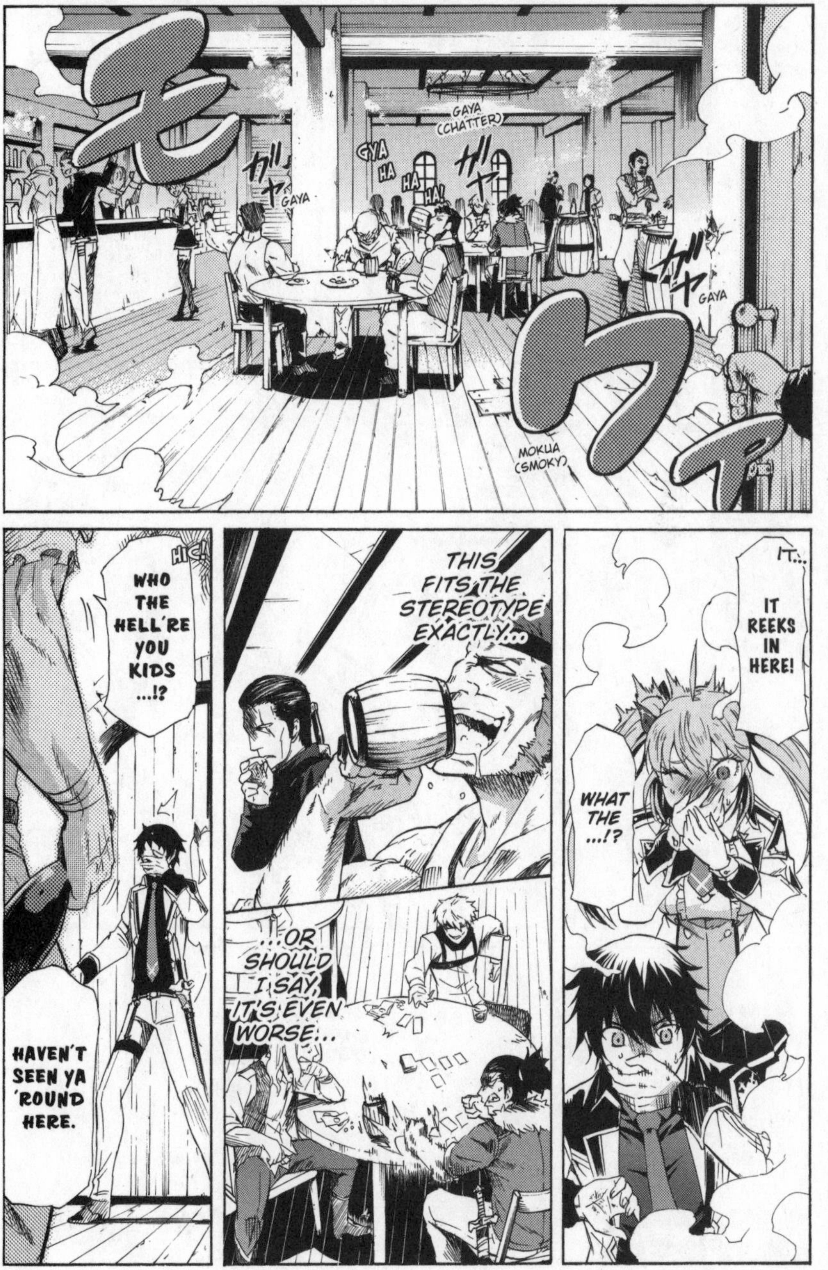
GAYA (CHATTER)
GYA HA HA HA!
GAYA
GAYA
MOKUA (SMOKY)
IT...
IT REEKS IN HERE!
WHAT THE ...!?
THIS FITS THE STEREOTYPE EXACTLY...
...OR SHOULD I SAY, IT'S EVEN WORSE...
HIC!
WHO THE HELL'RE YOU KIDS ...!?
HAVEN'T SEEN YA 'ROUND HERE.

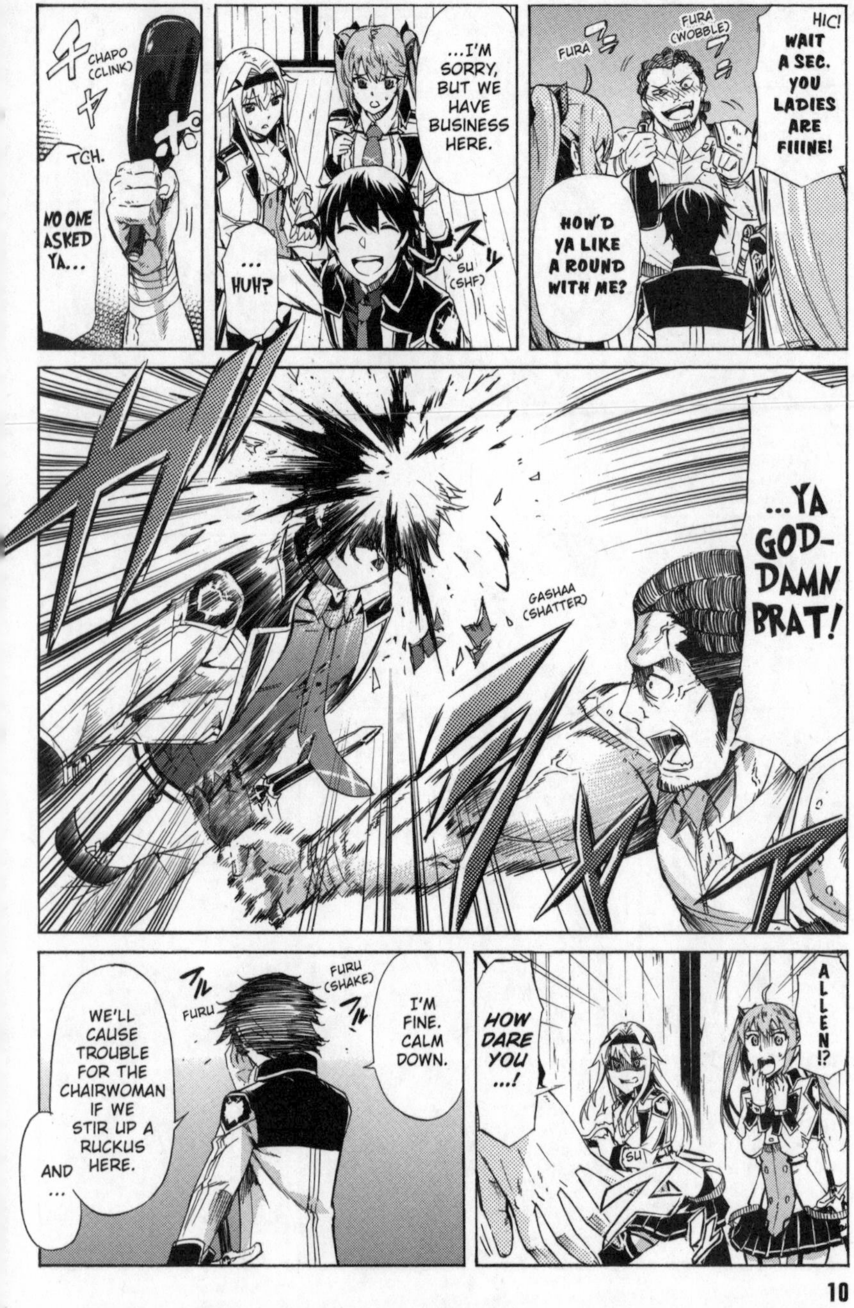
HIC! WAIT A SEC. YOU LADIES ARE FIIINE!
FURA (WOBBLE)
FURA
HOW'D YA LIKE A ROUND WITH ME?
...I'M SORRY, BUT WE HAVE BUSINESS HERE.
SU (SHF)
...HUH?
CHAPO (CLINK)
TCH.
NO ONE ASKED YA...
...YA GOD-DAMN BRAT!
GASHAA (SHATTER)
ALLEN!?
HOW DARE YOU...!
SU
FURU (SHAKE)
FURU
I'M FINE. CALM DOWN.
WE'LL CAUSE TROUBLE FOR THE CHAIRWOMAN IF WE STIR UP A RUCKUS HERE.
AND ...

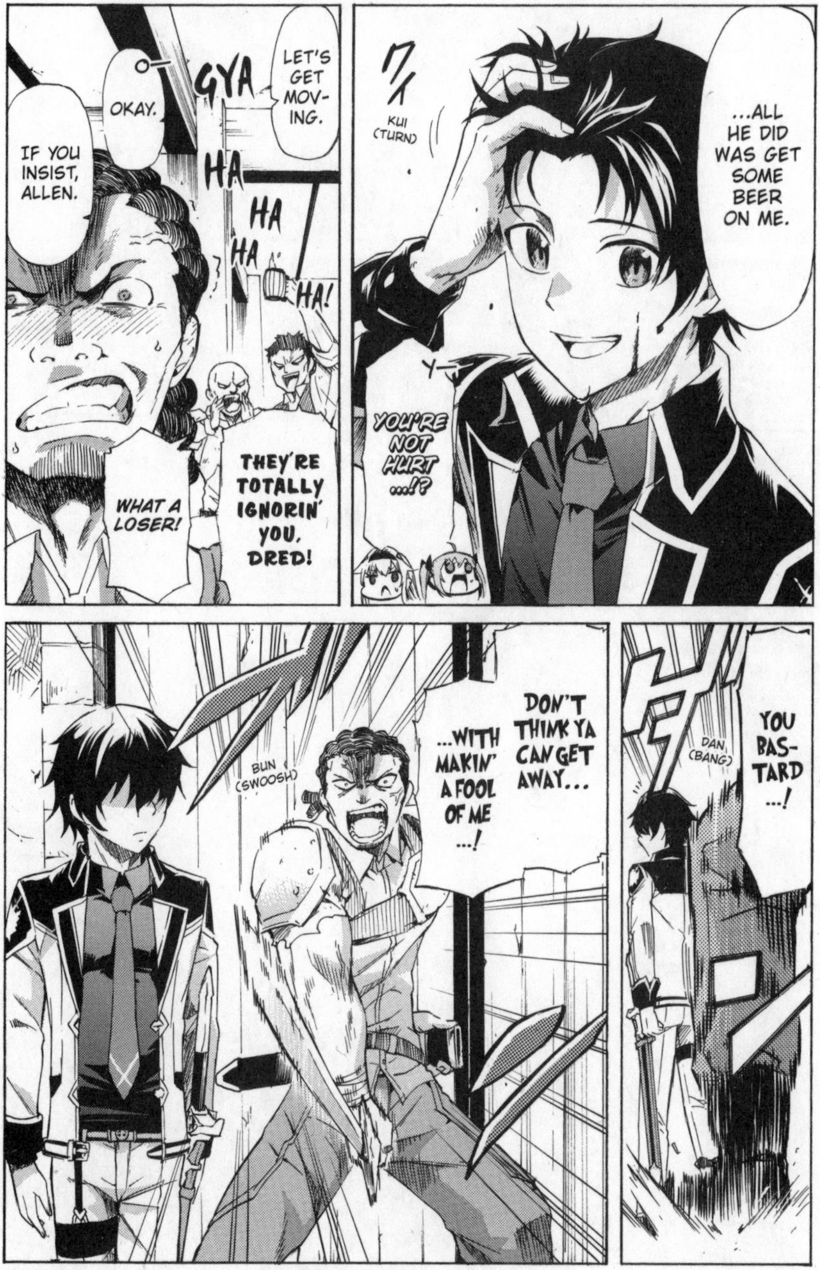
...ALL HE DID WAS GET SOME BEER ON ME.
KUI (TURN)
YOU'RE NOT HURT ...!?
LET'S GET MOVING.
O- OKAY.
IF YOU INSIST, ALLEN.
GYA HA HA HA HA!
THEY'RE TOTALLY IGNORIN' YOU, DRED!
WHAT A LOSER!
DAN (BANG)
YOU BASTARD ...!
DON'T THINK YA CAN GET AWAY...
...WITH MAKIN' A FOOL OF ME ...!
BUN (SWOOSH)

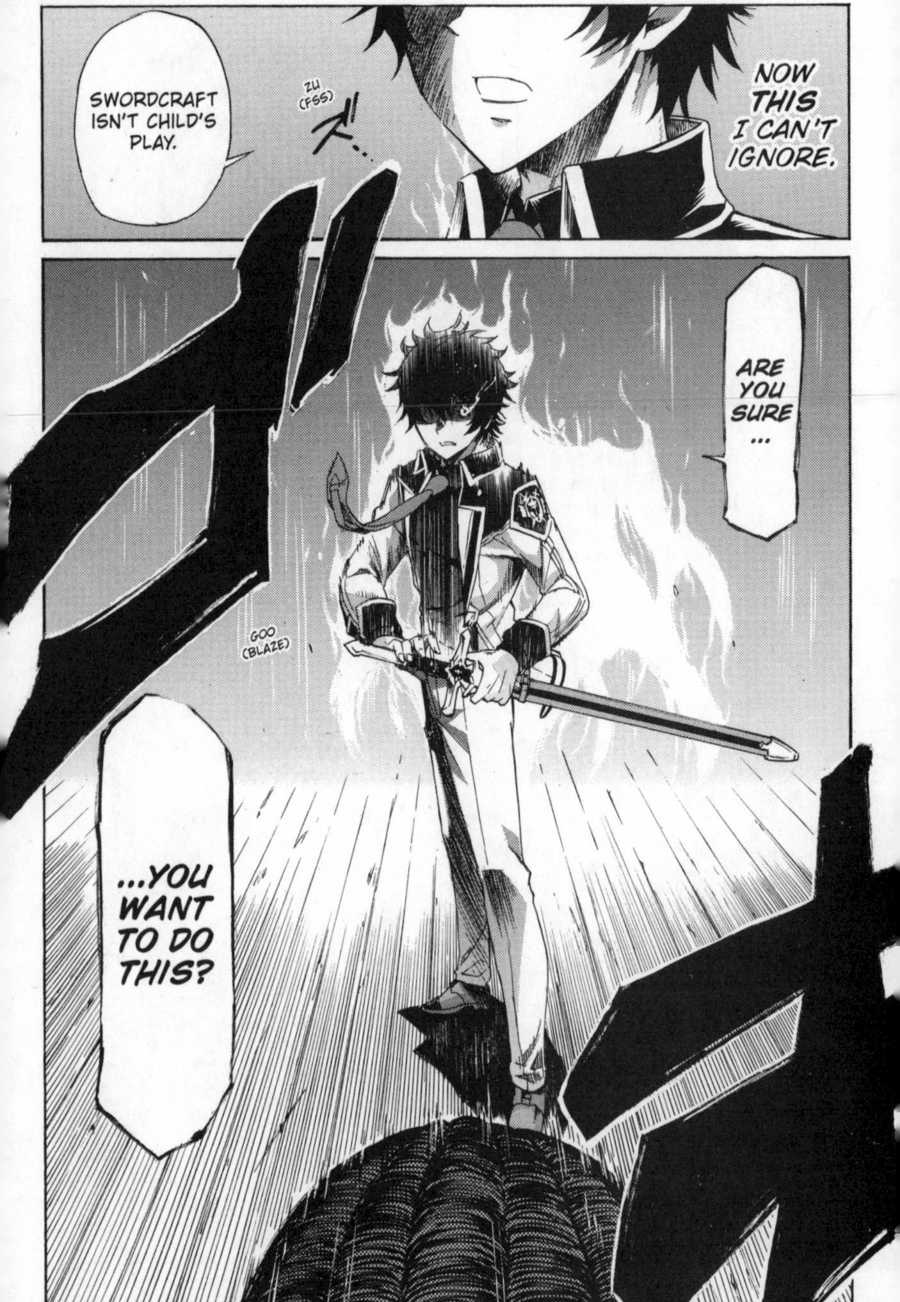
NOW THIS I CAN'T IGNORE.
ZU (FSS)
SWORDCRAFT ISN'T CHILD'S PLAY.
ARE YOU SURE...
GOO (BLAZE)
...YOU WANT TO DO THIS?

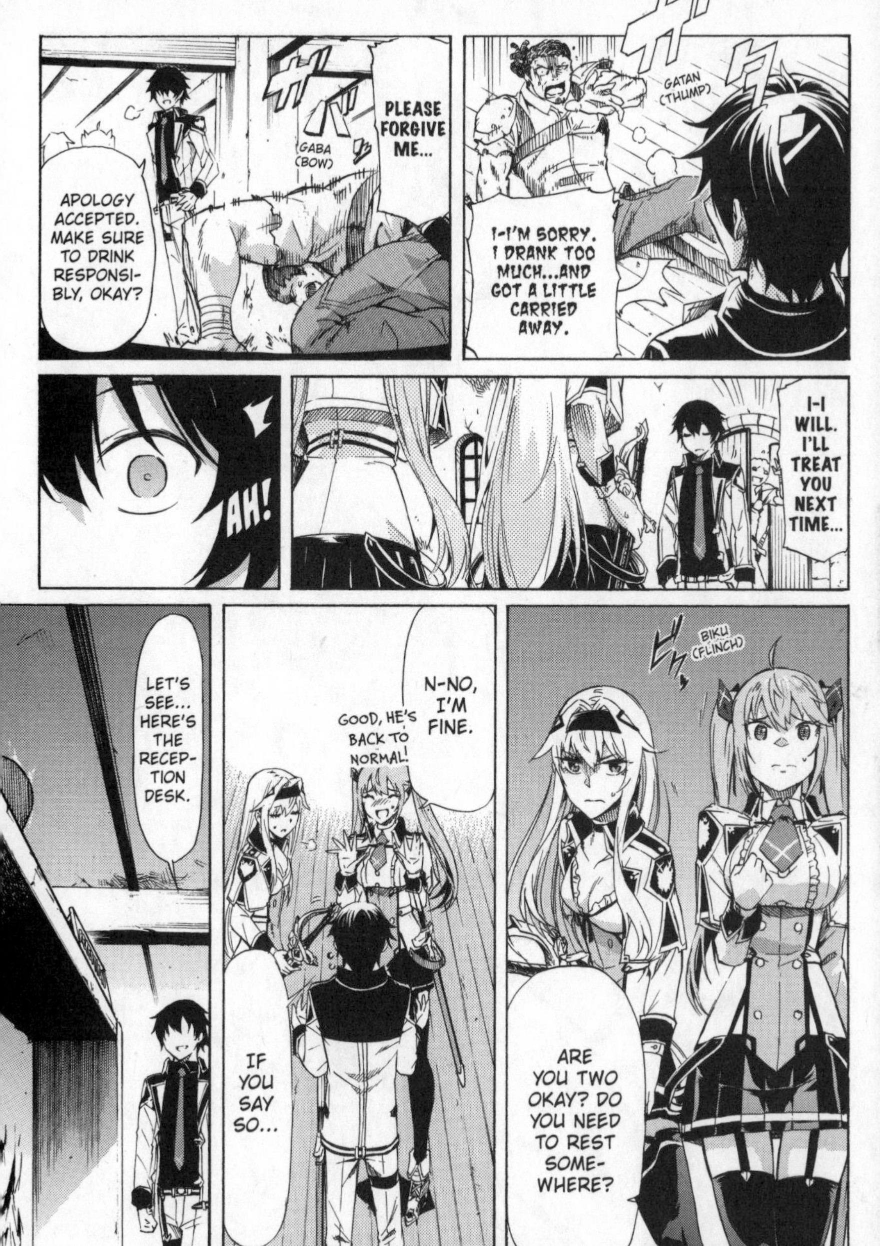
GATAN (THUMP)
I-I'M SORRY. I DRANK TOO MUCH...AND GOT A LITTLE CARRIED AWAY.
PLEASE FORGIVE ME...
GABA (BOW)
APOLOGY ACCEPTED. MAKE SURE TO DRINK RESPONSIBLY, OKAY?
I-I WILL. I'LL TREAT YOU NEXT TIME...
AH!
BIKU (FLINCH)
ARE YOU TWO OKAY? DO YOU NEED TO REST SOMEWHERE?
N-NO, I'M FINE.
GOOD, HE'S BACK TO NORMAL!
IF YOU SAY SO...
LET'S SEE... HERE'S THE RECEPTION DESK.

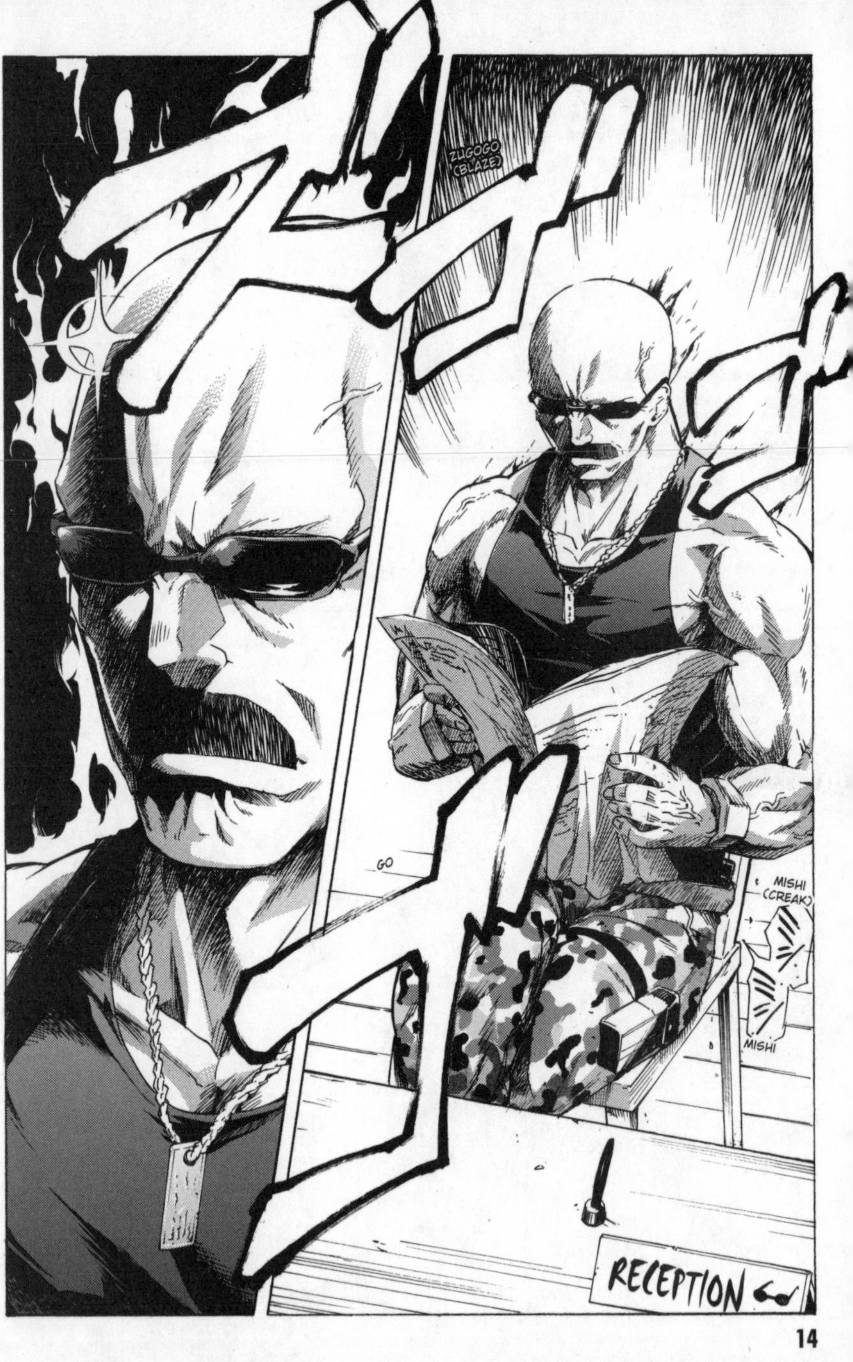
ZUGOGO
(BLAZE)
MISHI
(CREAK)
MISHI
GO
RECEPTION

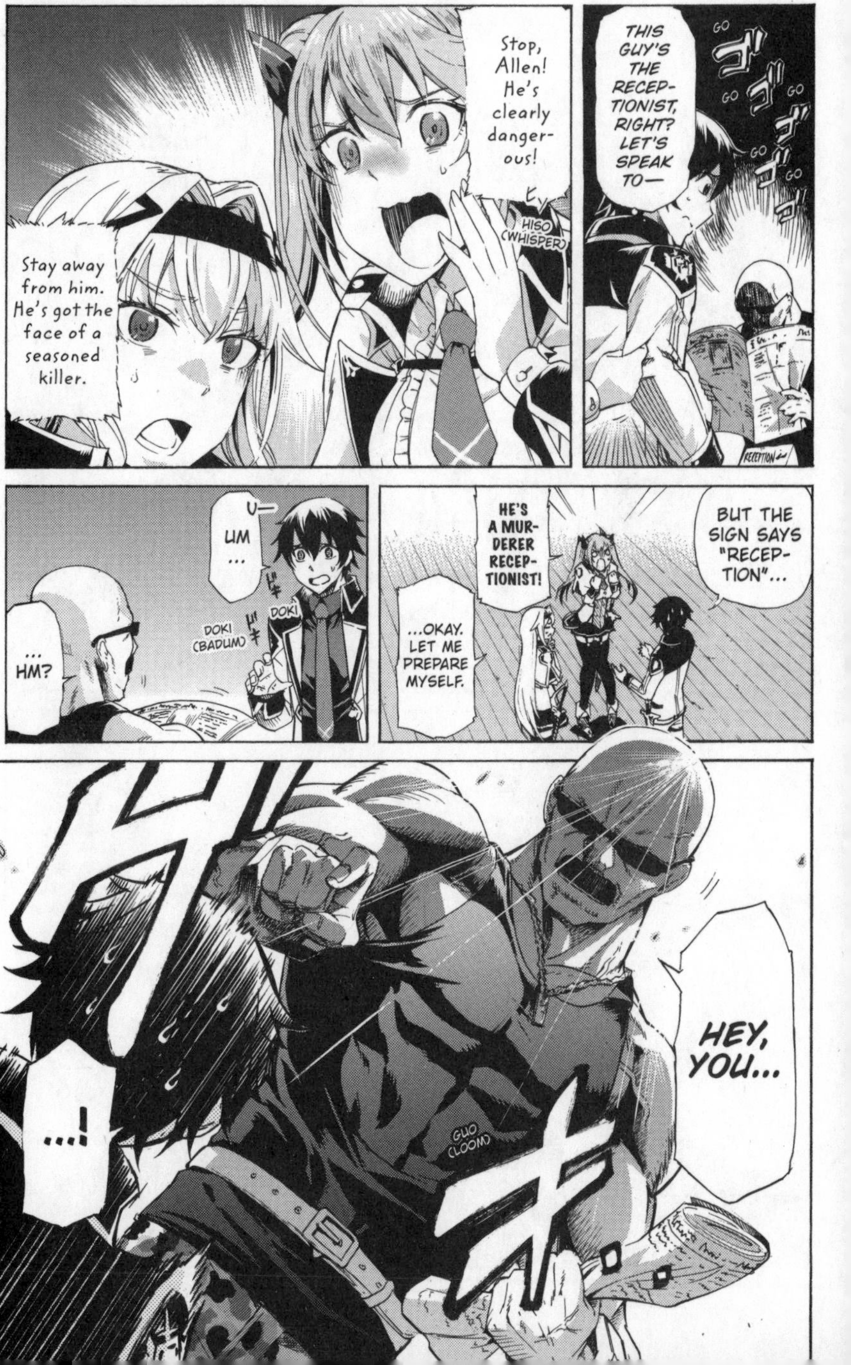
THIS GUY'S THE RECEPTIONIST, RIGHT? LET'S SPEAK TO—
GO
GO
GO
GO
GO
RECEPTION
Stop, Allen! He's clearly dangerous!
HISO (WHISPER)
Stay away from him. He's got the face of a seasoned killer.
BUT THE SIGN SAYS "RECEPTION"...
HE'S A MURDERER RECEPTIONIST!
...OKAY. LET ME PREPARE MYSELF.
U— UM ...
DOKI
DOKI (BADUM)
... HM?
HEY, YOU...
GUO (LOOM)
...!

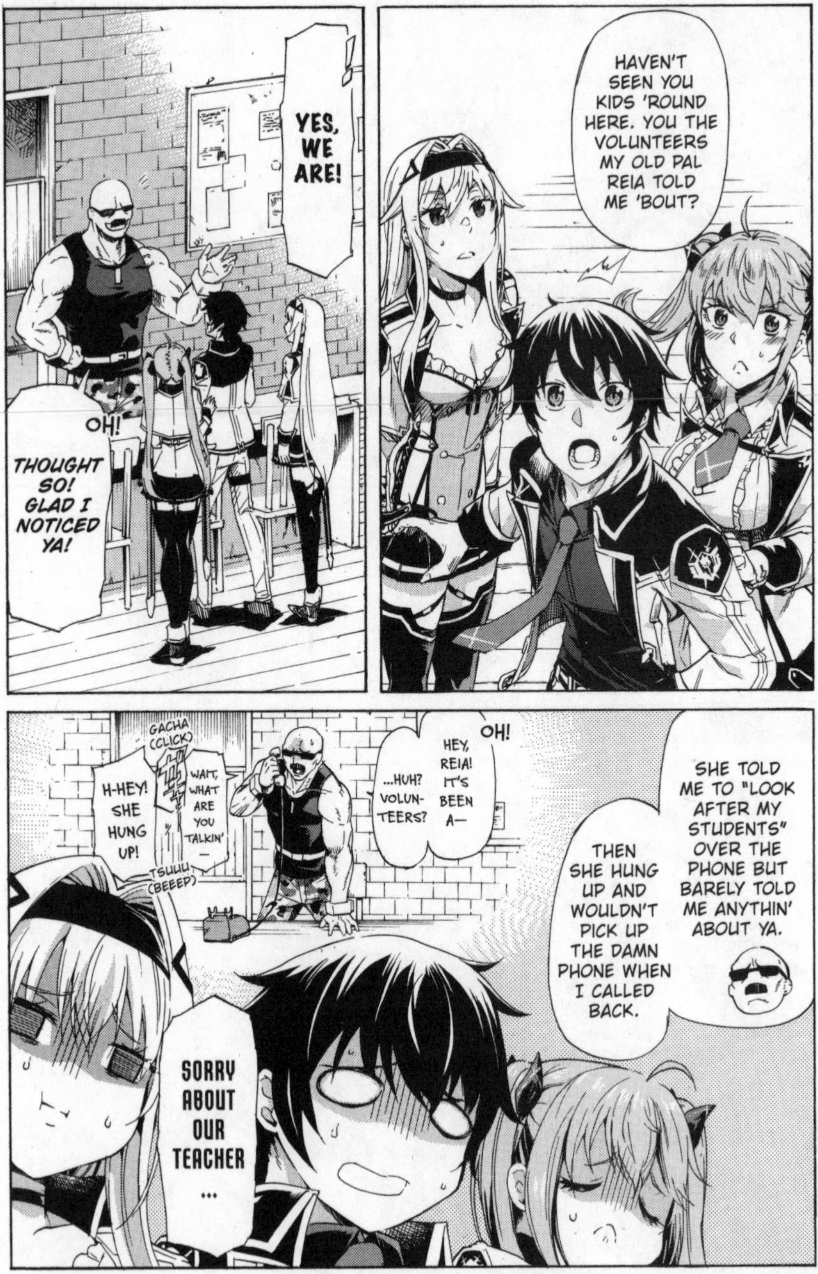
HAVEN'T SEEN YOU KIDS 'ROUND HERE. YOU THE VOLUNTEERS MY OLD PAL REIA TOLD ME 'BOUT?
YES, WE ARE!
OH!
THOUGHT SO! GLAD I NOTICED YA!
SHE TOLD ME TO "LOOK AFTER MY STUDENTS" OVER THE PHONE BUT BARELY TOLD ME ANYTHIN' ABOUT YA.
THEN SHE HUNG UP AND WOULDN'T PICK UP THE DAMN PHONE WHEN I CALLED BACK.
OH!
HEY, REIA! IT'S BEEN A—
...HUH? VOLUNTEERS?
WAIT, WHAT ARE YOU TALKIN'—
GACHA (CLICK)
H-HEY! SHE HUNG UP!
TSUUU (BEEEP)
SORRY ABOUT OUR TEACHER...

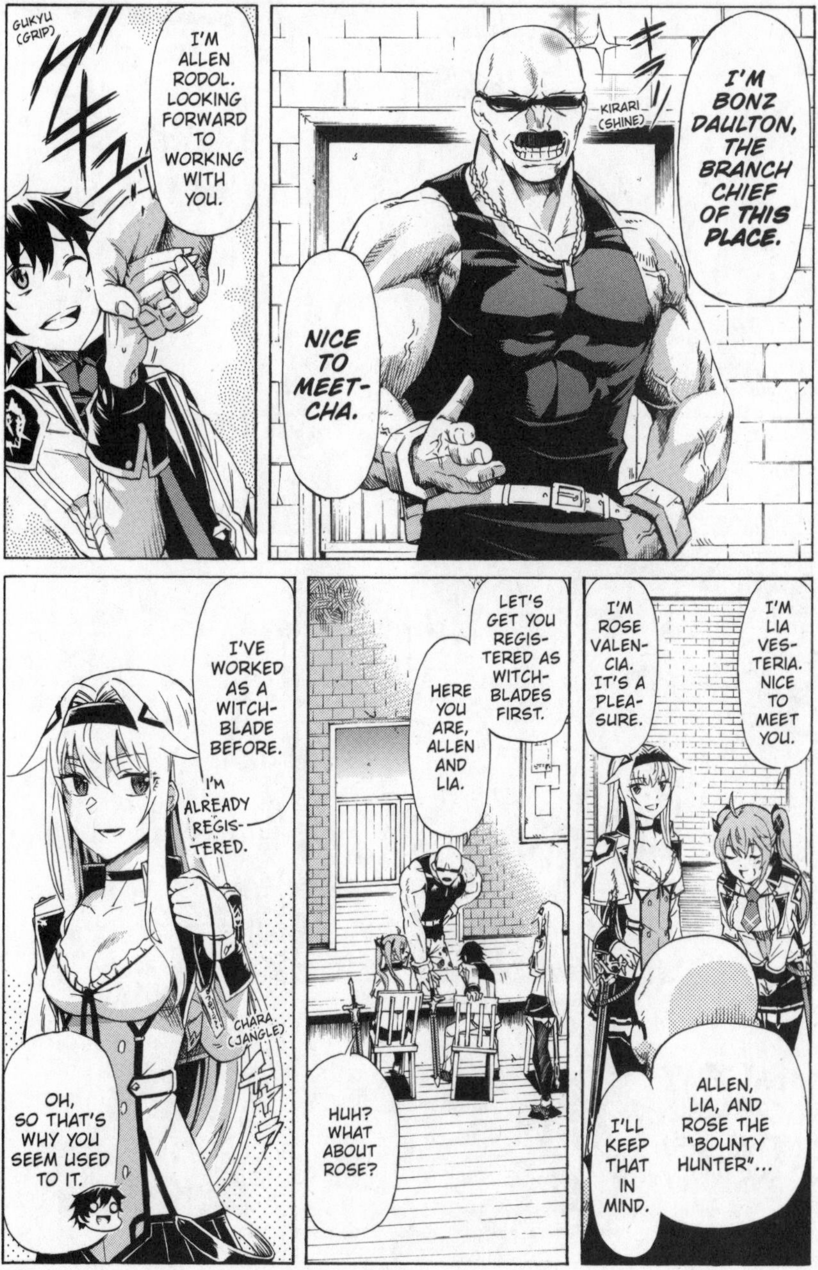
KIRARI (SHINE)
I'M BONZ DAULTON, THE BRANCH CHIEF OF THIS PLACE.
NICE TO MEET-CHA.
GUKYU (GRIP)
I'M ALLEN RODOL. LOOKING FORWARD TO WORKING WITH YOU.
I'M LIA VESTERIA. NICE TO MEET YOU.
I'M ROSE VALENCIA. IT'S A PLEASURE.
ALLEN, LIA, AND ROSE THE "BOUNTY HUNTER"...
I'LL KEEP THAT IN MIND.
LET'S GET YOU REGISTERED AS WITCH-BLADES FIRST.
HERE YOU ARE, ALLEN AND LIA.
HUH? WHAT ABOUT ROSE?
I'VE WORKED AS A WITCH-BLADE BEFORE.
I'M ALREADY REGISTERED.
CHARA (JANGLE)
OH, SO THAT'S WHY YOU SEEM USED TO IT.

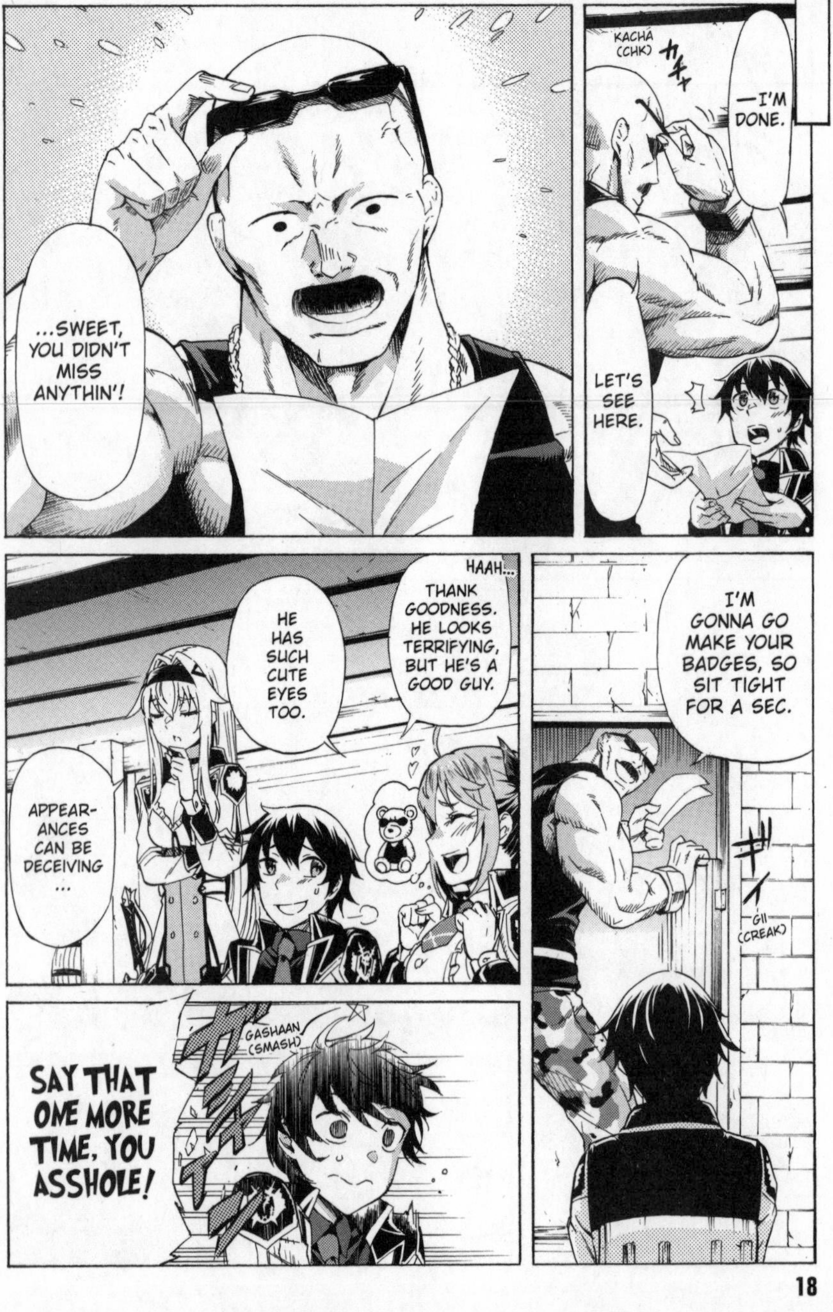
KACHA (CHK)
—I'M DONE.
LET'S SEE HERE.
...SWEET, YOU DIDN'T MISS ANYTHIN'!
I'M GONNA GO MAKE YOUR BADGES, SO SIT TIGHT FOR A SEC.
GII (CREAK)
HAAH...
THANK GOODNESS. HE LOOKS TERRIFYING, BUT HE'S A GOOD GUY.
HE HAS SUCH CUTE EYES TOO.
APPEARANCES CAN BE DECEIVING...
GASHAAN (SMASH)
SAY THAT ONE MORE TIME, YOU ASSHOLE!

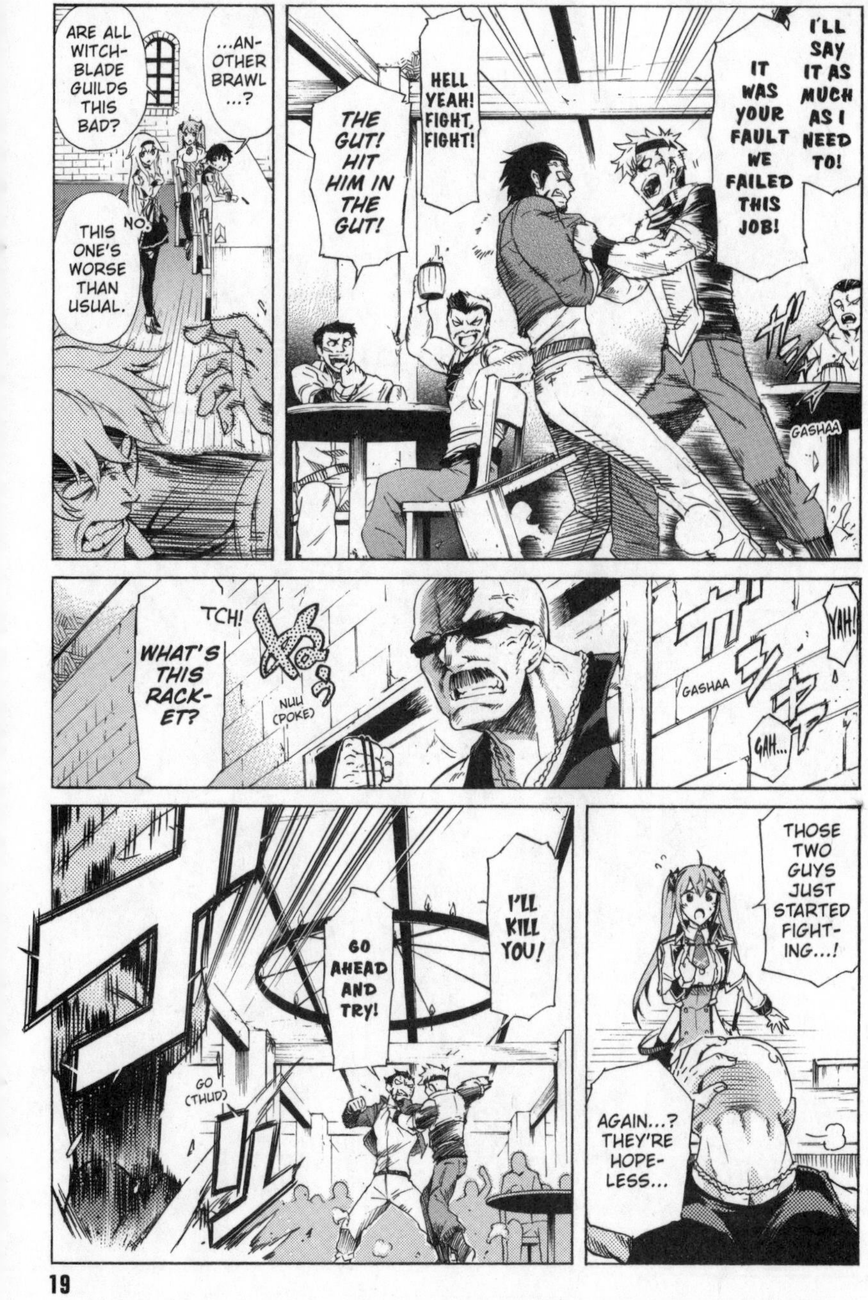
I'LL SAY IT AS MUCH AS I NEED TO!
IT WAS YOUR FAULT WE FAILED THIS JOB!
HELL YEAH! FIGHT, FIGHT!
THE GUT! HIT HIM IN THE GUT!
GASHAA
...AN-OTHER BRAWL...?
ARE ALL WITCH-BLADE GUILDS THIS BAD?
NO.
THIS ONE'S WORSE THAN USUAL.
YAH!
GASHAA
GAH...
TCH!
WHAT'S THIS RACK-ET?
NUU (POKE)
THOSE TWO GUYS JUST STARTED FIGHT-ING...!
AGAIN...? THEY'RE HOPE-LESS...
I'LL KILL YOU!
GO AHEAD AND TRY!
GO (THUD)

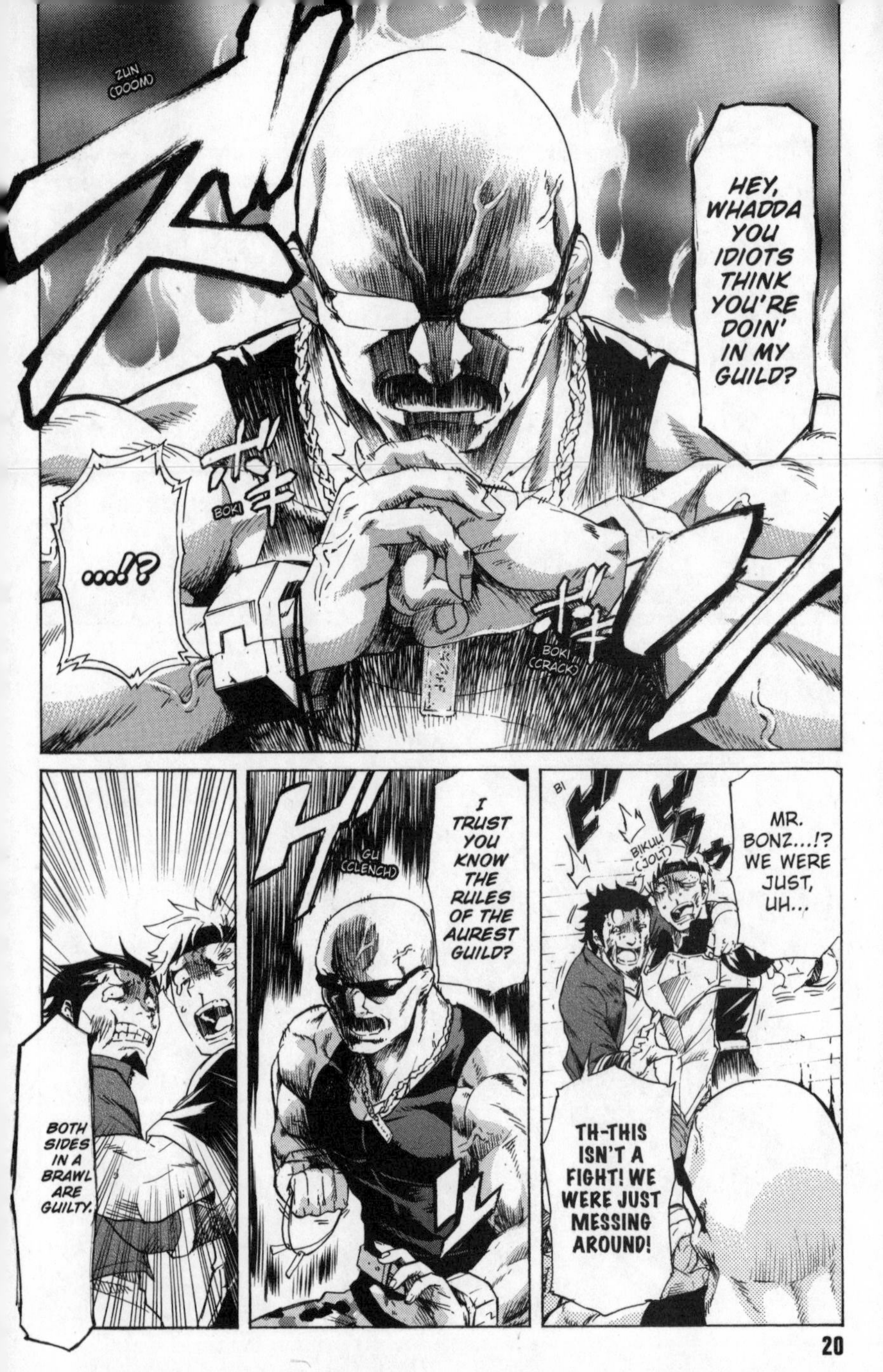
HEY, WHADDA YOU IDIOTS THINK YOU'RE DOIN' IN MY GUILD?
ZUN (DOOM)
BOKI
BOKI (CRACK)
...!?
MR. BONZ...!? WE WERE JUST, UH...
BI
BIKUU (JOLT)
TH-THIS ISN'T A FIGHT! WE WERE JUST MESSING AROUND!
I TRUST YOU KNOW THE RULES OF THE AUREST GUILD?
GU (CLENCH)
BOTH SIDES IN A BRAWL ARE GUILTY.

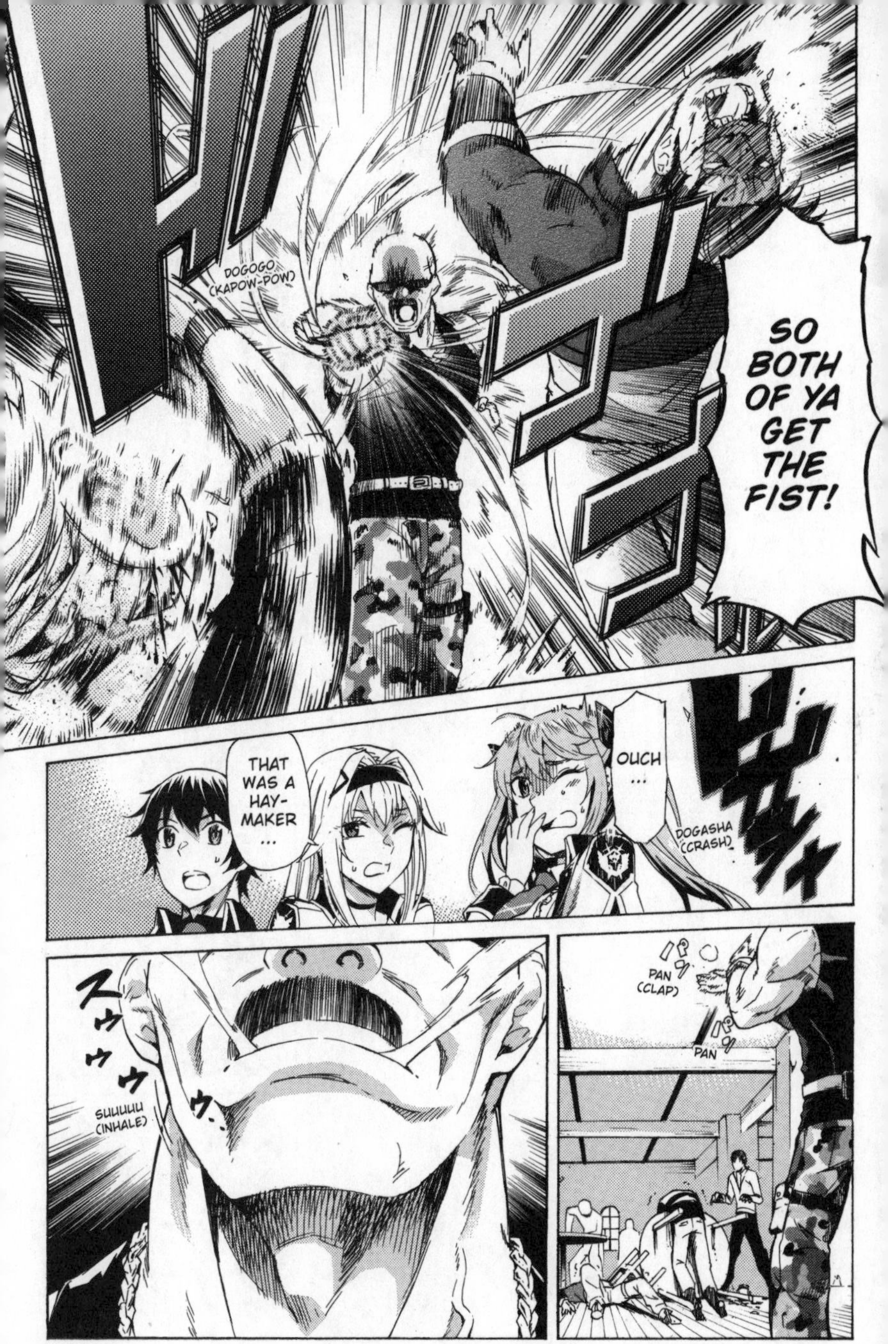
SO BOTH OF YA GET THE FIST!
DOGOGO (KAPOW-POW)
DOGASHA (CRASH)
OUCH ...
THAT WAS A HAY-MAKER ...
PAN (CLAP)
PAN
SUUUUU (INHALE)

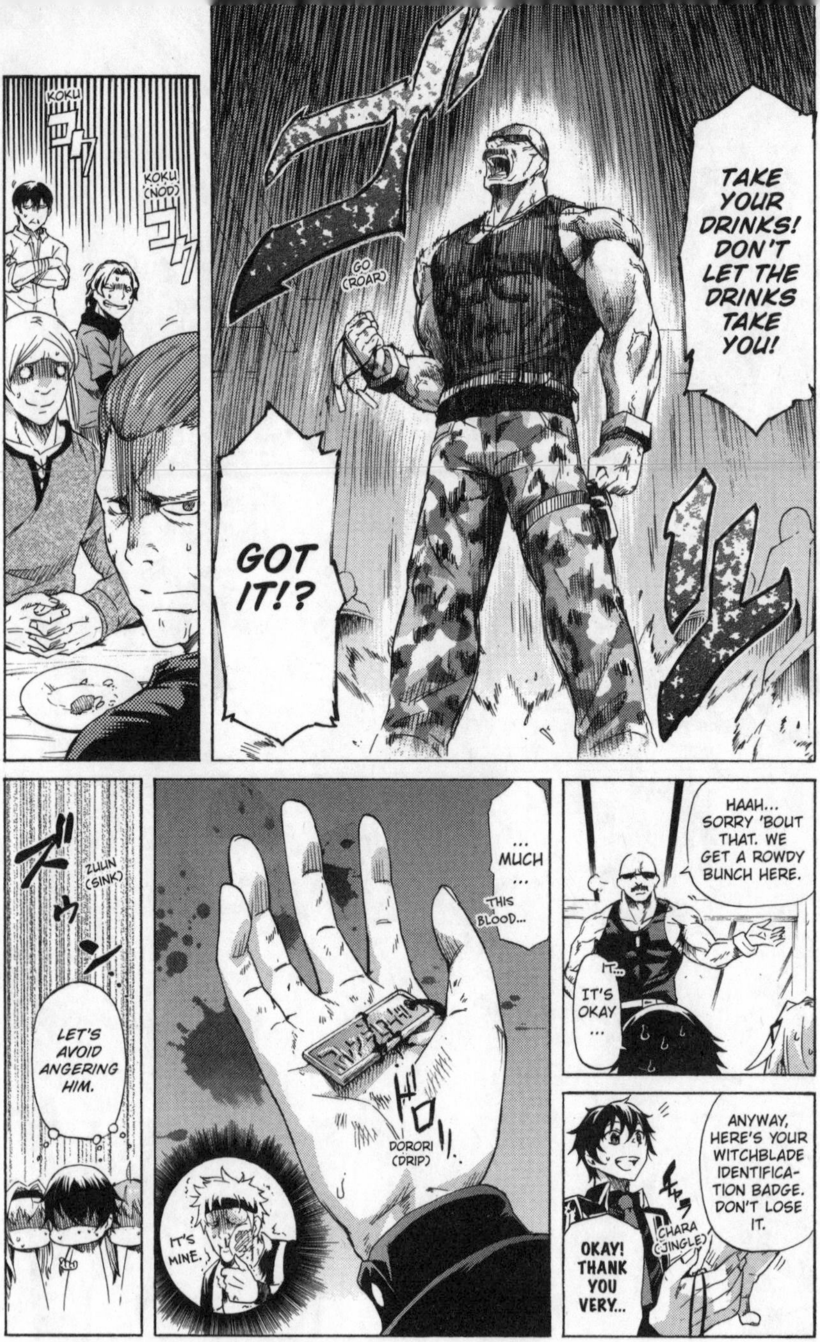
TAKE YOUR DRINKS! DON'T LET THE DRINKS TAKE YOU!
GO (ROAR)
GOT IT!?
KOKU
KOKU (NOD)
HAAH... SORRY 'BOUT THAT. WE GET A ROWDY BUNCH HERE.
IT... IT'S OKAY...
ANYWAY, HERE'S YOUR WITCHBLADE IDENTIFICATION BADGE. DON'T LOSE IT.
CHARA (JINGLE)
OKAY! THANK YOU VERY...
...MUCH...
THIS BLOOD...
DORORI (DRIP)
IT'S MINE.
ZUUN (SINK)
LET'S AVOID ANGERING HIM.

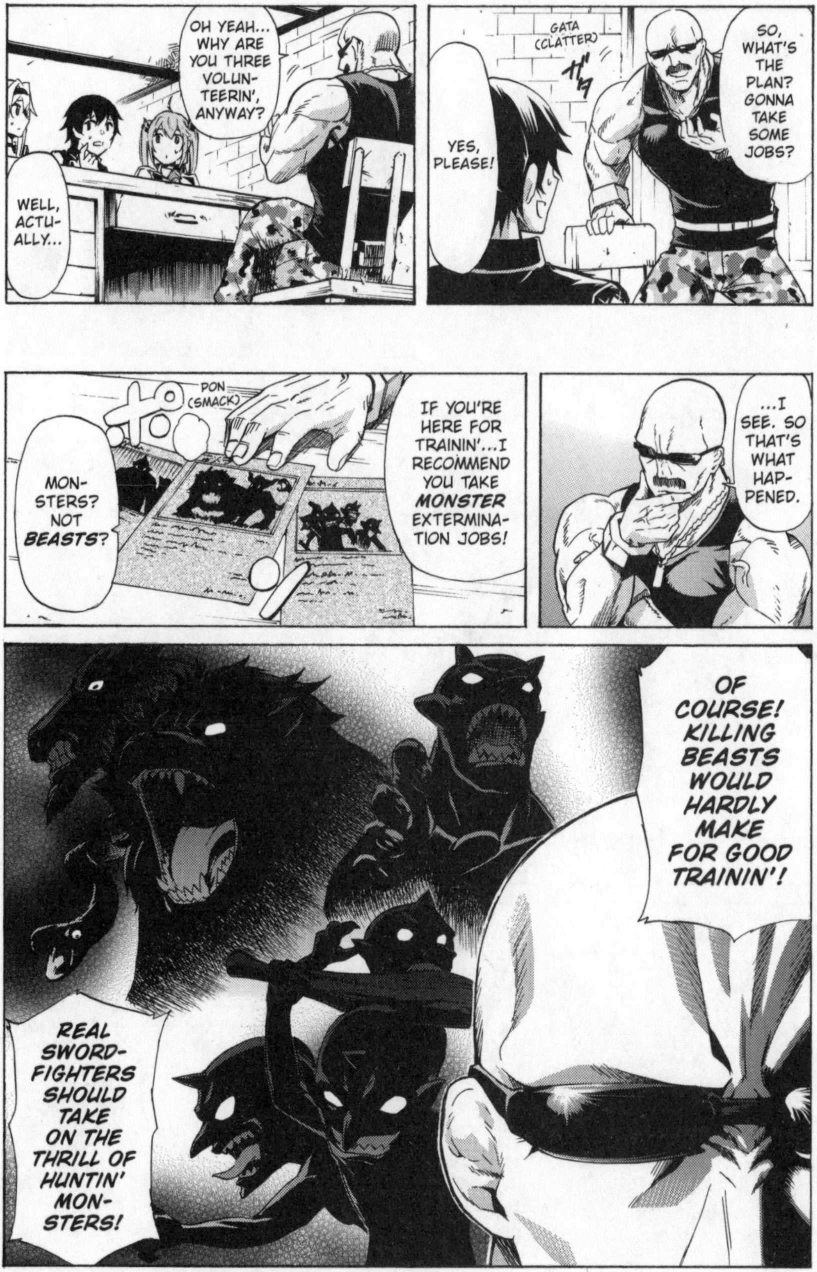
SO, WHAT'S THE PLAN? GONNA TAKE SOME JOBS?
GATA (CLATTER)
YES, PLEASE!
OH YEAH... WHY ARE YOU THREE VOLUNTEERIN', ANYWAY?
WELL, ACTUALLY...
...I SEE. SO THAT'S WHAT HAPPENED.
IF YOU'RE HERE FOR TRAININ'...I RECOMMEND YOU TAKE *MONSTER* EXTERMINATION JOBS!
PON (SMACK)
MONSTERS? NOT *BEASTS*?
OF COURSE! KILLING BEASTS WOULD HARDLY MAKE FOR GOOD TRAININ'!
REAL SWORDFIGHTERS SHOULD TAKE ON THE THRILL OF HUNTIN' MONSTERS!

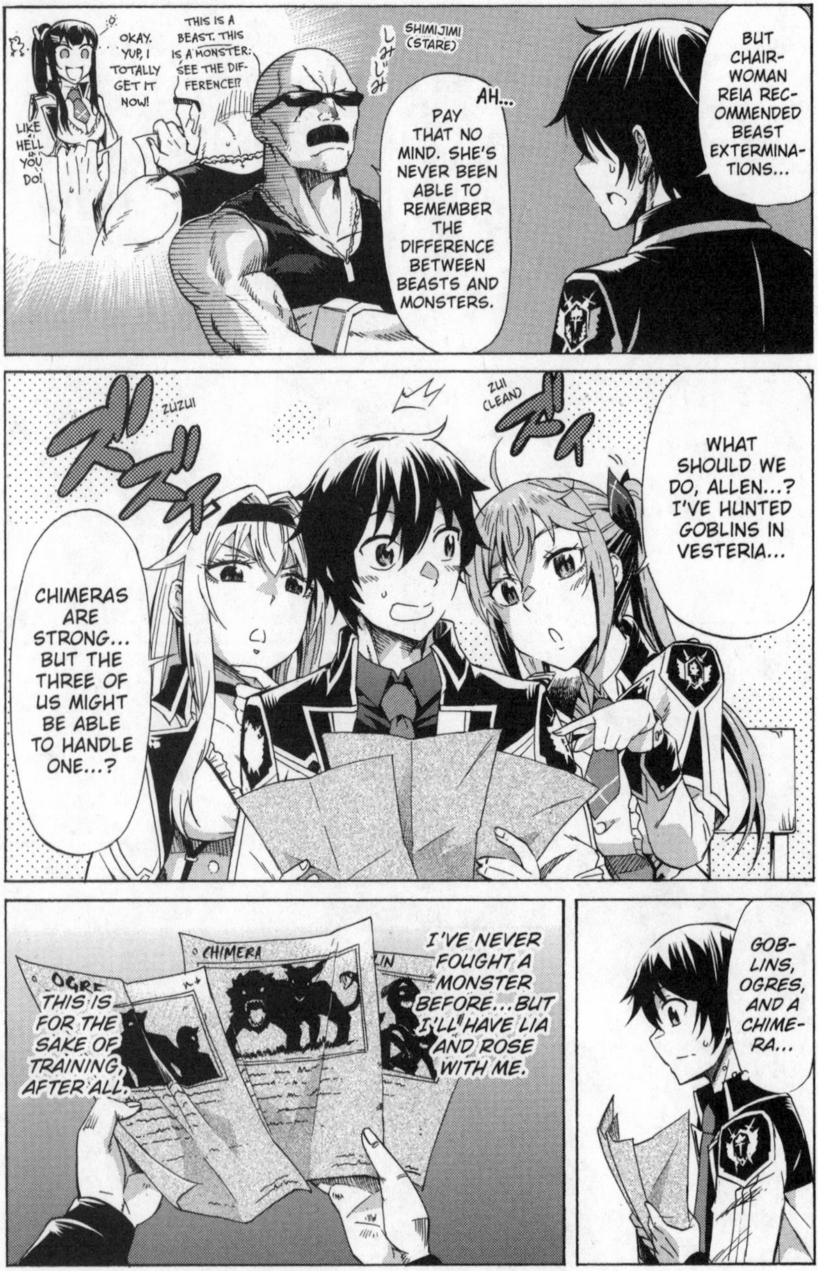
BUT CHAIR-WOMAN REIA RECOMMENDED BEAST EXTERMINATIONS...
AH... PAY THAT NO MIND. SHE'S NEVER BEEN ABLE TO REMEMBER THE DIFFERENCE BETWEEN BEASTS AND MONSTERS.
SHIMIJIMI (STARE)
THIS IS A BEAST. THIS IS A MONSTER. SEE THE DIFFERENCE!?
OKAY. YUP, I TOTALLY GET IT NOW!
LIKE HELL YOU DO!
WHAT SHOULD WE DO, ALLEN...? I'VE HUNTED GOBLINS IN VESTERIA...
ZUI (CLEAN)
ZUZUI
CHIMERAS ARE STRONG... BUT THE THREE OF US MIGHT BE ABLE TO HANDLE ONE...?
GOBLINS, OGRES, AND A CHIMERA...
I'VE NEVER FOUGHT A MONSTER BEFORE... BUT I'LL HAVE LIA AND ROSE WITH ME.
CHIMERA
OGRE
THIS IS FOR THE SAKE OF TRAINING, AFTER ALL.

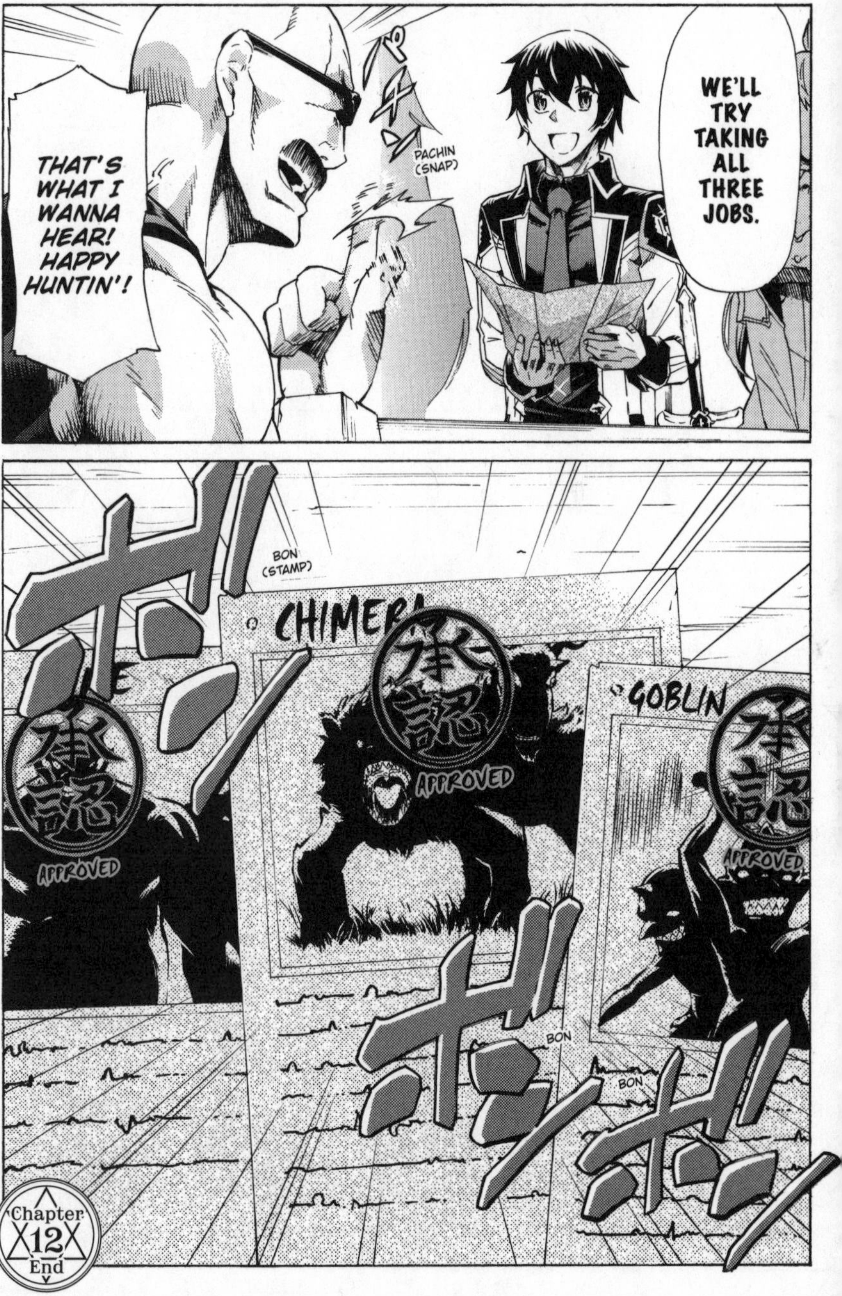
WE'LL TRY TAKING ALL THREE JOBS.
PACHIN (SNAP)
THAT'S WHAT I WANNA HEAR! HAPPY HUNTIN'!
GOBLIN
APPROVED
CHIMERA
APPROVED
BON (STAMP)
APPROVED
BON
BON
Chapter 12 End

I KEPT PRESSING THE 100-MILLION-YEAR BUTTON AND CAME OUT ON TOP

~THE UNBEATABLE REJECT SWORDSMAN~

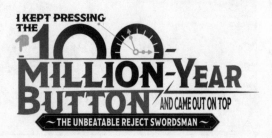

Chapter 13

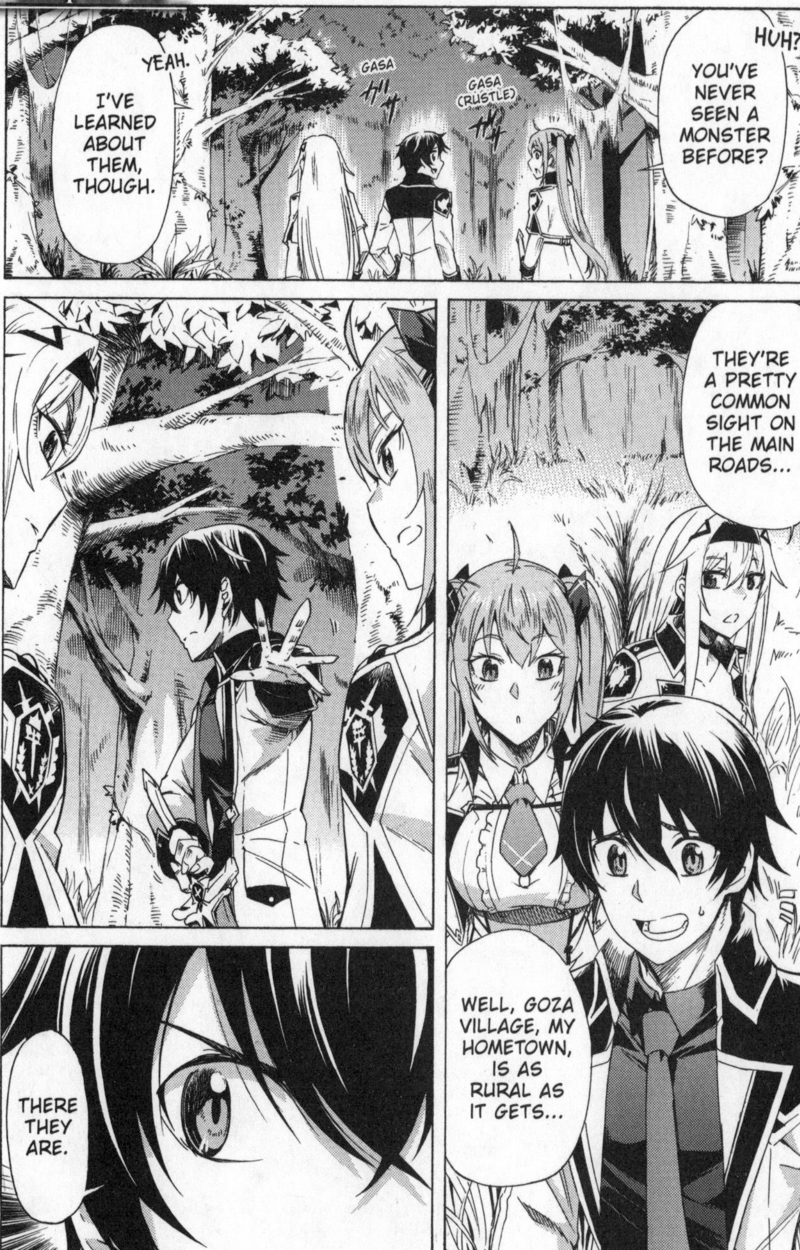
HUH?
YOU'VE NEVER SEEN A MONSTER BEFORE?
GASA (RUSTLE)
GASA
YEAH.
I'VE LEARNED ABOUT THEM, THOUGH.
THEY'RE A PRETTY COMMON SIGHT ON THE MAIN ROADS...
WELL, GOZA VILLAGE, MY HOMETOWN, IS AS RURAL AS IT GETS...
THERE THEY ARE.

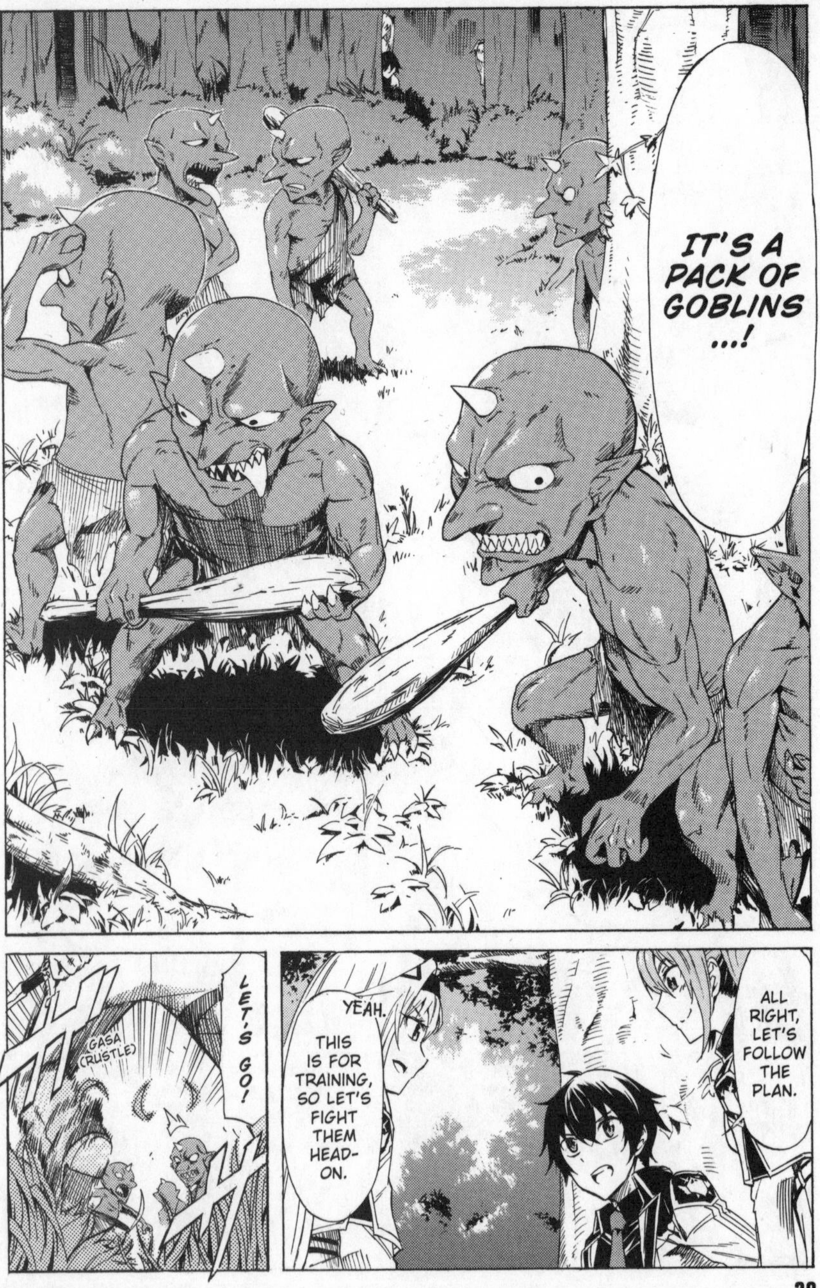
IT'S A PACK OF GOBLINS ...!
ALL RIGHT, LET'S FOLLOW THE PLAN.
YEAH.
THIS IS FOR TRAINING, SO LET'S FIGHT THEM HEAD-ON.
LET'S GO!
GASA (RUSTLE)

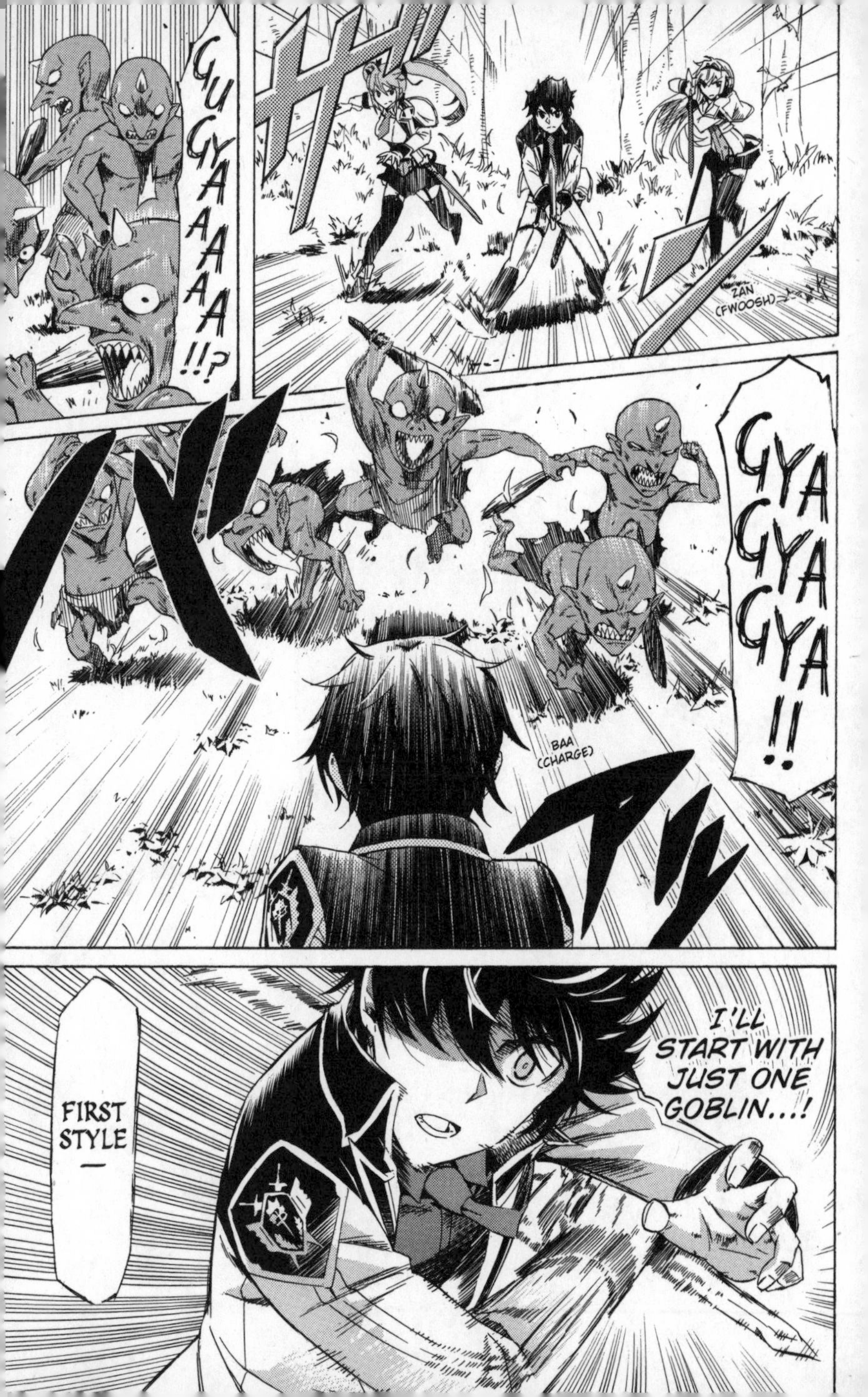
ZAN
(FWOOSH)
GUGYAAAAAA!!?
GYAGYAGYA!!
BAA
(CHARGE)
I'LL START WITH JUST ONE GOBLIN...!
FIRST STYLE —

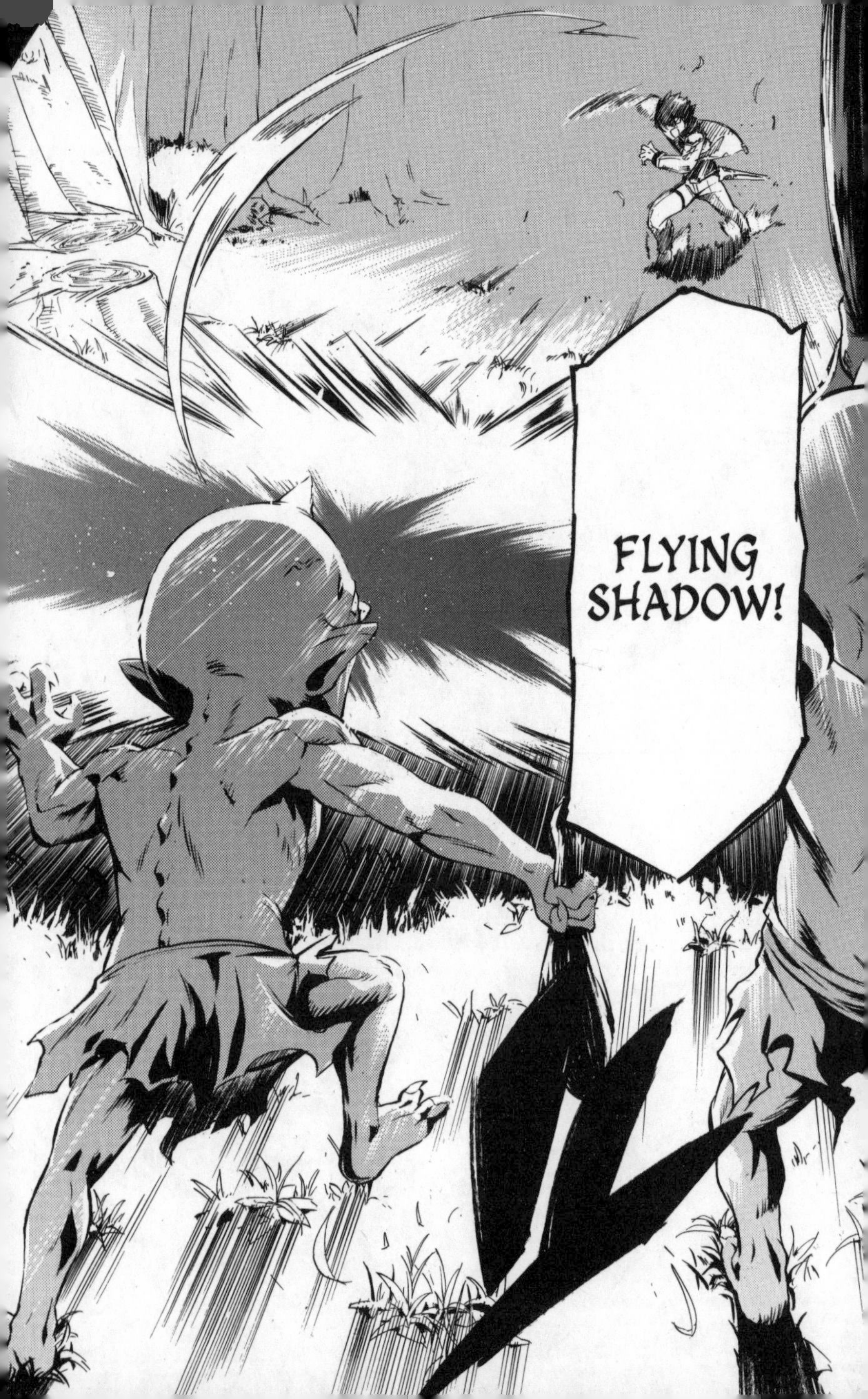
FLYING SHADOW!

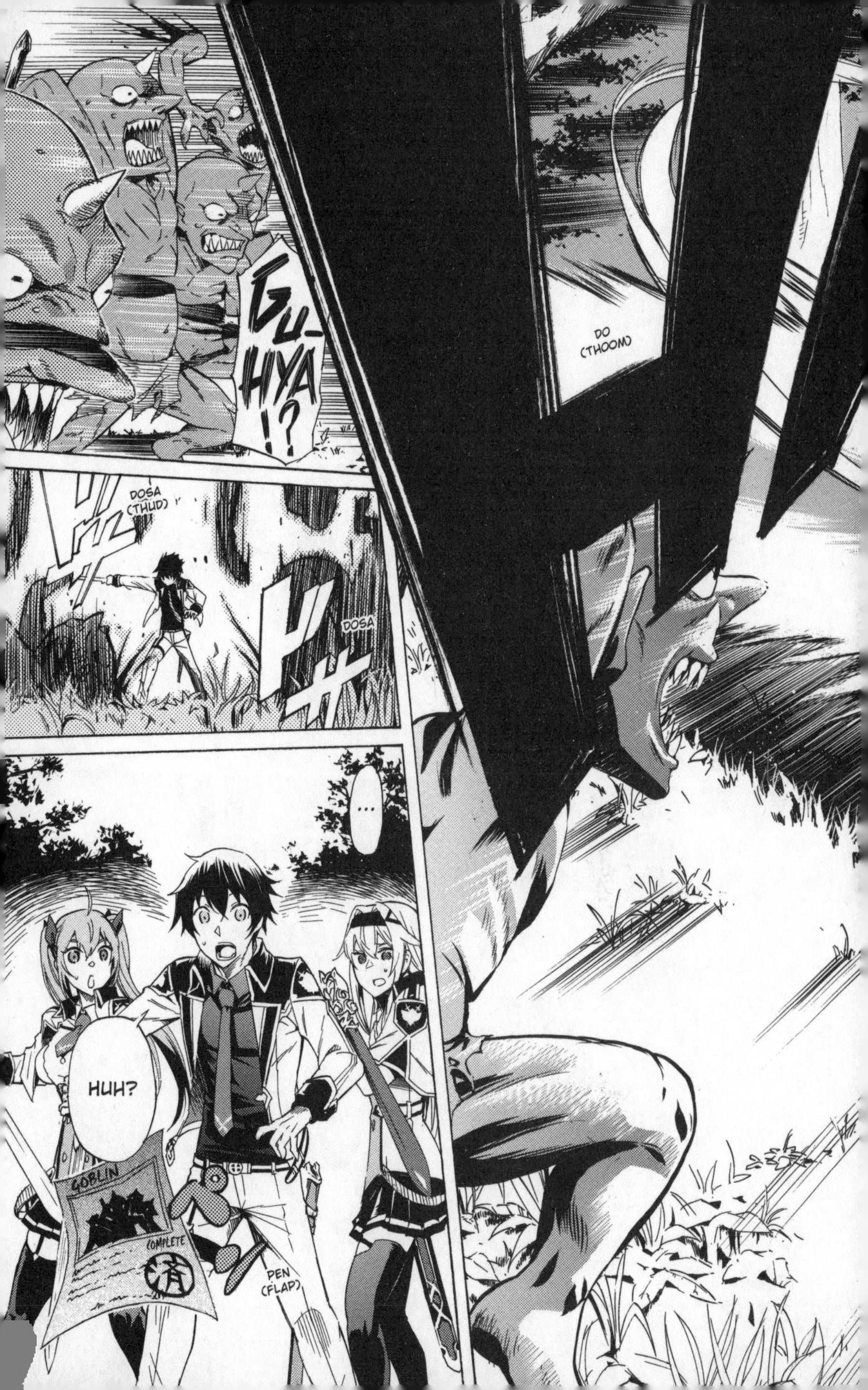
DO (THOOM)
GU-HYA!?
DOSA (THUD)
...
DOSA
...
HUH?
GOBLIN
COMPLETE
PEN (FLAP)

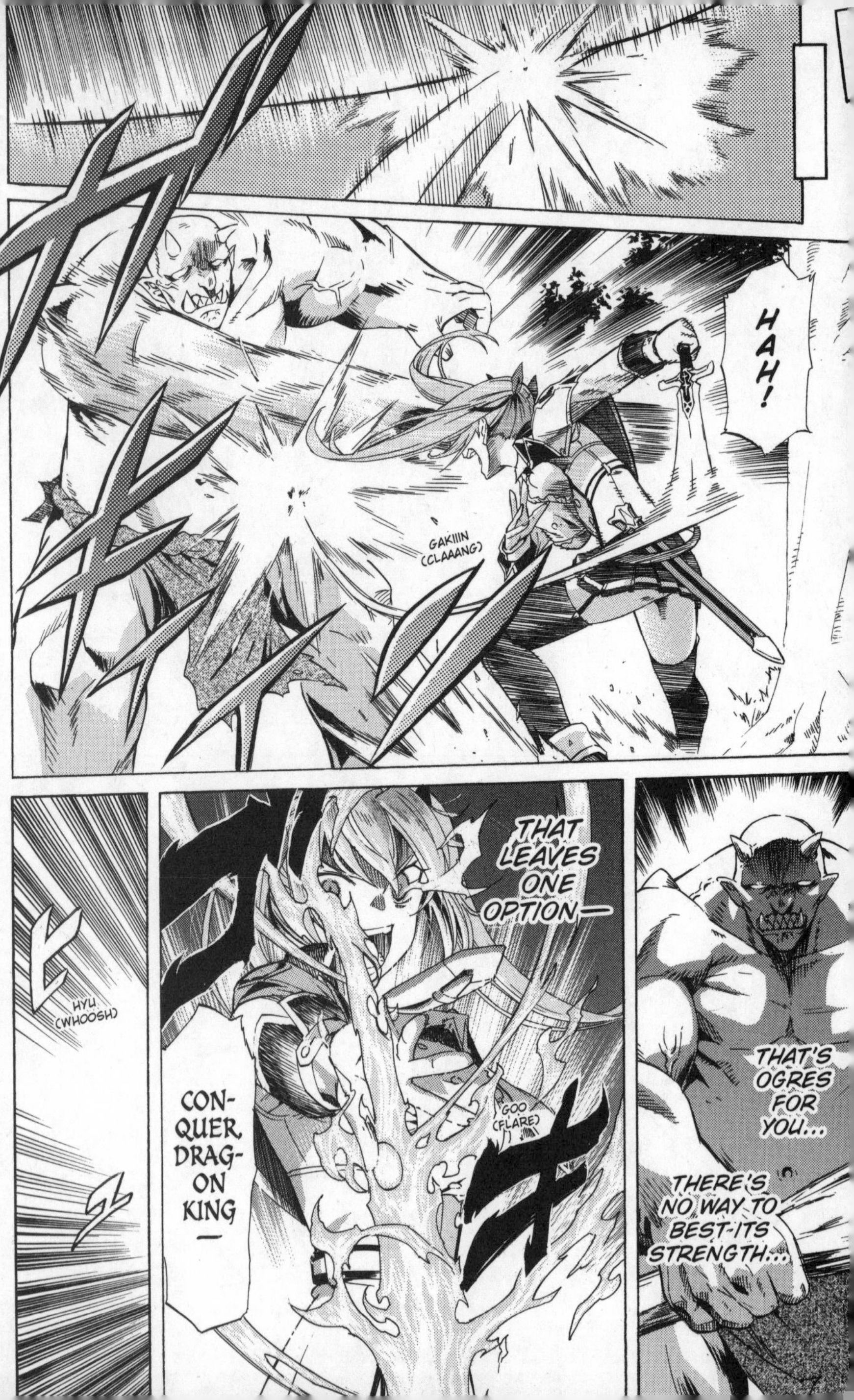
HAH!
GAKIIN (CLAAANG)
THAT'S OGRES FOR YOU...
THERE'S NO WAY TO BEST ITS STRENGTH...
THAT LEAVES ONE OPTION—
CONQUER DRAGON KING—
GOO (FLARE)
HYU (WHOOSH)

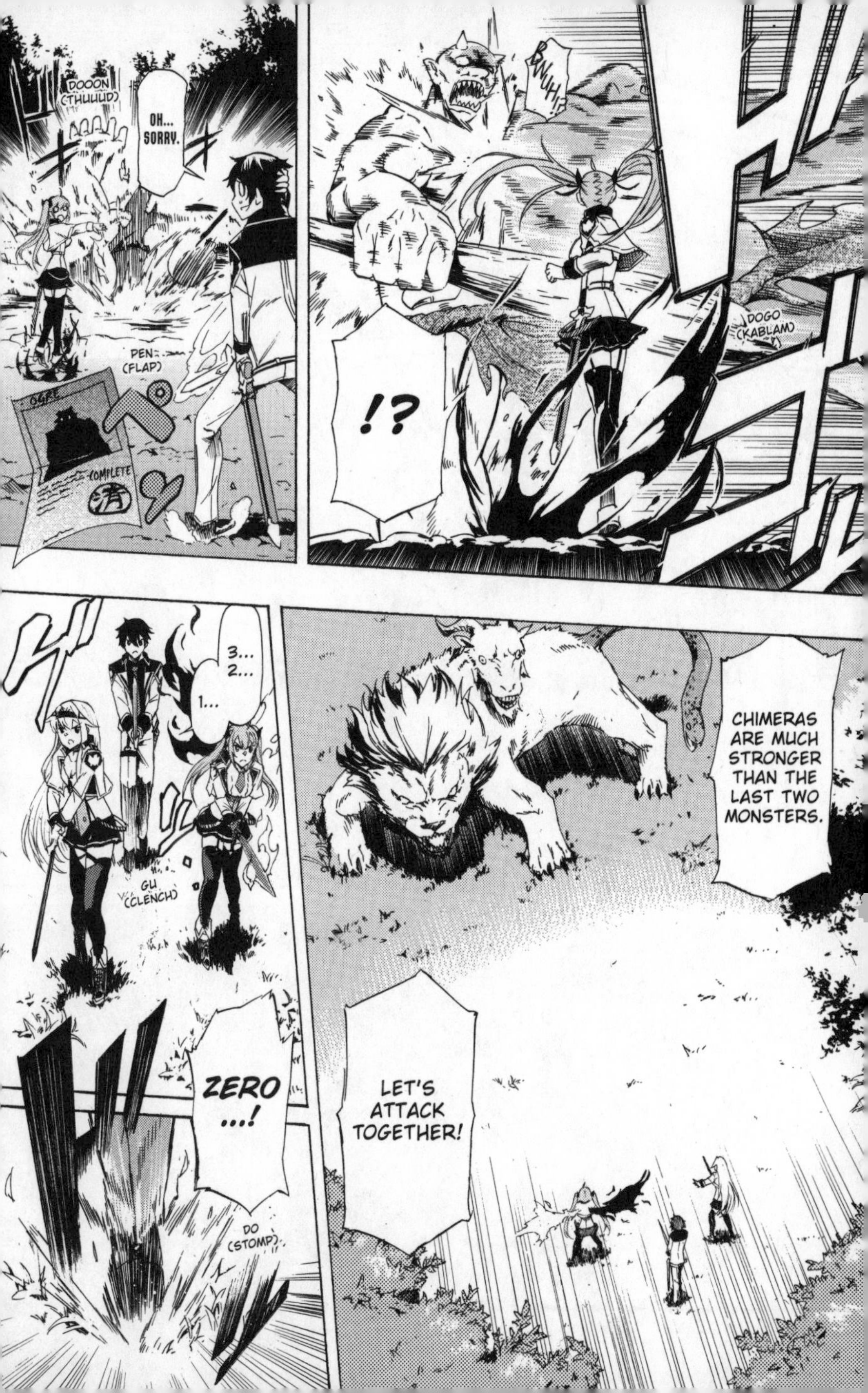
BNUH!?
!?
DOGO (KABLAM)
DOOON (THUUUD)
OH... SORRY.
PEN (FLAP)
OGRE
COMPLETE
CHIMERAS ARE MUCH STRONGER THAN THE LAST TWO MONSTERS.
LET'S ATTACK TOGETHER!
3... 2... 1...
GU (CLENCH)
ZERO ...!
DO (STOMP)

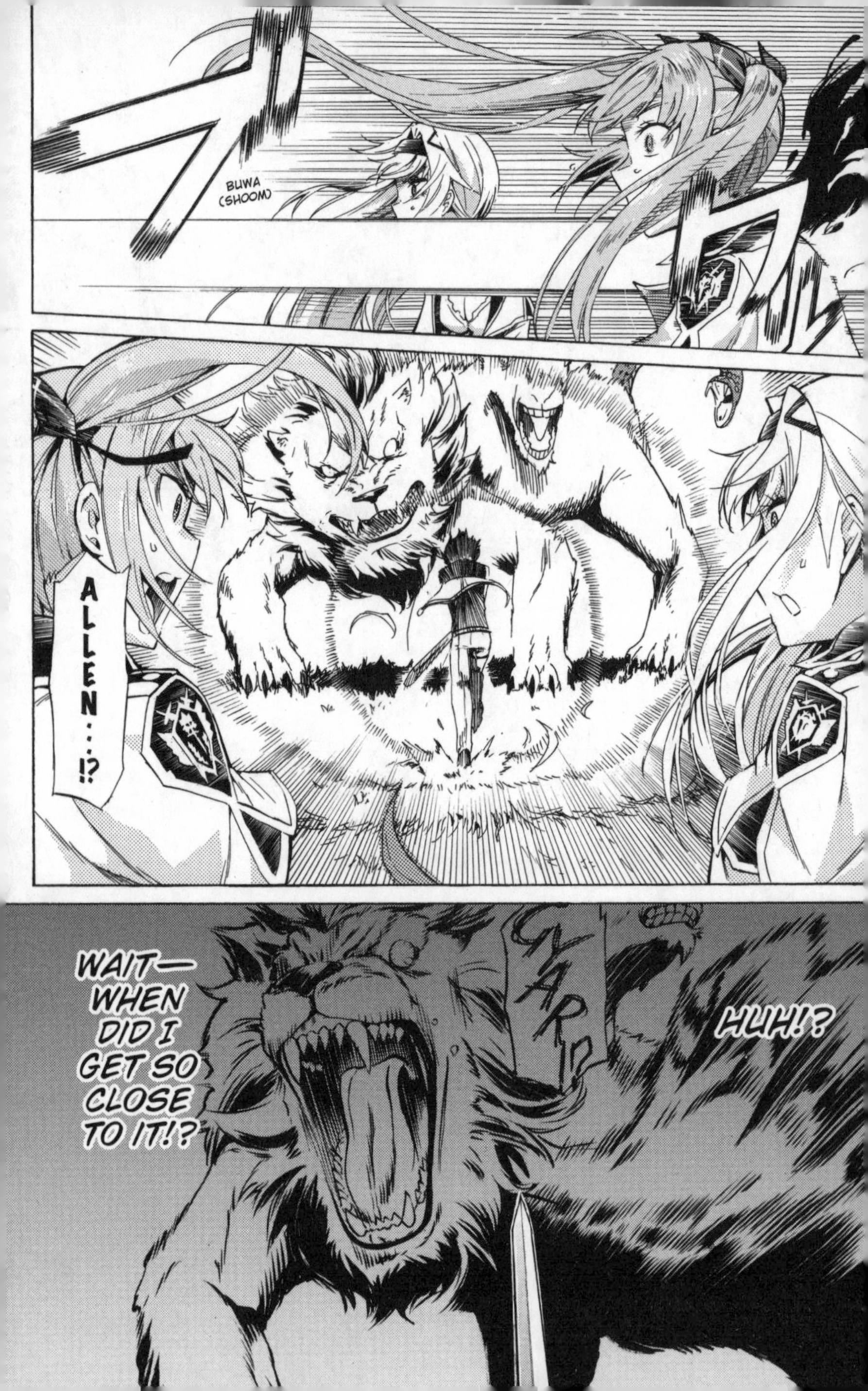
BUWA (SHOOM)
ALLEN...!?
HUH!?
GYAR
WAIT— WHEN DID I GET SO CLOSE TO IT!?

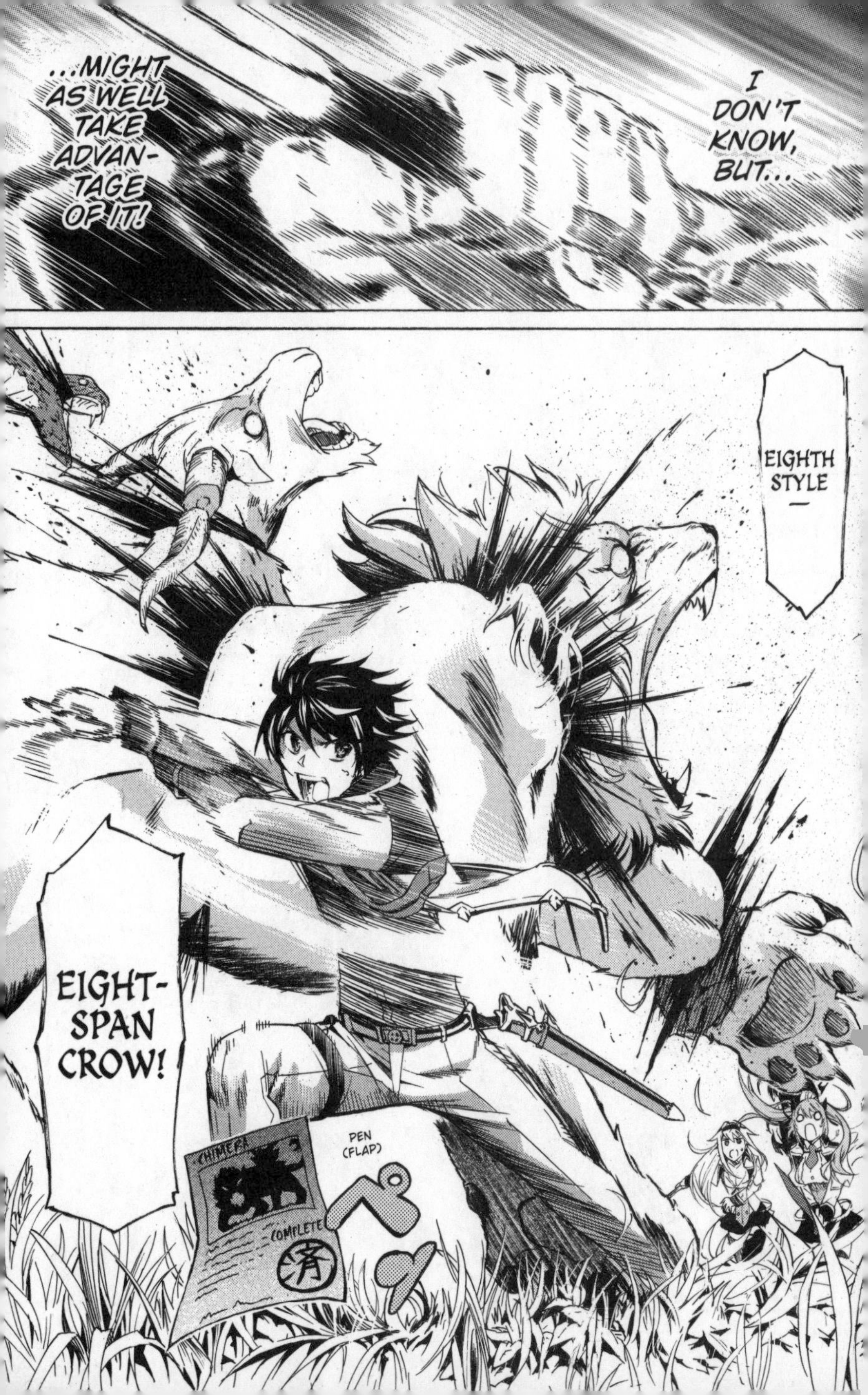
I DON'T KNOW, BUT...
...MIGHT AS WELL TAKE ADVAN-TAGE OF IT!
EIGHTH STYLE —
EIGHT-SPAN CROW!
PEN (FLAP)
ペ
CHIMERA
COMPLETE
済

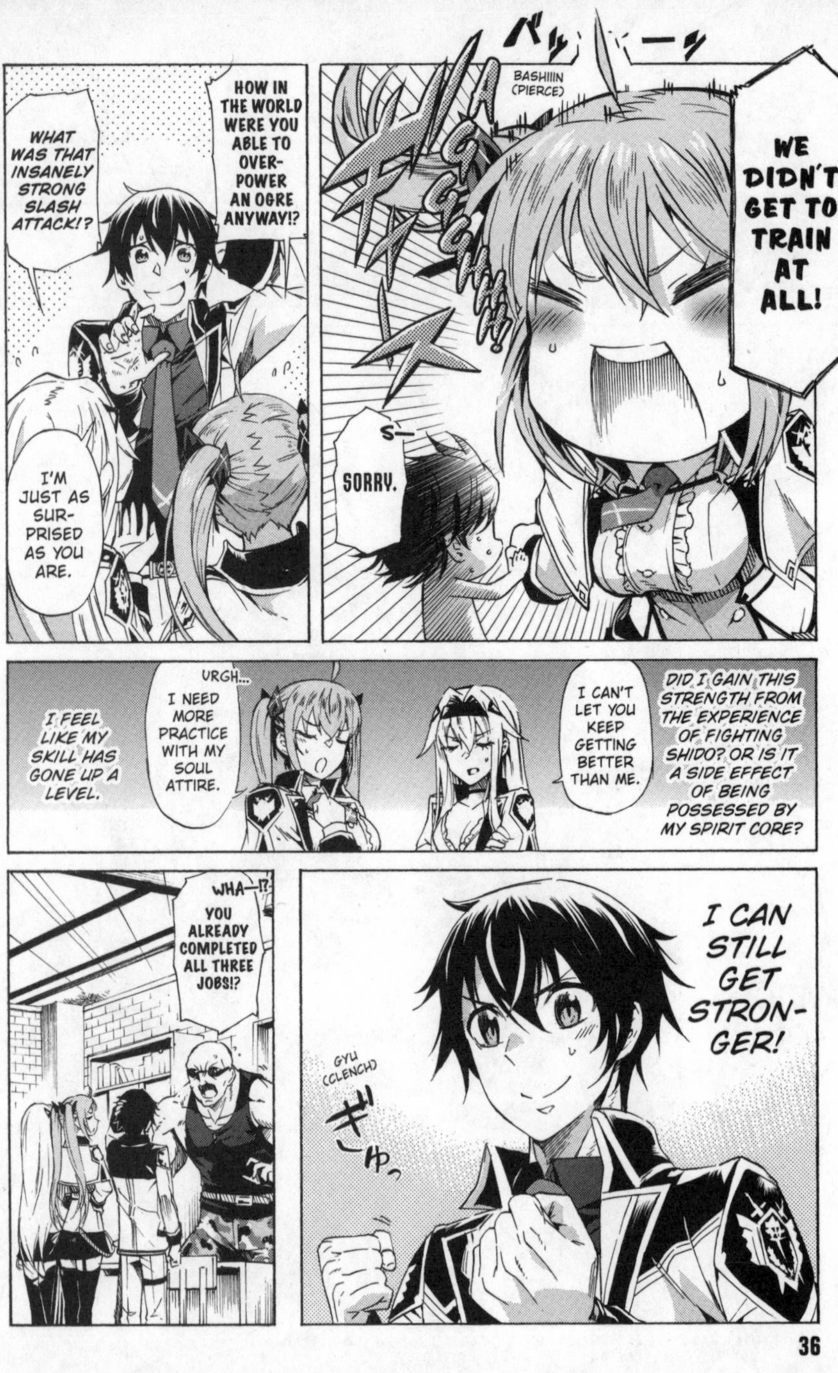
BASHIIIN (PIERCE)
WE DIDN'T GET TO TRAIN AT ALL!
S— SORRY.
HOW IN THE WORLD WERE YOU ABLE TO OVER-POWER AN OGRE ANYWAY!?
WHAT WAS THAT INSANELY STRONG SLASH ATTACK!?
I'M JUST AS SUR-PRISED AS YOU ARE.
DID I GAIN THIS STRENGTH FROM THE EXPERIENCE OF FIGHTING SHIDO? OR IS IT A SIDE EFFECT OF BEING POSSESSED BY MY SPIRIT CORE?
I CAN'T LET YOU KEEP GETTING BETTER THAN ME.
URGH... I NEED MORE PRACTICE WITH MY SOUL ATTIRE.
I FEEL LIKE MY SKILL HAS GONE UP A LEVEL.
I CAN STILL GET STRON-GER!
GYU (CLENCH)
WHA—!? YOU ALREADY COMPLETED ALL THREE JOBS!?

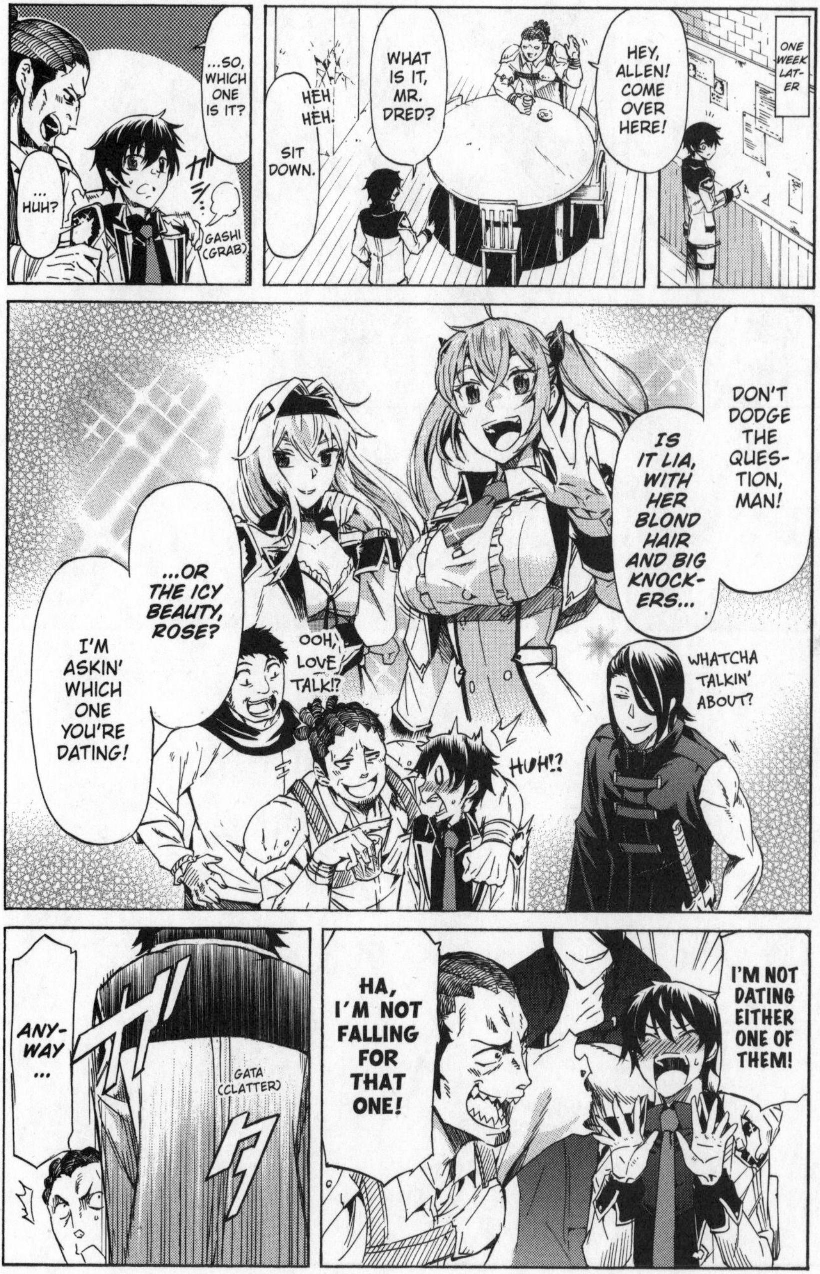
ONE WEEK LATER
HEY, ALLEN! COME OVER HERE!
WHAT IS IT, MR. DRED?
HEH HEH.
SIT DOWN.
...SO, WHICH ONE IS IT?
... HUH?
GASHI (GRAB)
DON'T DODGE THE QUESTION, MAN!
IS IT LIA, WITH HER BLOND HAIR AND BIG KNOCKERS...
...OR THE ICY BEAUTY, ROSE?
I'M ASKIN' WHICH ONE YOU'RE DATING!
WHATCHA TALKIN' ABOUT?
OOH, LOVE TALK!?
HUH!?
I'M NOT DATING EITHER ONE OF THEM!
HA, I'M NOT FALLING FOR THAT ONE!
ANY-WAY...
GATA (CLATTER)

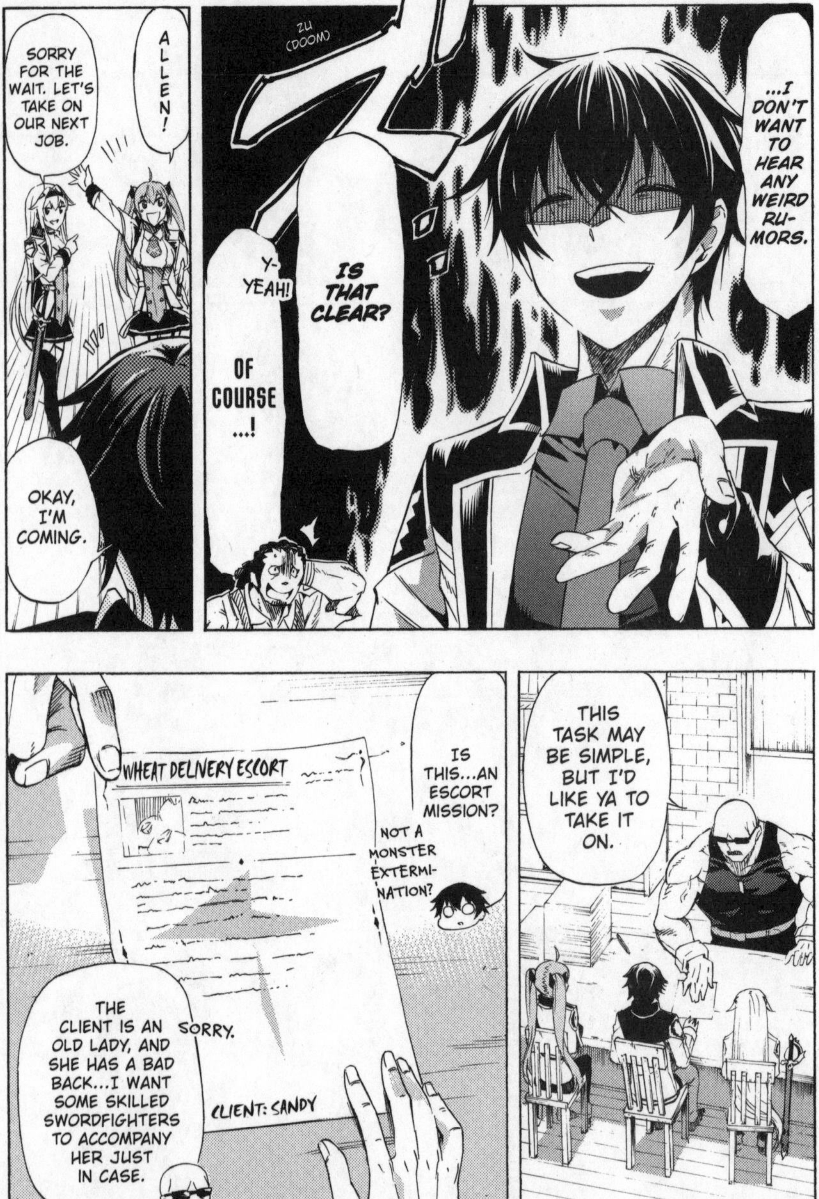
ZU (DOOM)
...I DON'T WANT TO HEAR ANY WEIRD RU-MORS.
IS THAT CLEAR?
Y-YEAH!
OF COURSE ...!
ALLEN!
SORRY FOR THE WAIT. LET'S TAKE ON OUR NEXT JOB.
OKAY, I'M COMING.
THIS TASK MAY BE SIMPLE, BUT I'D LIKE YA TO TAKE IT ON.
IS THIS...AN ESCORT MISSION?
NOT A MONSTER EXTERMI-NATION?
WHEAT DELIVERY ESCORT
THE CLIENT IS AN OLD LADY, AND SHE HAS A BAD BACK...I WANT SOME SKILLED SWORDFIGHTERS TO ACCOMPANY HER JUST IN CASE.
SORRY.
CLIENT: SANDY

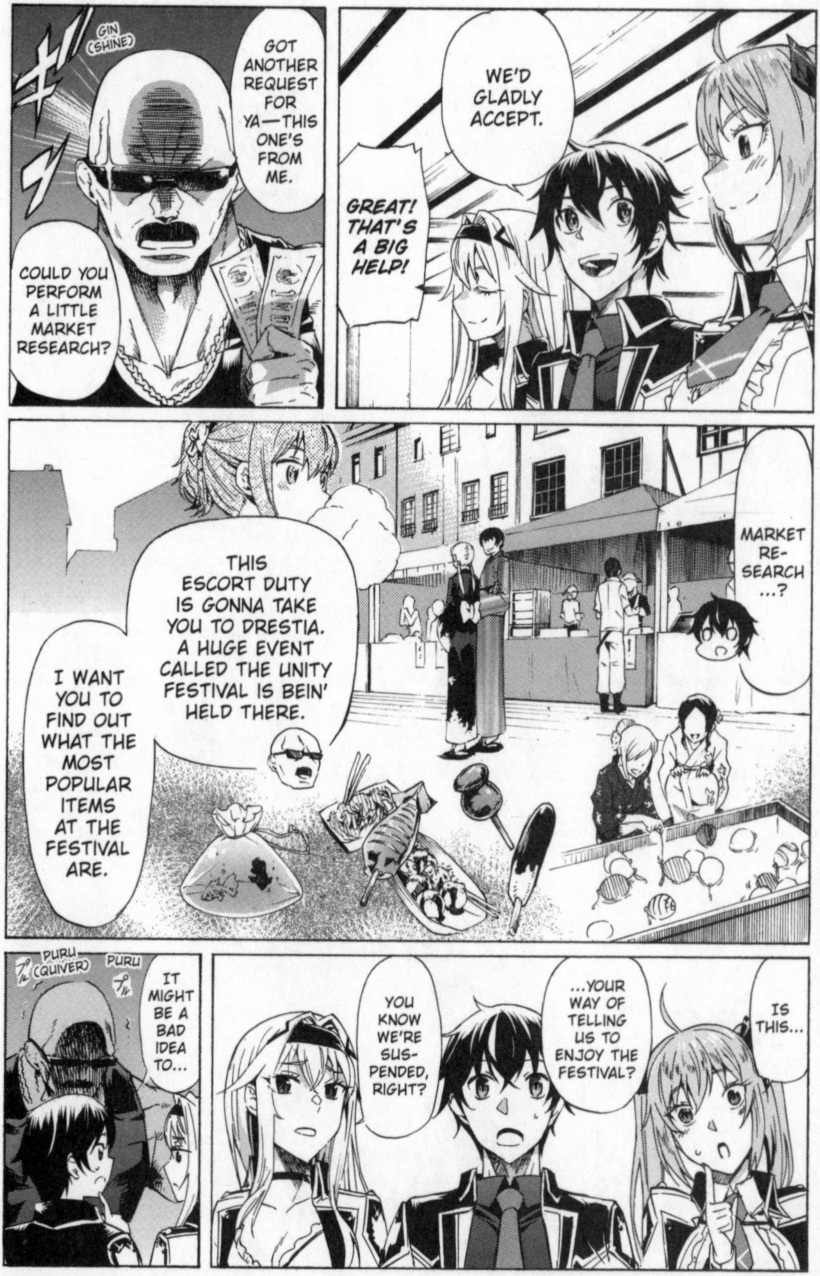
WE'D GLADLY ACCEPT.
GREAT! THAT'S A BIG HELP!
GIN (SHINE)
GOT ANOTHER REQUEST FOR YA—THIS ONE'S FROM ME.
COULD YOU PERFORM A LITTLE MARKET RESEARCH?
MARKET RE-SEARCH...?
THIS ESCORT DUTY IS GONNA TAKE YOU TO DRESTIA. A HUGE EVENT CALLED THE UNITY FESTIVAL IS BEIN' HELD THERE.
I WANT YOU TO FIND OUT WHAT THE MOST POPULAR ITEMS AT THE FESTIVAL ARE.
IS THIS...
...YOUR WAY OF TELLING US TO ENJOY THE FESTIVAL?
YOU KNOW WE'RE SUS-PENDED, RIGHT?
PURU (QUIVER)
PURU
IT MIGHT BE A BAD IDEA TO...

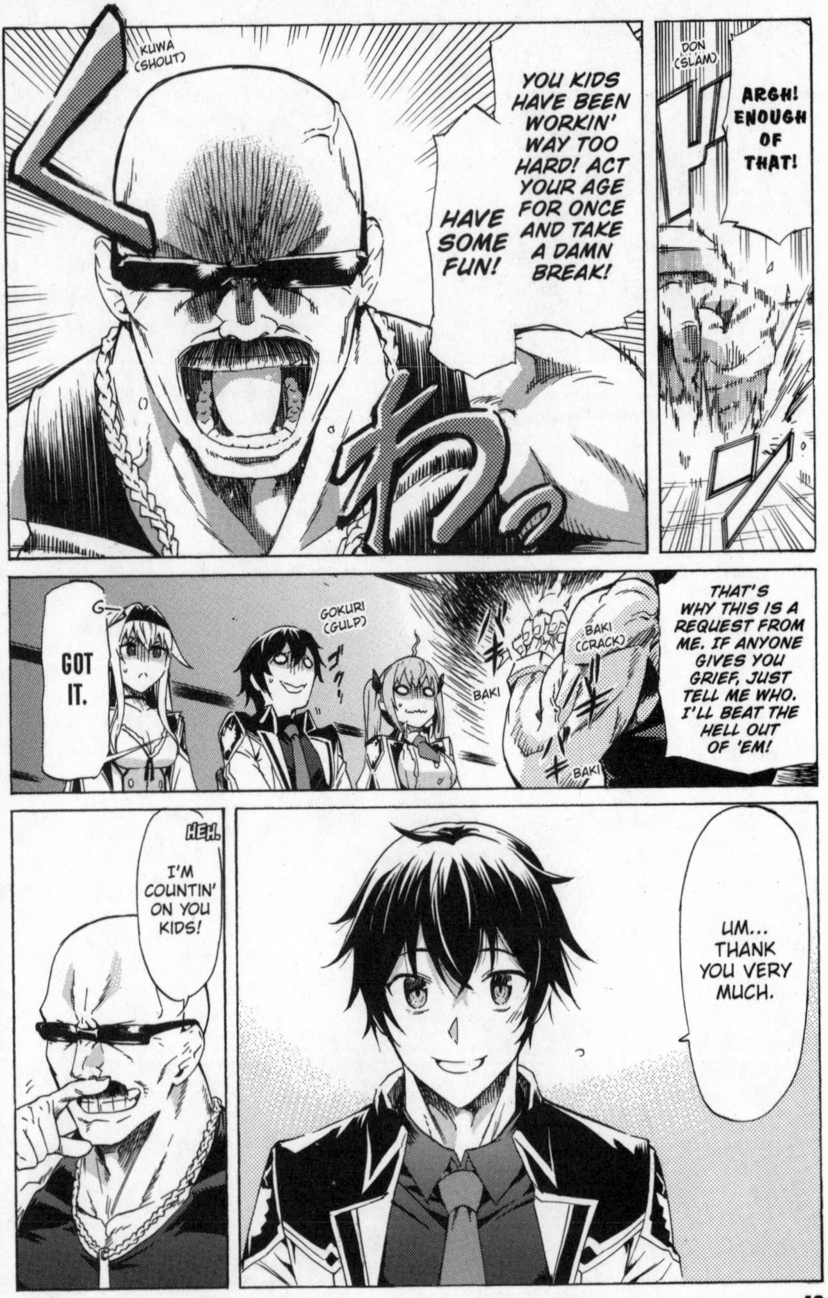
DON (SLAM)
ARGH! ENOUGH OF THAT!
KUWA (SHOUT)
YOU KIDS HAVE BEEN WORKIN' WAY TOO HARD! ACT YOUR AGE FOR ONCE AND TAKE A DAMN BREAK!
HAVE SOME FUN!
THAT'S WHY THIS IS A REQUEST FROM ME. IF ANYONE GIVES YOU GRIEF, JUST TELL ME WHO. I'LL BEAT THE HELL OUT OF 'EM!
BAKI (CRACK)
BAKI
BAKI
GOKURI (GULP)
GOT IT.
UM... THANK YOU VERY MUCH.
HEH.
I'M COUNTIN' ON YOU KIDS!

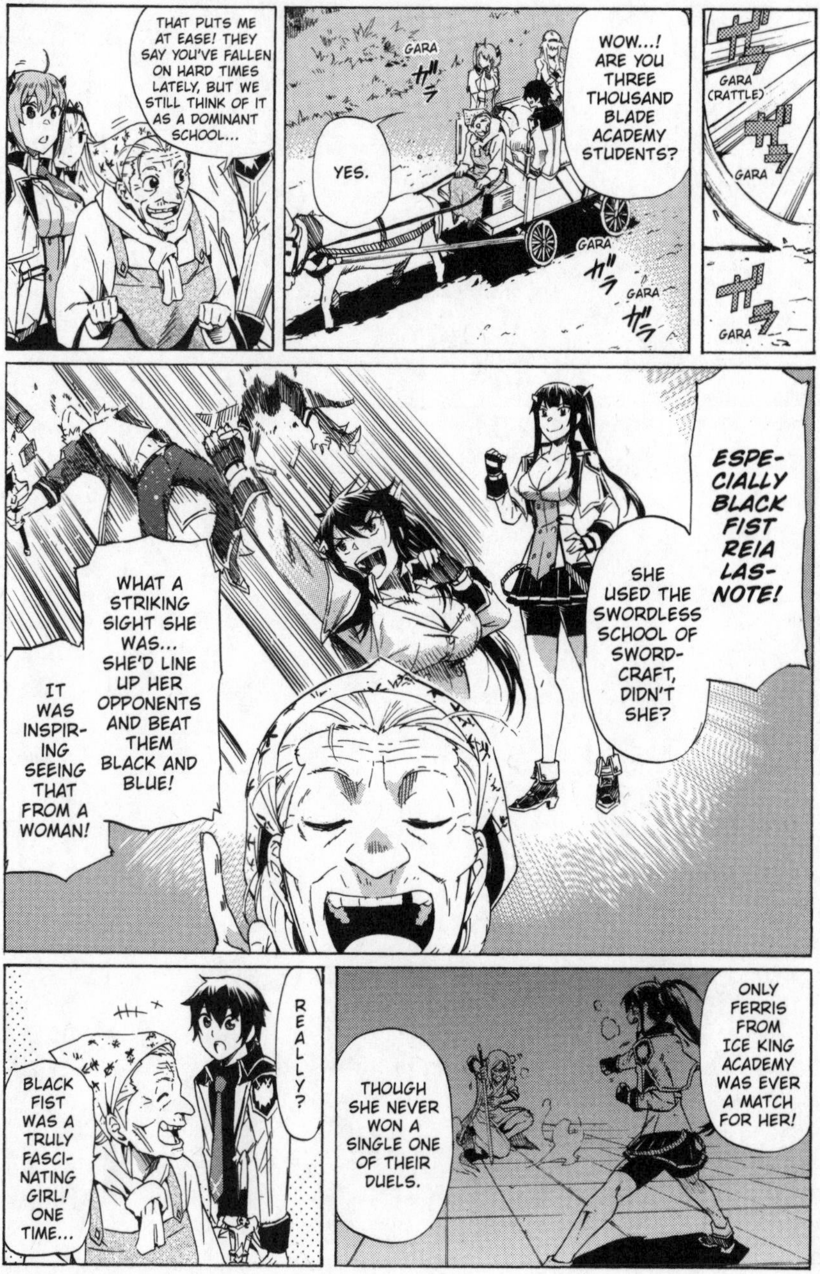
GARA (RATTLE)
GARA
GARA
WOW...! ARE YOU THREE THOUSAND BLADE ACADEMY STUDENTS?
GARA
YES.
GARA
GARA
THAT PUTS ME AT EASE! THEY SAY YOU'VE FALLEN ON HARD TIMES LATELY, BUT WE STILL THINK OF IT AS A DOMINANT SCHOOL...
ESPECIALLY BLACK FIST REIA LASNOTE!
SHE USED THE SWORDLESS SCHOOL OF SWORDCRAFT, DIDN'T SHE?
WHAT A STRIKING SIGHT SHE WAS... SHE'D LINE UP HER OPPONENTS AND BEAT THEM BLACK AND BLUE!
IT WAS INSPIRING SEEING THAT FROM A WOMAN!
ONLY FERRIS FROM ICE KING ACADEMY WAS EVER A MATCH FOR HER!
THOUGH SHE NEVER WON A SINGLE ONE OF THEIR DUELS.
REALLY?
BLACK FIST WAS A TRULY FASCINATING GIRL! ONE TIME...

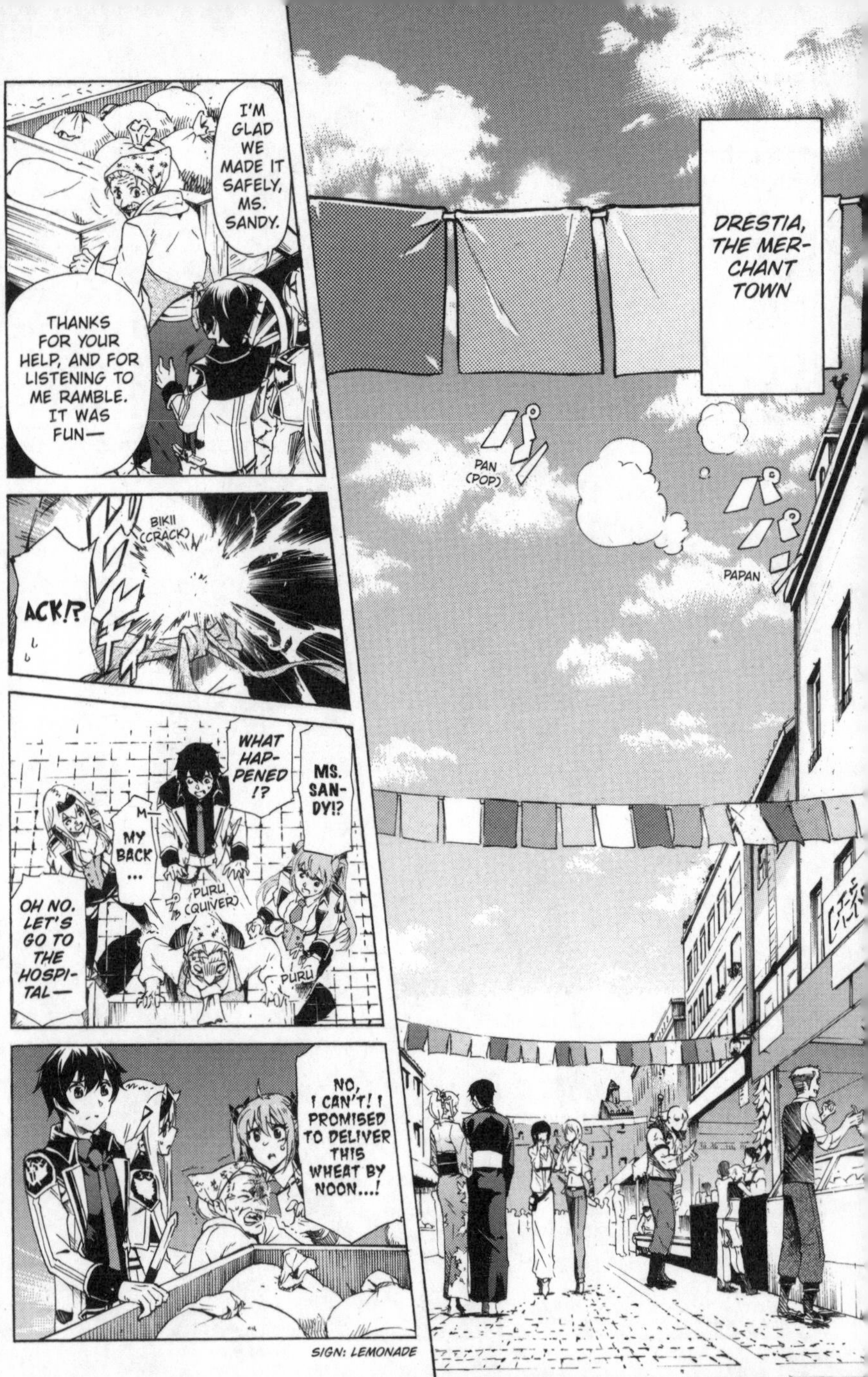
DRESTIA, THE MER-CHANT TOWN
PAN (POP)
PAPAN
I'M GLAD WE MADE IT SAFELY, MS. SANDY.
THANKS FOR YOUR HELP, AND FOR LISTENING TO ME RAMBLE. IT WAS FUN—
BIKII (CRACK)
ACK!?
MS. SANDY!?
WHAT HAP-PENED!?
M— MY BACK...
PURU (QUIVER)
PURU
OH NO. LET'S GO TO THE HOSPI-TAL—
NO, I CAN'T! I PROMISED TO DELIVER THIS WHEAT BY NOON...!
SIGN: LEMONADE

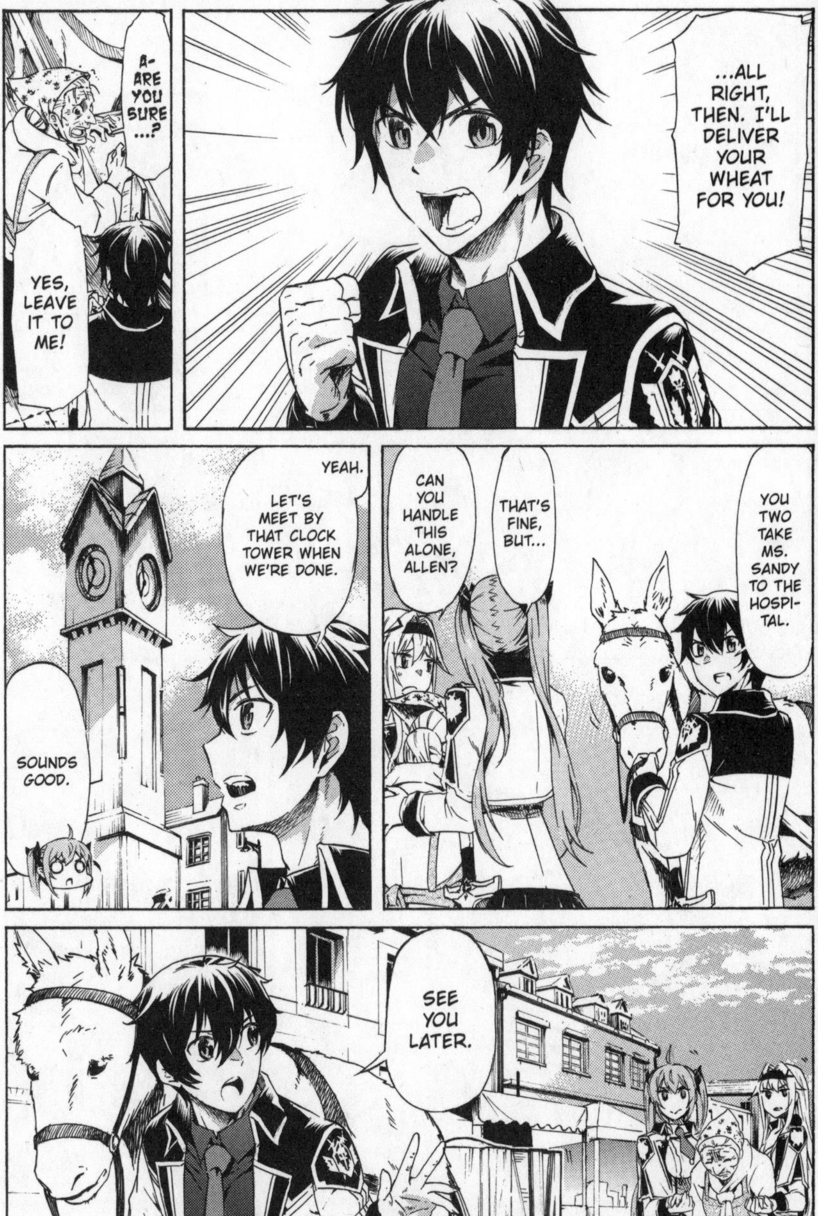
...ALL RIGHT, THEN. I'LL DELIVER YOUR WHEAT FOR YOU!
A-ARE YOU SURE...?
YES, LEAVE IT TO ME!
YOU TWO TAKE MS. SANDY TO THE HOSPITAL.
THAT'S FINE, BUT...
CAN YOU HANDLE THIS ALONE, ALLEN?
YEAH.
LET'S MEET BY THAT CLOCK TOWER WHEN WE'RE DONE.
SOUNDS GOOD.
SEE YOU LATER.

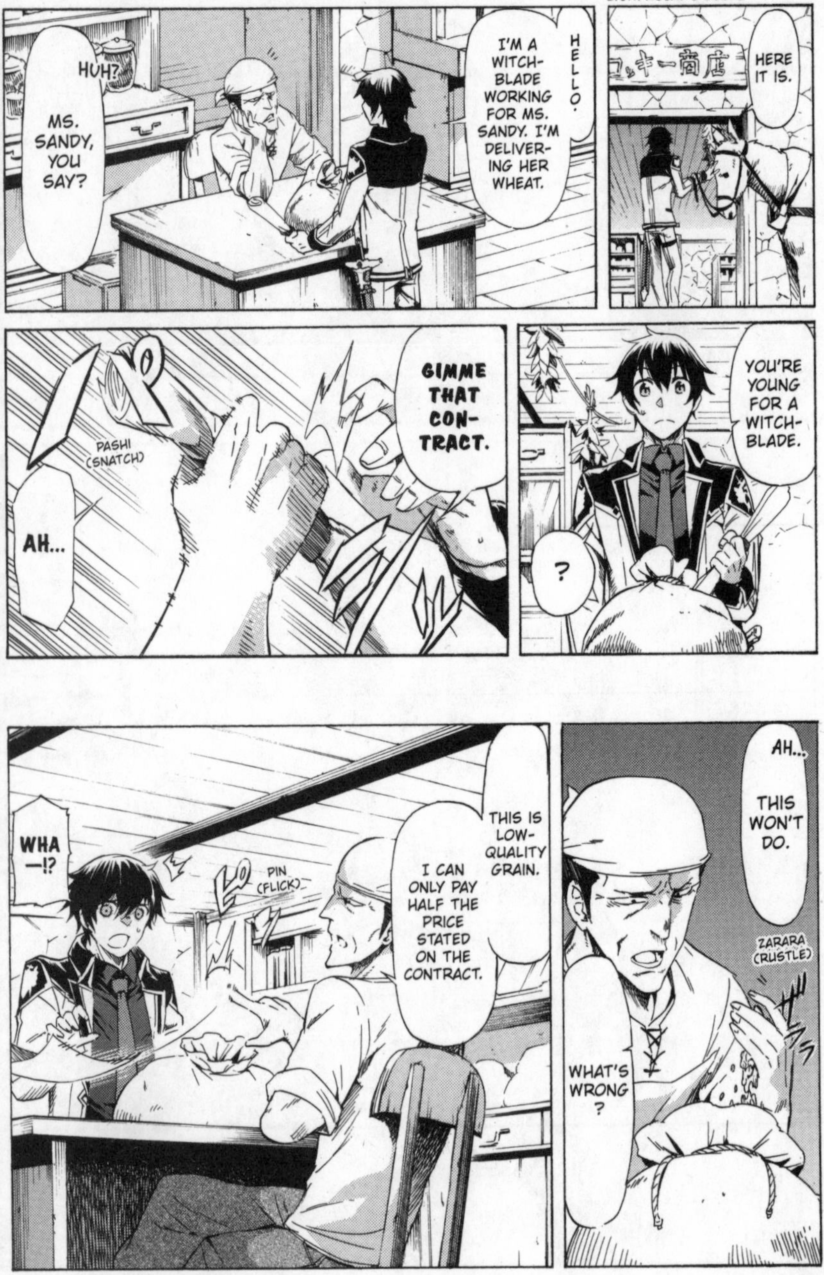
SIGN: ROCKY'S GOODS
HERE IT IS.
HELLO.
I'M A WITCH-BLADE WORKING FOR MS. SANDY. I'M DELIVER-ING HER WHEAT.
HUH?
MS. SANDY, YOU SAY?
YOU'RE YOUNG FOR A WITCH-BLADE.
?
GIMME THAT CON-TRACT.
PASHI (SNATCH)
AH...
AH...
THIS WON'T DO.
ZARARA (RUSTLE)
WHAT'S WRONG ?
THIS IS LOW-QUALITY GRAIN.
I CAN ONLY PAY HALF THE PRICE STATED ON THE CONTRACT.
PIN (FLICK)
WHA —!?

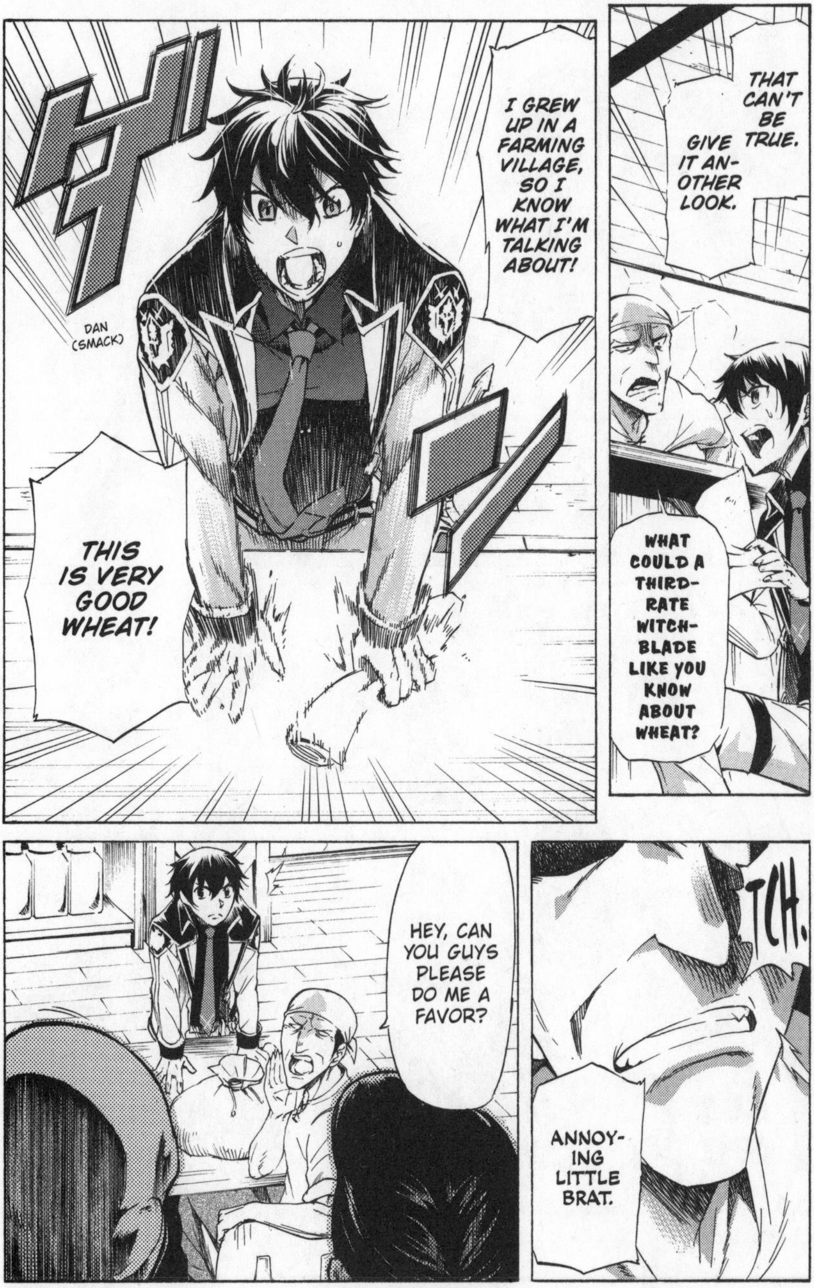
THAT CAN'T BE TRUE.
GIVE IT AN-OTHER LOOK.
WHAT COULD A THIRD-RATE WITCH-BLADE LIKE YOU KNOW ABOUT WHEAT?
I GREW UP IN A FARMING VILLAGE, SO I KNOW WHAT I'M TALKING ABOUT!
DAN (SMACK)
THIS IS VERY GOOD WHEAT!
TCH.
ANNOY-ING LITTLE BRAT.
HEY, CAN YOU GUYS PLEASE DO ME A FAVOR?

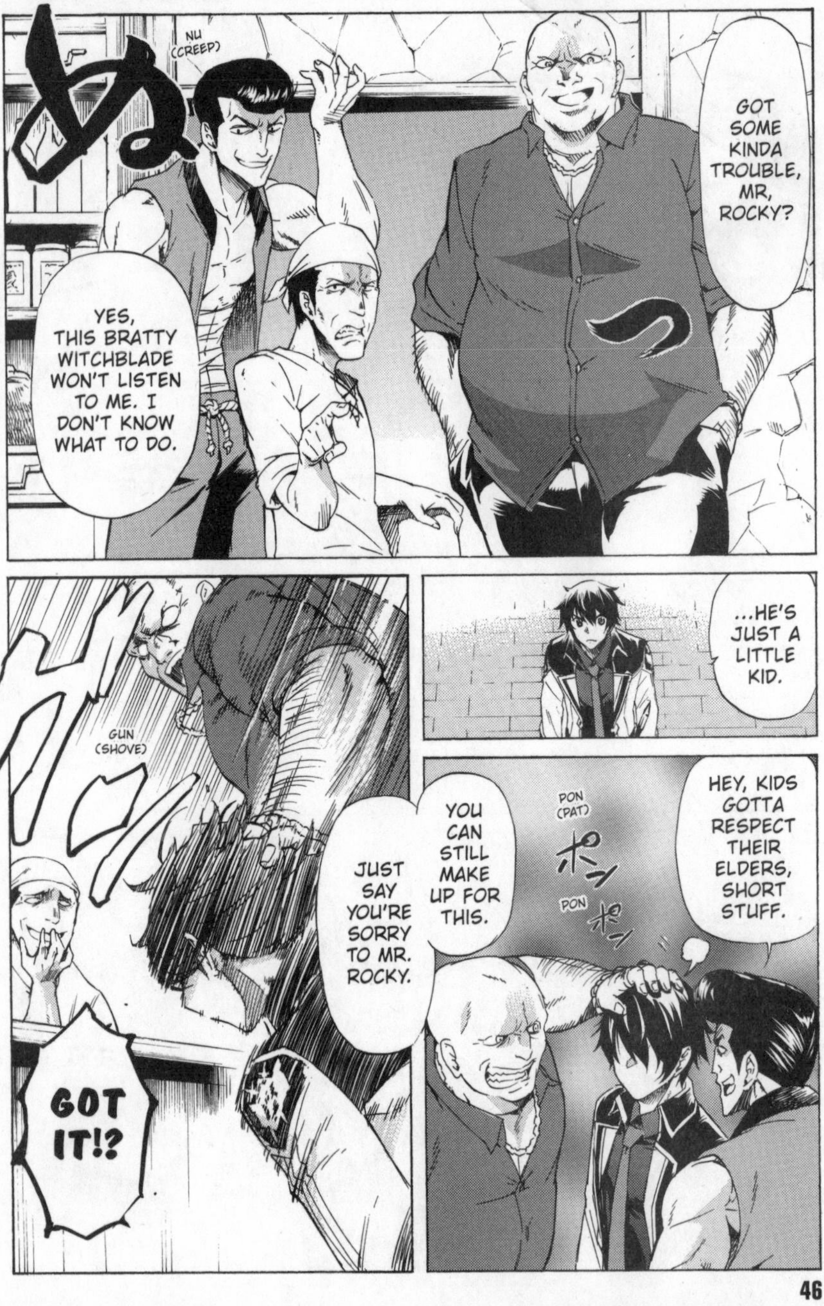
GOT SOME KINDA TROUBLE, MR, ROCKY?
ぬ
NU (CREEP)
YES, THIS BRATTY WITCHBLADE WON'T LISTEN TO ME. I DON'T KNOW WHAT TO DO.
...HE'S JUST A LITTLE KID.
HEY, KIDS GOTTA RESPECT THEIR ELDERS, SHORT STUFF.
ポン
PON (PAT)
ポン
PON
YOU CAN STILL MAKE UP FOR THIS.
JUST SAY YOU'RE SORRY TO MR. ROCKY.
GUN (SHOVE)
GOT IT!?

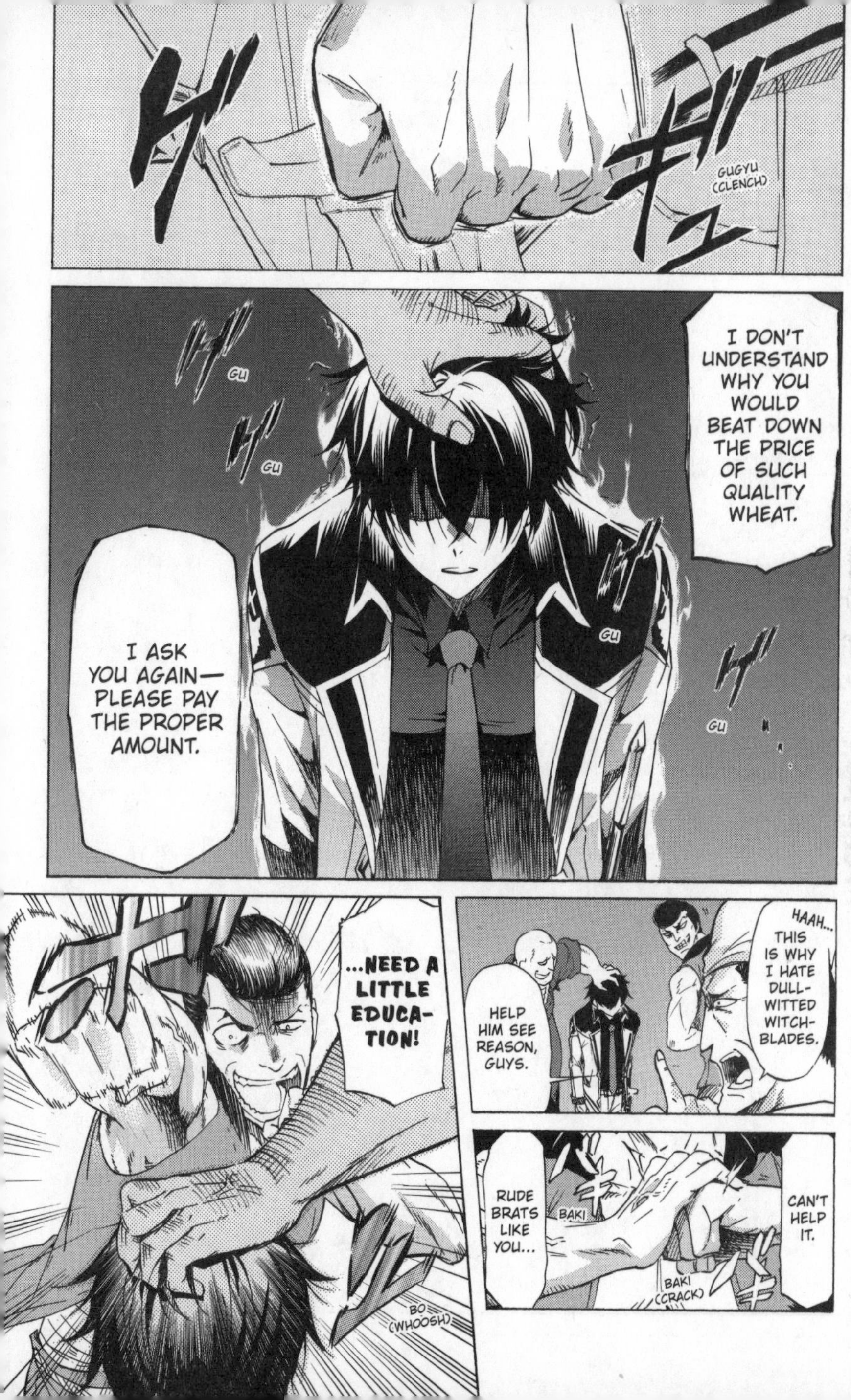
GUGYU (CLENCH)
I DON'T UNDERSTAND WHY YOU WOULD BEAT DOWN THE PRICE OF SUCH QUALITY WHEAT.
GU
GU
GU
GU
I ASK YOU AGAIN—PLEASE PAY THE PROPER AMOUNT.
HAAH... THIS IS WHY I HATE DULL-WITTED WITCH-BLADES.
HELP HIM SEE REASON, GUYS.
CAN'T HELP IT.
BAKI (CRACK)
BAKI
RUDE BRATS LIKE YOU...
...NEED A LITTLE EDUCATION!
BO (WHOOSH)

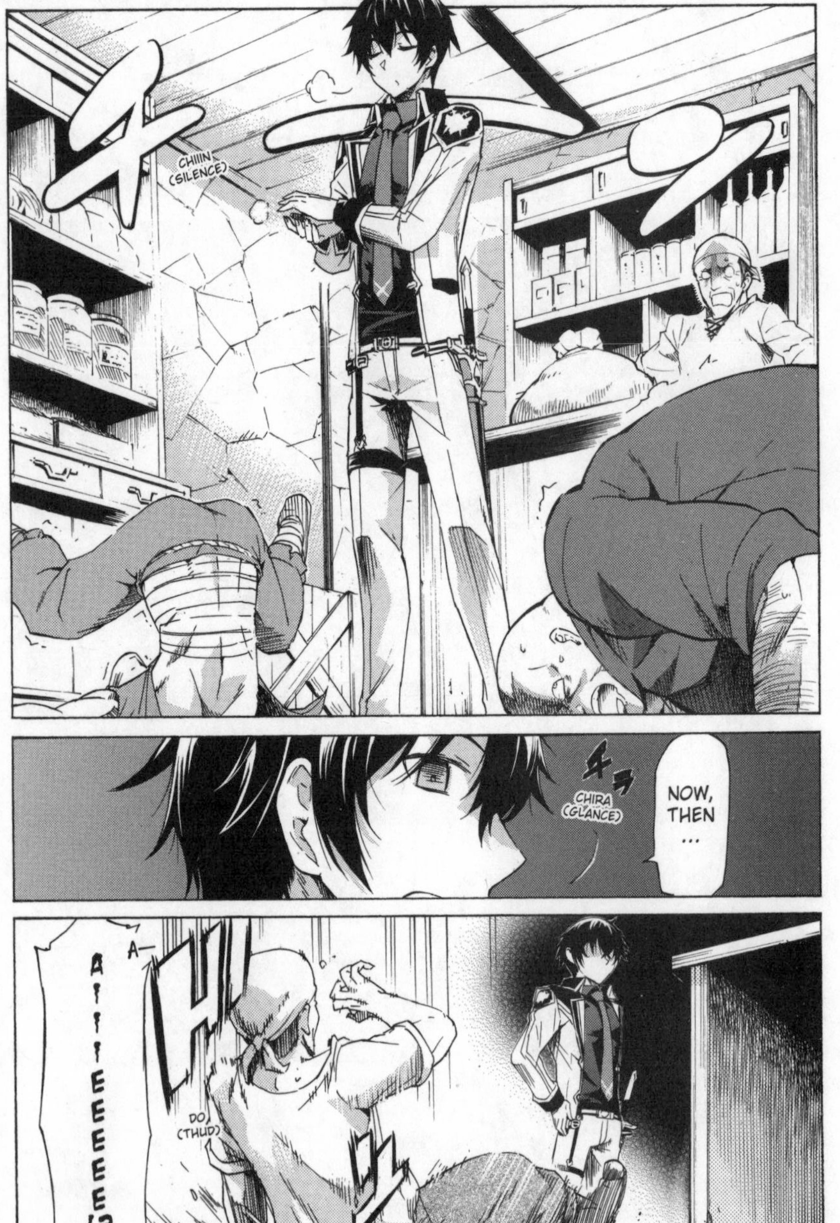
CHIIIN
(SILENCE)
NOW, THEN ...
CHIRA
(GLANCE)
DO
(THUD)
A—
AIIIEEEEEE!?

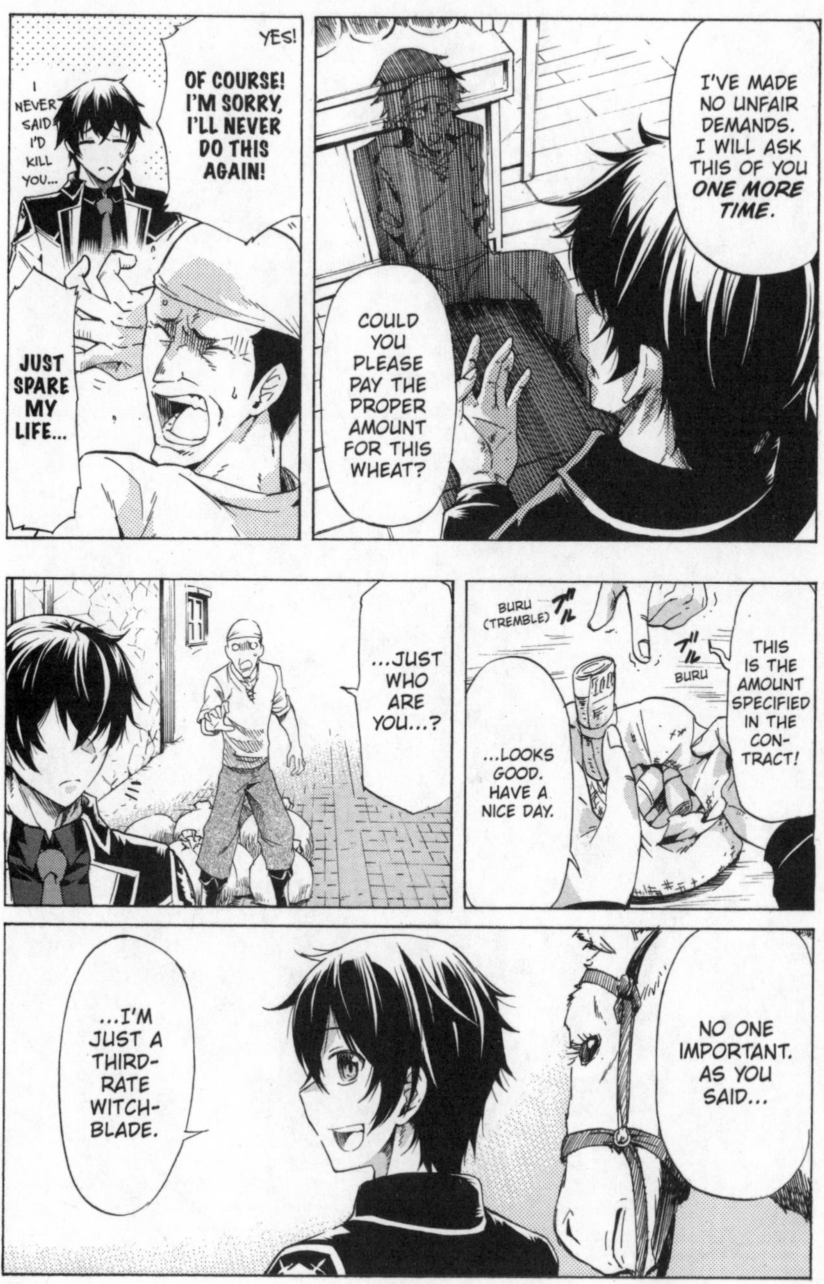
I'VE MADE NO UNFAIR DEMANDS. I WILL ASK THIS OF YOU *ONE MORE TIME.*
COULD YOU PLEASE PAY THE PROPER AMOUNT FOR THIS WHEAT?
YES!
OF COURSE! I'M SORRY, I'LL NEVER DO THIS AGAIN!
I NEVER SAID I'D KILL YOU...
JUST SPARE MY LIFE...
THIS IS THE AMOUNT SPECIFIED IN THE CONTRACT!
BURU (TREMBLE)
BURU
...LOOKS GOOD. HAVE A NICE DAY.
...JUST WHO ARE YOU...?
NO ONE IMPORTANT. AS YOU SAID...
...I'M JUST A THIRD-RATE WITCH-BLADE.

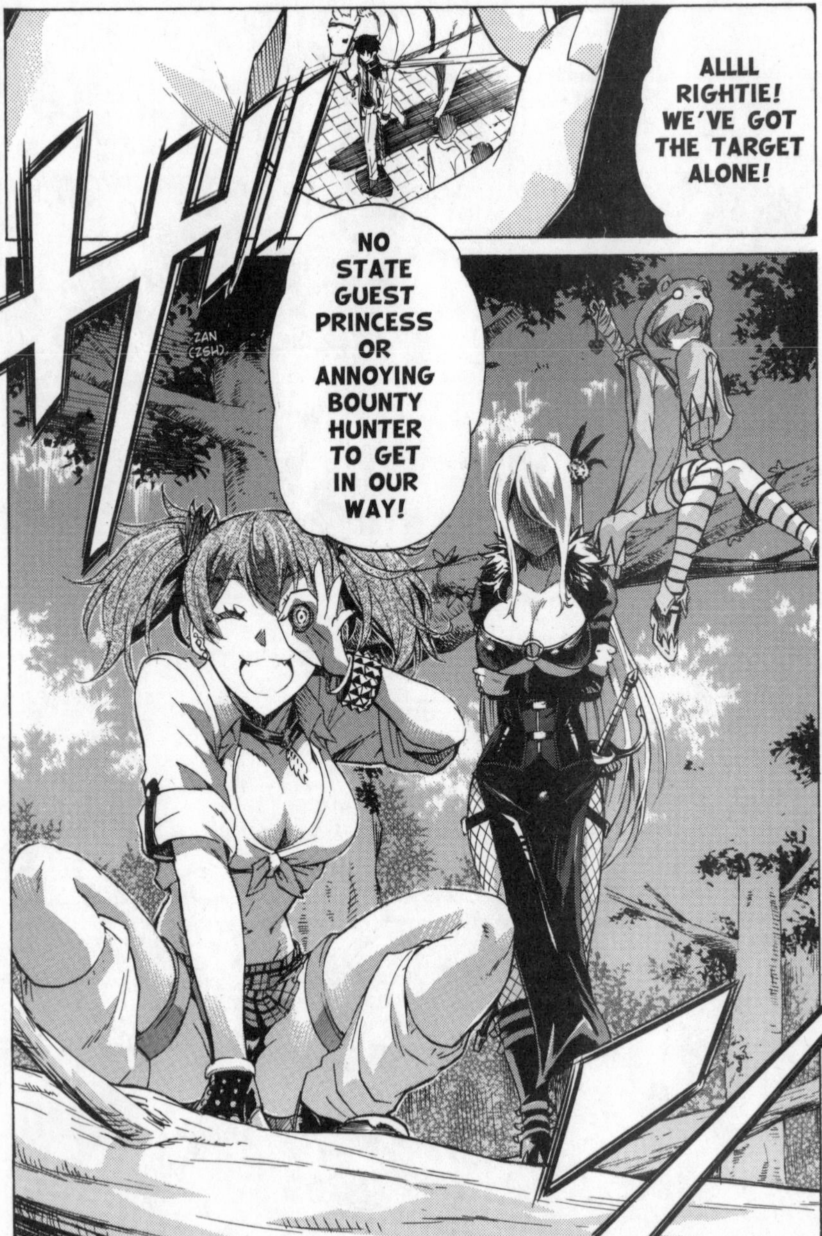
ALLLL RIGHTIE! WE'VE GOT THE TARGET ALONE!
ZAN (ZSH)
NO STATE GUEST PRINCESS OR ANNOYING BOUNTY HUNTER TO GET IN OUR WAY!

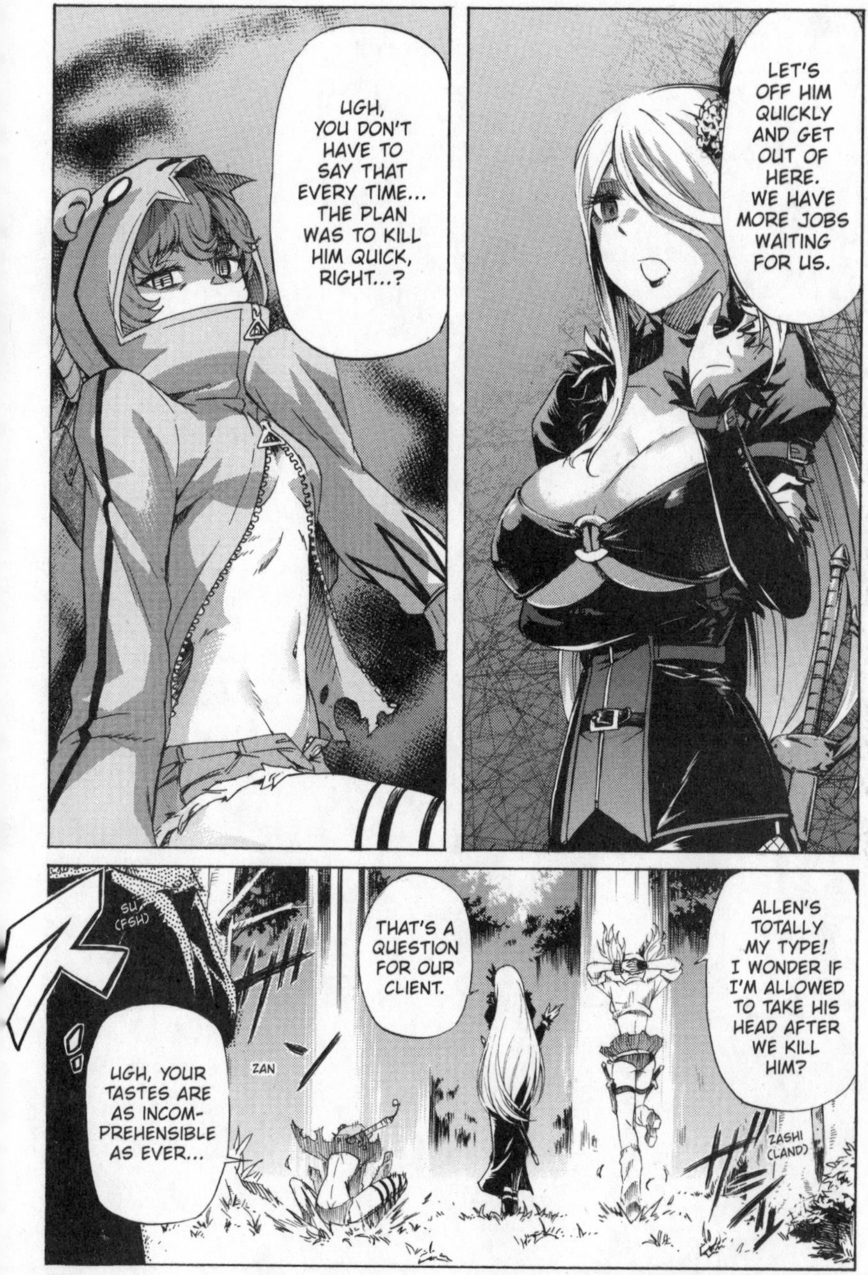
LET'S OFF HIM QUICKLY AND GET OUT OF HERE. WE HAVE MORE JOBS WAITING FOR US.
UGH, YOU DON'T HAVE TO SAY THAT EVERY TIME... THE PLAN WAS TO KILL HIM QUICK, RIGHT...?
ALLEN'S TOTALLY MY TYPE! I WONDER IF I'M ALLOWED TO TAKE HIS HEAD AFTER WE KILL HIM?
THAT'S A QUESTION FOR OUR CLIENT.
SU (FSH)
ZASHI (LAND)
ZAN
UGH, YOUR TASTES ARE AS INCOM-PREHENSIBLE AS EVER...

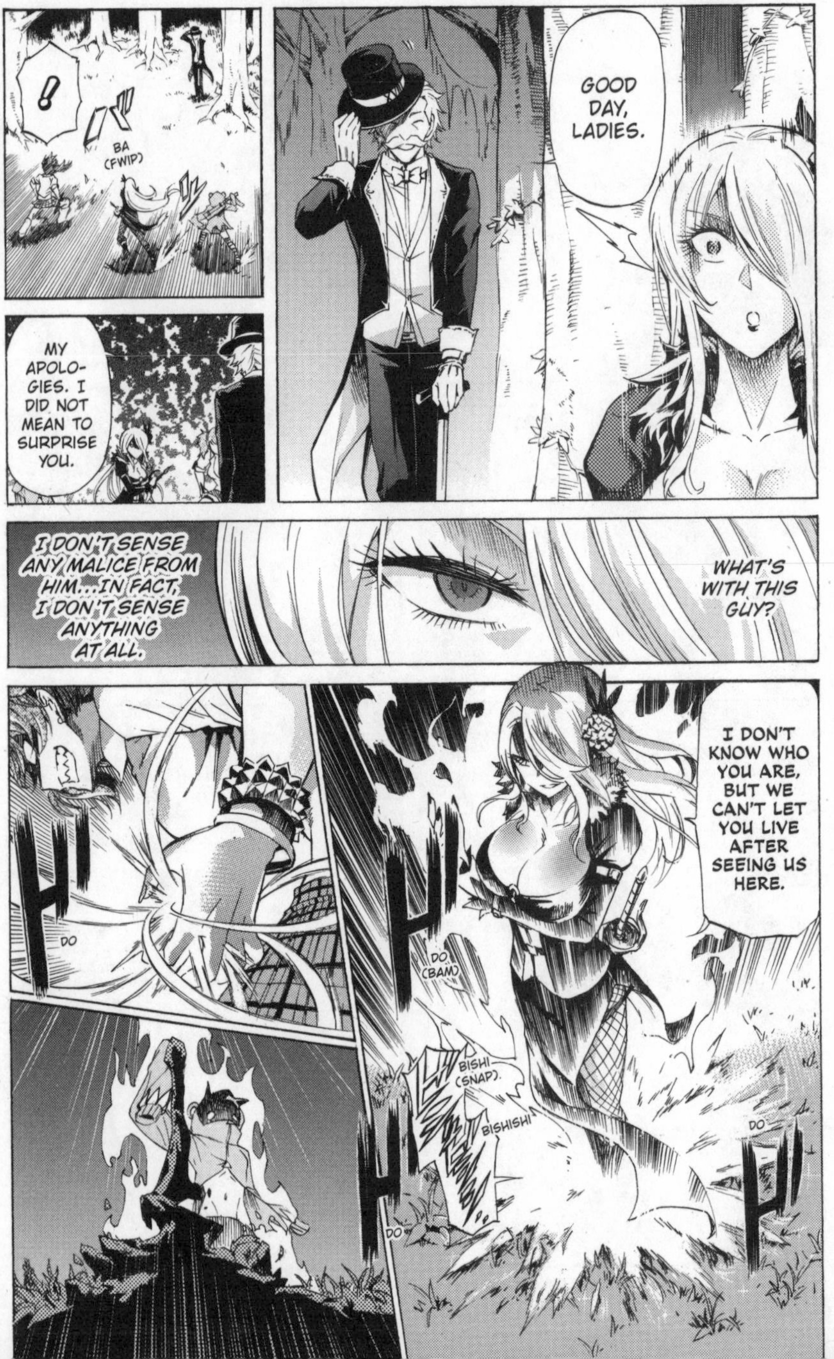
GOOD DAY, LADIES.
!
BA (FWIP)
MY APOLOGIES. I DID NOT MEAN TO SURPRISE YOU.
WHAT'S WITH THIS GUY?
I DON'T SENSE ANY MALICE FROM HIM...IN FACT, I DON'T SENSE ANYTHING AT ALL.
I DON'T KNOW WHO YOU ARE, BUT WE CAN'T LET YOU LIVE AFTER SEEING US HERE.
DO
DO (BAM)
BISHI (SNAP)
BISHISHI
DO
DO

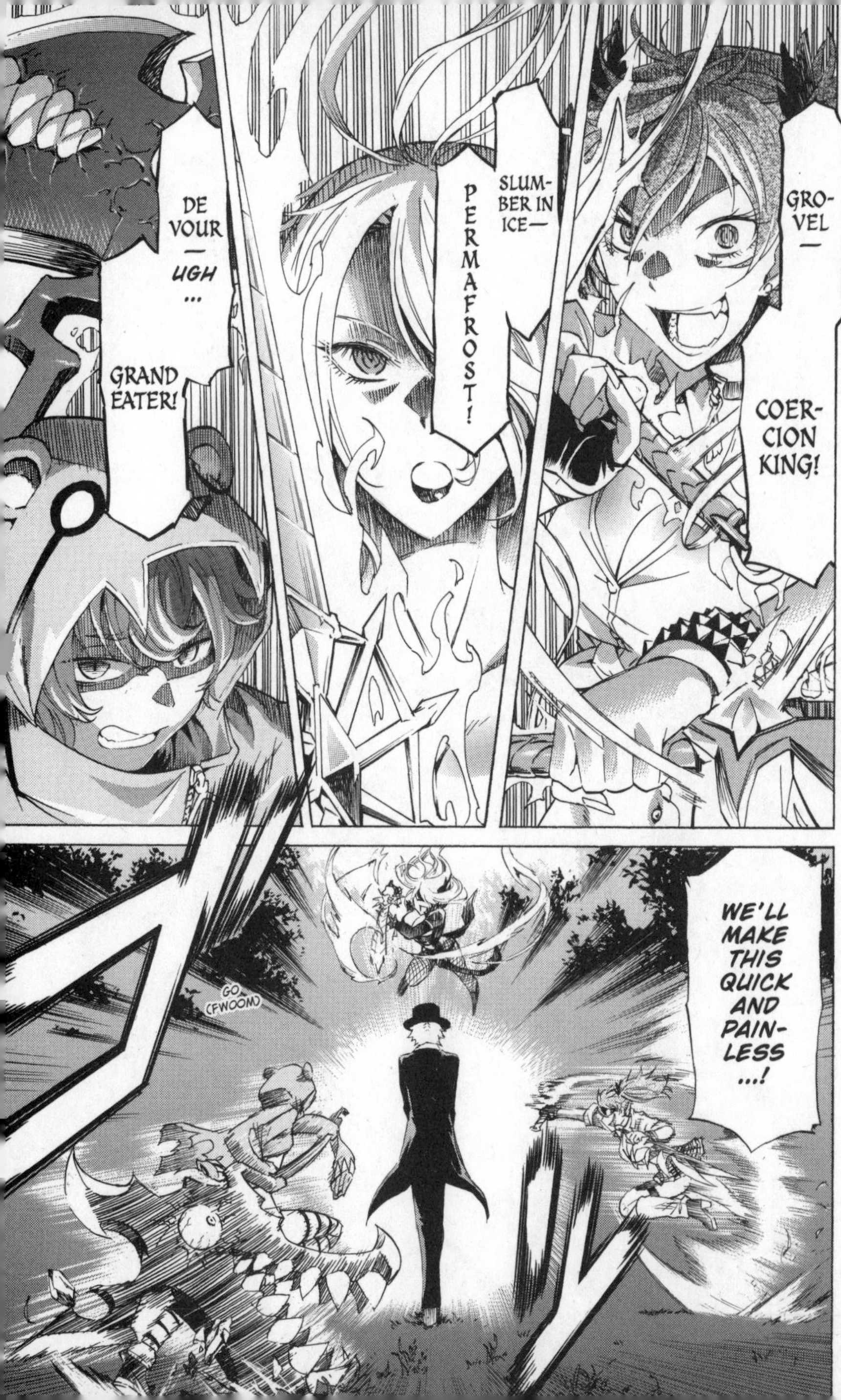

GRO-
VEL
—
COERCION KING!
SLUMBER IN ICE—
PERMAFROST!
DE
VOUR
—
UGH ...
GRAND EATER!
WE'LL MAKE THIS QUICK AND PAINLESS ...!
GO
(FWOOM)

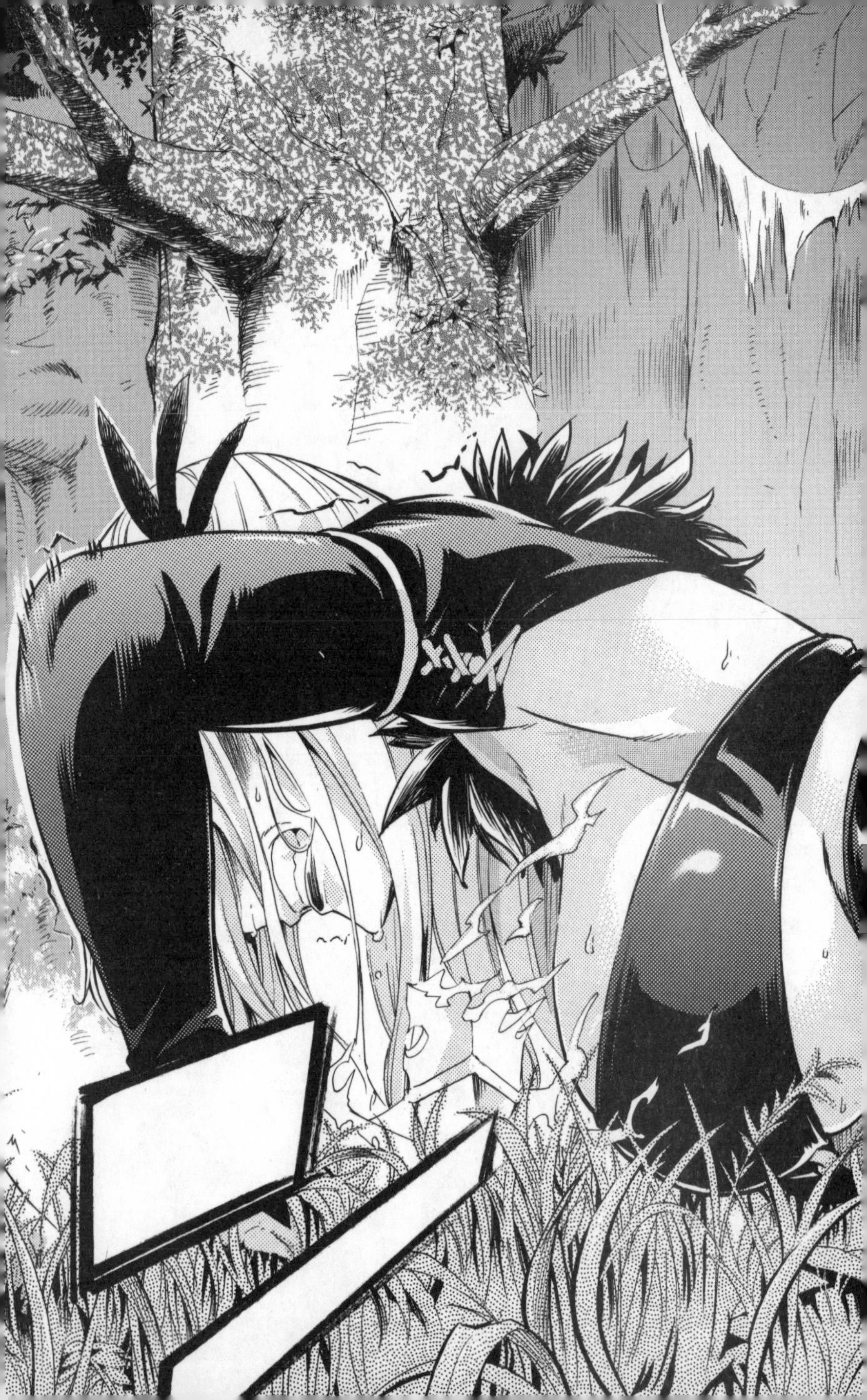

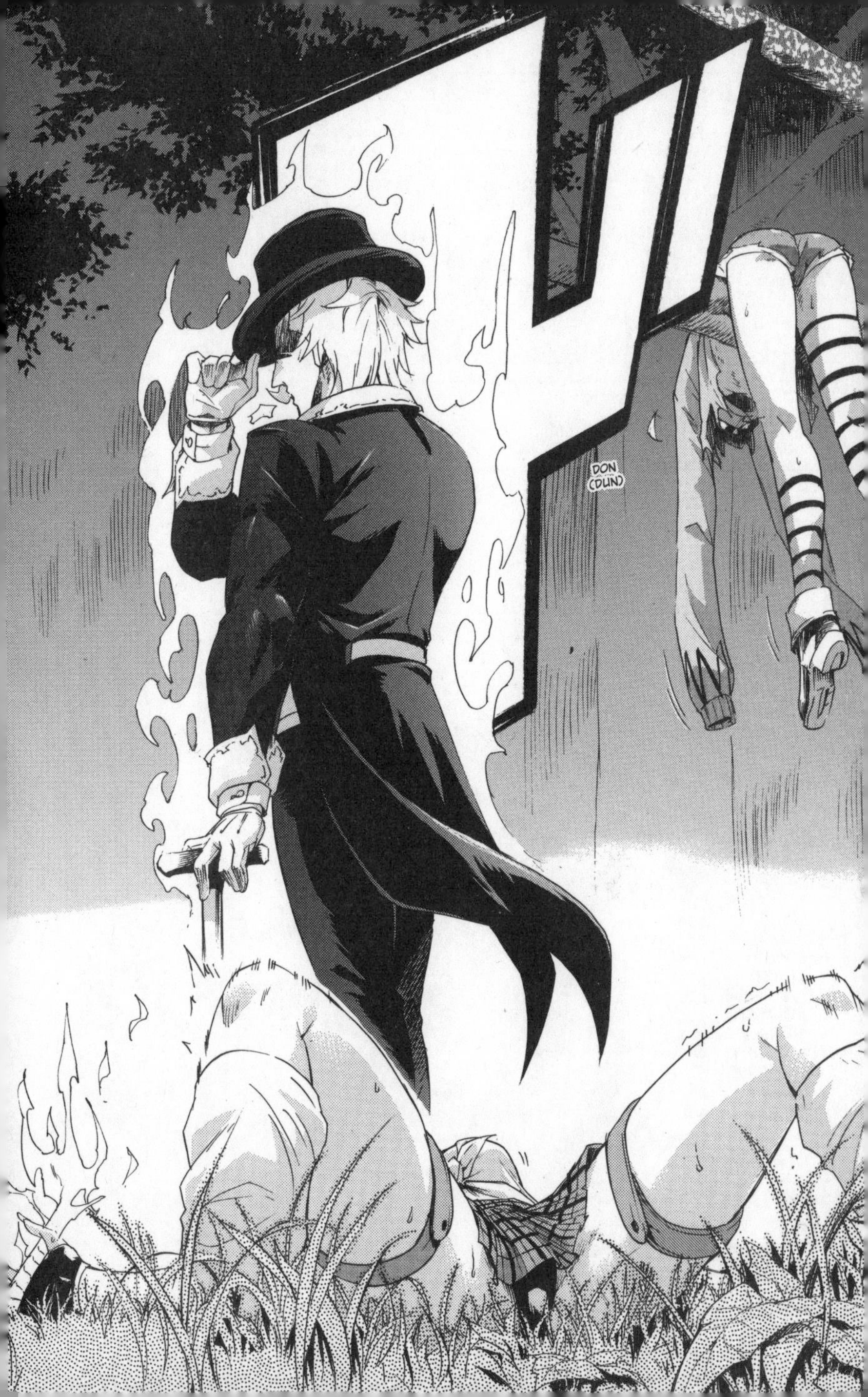
DON
(DUN)

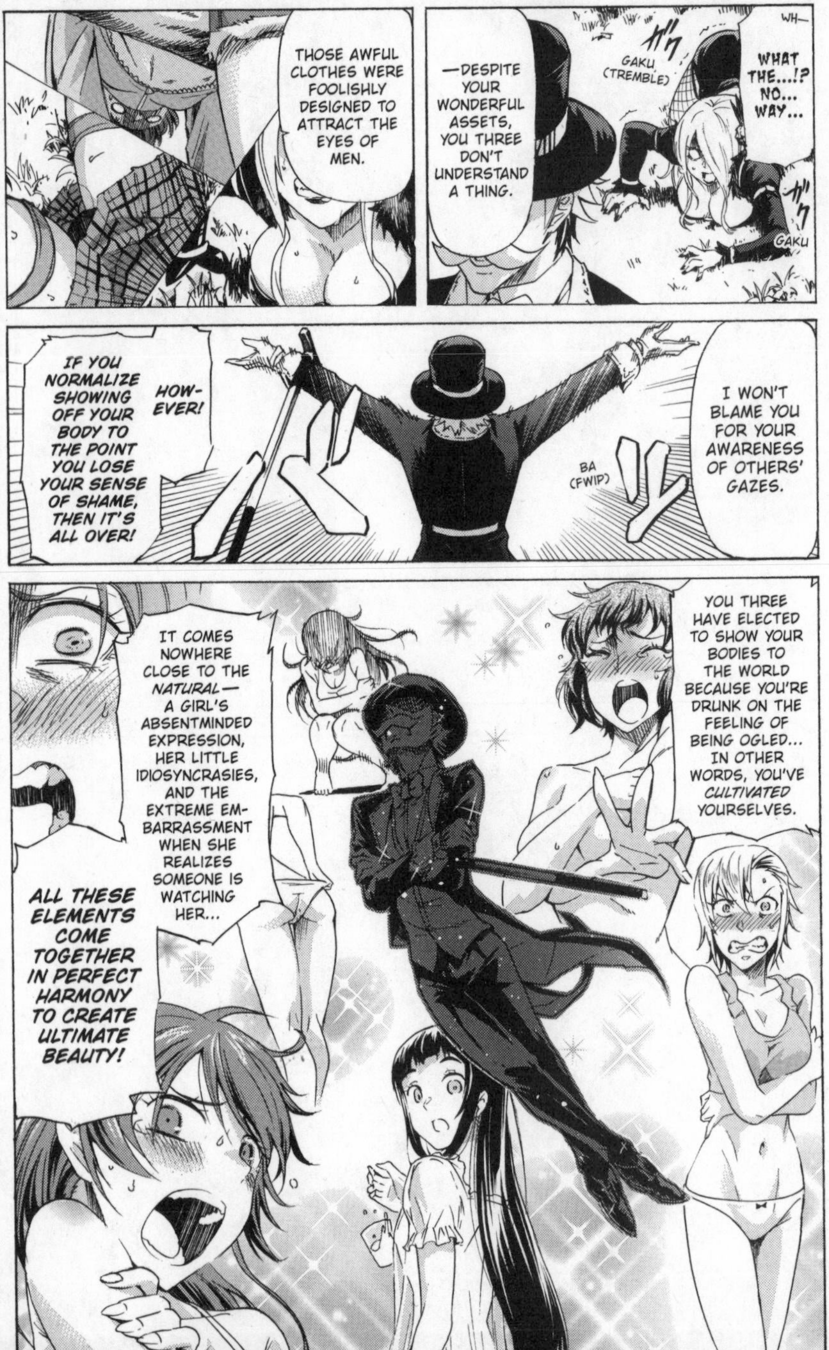
WH—
WHAT THE...!? NO... WAY...
GAKU (TREMBLE)
GAKU
—DESPITE YOUR WONDERFUL ASSETS, YOU THREE DON'T UNDERSTAND A THING.
THOSE AWFUL CLOTHES WERE FOOLISHLY DESIGNED TO ATTRACT THE EYES OF MEN.
I WON'T BLAME YOU FOR YOUR AWARENESS OF OTHERS' GAZES.
BA (FWIP)
HOW-EVER!
IF YOU NORMALIZE SHOWING OFF YOUR BODY TO THE POINT YOU LOSE YOUR SENSE OF SHAME, THEN IT'S ALL OVER!
YOU THREE HAVE ELECTED TO SHOW YOUR BODIES TO THE WORLD BECAUSE YOU'RE DRUNK ON THE FEELING OF BEING OGLED... IN OTHER WORDS, YOU'VE CULTIVATED YOURSELVES.
IT COMES NOWHERE CLOSE TO THE NATURAL— A GIRL'S ABSENTMINDED EXPRESSION, HER LITTLE IDIOSYNCRASIES, AND THE EXTREME EM-BARRASSMENT WHEN SHE REALIZES SOMEONE IS WATCHING HER...
ALL THESE ELEMENTS COME TOGETHER IN PERFECT HARMONY TO CREATE ULTIMATE BEAUTY!

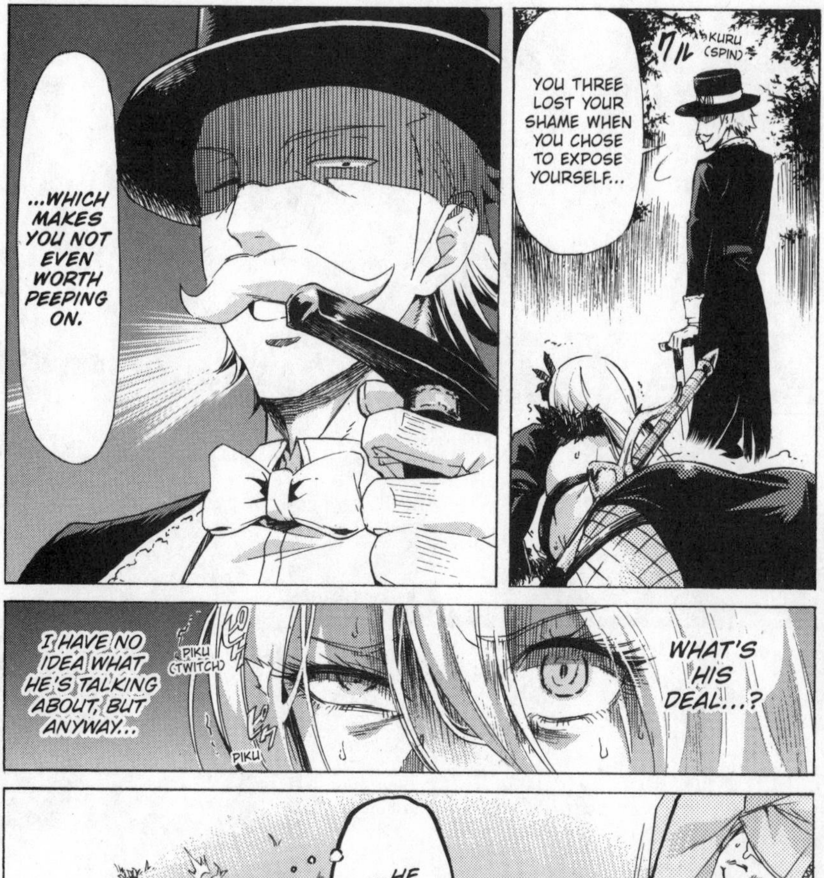
KURU (SPIN)
YOU THREE LOST YOUR SHAME WHEN YOU CHOSE TO EXPOSE YOURSELF...
...WHICH MAKES YOU NOT EVEN WORTH PEEPING ON.
WHAT'S HIS DEAL...?
PIKU (TWITCH)
PIKU
I HAVE NO IDEA WHAT HE'S TALKING ABOUT, BUT ANYWAY...
...HE CREEPS ME OUT...
GAKU

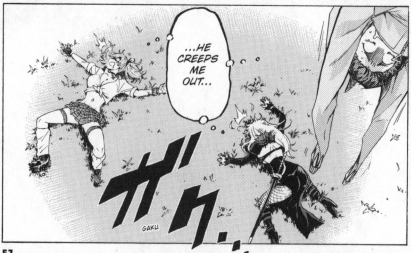

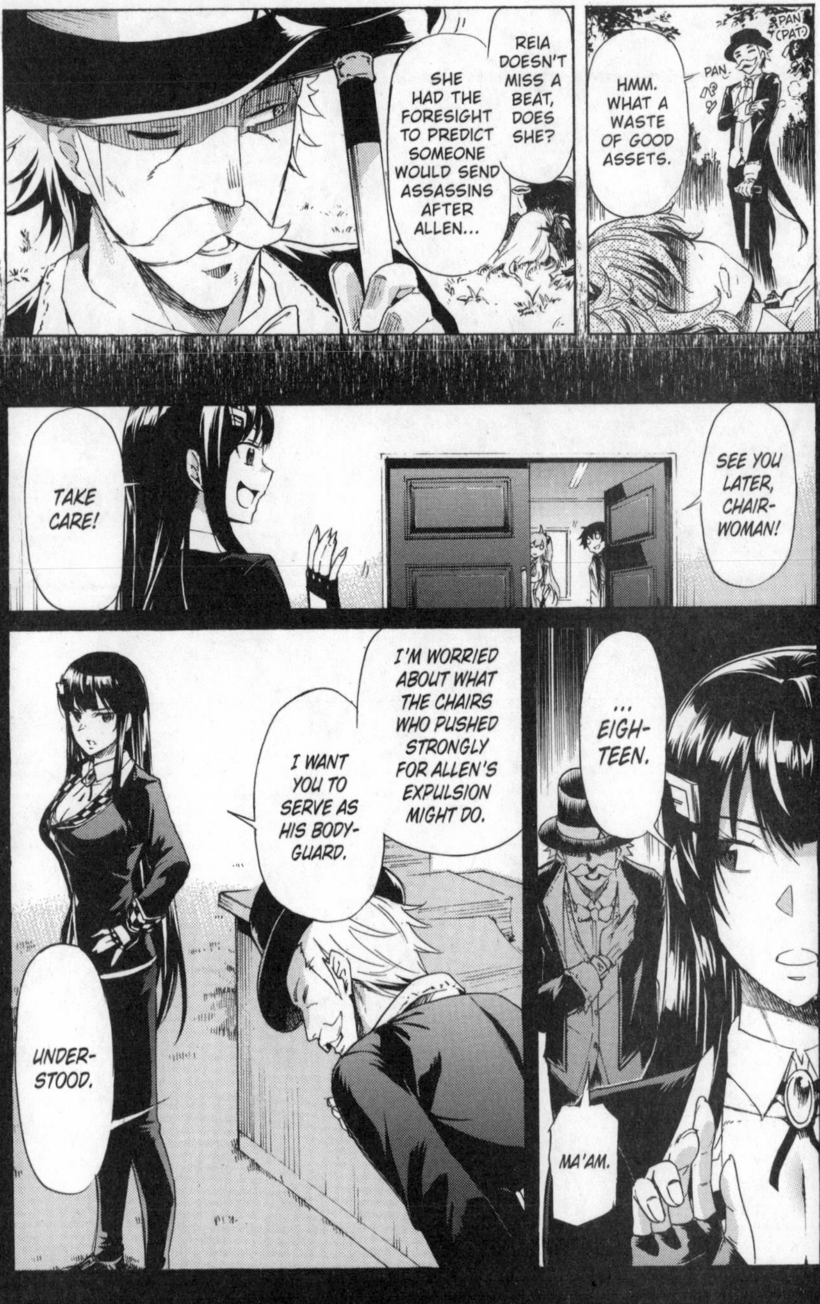
PAN (PAT-)
PAN
HMM. WHAT A WASTE OF GOOD ASSETS.
REIA DOESN'T MISS A BEAT, DOES SHE?
SHE HAD THE FORESIGHT TO PREDICT SOMEONE WOULD SEND ASSASSINS AFTER ALLEN...
SEE YOU LATER, CHAIR-WOMAN!
TAKE CARE!
...EIGH-TEEN.
MA'AM.
I'M WORRIED ABOUT WHAT THE CHAIRS WHO PUSHED STRONGLY FOR ALLEN'S EXPULSION MIGHT DO.
I WANT YOU TO SERVE AS HIS BODY-GUARD.
UNDER-STOOD.

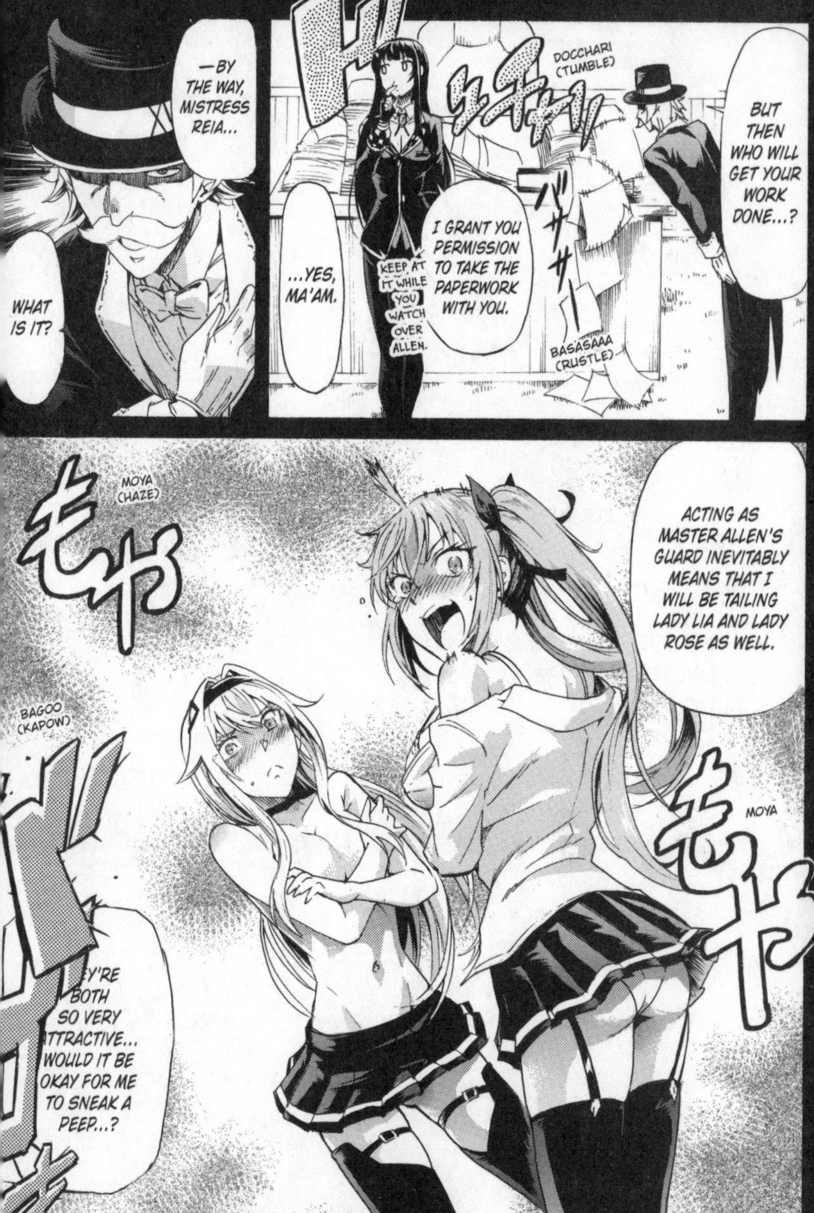
DOCCHARI (TUMBLE)
BUT THEN WHO WILL GET YOUR WORK DONE...?
BASASAAA (RUSTLE)
I GRANT YOU PERMISSION TO TAKE THE PAPERWORK WITH YOU.
KEEP AT IT WHILE YOU WATCH OVER ALLEN.
...YES, MA'AM.
—BY THE WAY, MISTRESS REIA...
WHAT IS IT?
ACTING AS MASTER ALLEN'S GUARD INEVITABLY MEANS THAT I WILL BE TAILING LADY LIA AND LADY ROSE AS WELL.
MOYA (HAZE)
MOYA
BAGOO (KAPOW)
EY'RE BOTH SO VERY TTRACTIVE... WOULD IT BE OKAY FOR ME TO SNEAK A PEEP...?
※ EIGHTEEN'S FANTASY

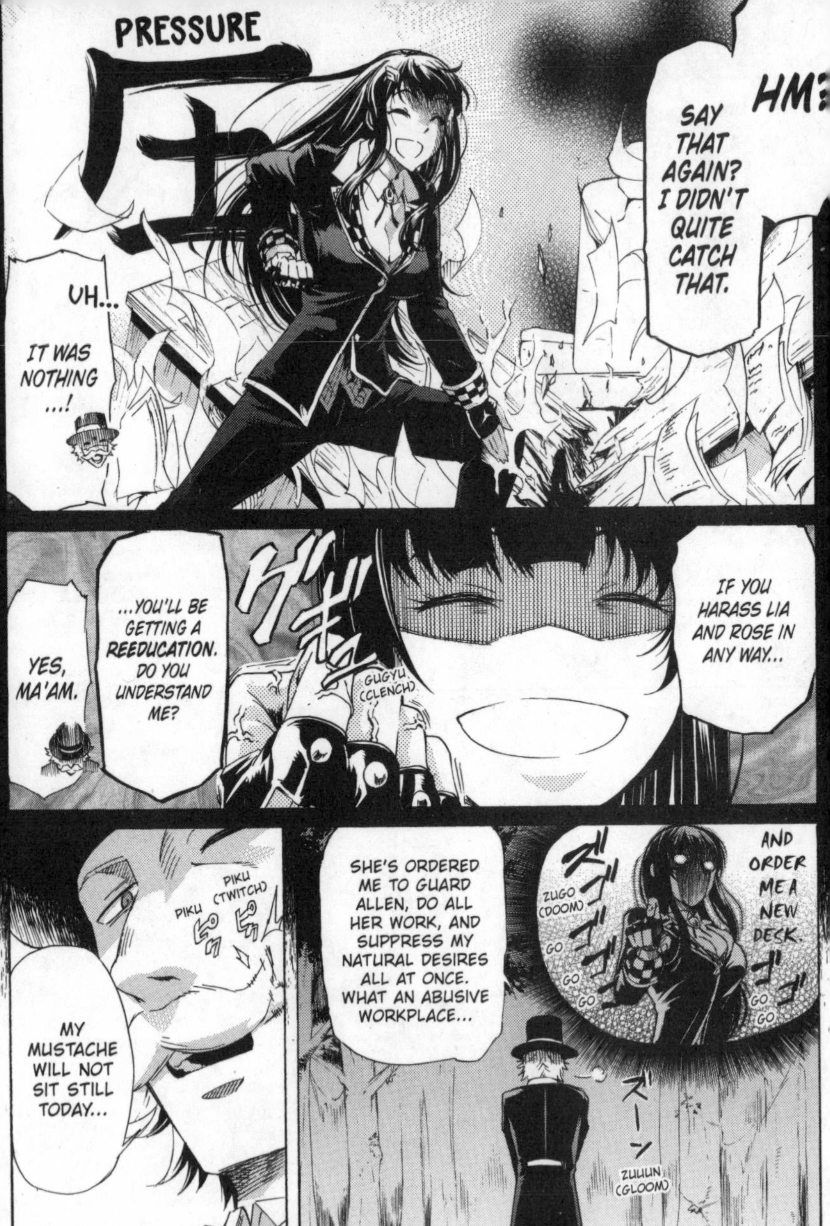
HM
SAY THAT AGAIN? I DIDN'T QUITE CATCH THAT.
PRESSURE
UH...
IT WAS NOTHING ...!
IF YOU HARASS LIA AND ROSE IN ANY WAY...
GUGYU (CLENCH)
...YOU'LL BE GETTING A REEDUCATION. DO YOU UNDERSTAND ME?
YES, MA'AM.
AND ORDER ME A NEW DECK.
ZUGO (DOOM)
GO GO GO
GO GO
SHE'S ORDERED ME TO GUARD ALLEN, DO ALL HER WORK, AND SUPPRESS MY NATURAL DESIRES ALL AT ONCE. WHAT AN ABUSIVE WORKPLACE...
ZUUUN (GLOOM)
PIKU (TWITCH)
PIKU
MY MUSTACHE WILL NOT SIT STILL TODAY...

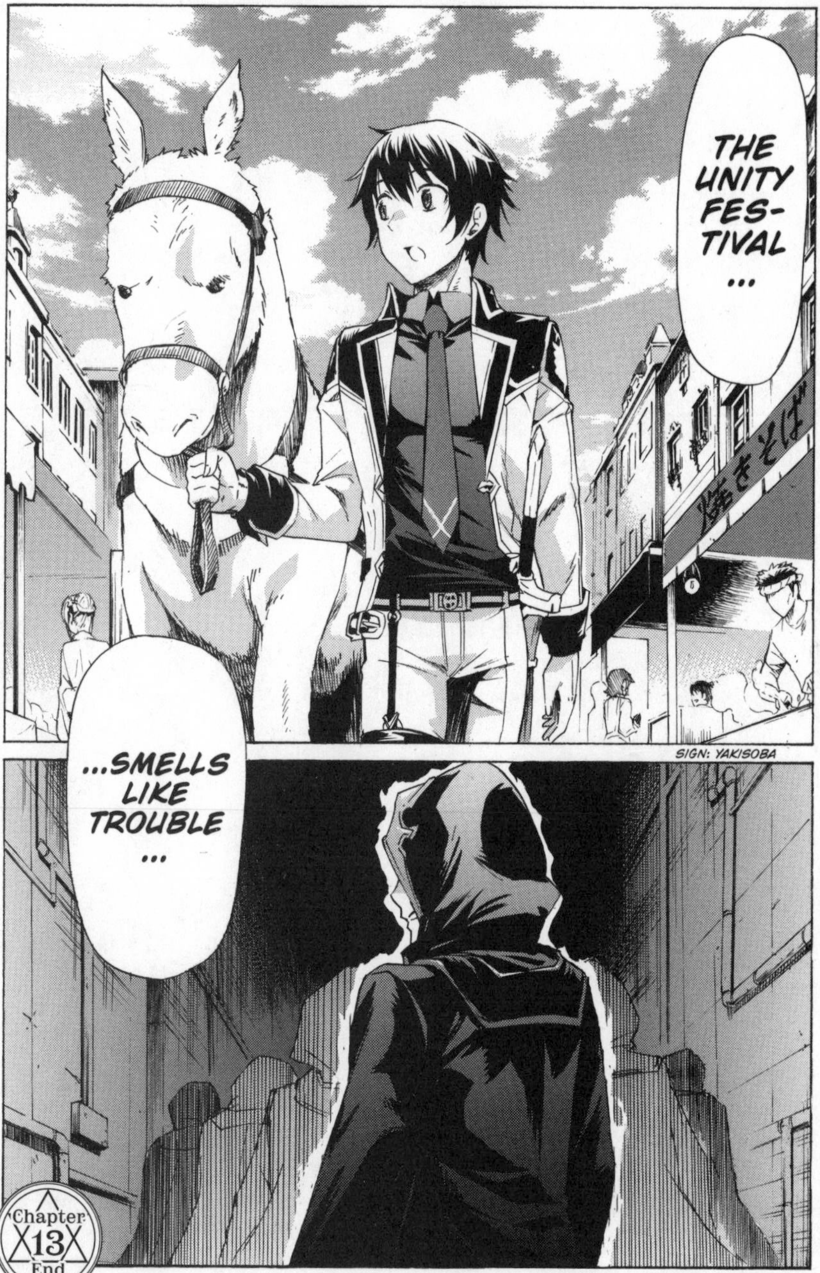
THE UNITY FES-TIVAL...
焼きそば
SIGN: YAKISOBA
...SMELLS LIKE TROUBLE...
Chapter 13 End

I KEPT PRESSING THE 100-MILLION-YEAR BUTTON AND CAME OUT ON TOP

~THE UNBEATABLE REJECT SWORDSMAN~

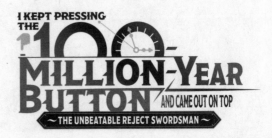

Chapter 14

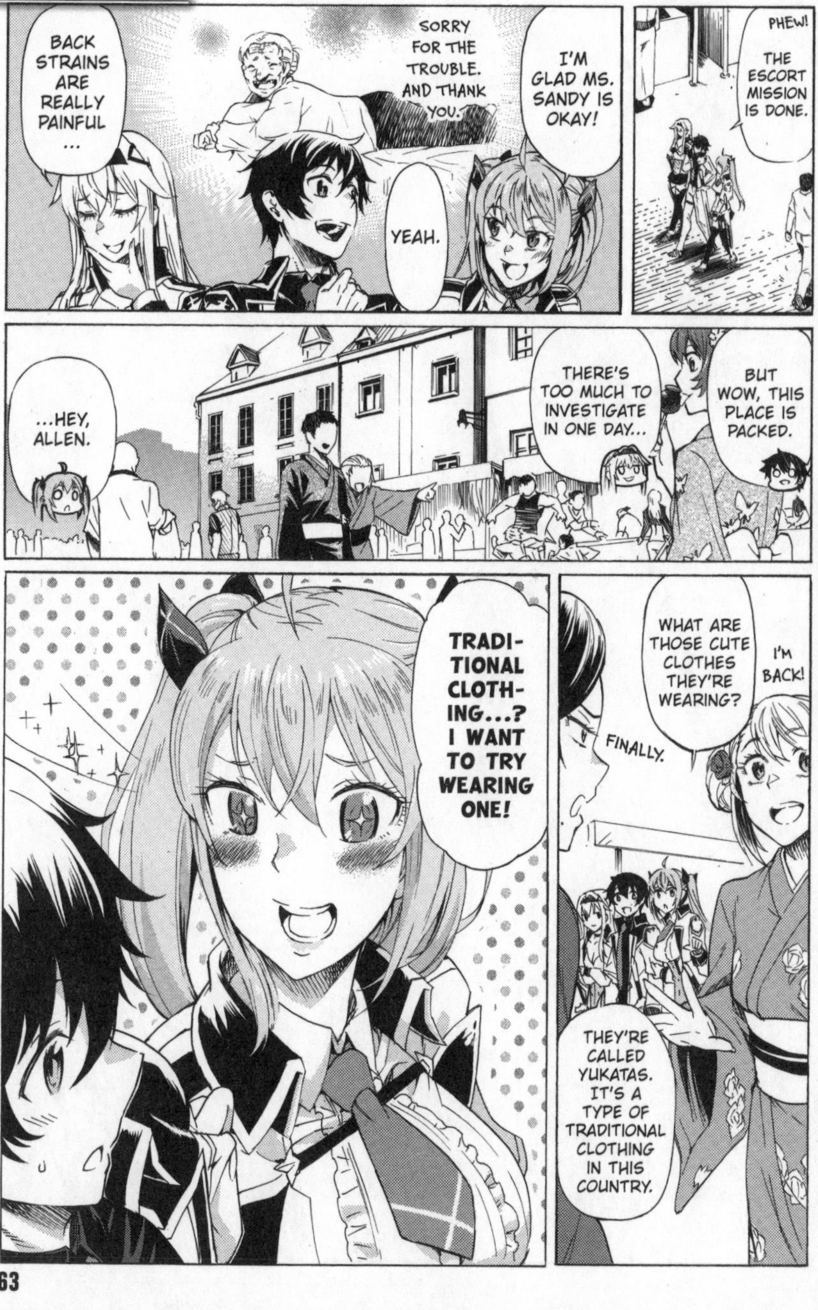
PHEW!
THE ESCORT MISSION IS DONE.
I'M GLAD MS. SANDY IS OKAY!
SORRY FOR THE TROUBLE. AND THANK YOU.
BACK STRAINS ARE REALLY PAINFUL...
YEAH.
BUT WOW, THIS PLACE IS PACKED.
THERE'S TOO MUCH TO INVESTIGATE IN ONE DAY...
...HEY, ALLEN.
I'M BACK!
WHAT ARE THOSE CUTE CLOTHES THEY'RE WEARING?
FINALLY.
THEY'RE CALLED YUKATAS. IT'S A TYPE OF TRADITIONAL CLOTHING IN THIS COUNTRY.
TRADITIONAL CLOTHING...? I WANT TO TRY WEARING ONE!

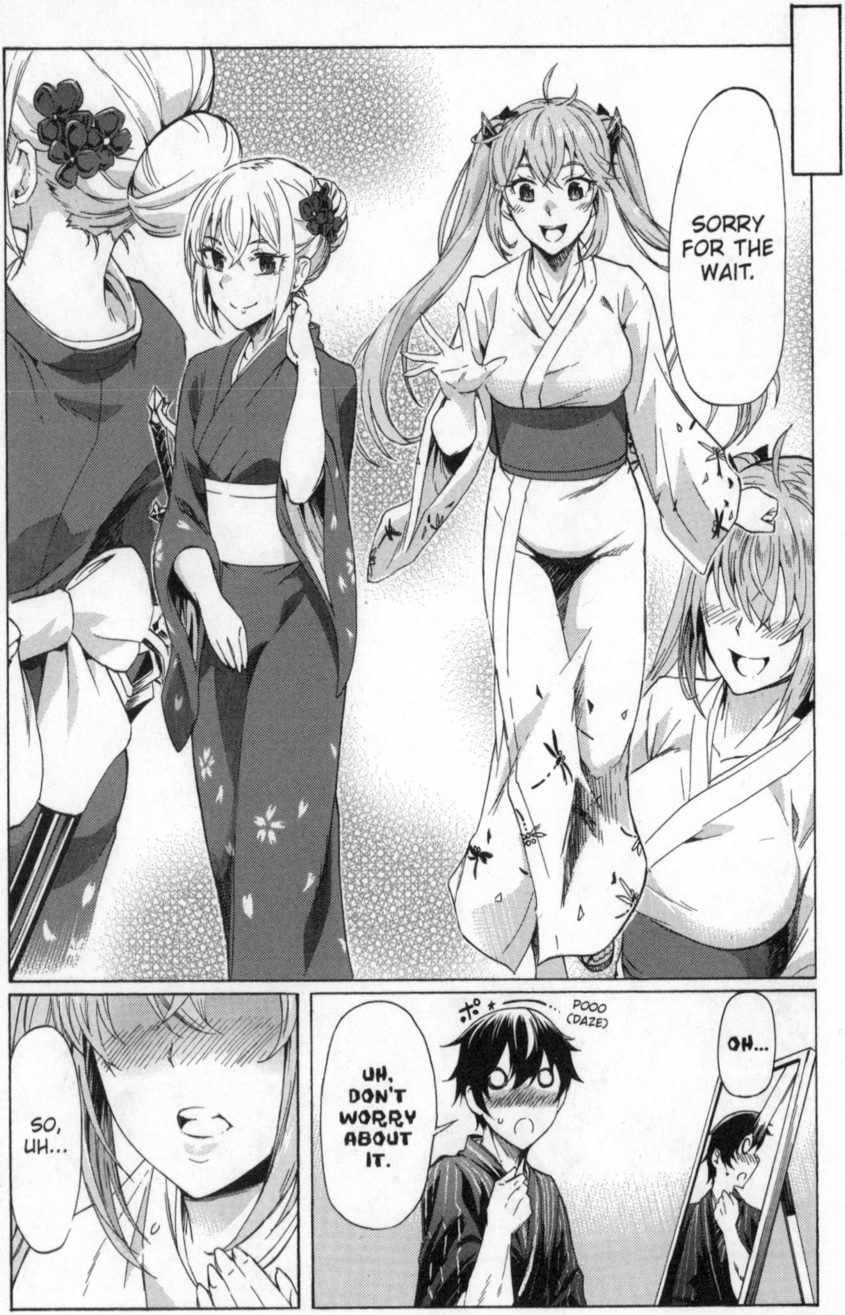
SORRY FOR THE WAIT.
OH...
POOO (DAZE)
UH, DON'T WORRY ABOUT IT.
SO, UH...

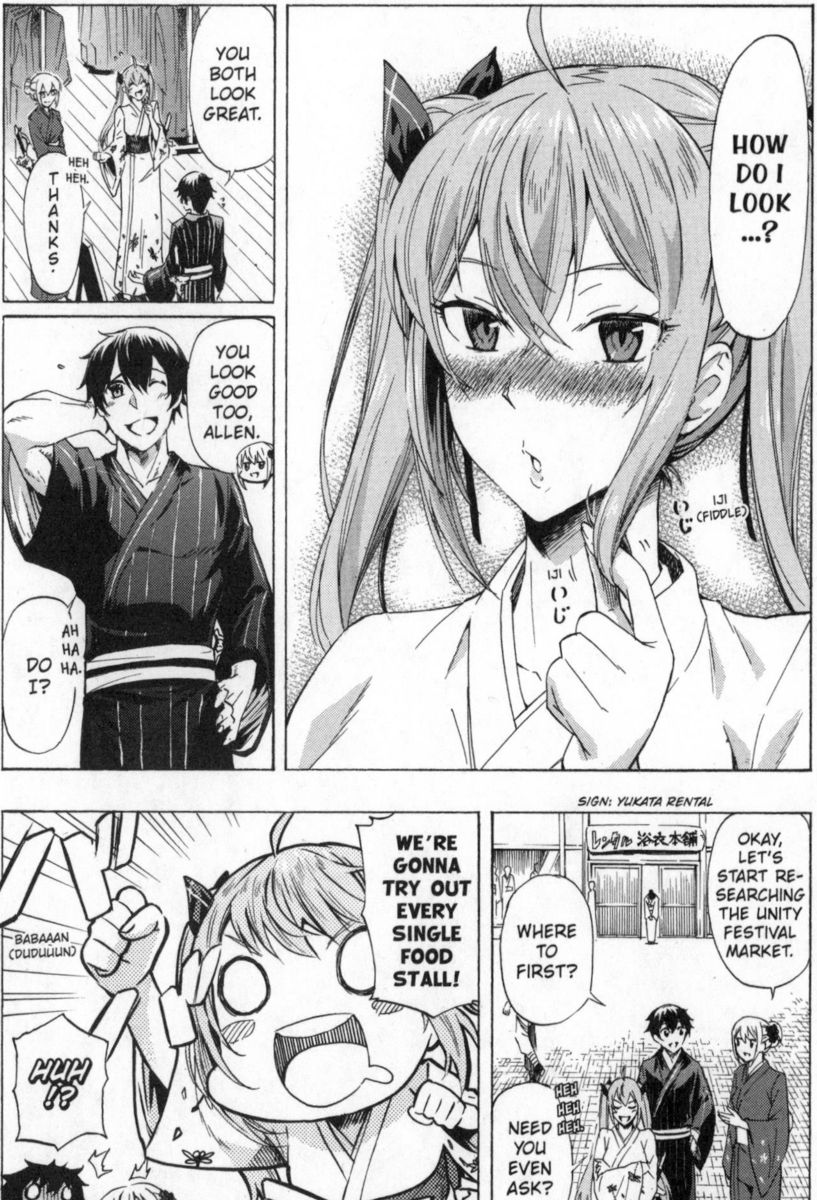
HOW DO I LOOK ...?
いじ
IJI (FIDDLE)
いじ
IJI
YOU BOTH LOOK GREAT.
HEH HEH.
THANKS.
YOU LOOK GOOD TOO, ALLEN.
AH HA HA.
DO I?
SIGN: YUKATA RENTAL
レンタル浴衣本舗
OKAY, LET'S START RE-SEARCHING THE UNITY FESTIVAL MARKET.
WHERE TO FIRST?
HEH HEH HEH.
NEED YOU EVEN ASK?
WE'RE GONNA TRY OUT EVERY SINGLE FOOD STALL!
BABAAAN (DUDUUUN)
HUH !?

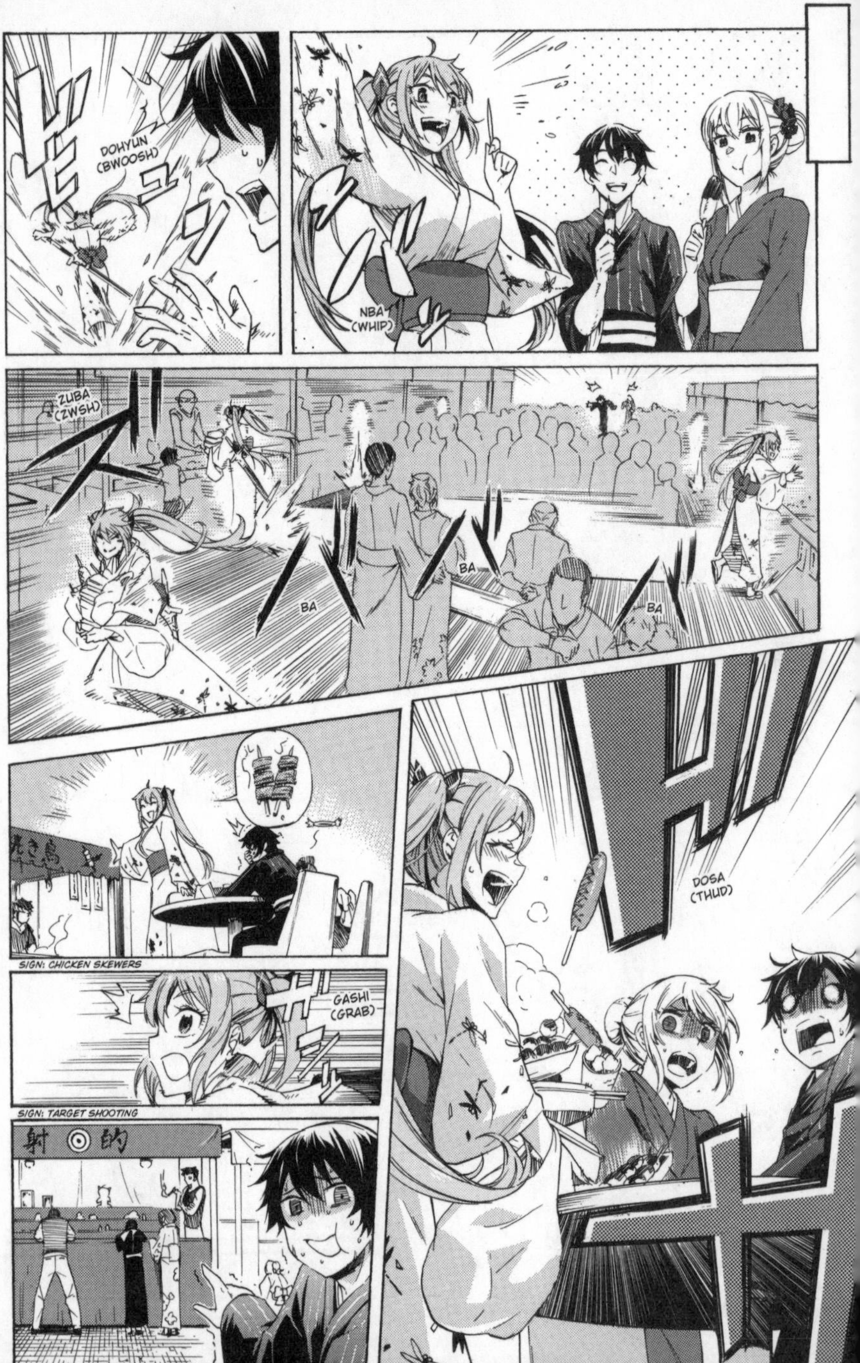
NBA (WHIP)
DOHYUN (BWOOSH)
ZUBA (ZWSH)
BA
BA
BA
DOSA (THUD)
SIGN: CHICKEN SKEWERS
GASHI (GRAB)
SIGN: TARGET SHOOTING
射的

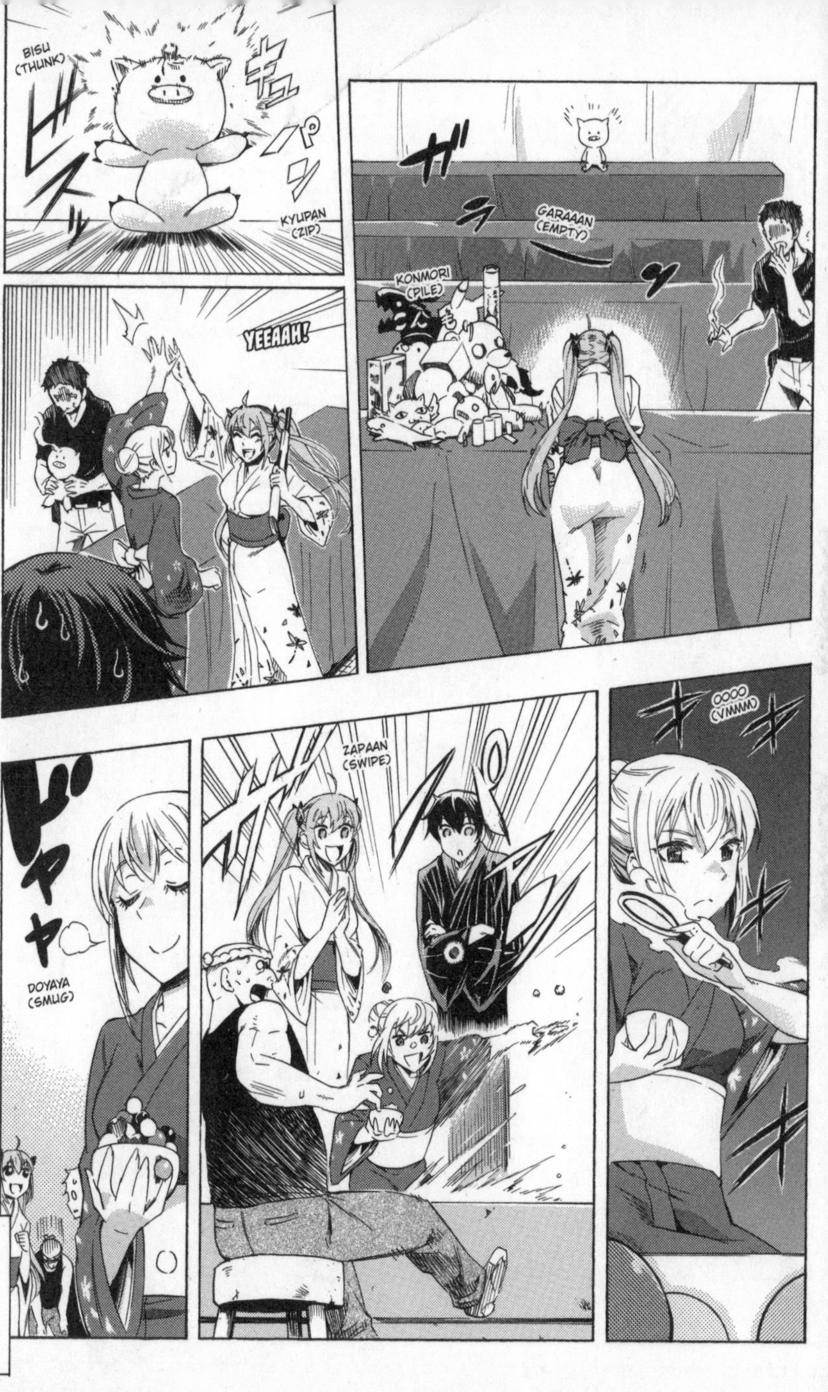
GARAAAN (EMPTY)
KONMORI (PILE)
KYUPAN (ZIP)
BISU (THUNK)
YEEAAH!
OOOO (VMMM)
ZAPAAN (SWIPE)
DOYAYA (SMUG)

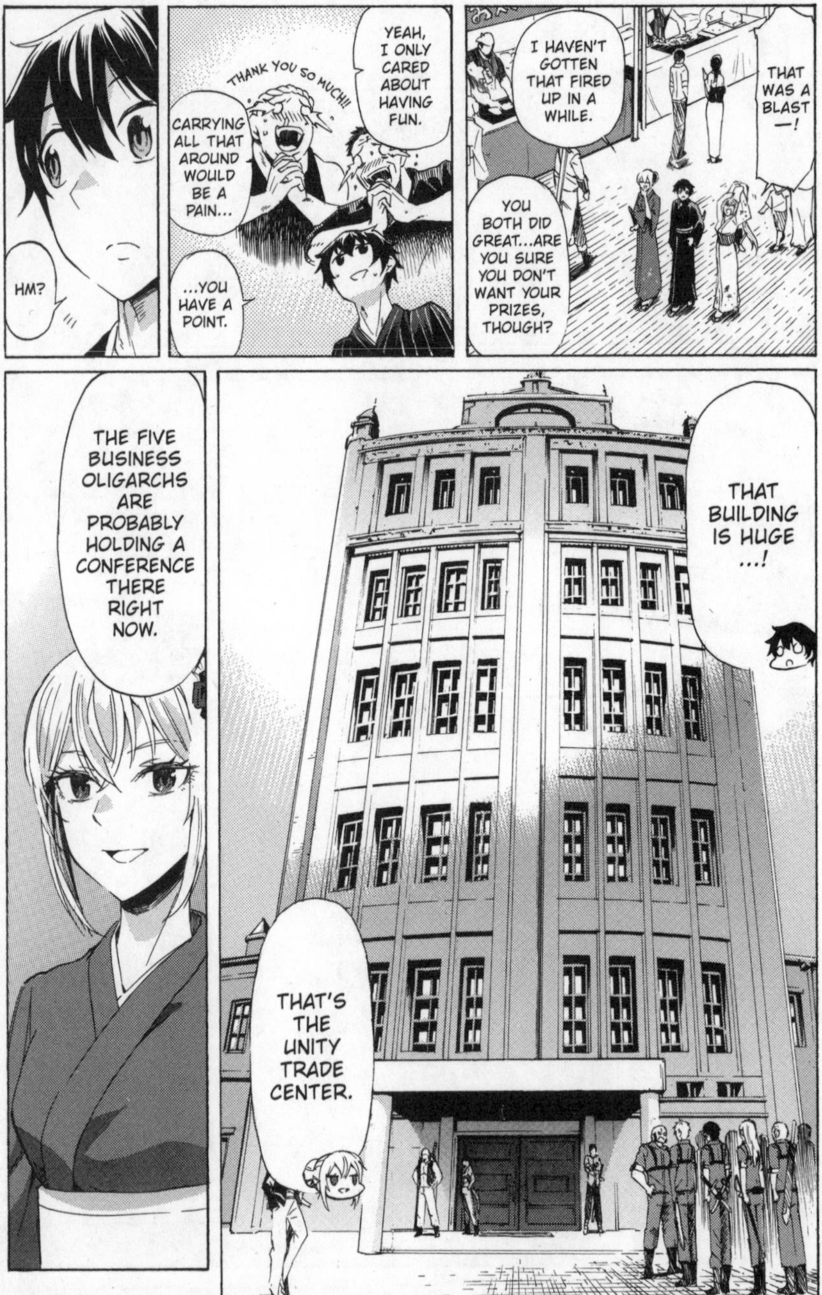
THAT WAS A BLAST—!
I HAVEN'T GOTTEN THAT FIRED UP IN A WHILE.
YOU BOTH DID GREAT...ARE YOU SURE YOU DON'T WANT YOUR PRIZES, THOUGH?
YEAH, I ONLY CARED ABOUT HAVING FUN.
THANK YOU SO MUCH!!
CARRYING ALL THAT AROUND WOULD BE A PAIN...
...YOU HAVE A POINT.
HM?
THAT BUILDING IS HUGE...!
THAT'S THE UNITY TRADE CENTER.
THE FIVE BUSINESS OLIGARCHS ARE PROBABLY HOLDING A CONFERENCE THERE RIGHT NOW.

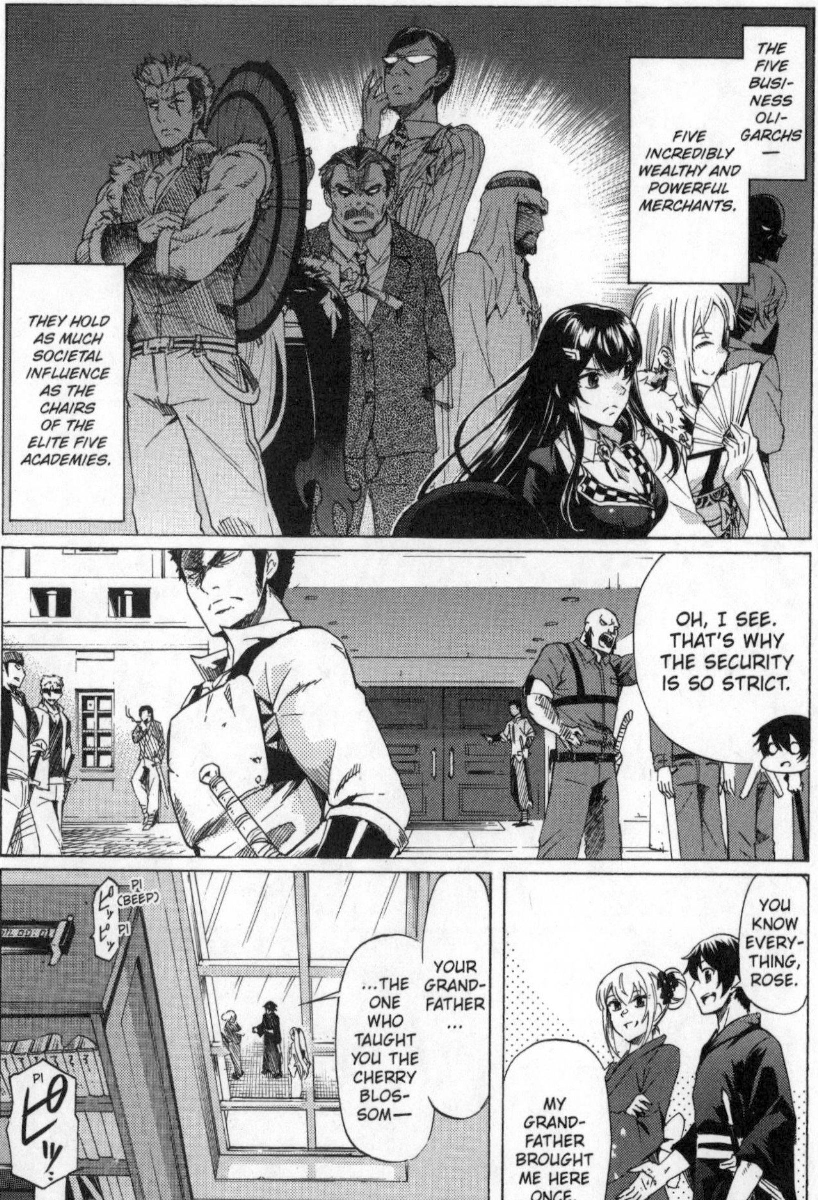
THE FIVE BUSINESS OLIGARCHS —
FIVE INCREDIBLY WEALTHY AND POWERFUL MERCHANTS.
THEY HOLD AS MUCH SOCIETAL INFLUENCE AS THE CHAIRS OF THE ELITE FIVE ACADEMIES.
OH, I SEE. THAT'S WHY THE SECURITY IS SO STRICT.
YOU KNOW EVERYTHING, ROSE.
MY GRANDFATHER BROUGHT ME HERE ONCE.
YOUR GRANDFATHER...
...THE ONE WHO TAUGHT YOU THE CHERRY BLOSSOM—
PI (BEEP)
PI
PI

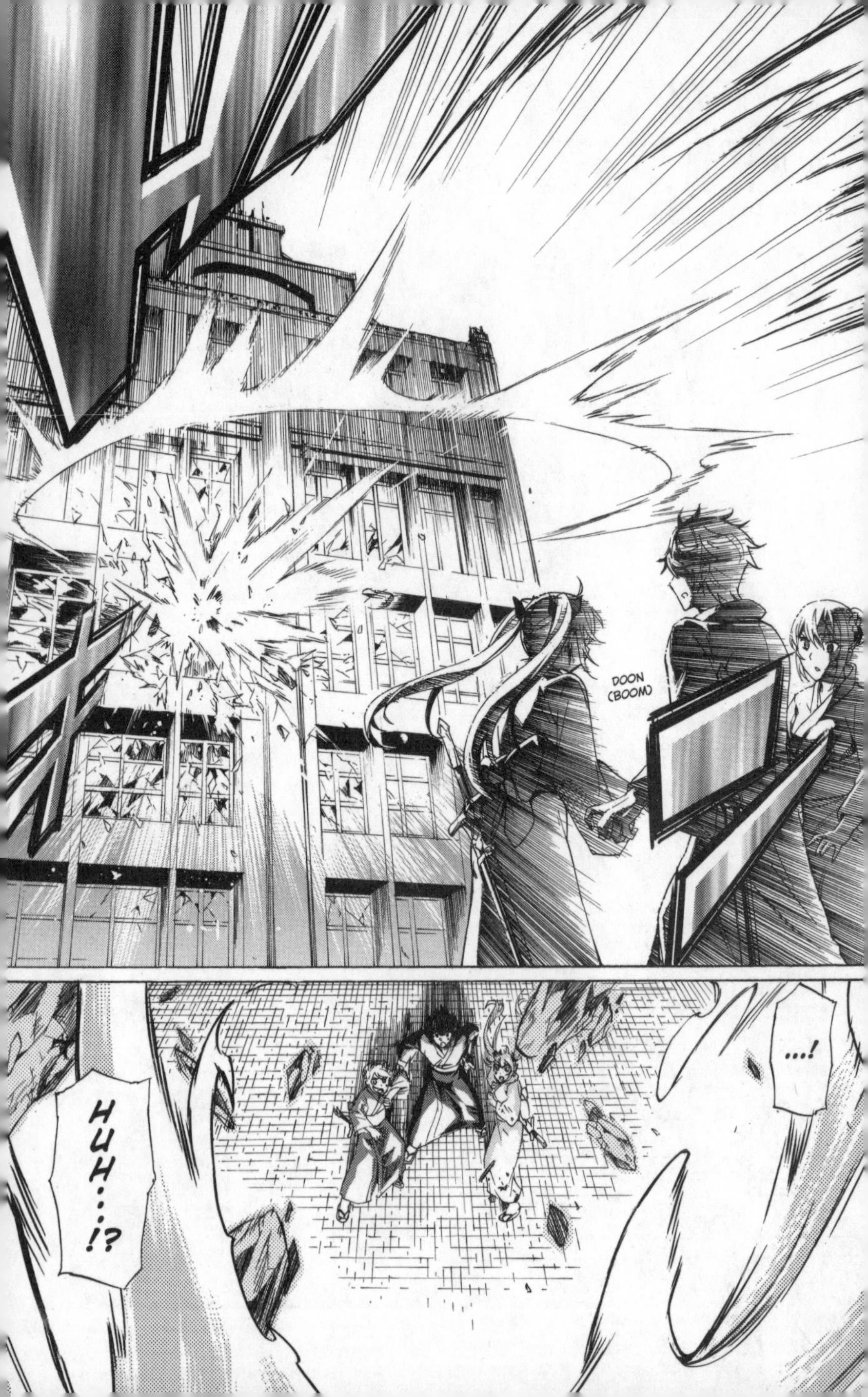
DOON
(BOOM)
...!
HUH...!?

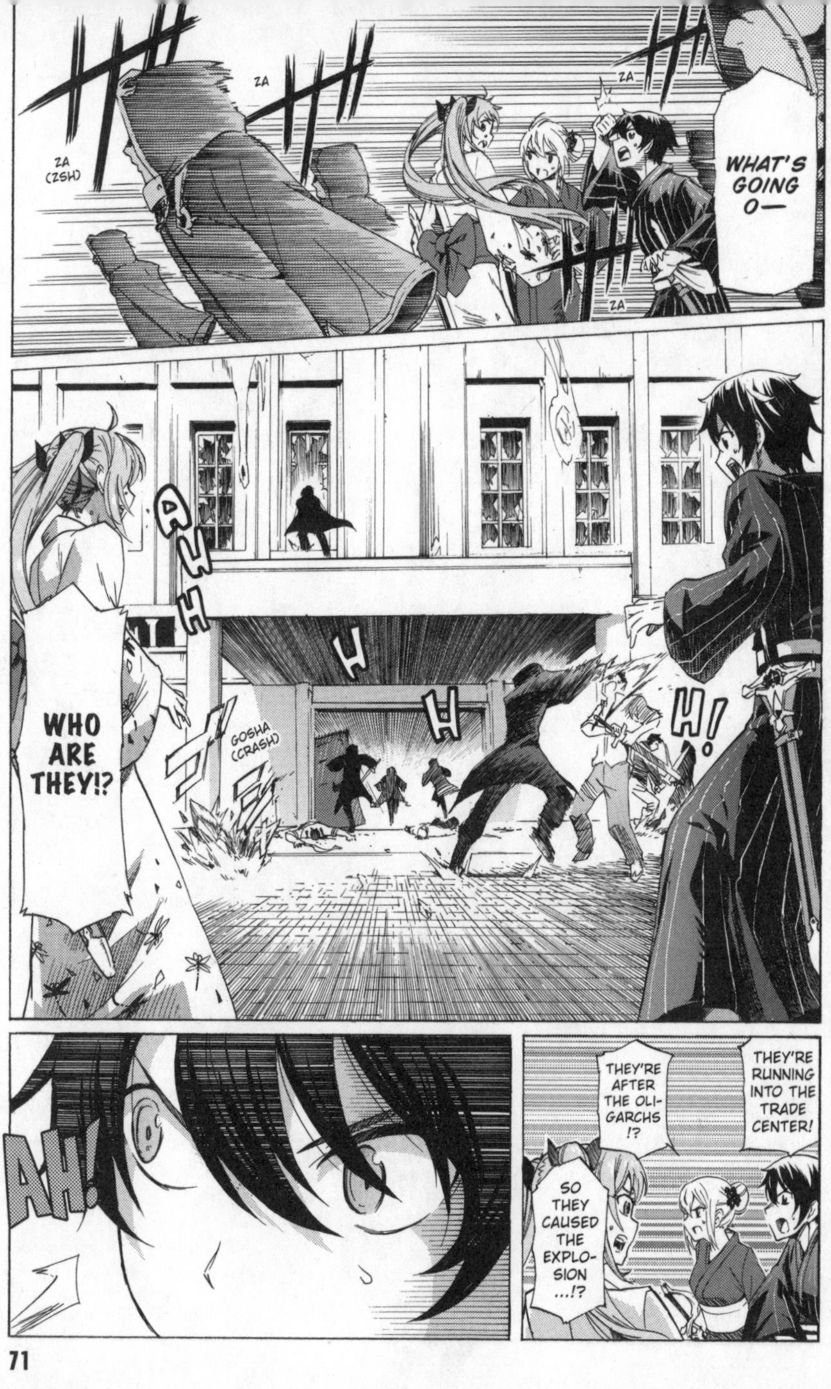
WHAT'S GOING O—
ZA
ZA
ZA (ZSH)
ZA
AHHHHH!
WHO ARE THEY!?
GOSHA (CRASH)
THEY'RE RUNNING INTO THE TRADE CENTER!
THEY'RE AFTER THE OLI-GARCHS!?
SO THEY CAUSED THE EXPLO-SION...!?
AH!

SIGN: APPLES

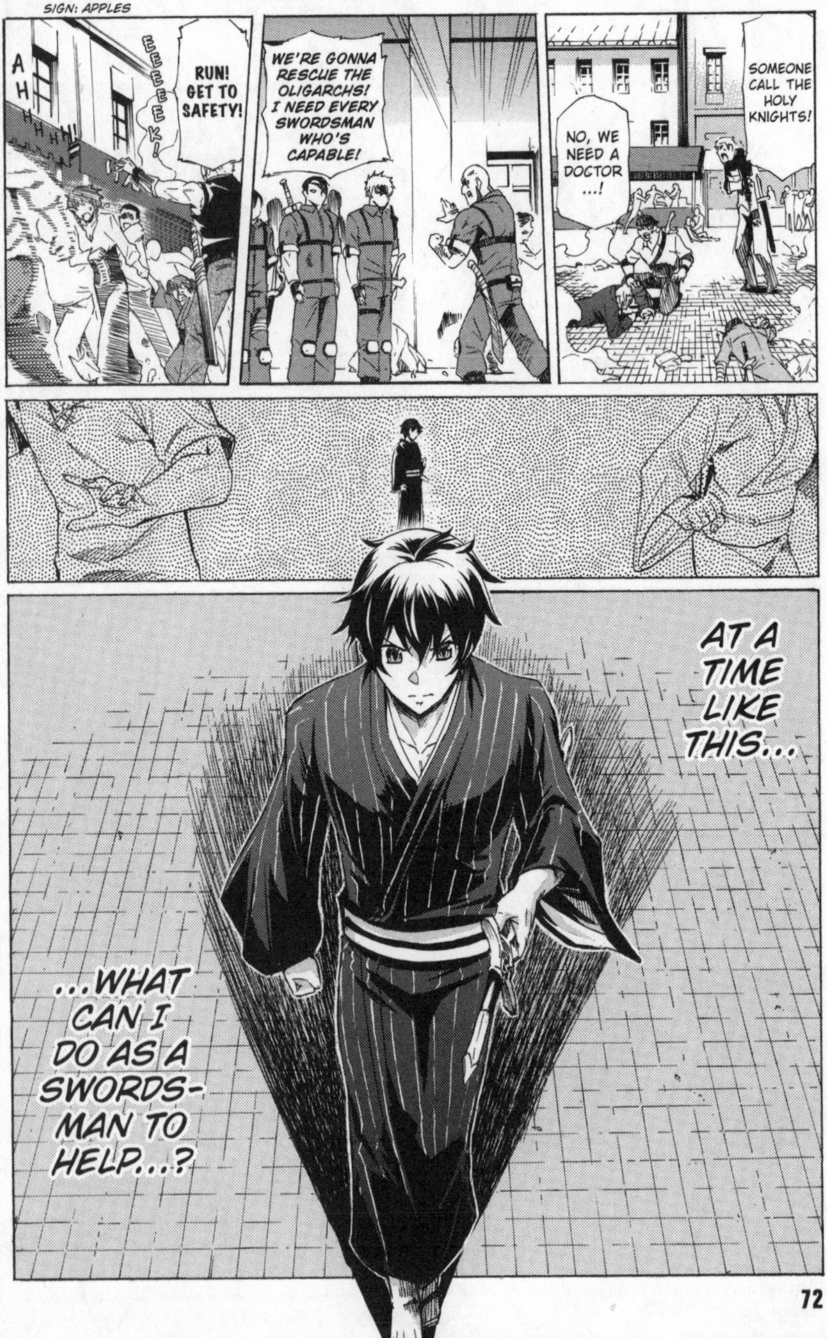
SOMEONE CALL THE HOLY KNIGHTS!
NO, WE NEED A DOCTOR ...!
WE'RE GONNA RESCUE THE OLIGARCHS! I NEED EVERY SWORDSMAN WHO'S CAPABLE!
RUN! GET TO SAFETY!
EEEEEEK!
AHHHHH!
AT A TIME LIKE THIS...
...WHAT CAN I DO AS A SWORDSMAN TO HELP...?

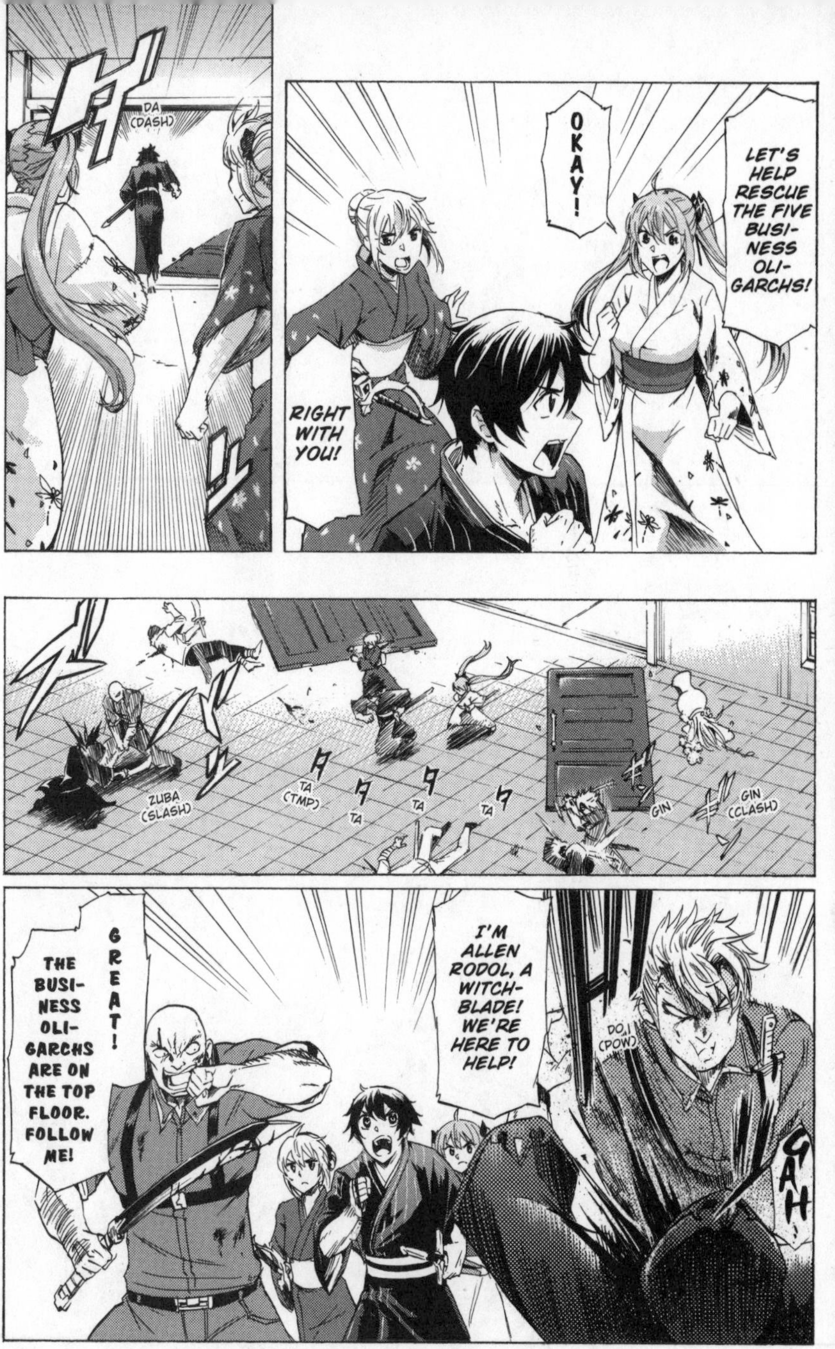
LET'S HELP RESCUE THE FIVE BUSINESS OLIGARCHS!
OKAY!
RIGHT WITH YOU!
DA (DASH)
GIN (CLASH)
GIN
TA
TA
TA
TA (TMP)
ZUBA (SLASH)
GAH
DO,I (POW)
I'M ALLEN RODOL, A WITCHBLADE! WE'RE HERE TO HELP!
GREAT!
THE BUSINESS OLIGARCHS ARE ON THE TOP FLOOR. FOLLOW ME!

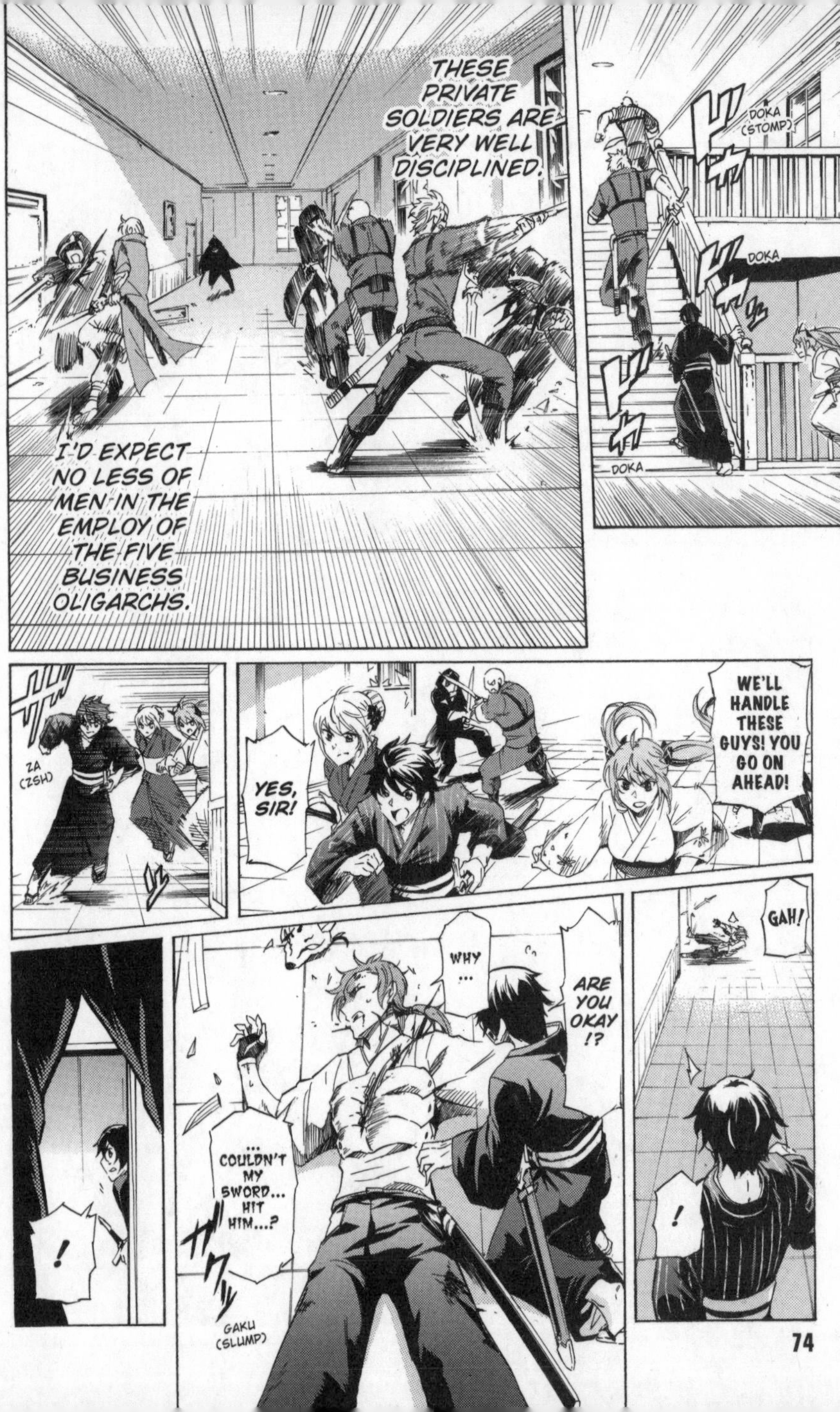
DOKA (STOMP)
DOKA
DOKA
THESE PRIVATE SOLDIERS ARE VERY WELL DISCIPLINED.
I'D EXPECT NO LESS OF MEN IN THE EMPLOY OF THE FIVE BUSINESS OLIGARCHS.
WE'LL HANDLE THESE GUYS! YOU GO ON AHEAD!
YES, SIR!
ZA (ZSH)
GAH!
!
ARE YOU OKAY !?
WHY ...
... COULDN'T MY SWORD... HIT HIM...?
GAKU (SLUMP)
!

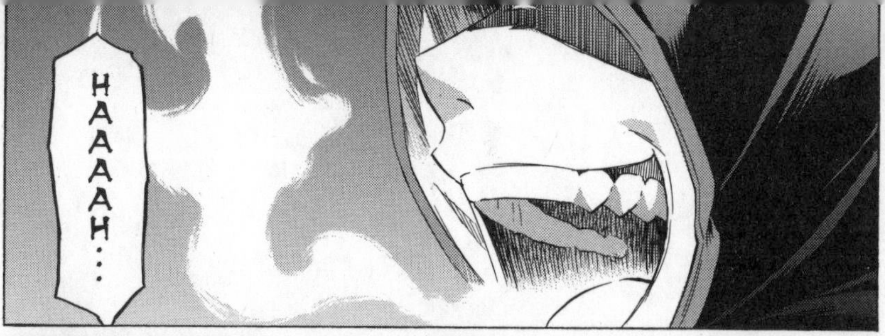
HAAAAAH...
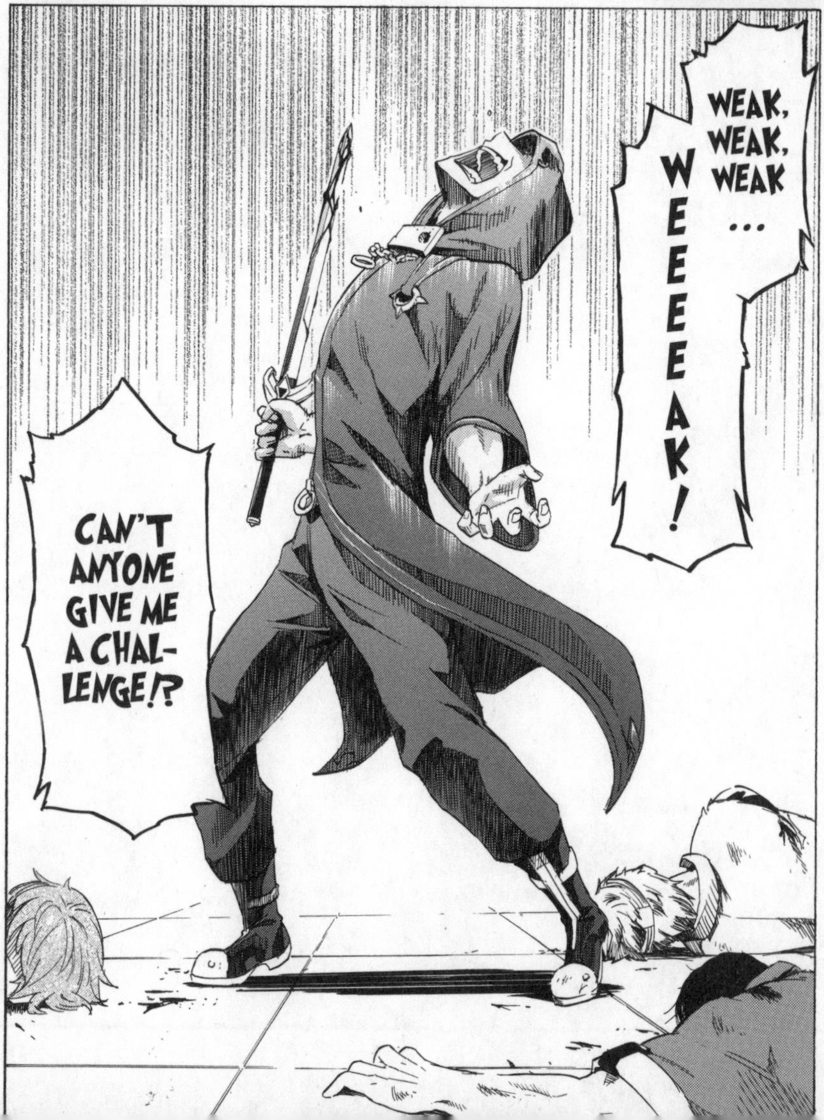
WEAK, WEAK, WEAK...
WEEEEAK!
CAN'T ANYONE GIVE ME A CHAL-LENGE!?

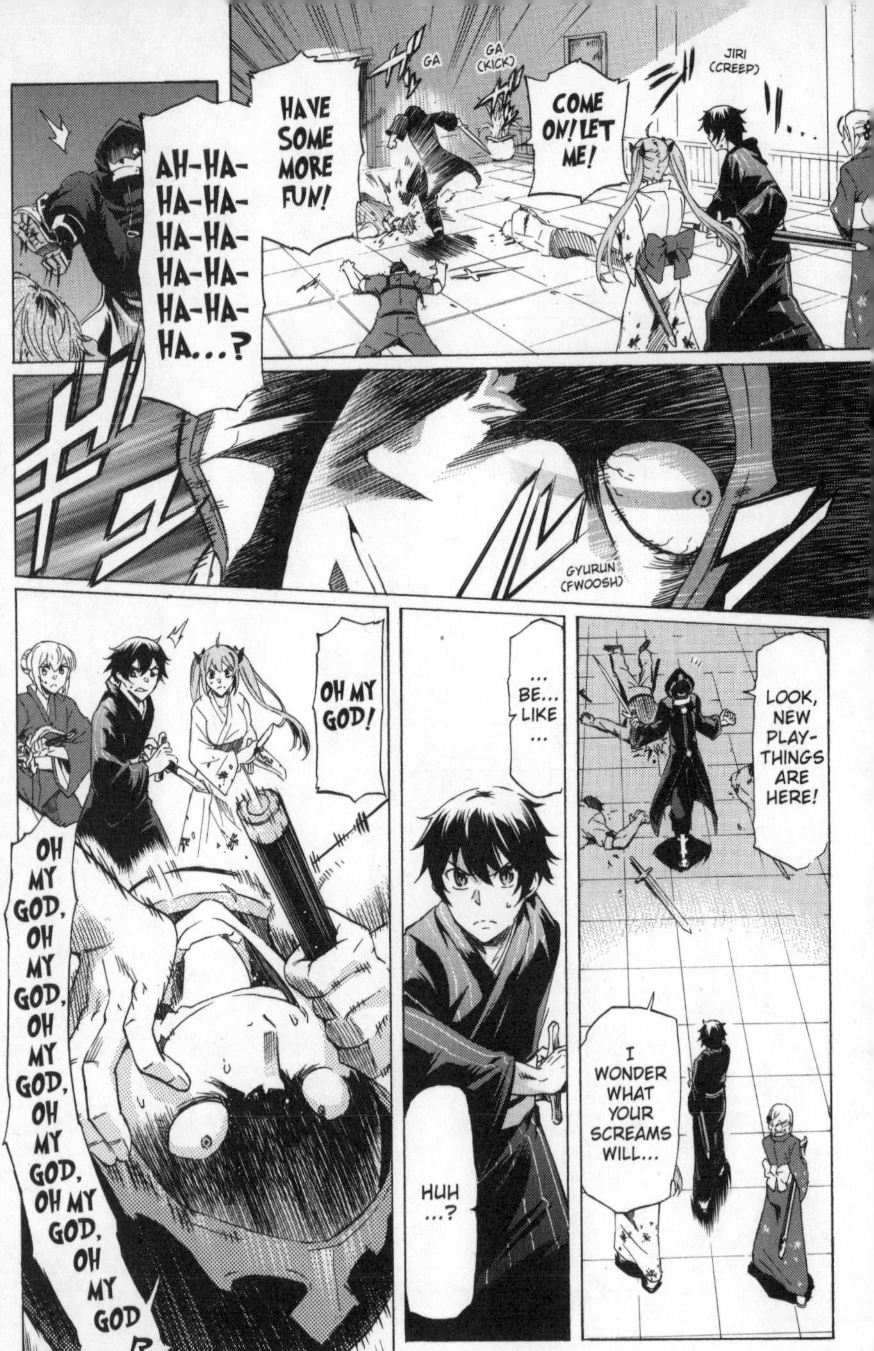
JIRI (CREEP)
!!...
COME ON! LET ME!
GA (KICK)
GA
HAVE SOME MORE FUN!
AH-HA-HA-HA-HA-HA-HA-HA-HA-HA-HA...?
GYURUN (FWOOSH)
LOOK, NEW PLAY-THINGS ARE HERE!
I WONDER WHAT YOUR SCREAMS WILL...
... BE... LIKE ...
HUH ...?
OH MY GOD!
OH MY GOD, OH MY GOD, OH MY GOD, OH MY GOD, OH MY GOD, OH MY GOD ...!?

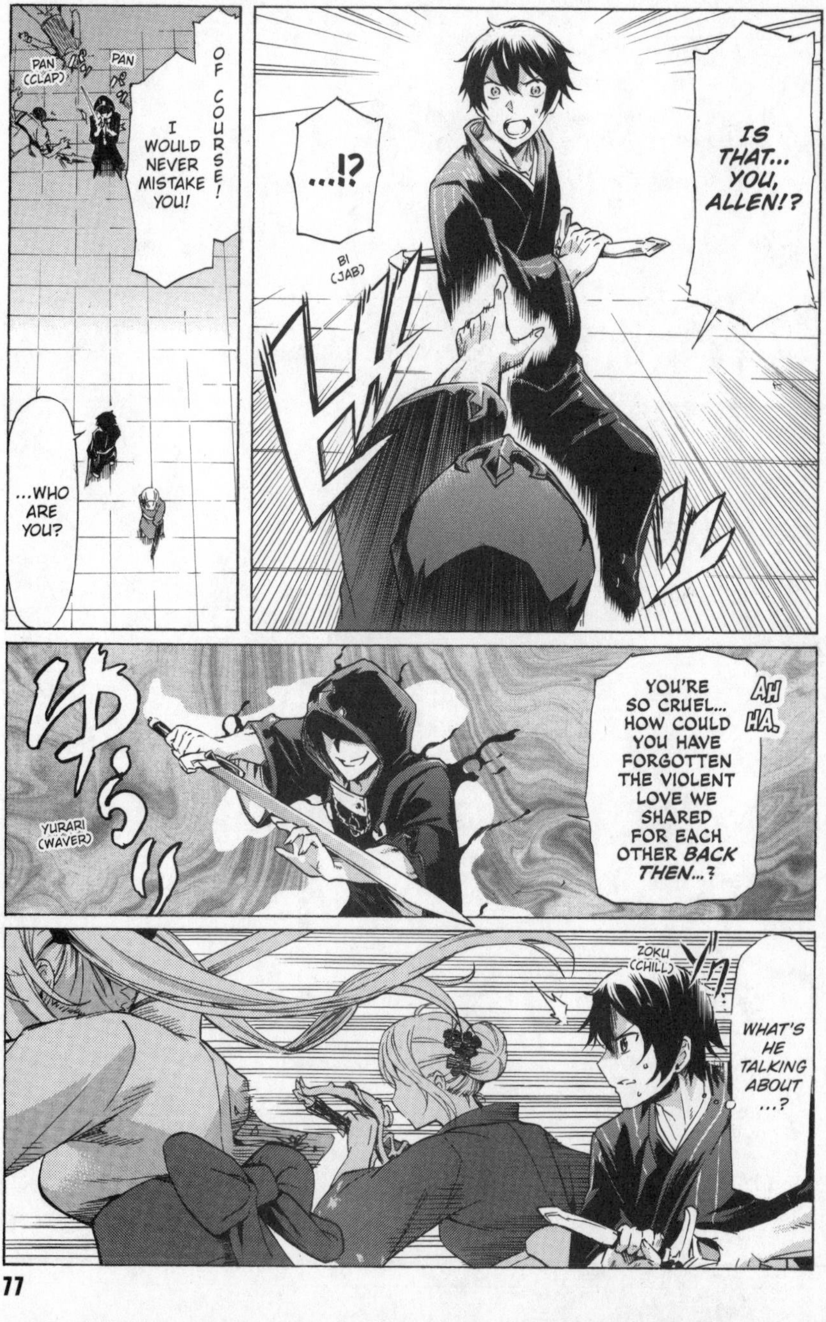

IS THAT... YOU, ALLEN!?
...!?
BI (JAB)
OF COURSE! I WOULD NEVER MISTAKE YOU!
PAN (CLAP)
PAN
...WHO ARE YOU?
AH HA.
YOU'RE SO CRUEL... HOW COULD YOU HAVE FORGOTTEN THE VIOLENT LOVE WE SHARED FOR EACH OTHER *BACK THEN*...?
YURARI (WAVER)
ZOKU (CHILL)
WHAT'S HE TALKING ABOUT ...?

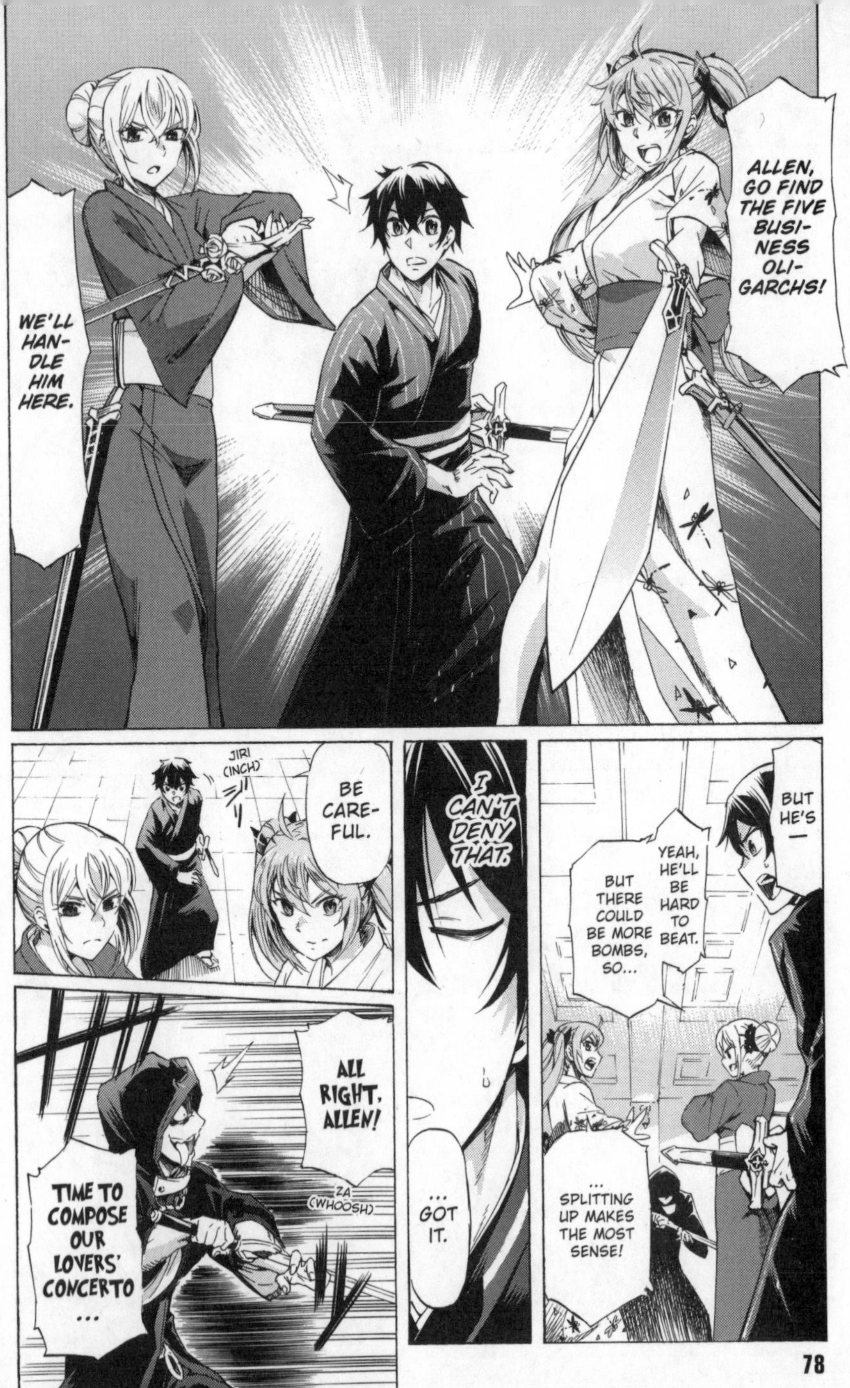
ALLEN, GO FIND THE FIVE BUSI-NESS OLI-GARCHS!
WE'LL HAN-DLE HIM HERE.
BUT HE'S—
YEAH, HE'LL BE HARD TO BEAT.
BUT THERE COULD BE MORE BOMBS, SO...
...SPLITTING UP MAKES THE MOST SENSE!
I CAN'T DENY THAT.
...GOT IT.
BE CARE-FUL.
JIRI (INCH)
ALL RIGHT, ALLEN!
ZA (WHOOSH)
TIME TO COMPOSE OUR LOVERS' CONCERTO...

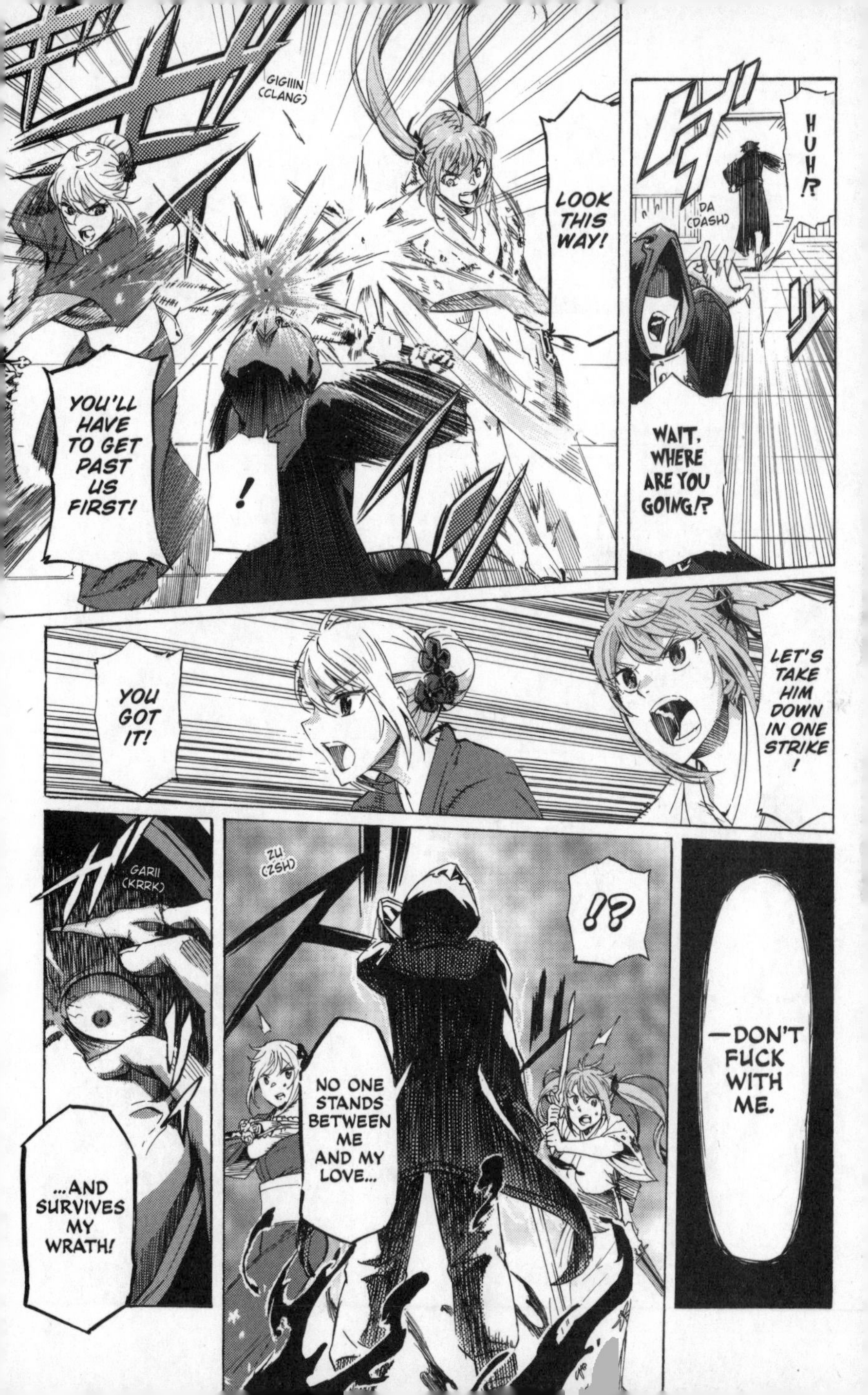
HUH!?
DA (DASH)
WAIT, WHERE ARE YOU GOING!?
GIGIIN (CLANG)
LOOK THIS WAY!
!
YOU'LL HAVE TO GET PAST US FIRST!
LET'S TAKE HIM DOWN IN ONE STRIKE!
YOU GOT IT!
—DON'T FUCK WITH ME.
!?
ZU (ZSH)
NO ONE STANDS BETWEEN ME AND MY LOVE...
GARII (KRRK)
...AND SURVIVES MY WRATH!

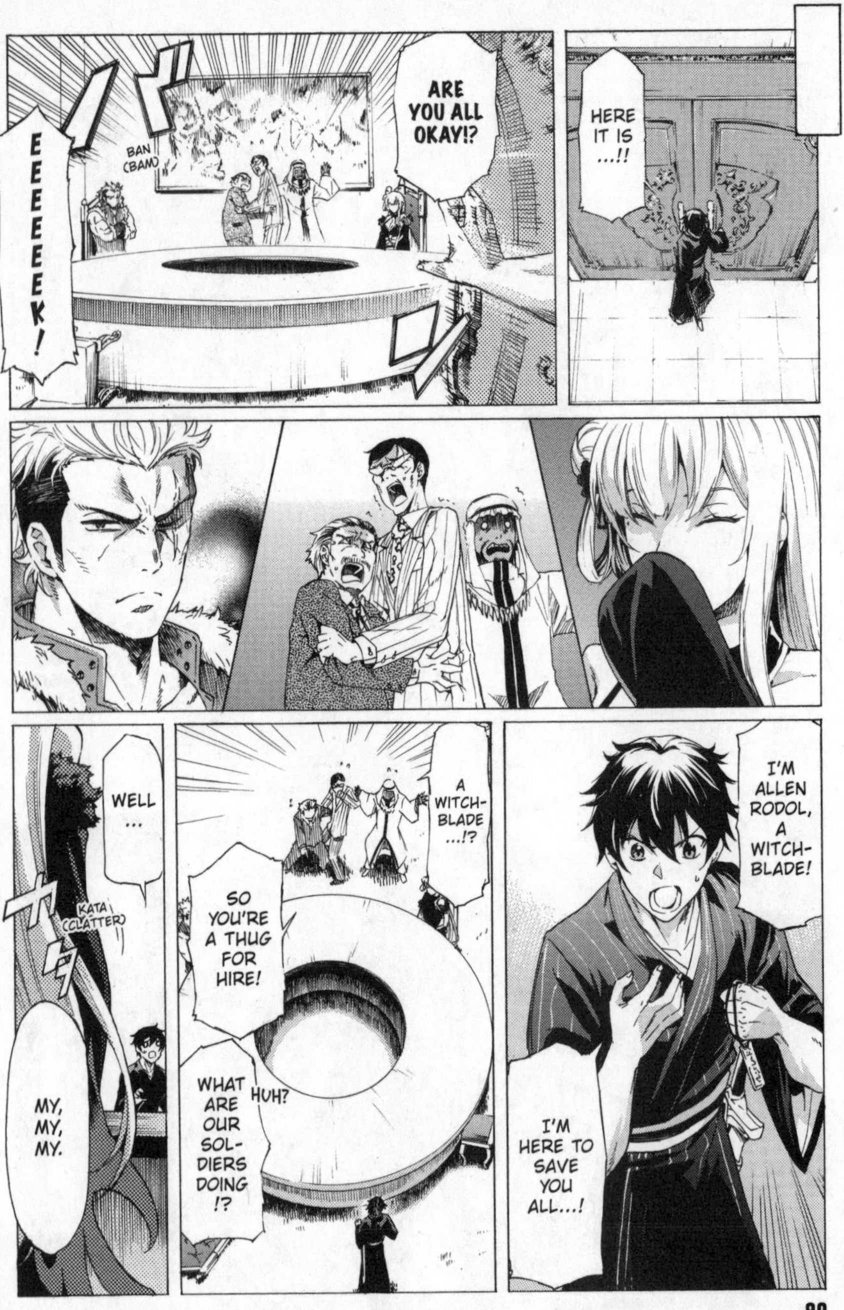
HERE IT IS ...!!
ARE YOU ALL OKAY!?
BAN (BAM)
EEEEEEEK!
I'M ALLEN RODOL, A WITCH-BLADE!
I'M HERE TO SAVE YOU ALL...!
A WITCH-BLADE ...!?
SO YOU'RE A THUG FOR HIRE!
HUH?
WHAT ARE OUR SOL-DIERS DOING !?
WELL ...
KATA (CLATTER)
MY, MY, MY.

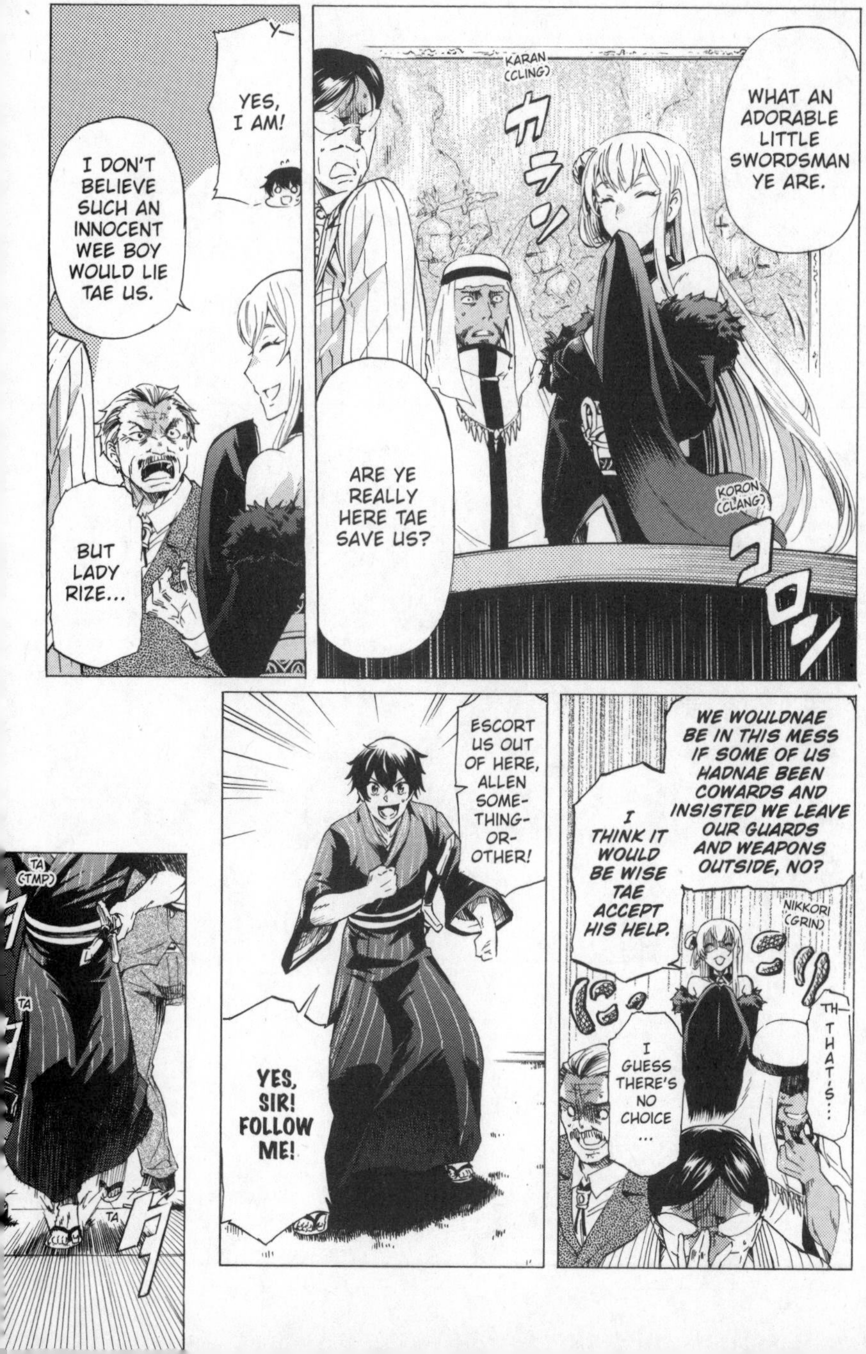
WHAT AN ADORABLE LITTLE SWORDSMAN YE ARE.
KARAN (CLING)
KORON (CLANG)
ARE YE REALLY HERE TAE SAVE US?
Y—
YES, I AM!
I DON'T BELIEVE SUCH AN INNOCENT WEE BOY WOULD LIE TAE US.
BUT LADY RIZE...
WE WOULDNAE BE IN THIS MESS IF SOME OF US HADNAE BEEN COWARDS AND INSISTED WE LEAVE OUR GUARDS AND WEAPONS OUTSIDE, NO?
I THINK IT WOULD BE WISE TAE ACCEPT HIS HELP.
NIKKORI (GRIN)
TH— THAT'S...
I GUESS THERE'S NO CHOICE...
ESCORT US OUT OF HERE, ALLEN SOME-THING-OR-OTHER!
YES, SIR! FOLLOW ME!
TA (TMP)
TA
TA

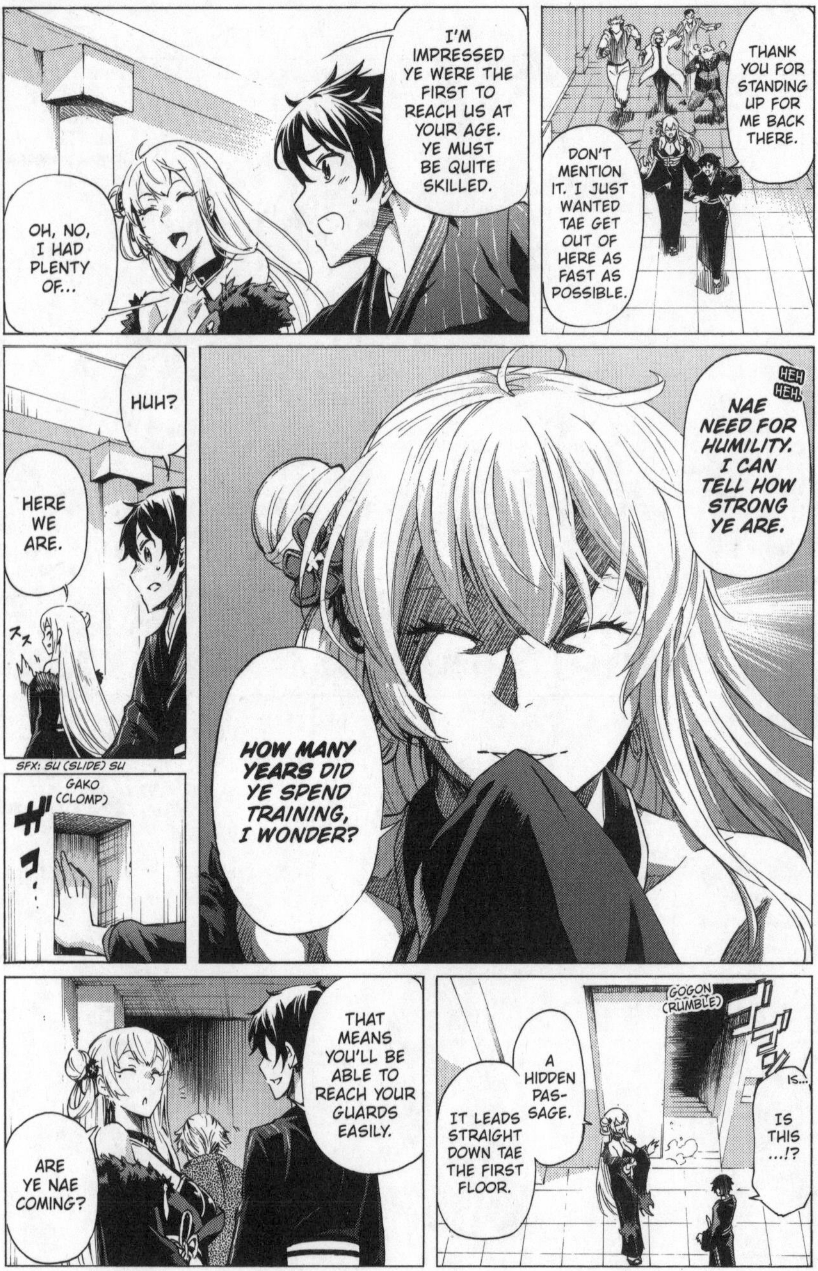
THANK YOU FOR STANDING UP FOR ME BACK THERE.
DON'T MENTION IT. I JUST WANTED TAE GET OUT OF HERE AS FAST AS POSSIBLE.
I'M IMPRESSED YE WERE THE FIRST TO REACH US AT YOUR AGE. YE MUST BE QUITE SKILLED.
OH, NO, I HAD PLENTY OF...
HEH HEH.
NAE NEED FOR HUMILITY. I CAN TELL HOW STRONG YE ARE.
HOW MANY YEARS DID YE SPEND TRAINING, I WONDER?
HUH?
HERE WE ARE.
SFX: SU (SLIDE) SU
GAKO (CLOMP)
GOGON (RUMBLE)
IS...
IS THIS ...!?
A HIDDEN PASSAGE.
IT LEADS STRAIGHT DOWN TAE THE FIRST FLOOR.
THAT MEANS YOU'LL BE ABLE TO REACH YOUR GUARDS EASILY.
ARE YE NAE COMING?

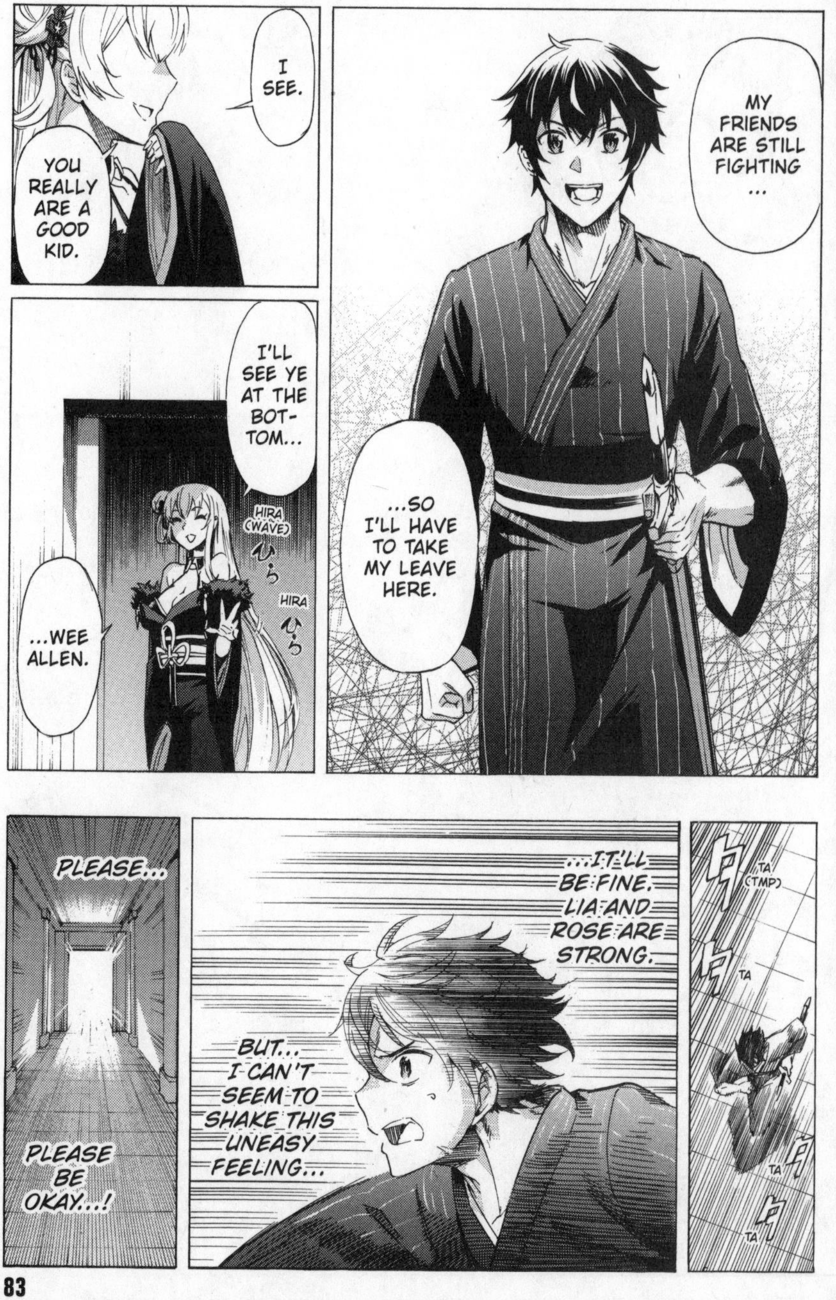
MY FRIENDS ARE STILL FIGHTING...
...SO I'LL HAVE TO TAKE MY LEAVE HERE.
I SEE.
YOU REALLY ARE A GOOD KID.
I'LL SEE YE AT THE BOT-TOM...
HIRA (WAVE)
ひら
HIRA
ひら
...WEE ALLEN.
TA (TMP)
TA
TA
TA
...IT'LL BE FINE. LIA AND ROSE ARE STRONG.
BUT... I CAN'T SEEM TO SHAKE THIS UNEASY FEELING...
PLEASE...
PLEASE BE OKAY...!

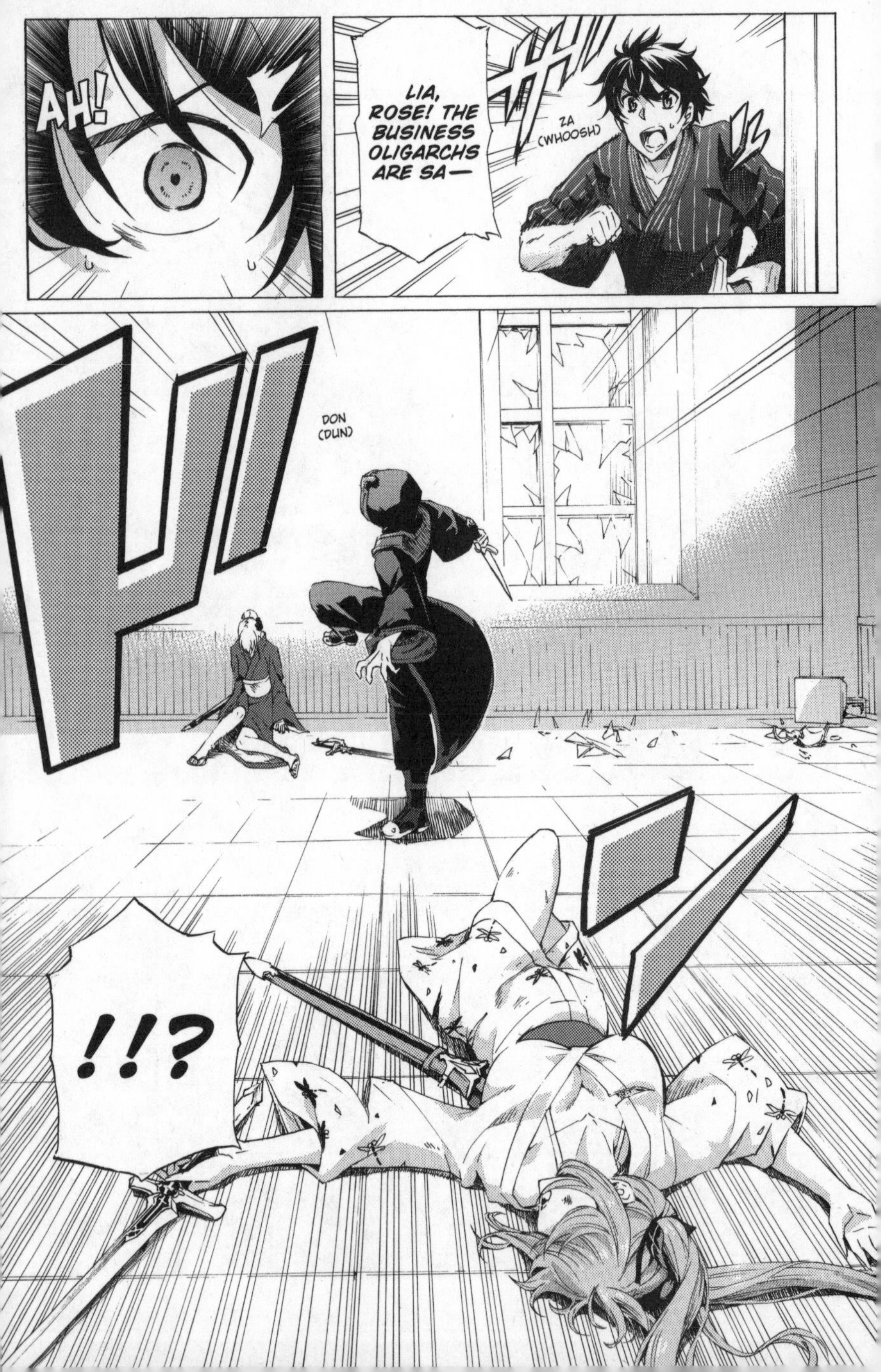
ZA (WHOOSH)
LIA, ROSE! THE BUSINESS OLIGARCHS ARE SA—
AH!
DON (DUN)
!!?

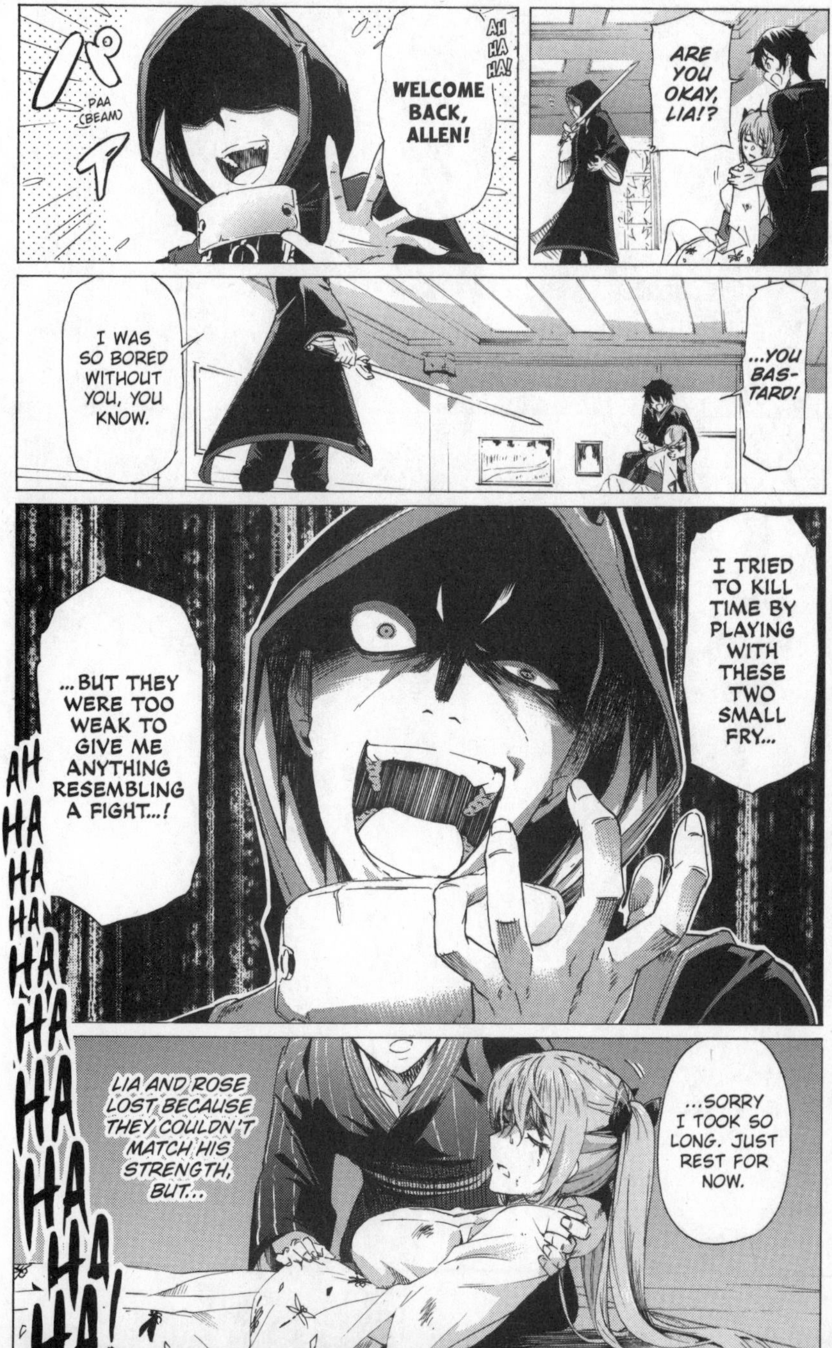
ARE YOU OKAY, LIA!?
AH HA HA!
WELCOME BACK, ALLEN!
PAA (BEAM)
...YOU BAS-TARD!
I WAS SO BORED WITHOUT YOU, YOU KNOW.
I TRIED TO KILL TIME BY PLAYING WITH THESE TWO SMALL FRY...
...BUT THEY WERE TOO WEAK TO GIVE ME ANYTHING RESEMBLING A FIGHT...!
AH HA HA HA HA HA HA HA HA HA HA HA HA!
...SORRY I TOOK SO LONG. JUST REST FOR NOW.
LIA AND ROSE LOST BECAUSE THEY COULDN'T MATCH HIS STRENGTH, BUT...

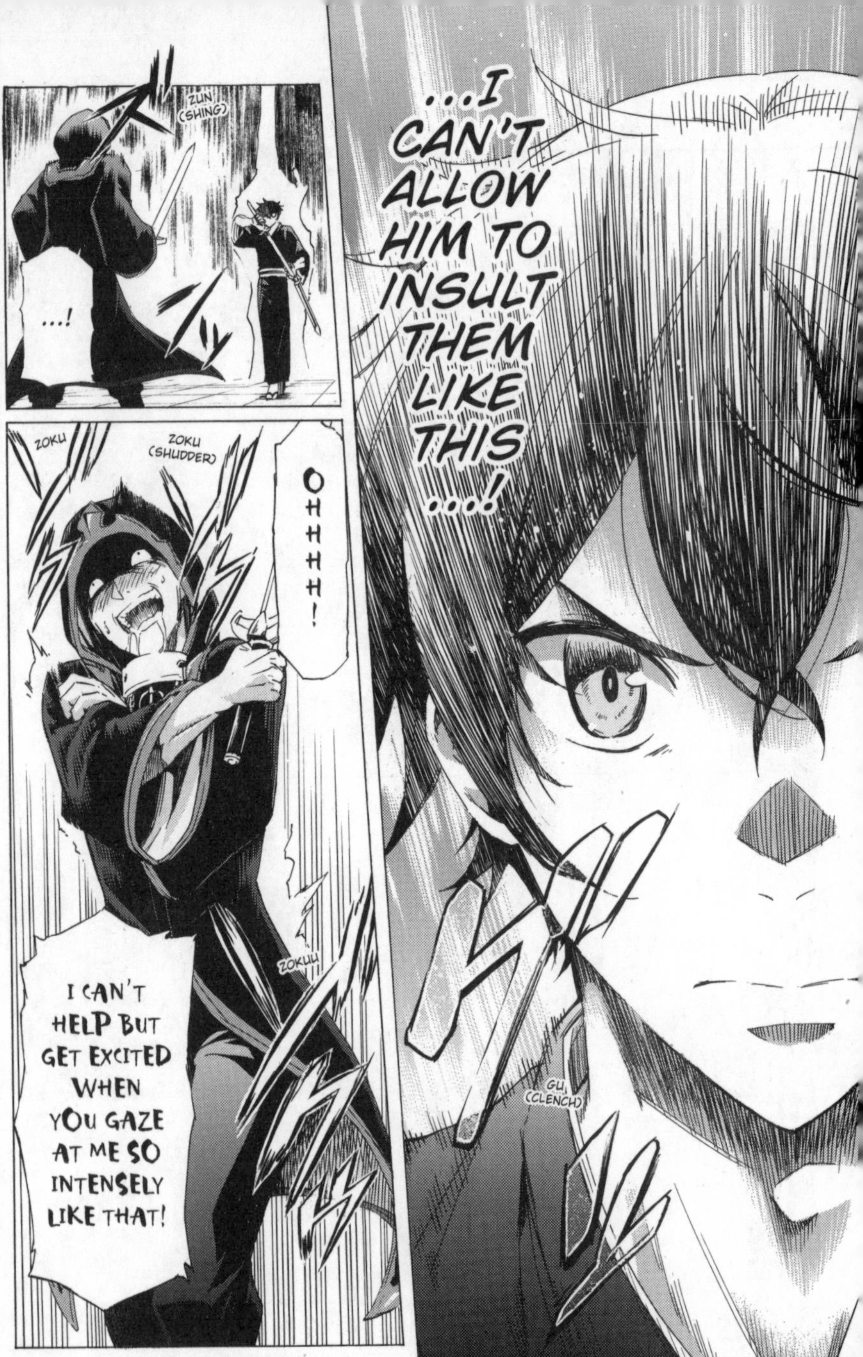
...I CAN'T ALLOW HIM TO INSULT THEM LIKE THIS...!
GU (CLENCH)
ZUN (SHING)
...!
ZOKU
ZOKU (SHUDDER)
OHHHHH!
ZOKUU
I CAN'T HELP BUT GET EXCITED WHEN YOU GAZE AT ME SO INTENSELY LIKE THAT!

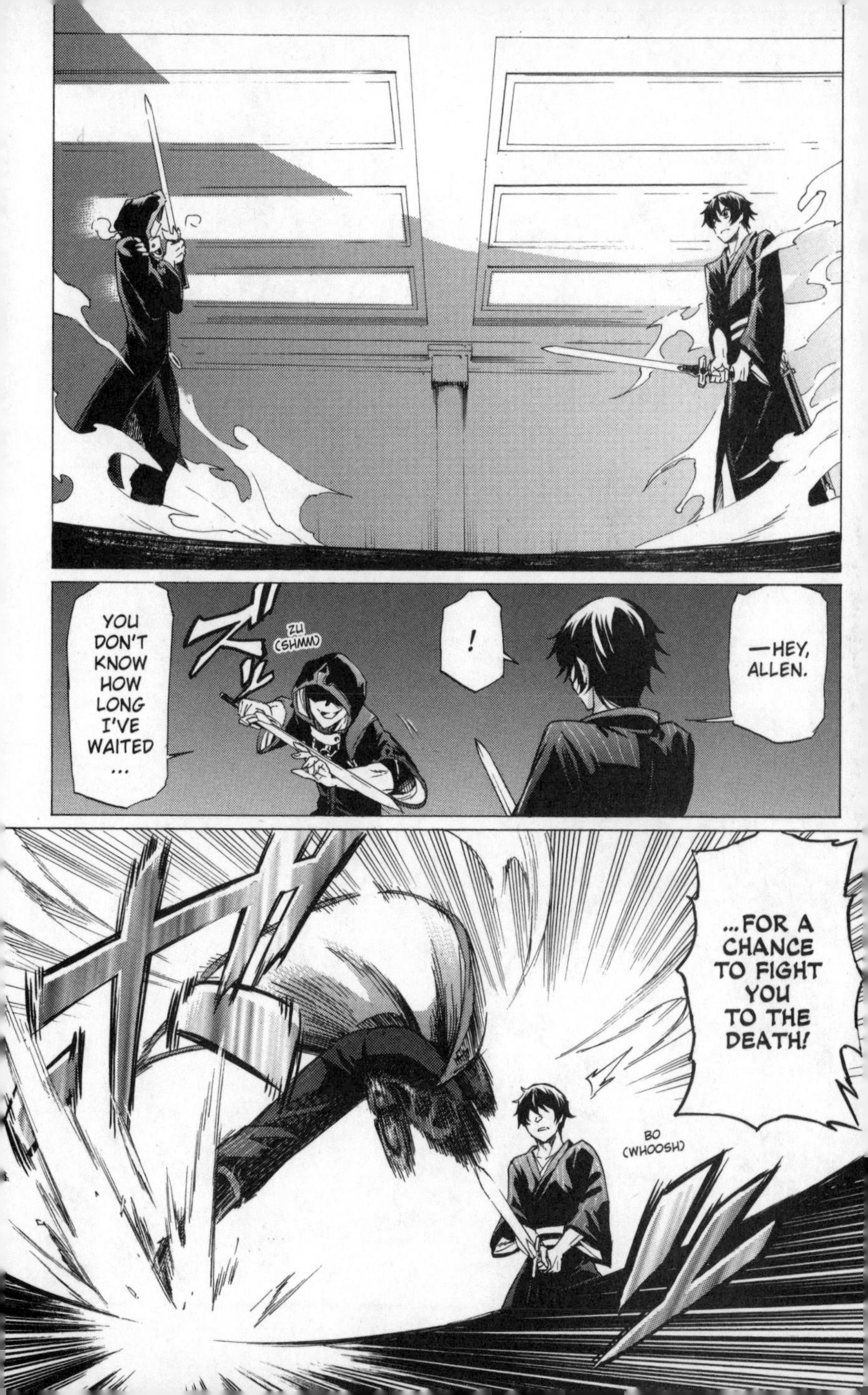
—HEY, ALLEN.
!
ZU (SHMM)
YOU DON'T KNOW HOW LONG I'VE WAITED ...
...FOR A CHANCE TO FIGHT YOU TO THE DEATH!
BO (WHOOSH)

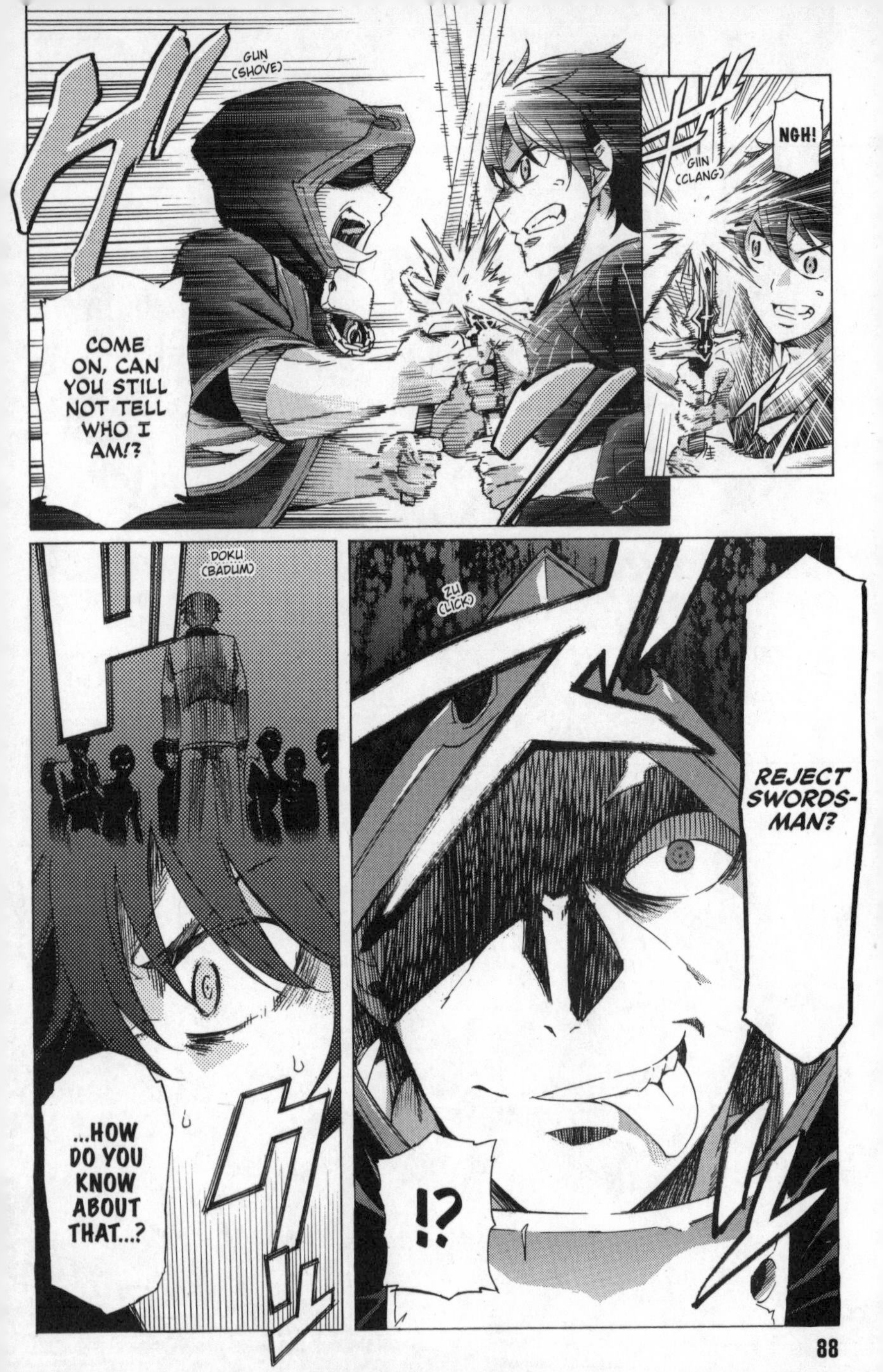
GIIN (CLANG)
NGH!
GUN (SHOVE)
COME ON, CAN YOU STILL NOT TELL WHO I AM!?
ZU (LICK)
REJECT SWORDS-MAN?
!?
DOKU (BADUM)
...HOW DO YOU KNOW ABOUT THAT...?

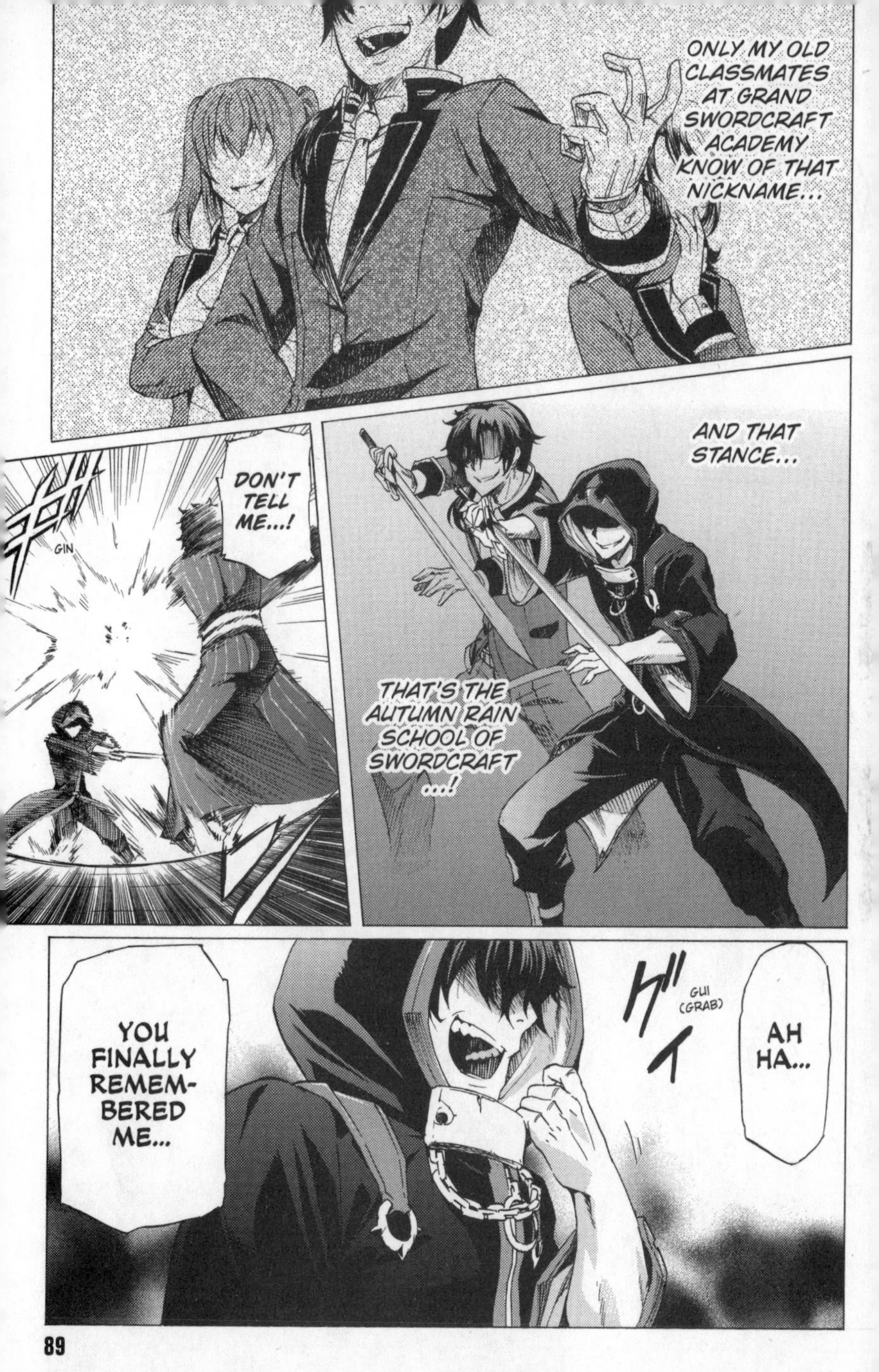
ONLY MY OLD CLASSMATES AT GRAND SWORDCRAFT ACADEMY KNOW OF THAT NICKNAME...
AND THAT STANCE...
THAT'S THE AUTUMN RAIN SCHOOL OF SWORDCRAFT ...!
DON'T TELL ME...!
GIN
AH HA...
GUI (GRAB)
YOU FINALLY REMEM-BERED ME...

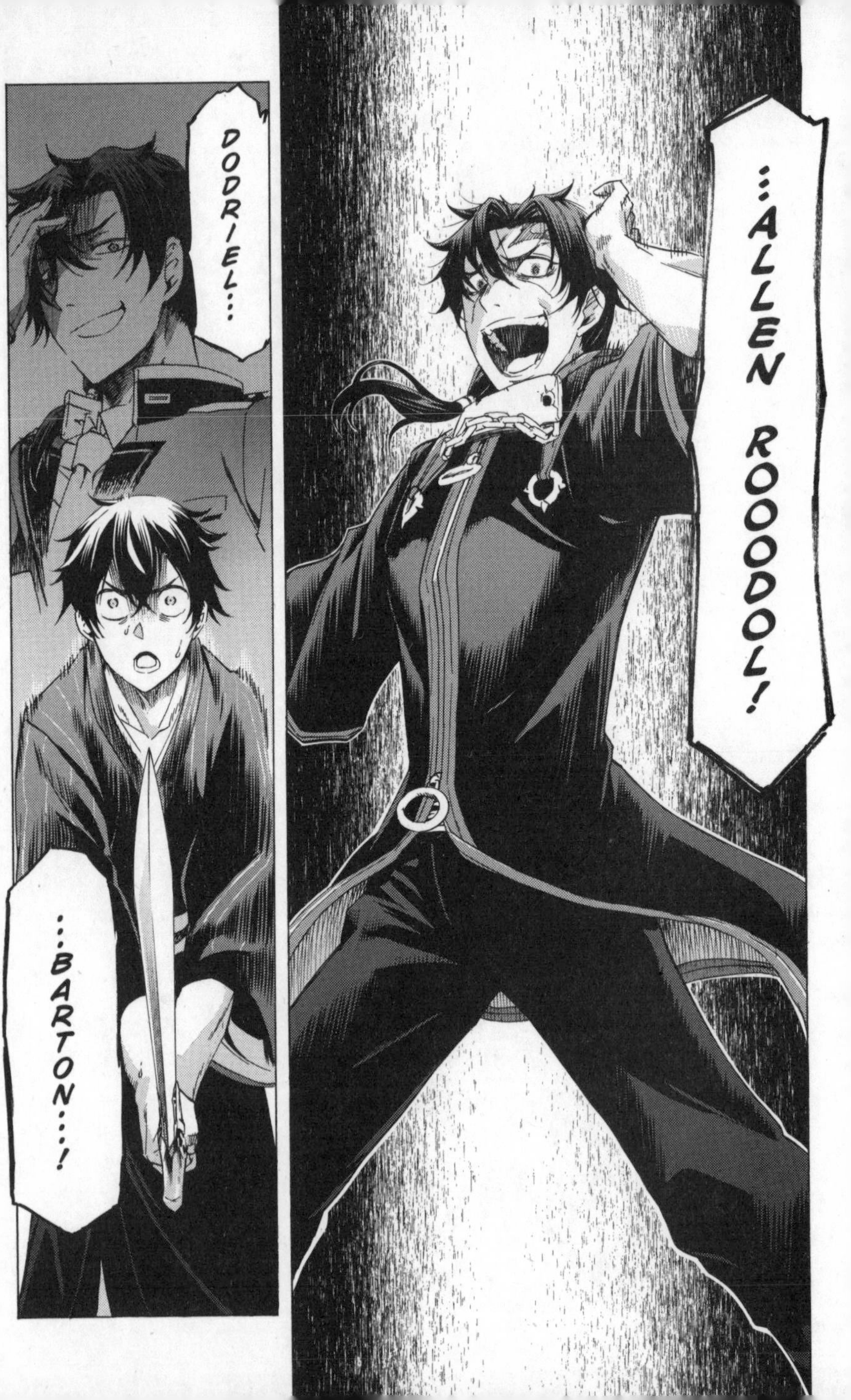
...ALLEN ROOOODOL!
DODRIEL...
...BARTON...!

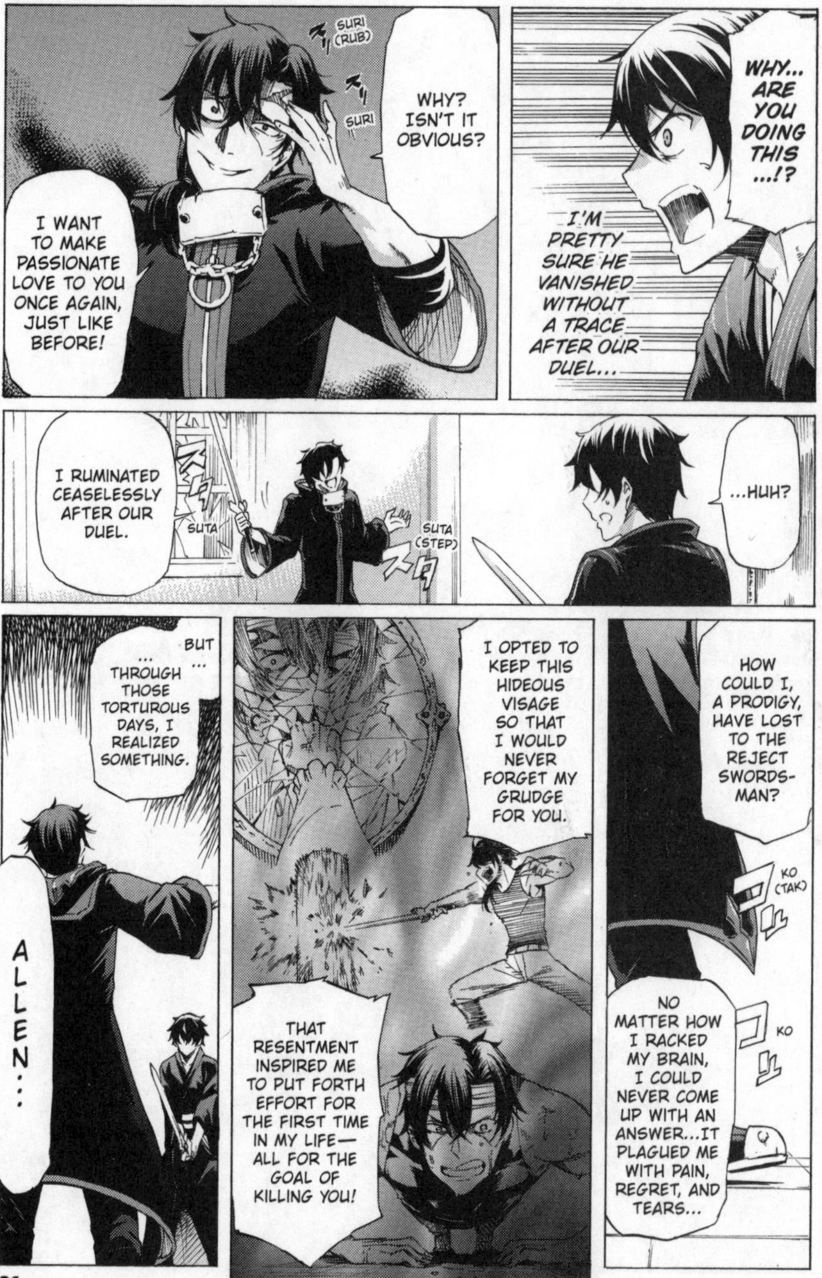
WHY... ARE YOU DOING THIS ...!?
I'M PRETTY SURE HE VANISHED WITHOUT A TRACE AFTER OUR DUEL...
SURI (RUB)
SURI
WHY? ISN'T IT OBVIOUS?
I WANT TO MAKE PASSIONATE LOVE TO YOU ONCE AGAIN, JUST LIKE BEFORE!
...HUH?
SUTA (STEP)
SUTA
I RUMINATED CEASELESSLY AFTER OUR DUEL.
HOW COULD I, A PRODIGY, HAVE LOST TO THE REJECT SWORDS-MAN?
KO (TAK)
NO MATTER HOW I RACKED MY BRAIN, I COULD NEVER COME UP WITH AN ANSWER...IT PLAGUED ME WITH PAIN, REGRET, AND TEARS...
KO
I OPTED TO KEEP THIS HIDEOUS VISAGE SO THAT I WOULD NEVER FORGET MY GRUDGE FOR YOU.
THAT RESENTMENT INSPIRED ME TO PUT FORTH EFFORT FOR THE FIRST TIME IN MY LIFE—ALL FOR THE GOAL OF KILLING YOU!
BUT... ...THROUGH THOSE TORTUROUS DAYS, I REALIZED SOMETHING.
ALLEN...

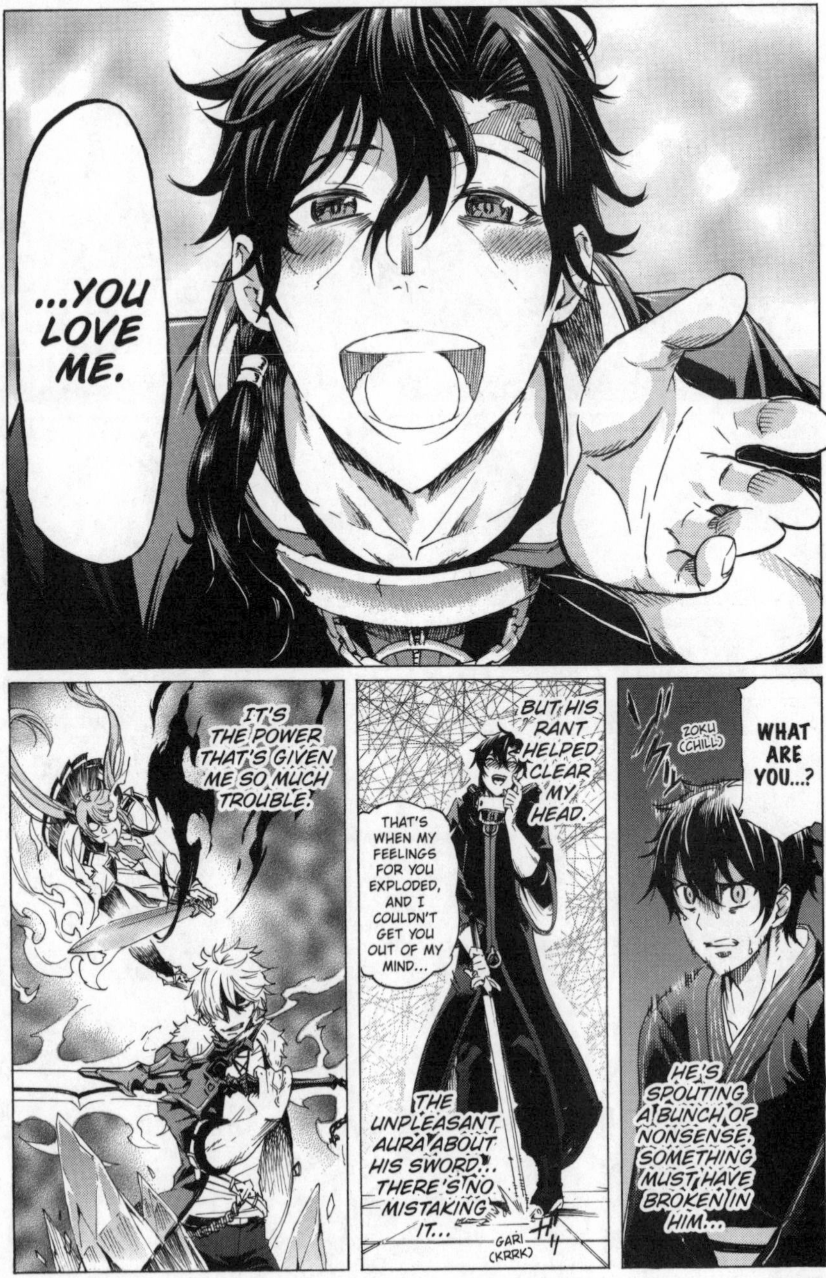
...YOU LOVE ME.
WHAT ARE YOU...?
ZOKU (CHILL)
HE'S SPOUTING A BUNCH OF NONSENSE. SOMETHING MUST HAVE BROKEN IN HIM...
BUT HIS RANT HELPED CLEAR MY HEAD.
THAT'S WHEN MY FEELINGS FOR YOU EXPLODED, AND I COULDN'T GET YOU OUT OF MY MIND...
THE UNPLEASANT AURA ABOUT HIS SWORD... THERE'S NO MISTAKING IT...
GARI (KRRK)
IT'S THE POWER THAT'S GIVEN ME SO MUCH TROUBLE.

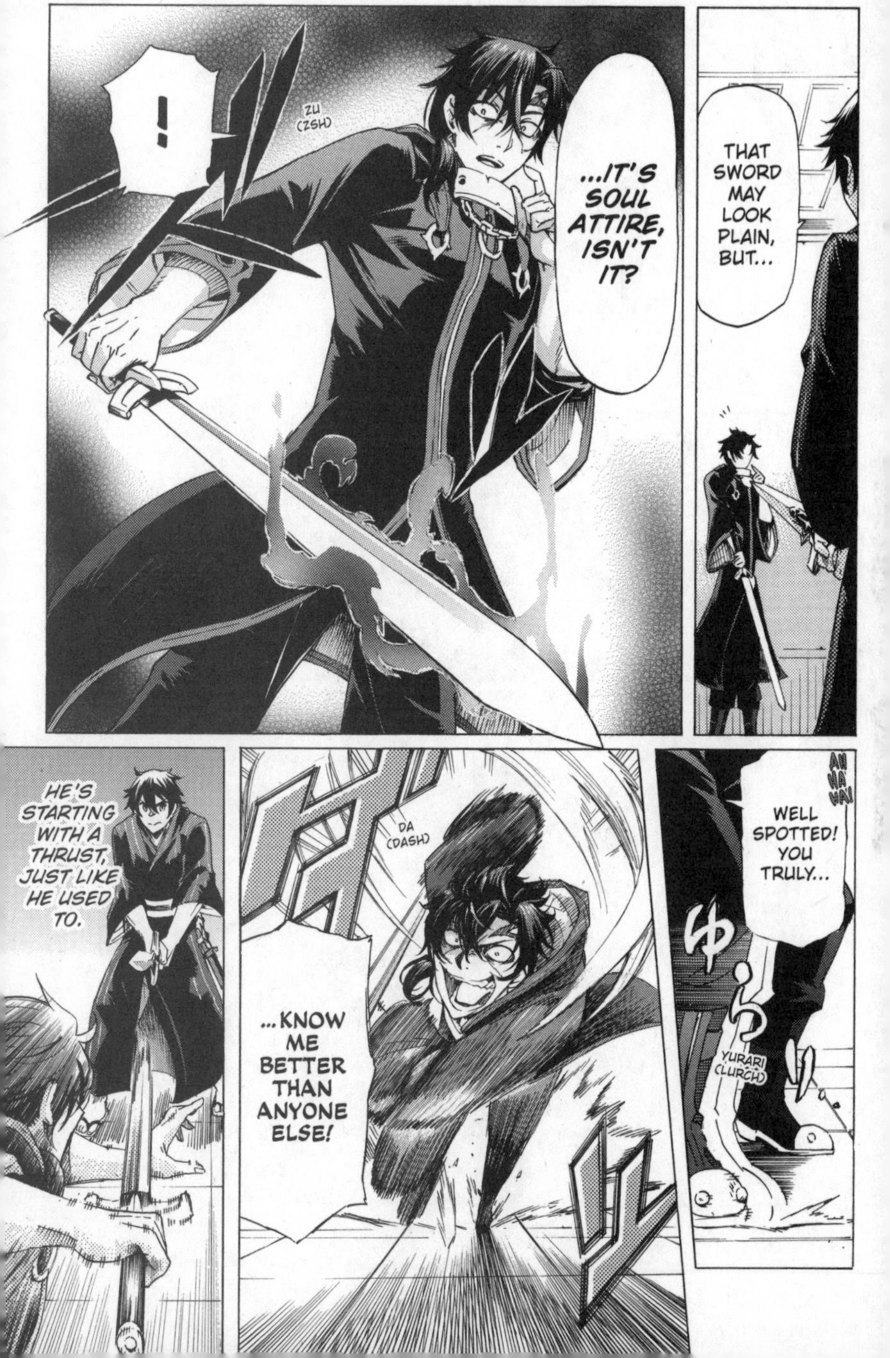
THAT SWORD MAY LOOK PLAIN, BUT...
...IT'S SOUL ATTIRE, ISN'T IT?
ZU (ZSH)
!
WELL SPOTTED! YOU TRULY...
AH HA HA!
YURARI (LURCH)
...KNOW ME BETTER THAN ANYONE ELSE!
DA (DASH)
HE'S STARTING WITH A THRUST, JUST LIKE HE USED TO.

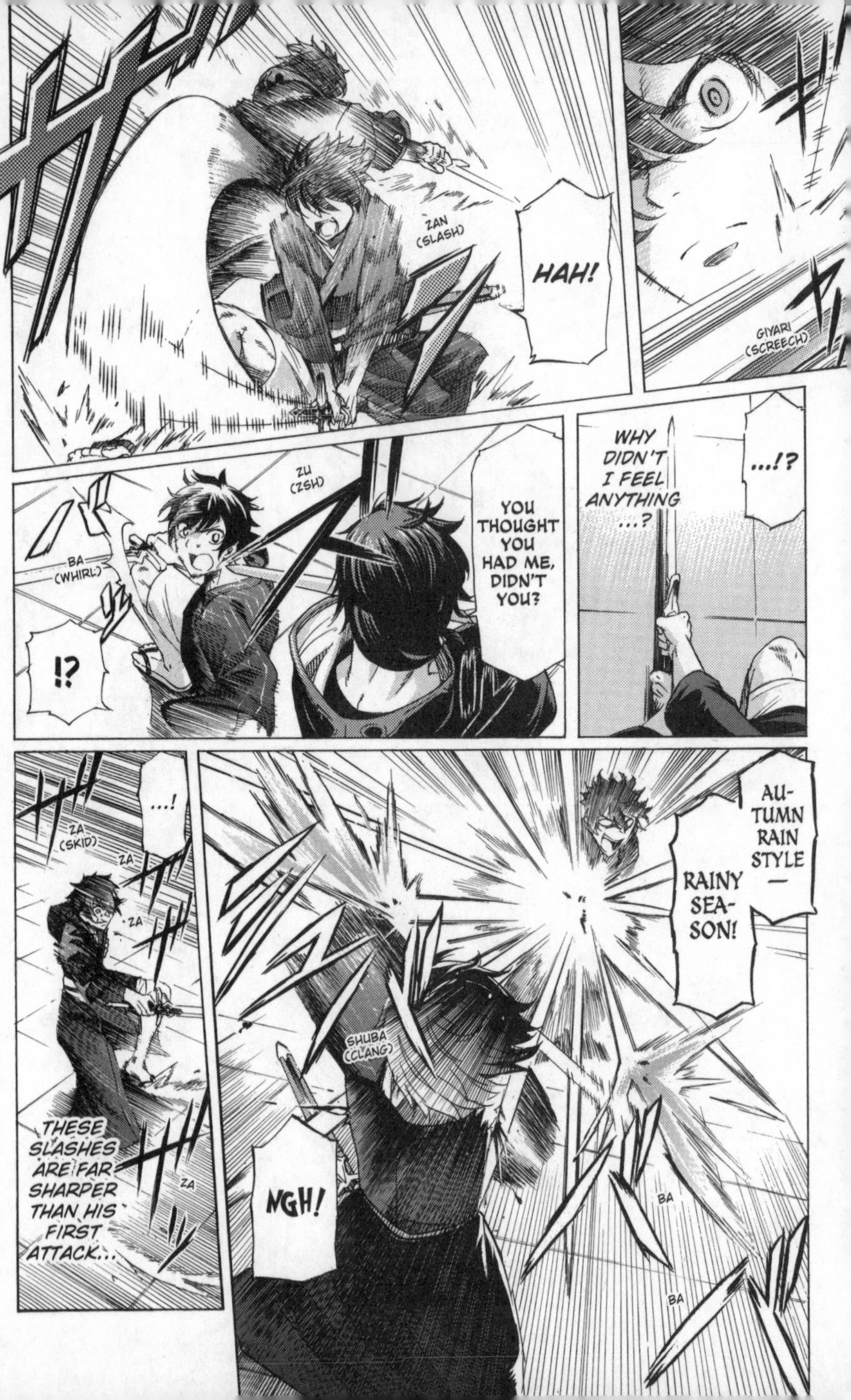
GIYARI (SCREECH)
HAH!
ZAN (SLASH)
...!?
WHY DIDN'T I FEEL ANYTHING ...?
YOU THOUGHT YOU HAD ME, DIDN'T YOU?
ZU (ZSH)
BA (WHIRL)
!?
AU-TUMN RAIN STYLE—
RAINY SEA-SON!
SHUBA (CLANG)
NGH!
BA
BA
...!
ZA (SKID)
ZA
ZA
THESE SLASHES ARE FAR SHARPER THAN HIS FIRST ATTACK...
ZA

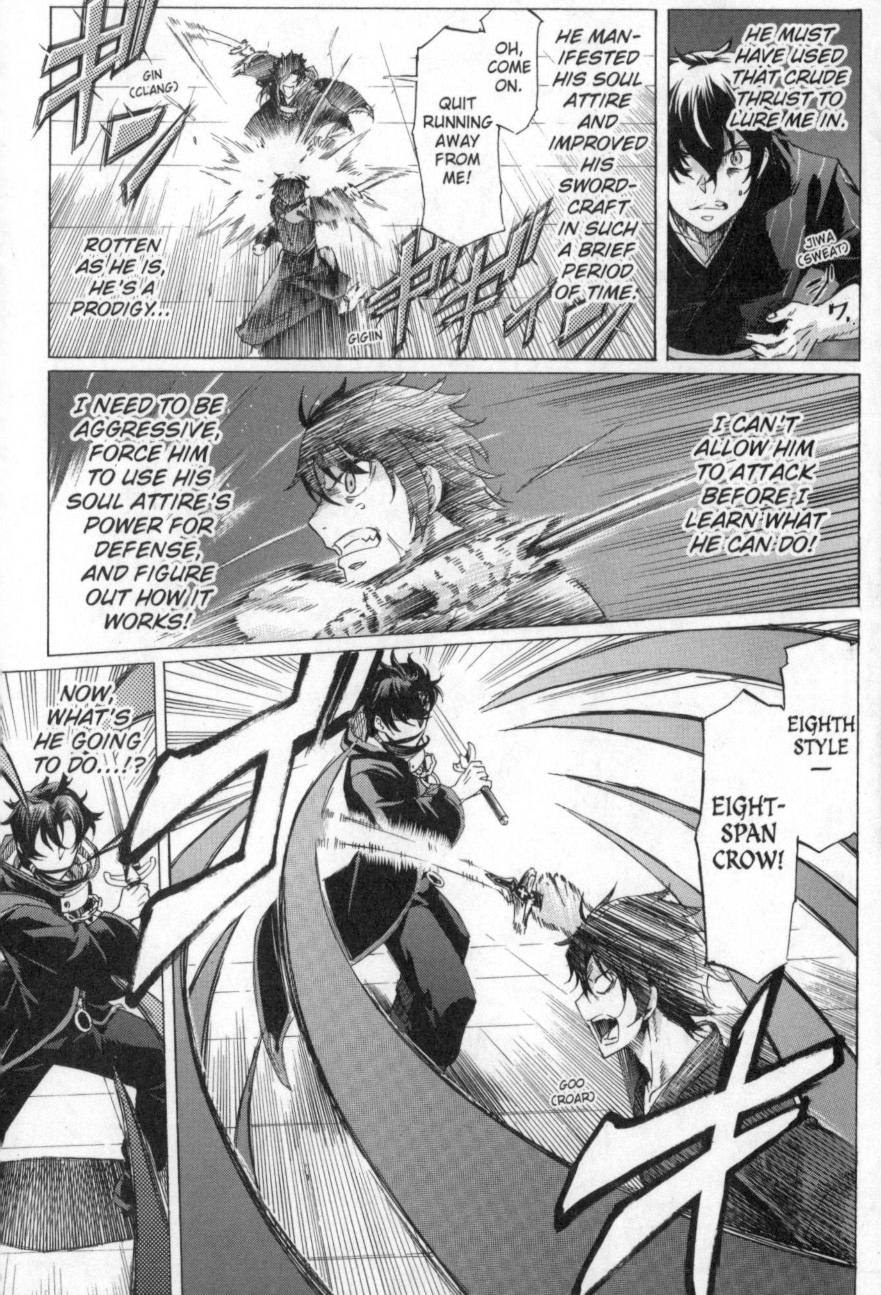

HE MUST HAVE USED THAT CRUDE THRUST TO LURE ME IN.
JIWA (SWEAT)
HE MAN-IFESTED HIS SOUL ATTIRE AND IMPROVED HIS SWORD-CRAFT IN SUCH A BRIEF PERIOD OF TIME.
OH, COME ON.
QUIT RUNNING AWAY FROM ME!
GIN (CLANG)
GIGIIN
ROTTEN AS HE IS, HE'S A PRODIGY...
I CAN'T ALLOW HIM TO ATTACK BEFORE I LEARN WHAT HE CAN DO!
I NEED TO BE AGGRESSIVE, FORCE HIM TO USE HIS SOUL ATTIRE'S POWER FOR DEFENSE, AND FIGURE OUT HOW IT WORKS!
EIGHTH STYLE —
EIGHT-SPAN CROW!
NOW, WHAT'S HE GOING TO DO...!?
GOO (ROAR)

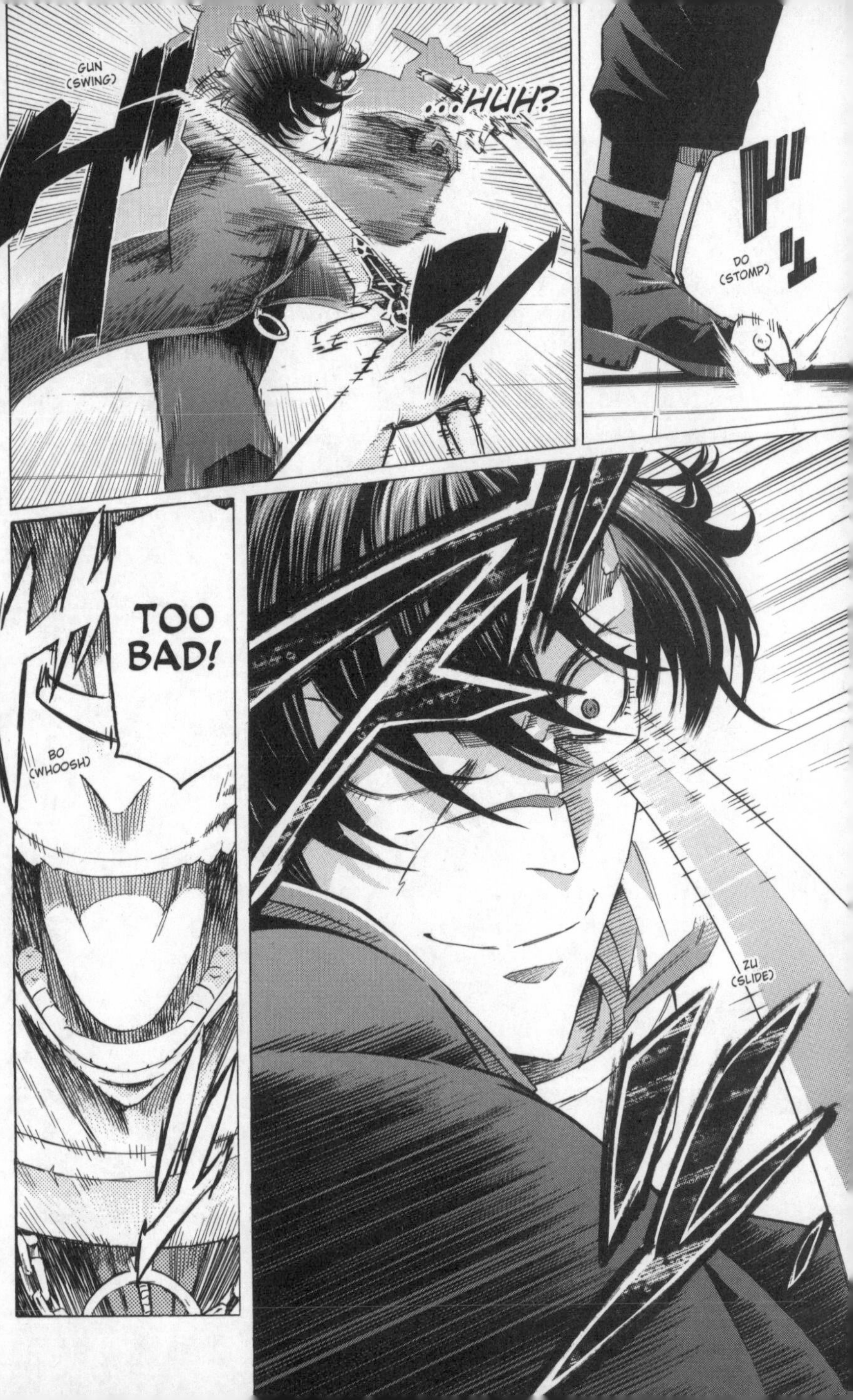
DO (STOMP)
...HUH?
GUN (SWING)
ZU (SLIDE)
TOO BAD!
BO (WHOOSH)

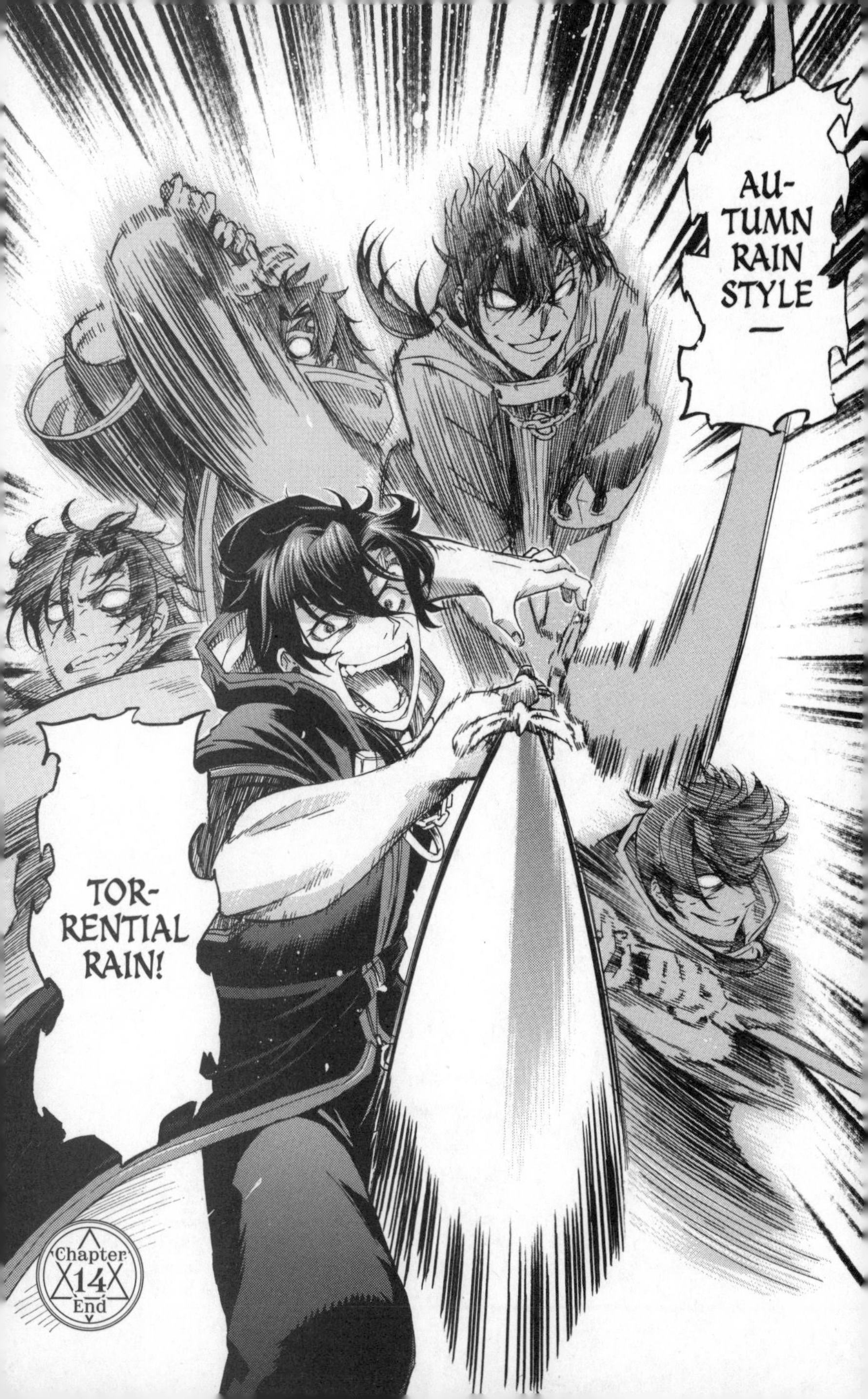
AU-
TUMN
RAIN
STYLE
—
TOR-
RENTIAL
RAIN!
Chapter
14
End

I KEPT PRESSING THE 100-MILLION-YEAR BUTTON AND CAME OUT ON TOP

~THE UNBEATABLE REJECT SWORDSMAN~

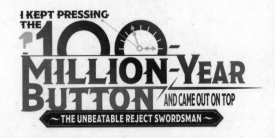

Chapter 15

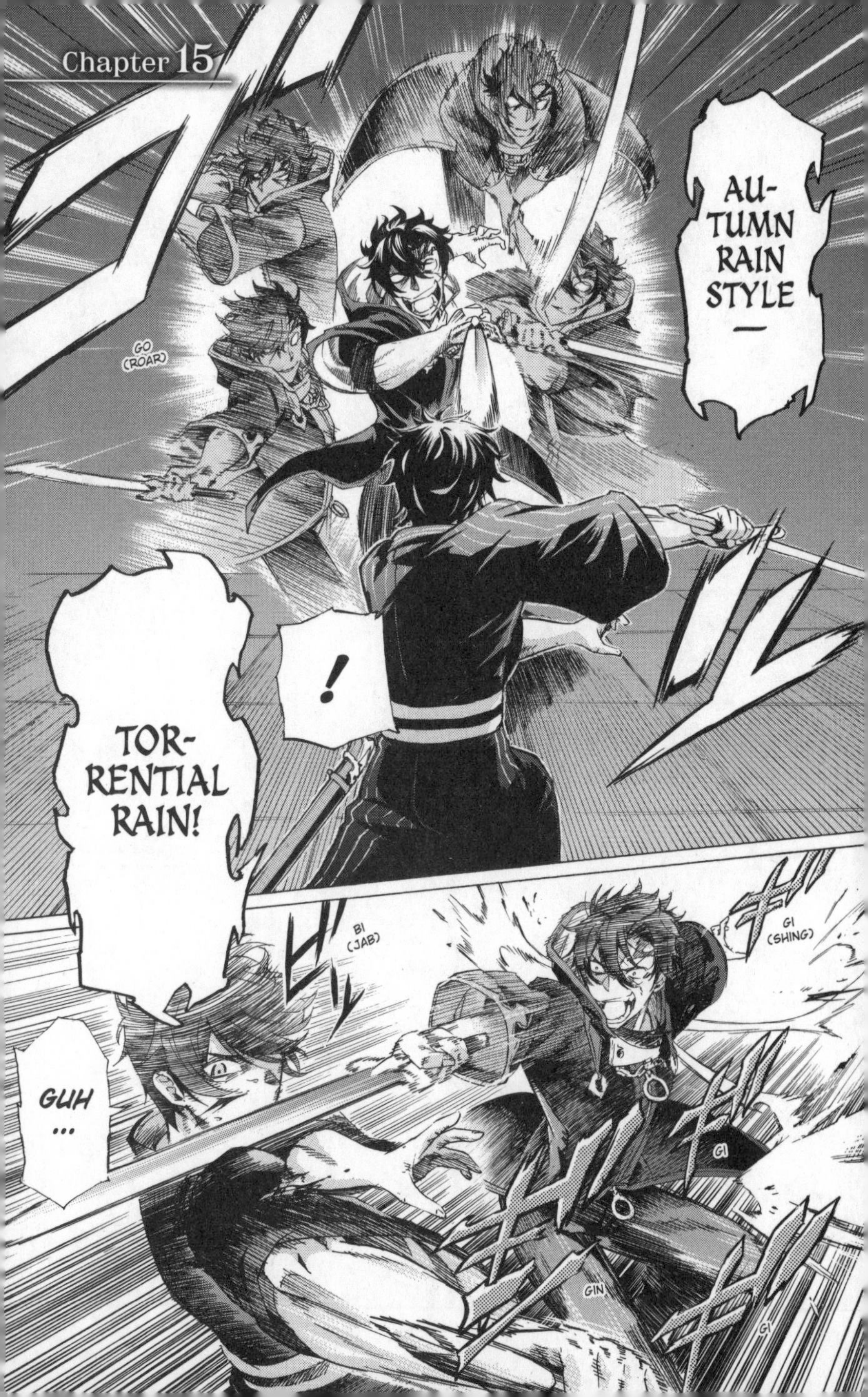
AU-TUMN RAIN STYLE —
GO (ROAR)
!
TOR-RENTIAL RAIN!
GI (SHING)
BI (JAB)
GUH ...
GI
GIN
GI

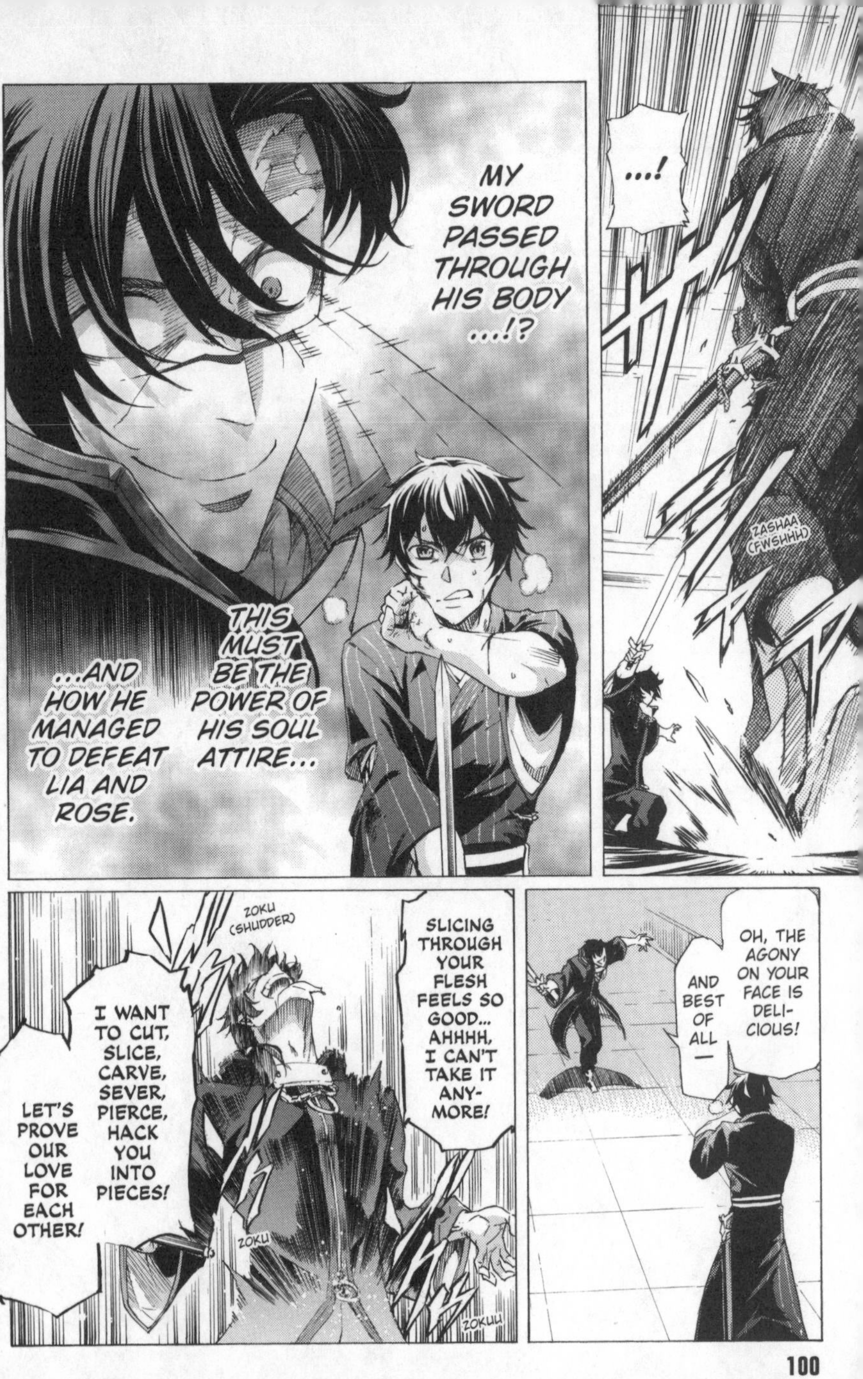
...!
ZASHAA (FWSHHH)
MY SWORD PASSED THROUGH HIS BODY ...!?
THIS MUST BE THE POWER OF HIS SOUL ATTIRE...
...AND HOW HE MANAGED TO DEFEAT LIA AND ROSE.
OH, THE AGONY ON YOUR FACE IS DELI-CIOUS!
AND BEST OF ALL —
ZOKU (SHUDDER)
SLICING THROUGH YOUR FLESH FEELS SO GOOD... AHHHH, I CAN'T TAKE IT ANY-MORE!
I WANT TO CUT, SLICE, CARVE, SEVER, PIERCE, HACK YOU INTO PIECES!
LET'S PROVE OUR LOVE FOR EACH OTHER!
ZOKU
ZOKUU

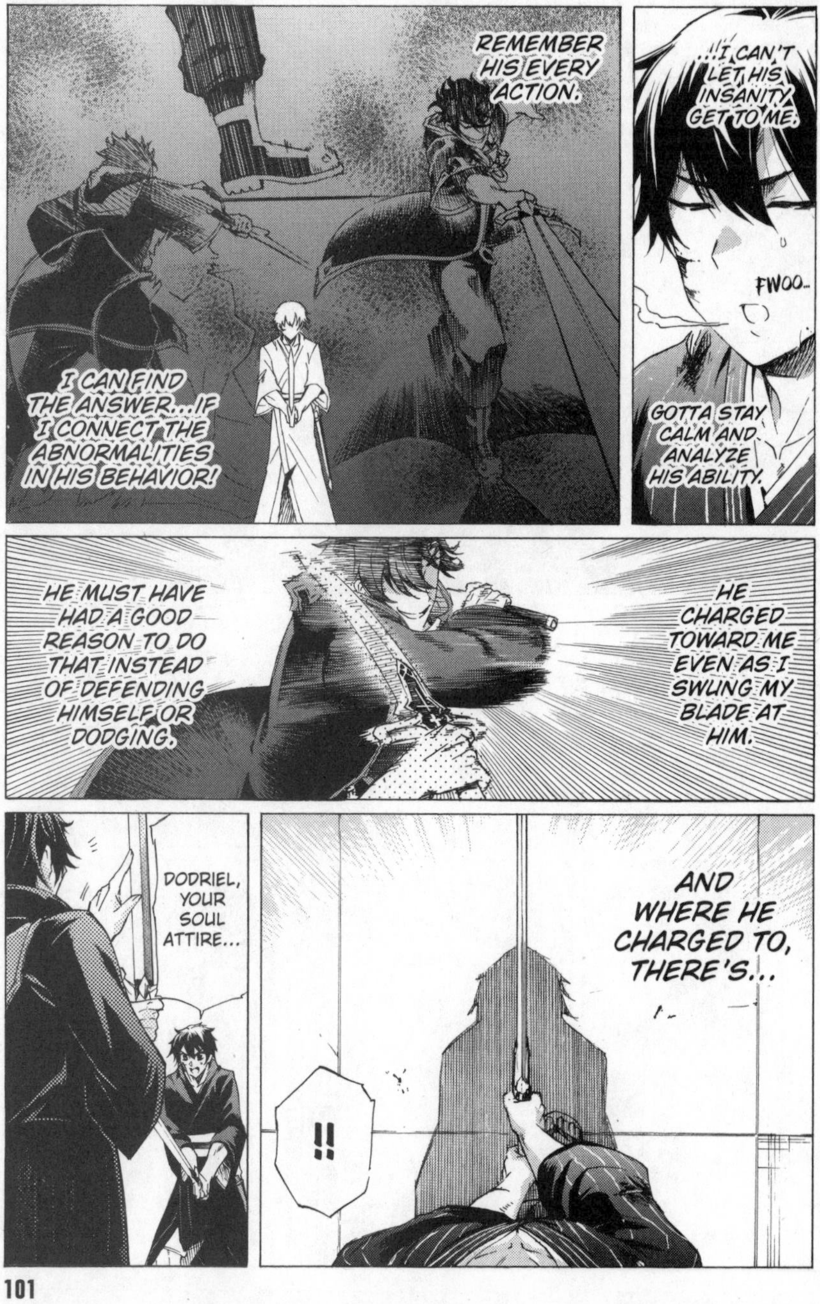
...!I CAN'T LET HIS INSANITY GET TO ME.
FWOO...
GOTTA STAY CALM AND ANALYZE HIS ABILITY.
REMEMBER HIS EVERY ACTION.
I CAN FIND THE ANSWER...IF I CONNECT THE ABNORMALITIES IN HIS BEHAVIOR!
HE CHARGED TOWARD ME EVEN AS I SWUNG MY BLADE AT HIM.
HE MUST HAVE HAD A GOOD REASON TO DO THAT INSTEAD OF DEFENDING HIMSELF OR DODGING.
AND WHERE HE CHARGED TO, THERE'S...
!!
DODRIEL, YOUR SOUL ATTIRE...

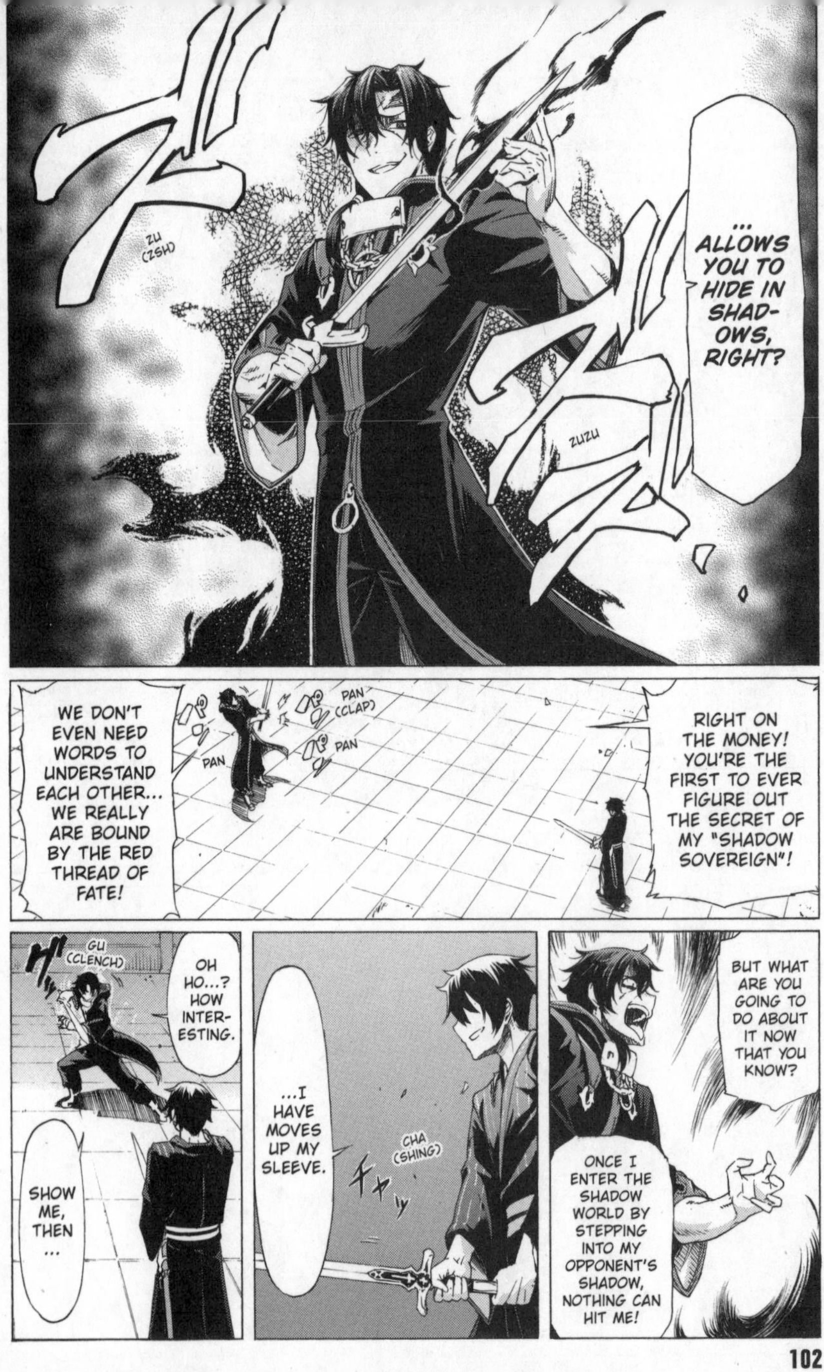

...ALLOWS YOU TO HIDE IN SHADOWS, RIGHT?
ZUZU
ZU (ZSH)
RIGHT ON THE MONEY! YOU'RE THE FIRST TO EVER FIGURE OUT THE SECRET OF MY "SHADOW SOVEREIGN"!
PAN (CLAP)
PAN
PAN
WE DON'T EVEN NEED WORDS TO UNDERSTAND EACH OTHER... WE REALLY ARE BOUND BY THE RED THREAD OF FATE!
BUT WHAT ARE YOU GOING TO DO ABOUT IT NOW THAT YOU KNOW?
ONCE I ENTER THE SHADOW WORLD BY STEPPING INTO MY OPPONENT'S SHADOW, NOTHING CAN HIT ME!
...I HAVE MOVES UP MY SLEEVE.
CHA (SHING)
GU (CLENCH)
OH HO...? HOW INTERESTING.
SHOW ME, THEN...

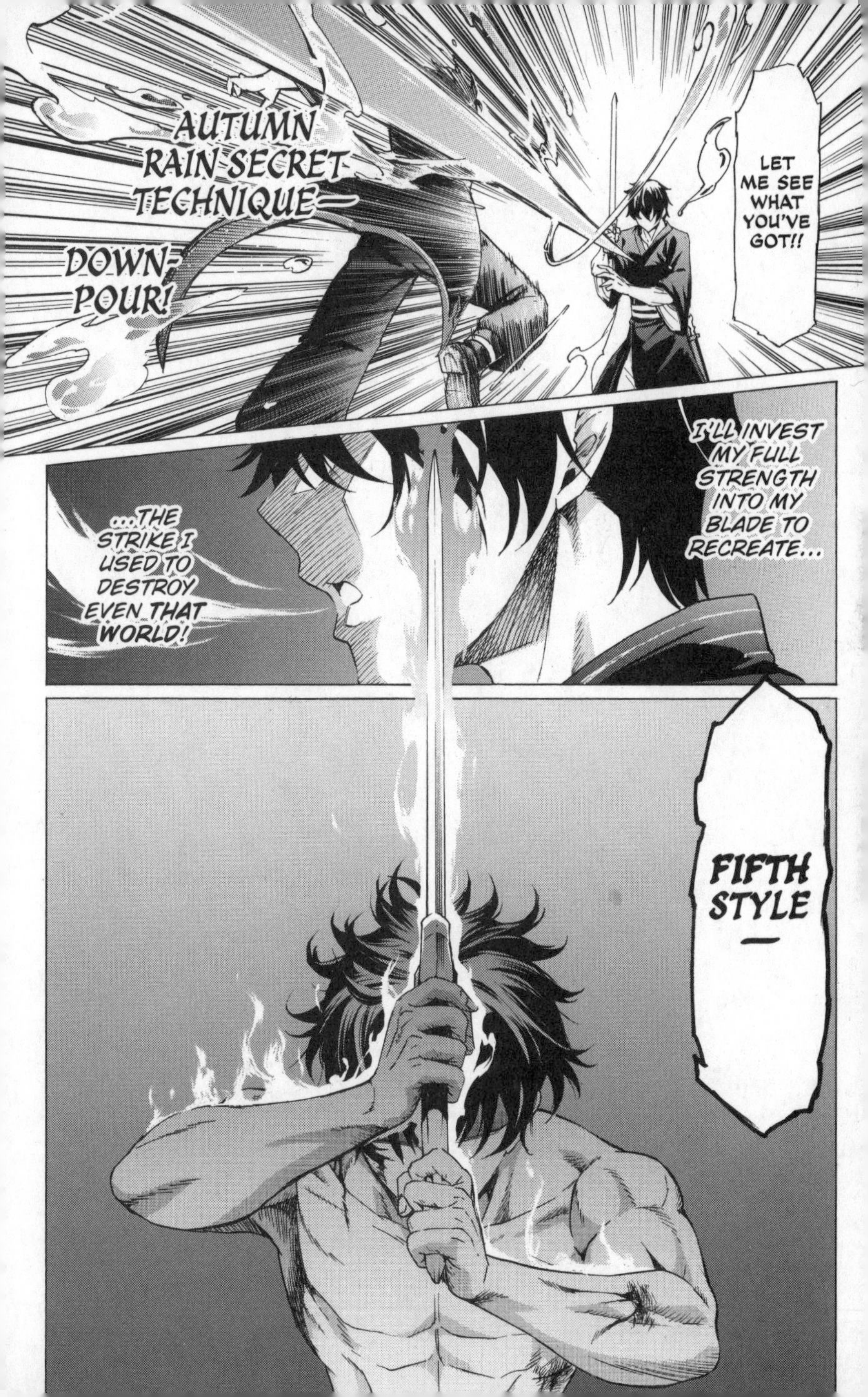
LET ME SEE WHAT YOU'VE GOT!!
AUTUMN RAIN SECRET TECHNIQUE—
DOWN-POUR!
I'LL INVEST MY FULL STRENGTH INTO MY BLADE TO RECREATE...
...THE STRIKE I USED TO DESTROY EVEN THAT WORLD!
FIFTH STYLE
—

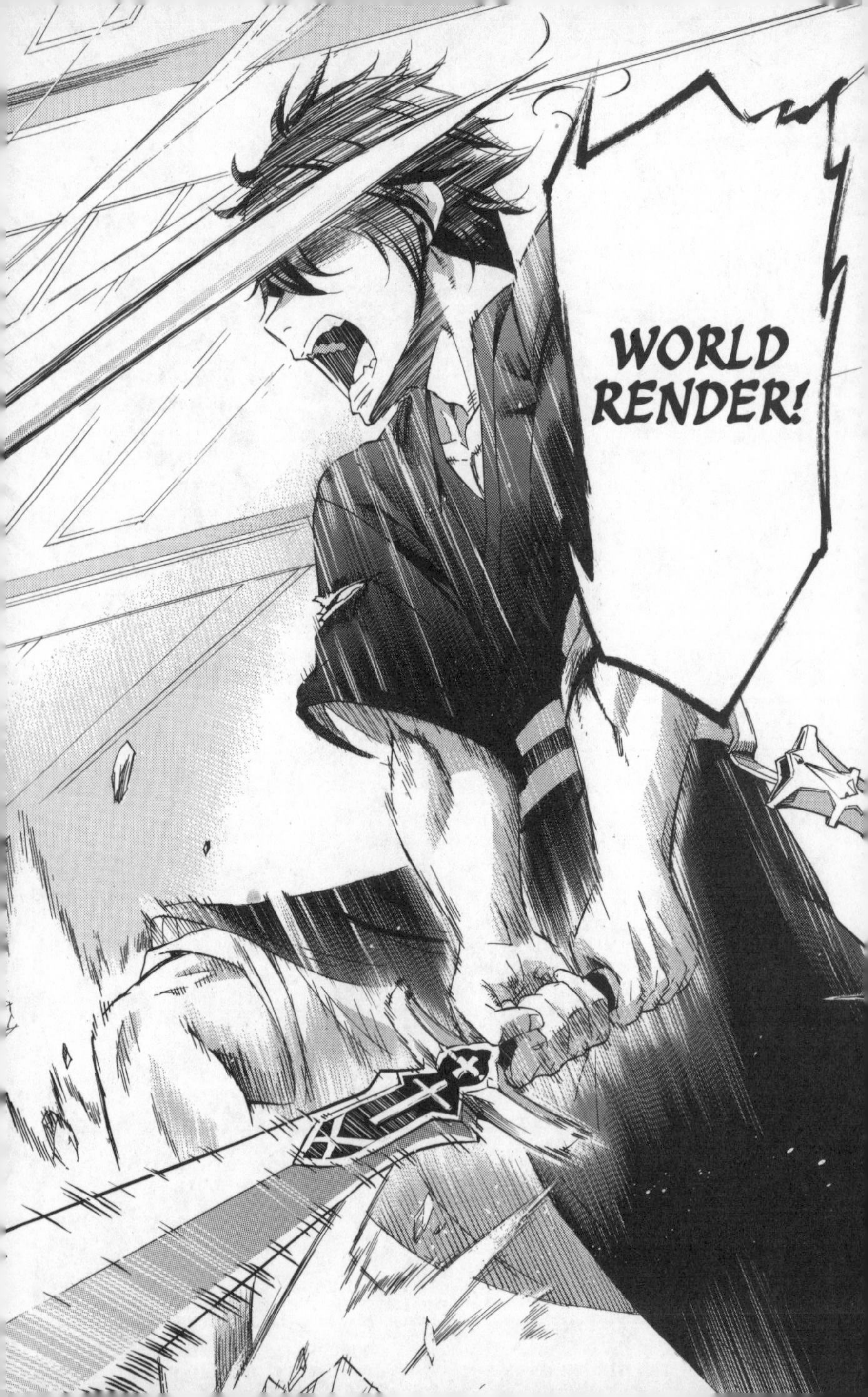
WORLD RENDER!

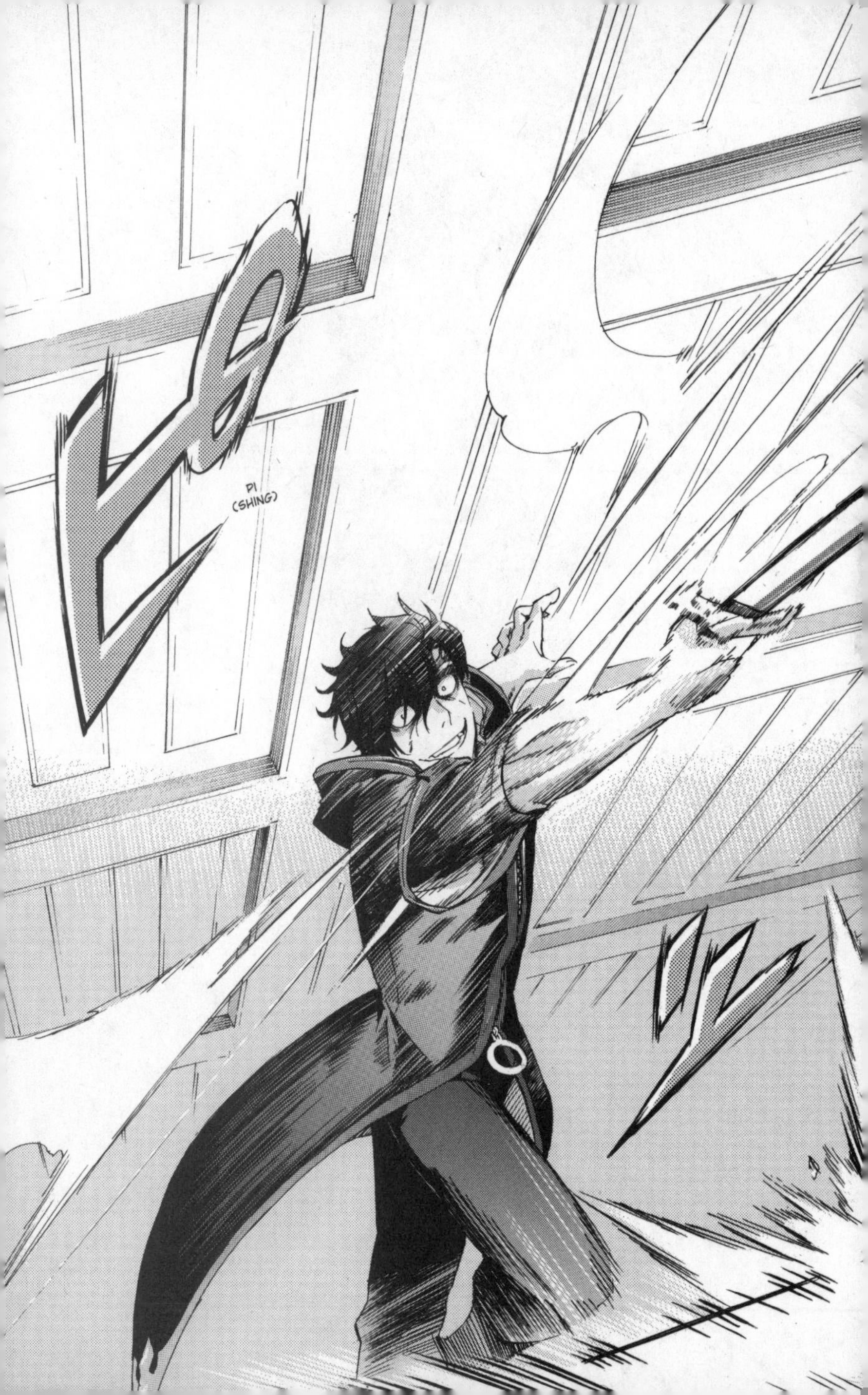
PI
(SHING)

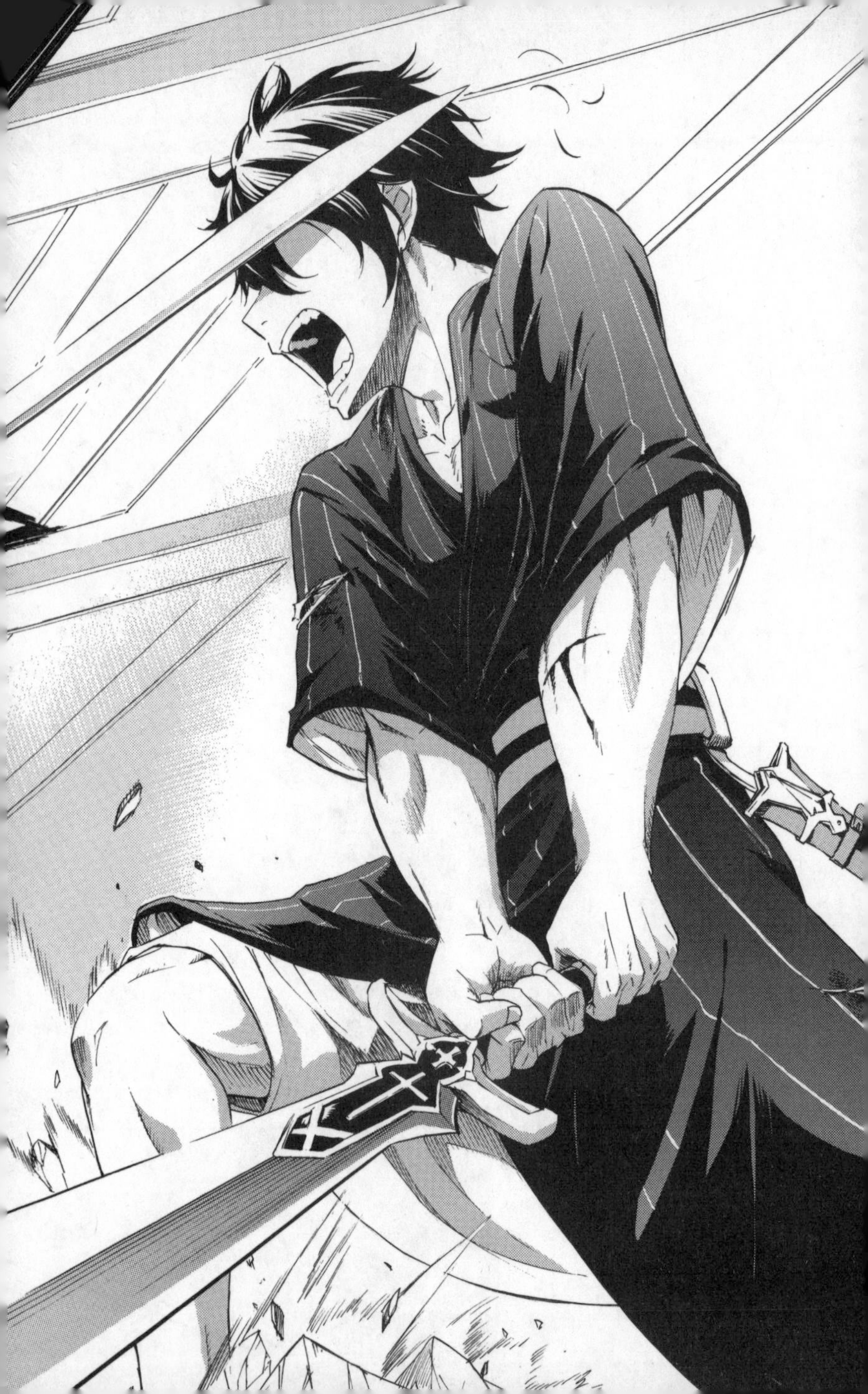

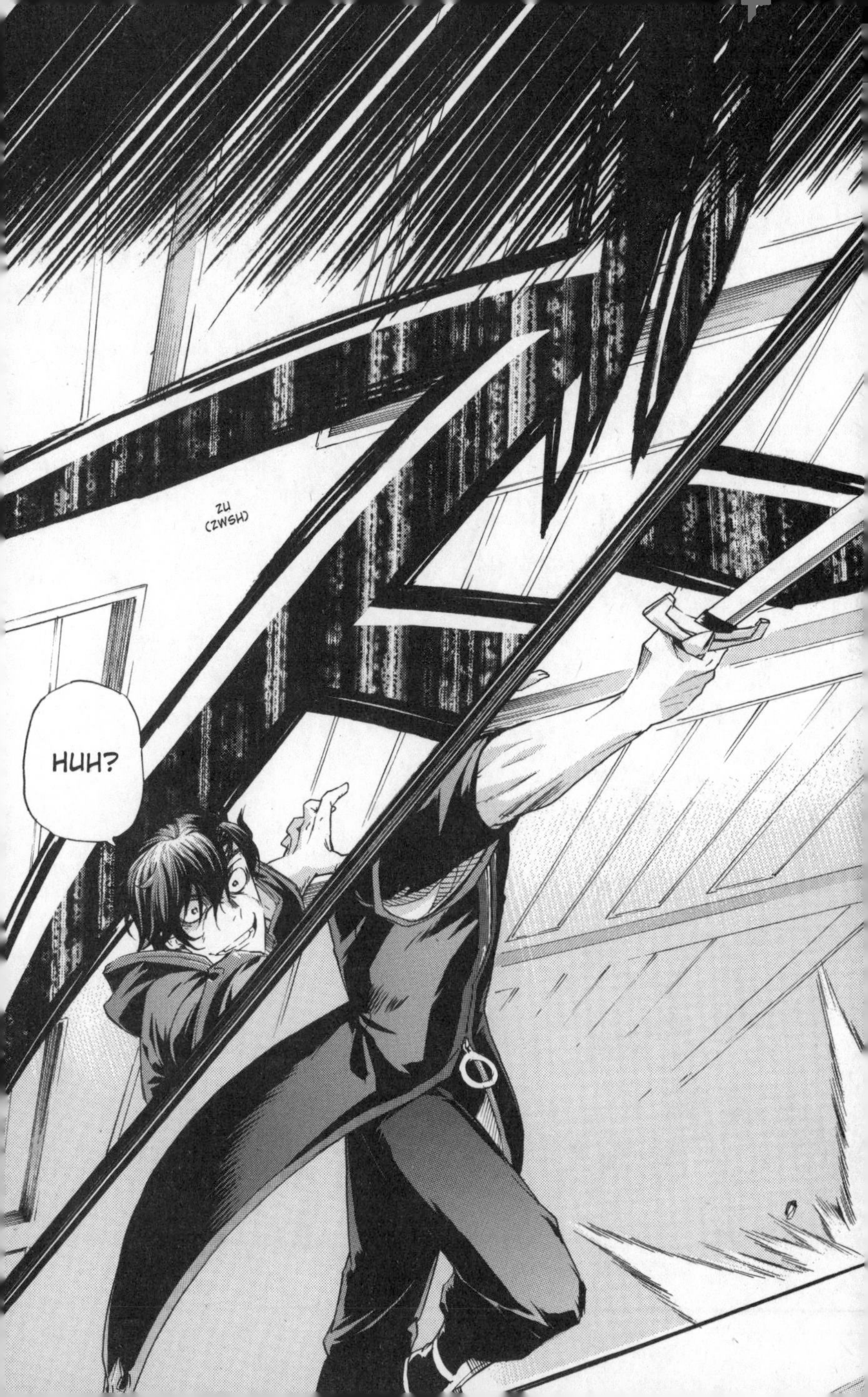
ZU
(ZWSH)
HUH?

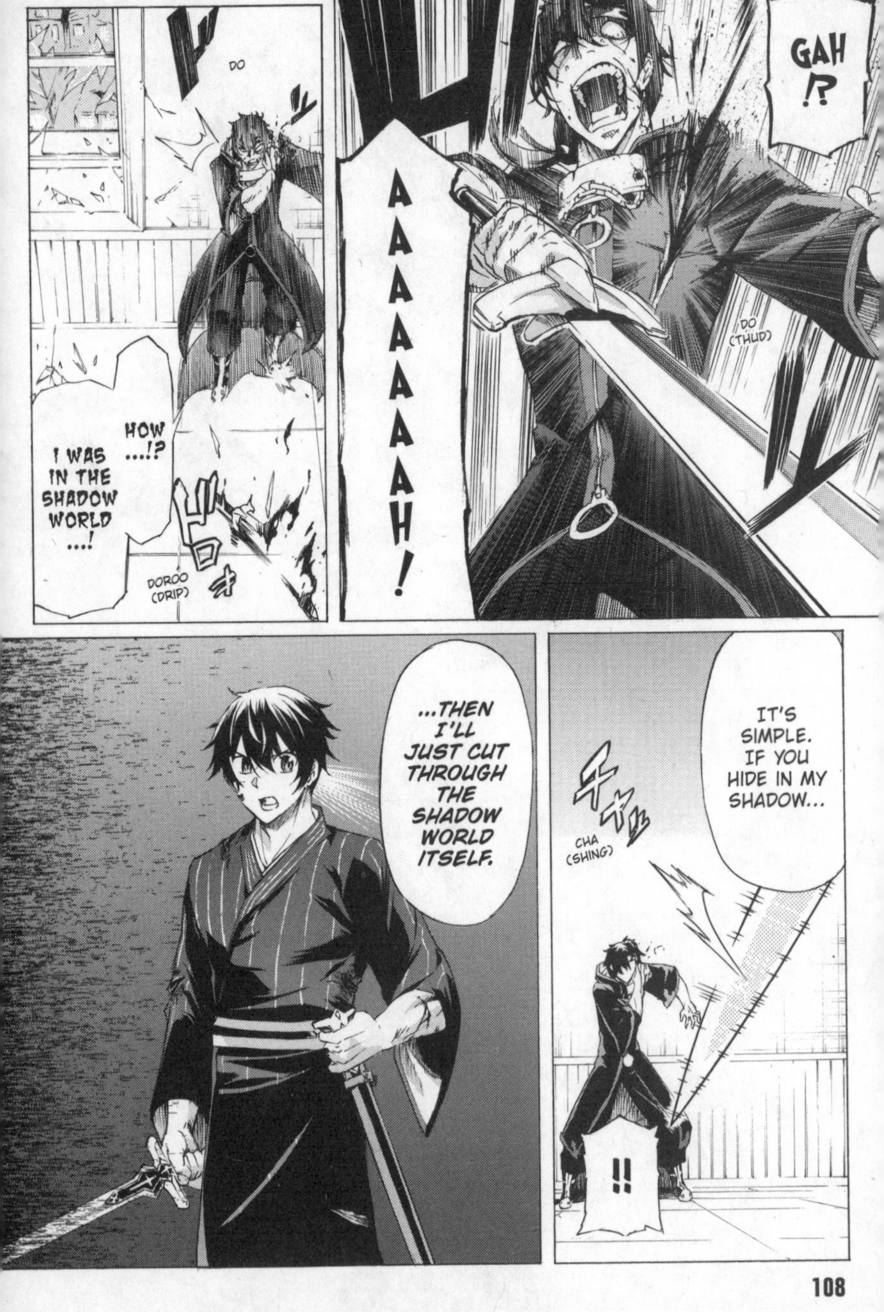
GAH !?
AAAAAAAAH!
DO (THUD)
DO
HOW ....!?
I WAS IN THE SHADOW WORLD ....!
DOROO (DRIP)
IT'S SIMPLE. IF YOU HIDE IN MY SHADOW...
CHA (SHING)
!!
...THEN I'LL JUST CUT THROUGH THE SHADOW WORLD ITSELF.

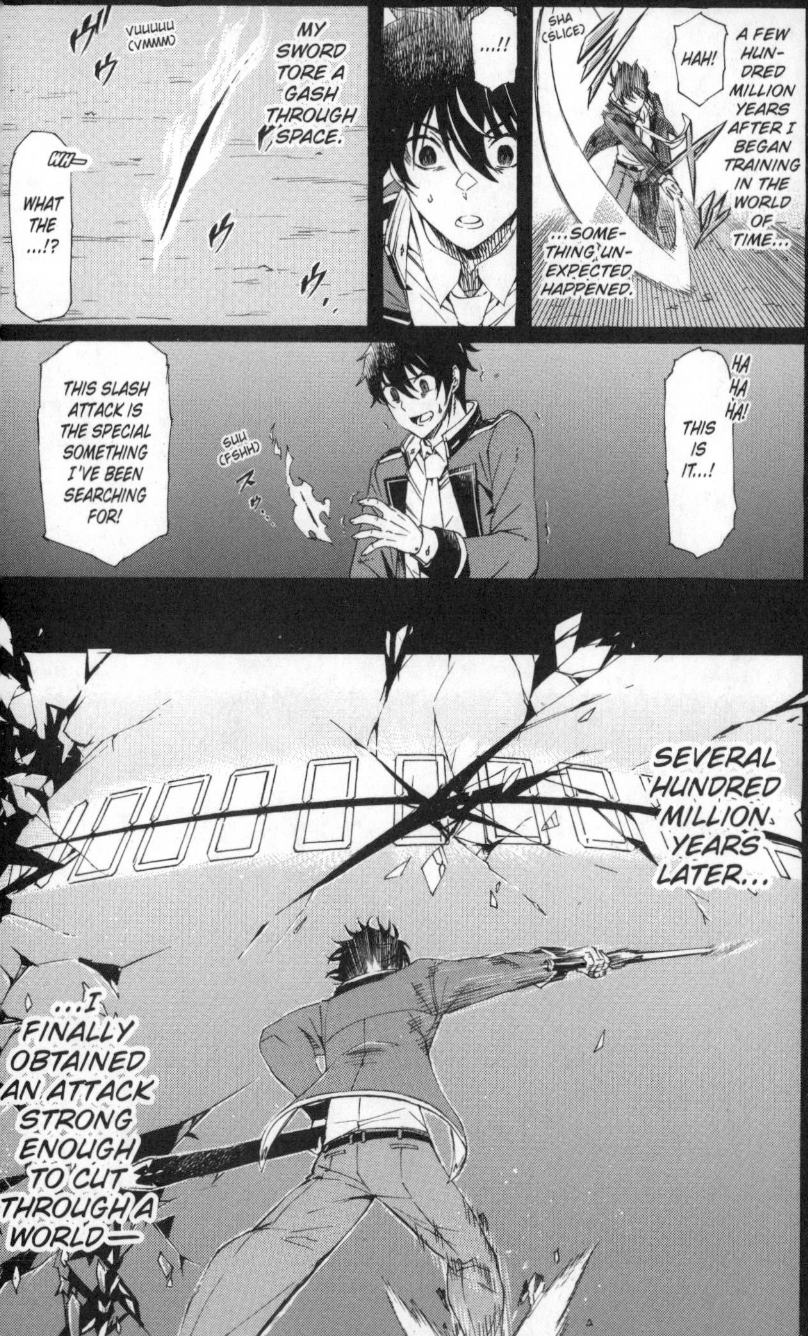
SHA (SLICE)
HAH!
A FEW HUNDRED MILLION YEARS AFTER I BEGAN TRAINING IN THE WORLD OF TIME...
...SOMETHING UNEXPECTED HAPPENED.
...!!
MY SWORD TORE A GASH THROUGH SPACE.
VUUUUU (VMMMM)
WH—
WHAT THE ...!?
HA HA HA!
THIS IS IT...!
SUU (FSHH)
THIS SLASH ATTACK IS THE SPECIAL SOMETHING I'VE BEEN SEARCHING FOR!
SEVERAL HUNDRED MILLION YEARS LATER...
...I FINALLY OBTAINED AN ATTACK STRONG ENOUGH TO CUT THROUGH A WORLD—

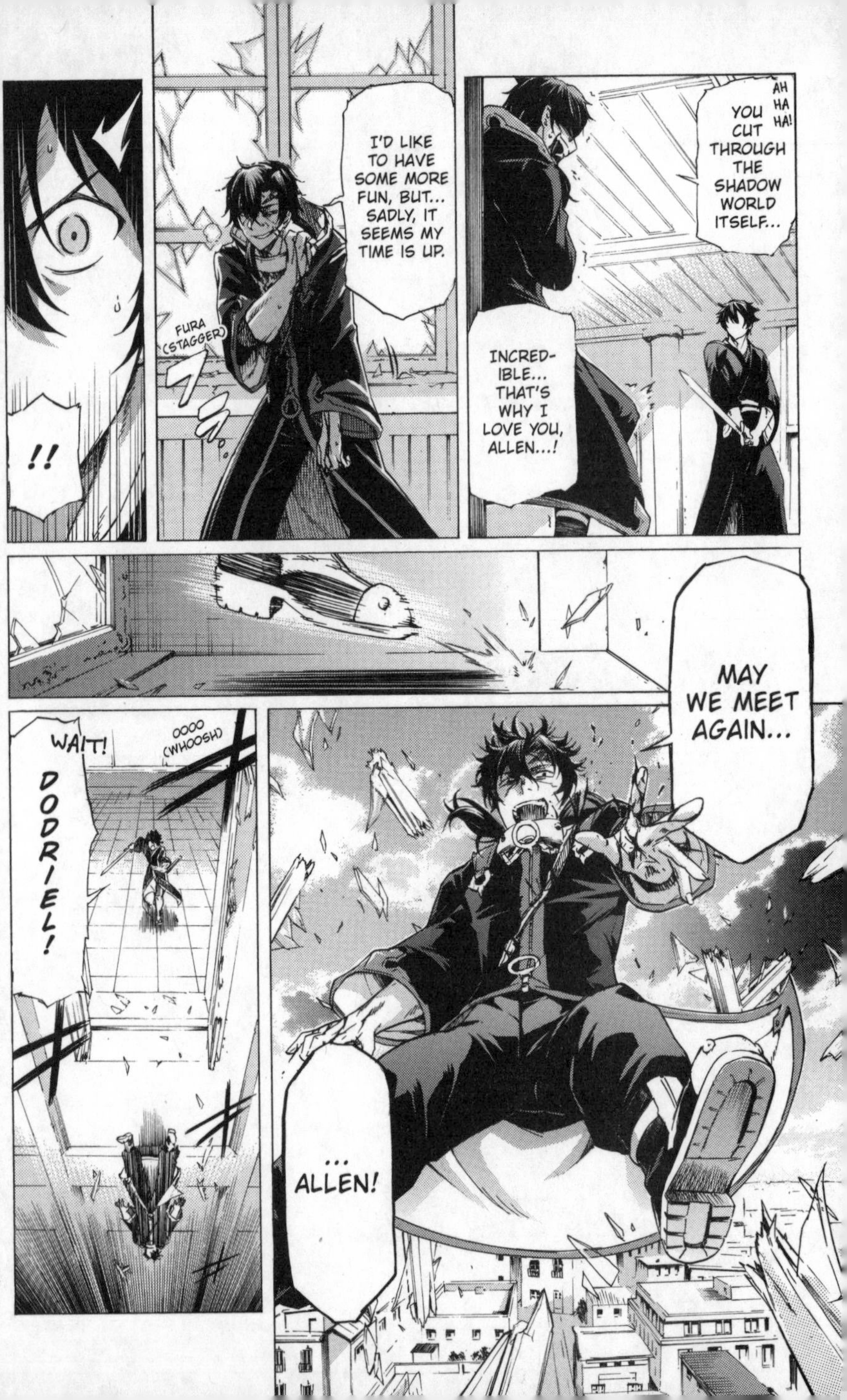
AH HA HA!
YOU CUT THROUGH THE SHADOW WORLD ITSELF...
INCREDIBLE... THAT'S WHY I LOVE YOU, ALLEN...!
I'D LIKE TO HAVE SOME MORE FUN, BUT... SADLY, IT SEEMS MY TIME IS UP.
FURA (STAGGER)
!!
MAY WE MEET AGAIN...
... ALLEN!
WAIT!
OOOO (WHOOSH)
DODRIEL!

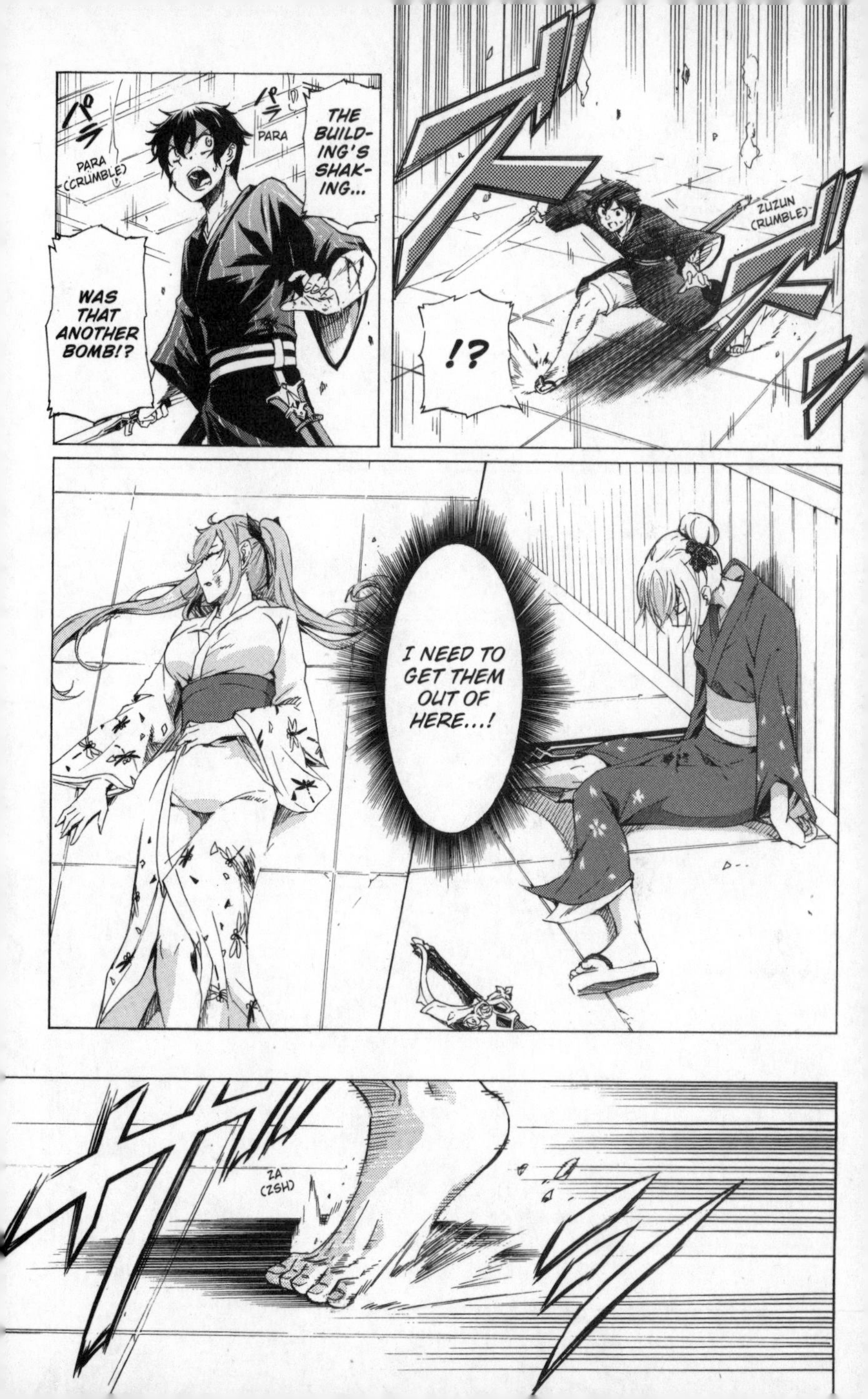
THE BUILD-ING'S SHAK-ING...
PARA
PARA (CRUMBLE)
WAS THAT ANOTHER BOMB!?
ZUZUN (RUMBLE)
!?
I NEED TO GET THEM OUT OF HERE...!
ZA (ZSH)

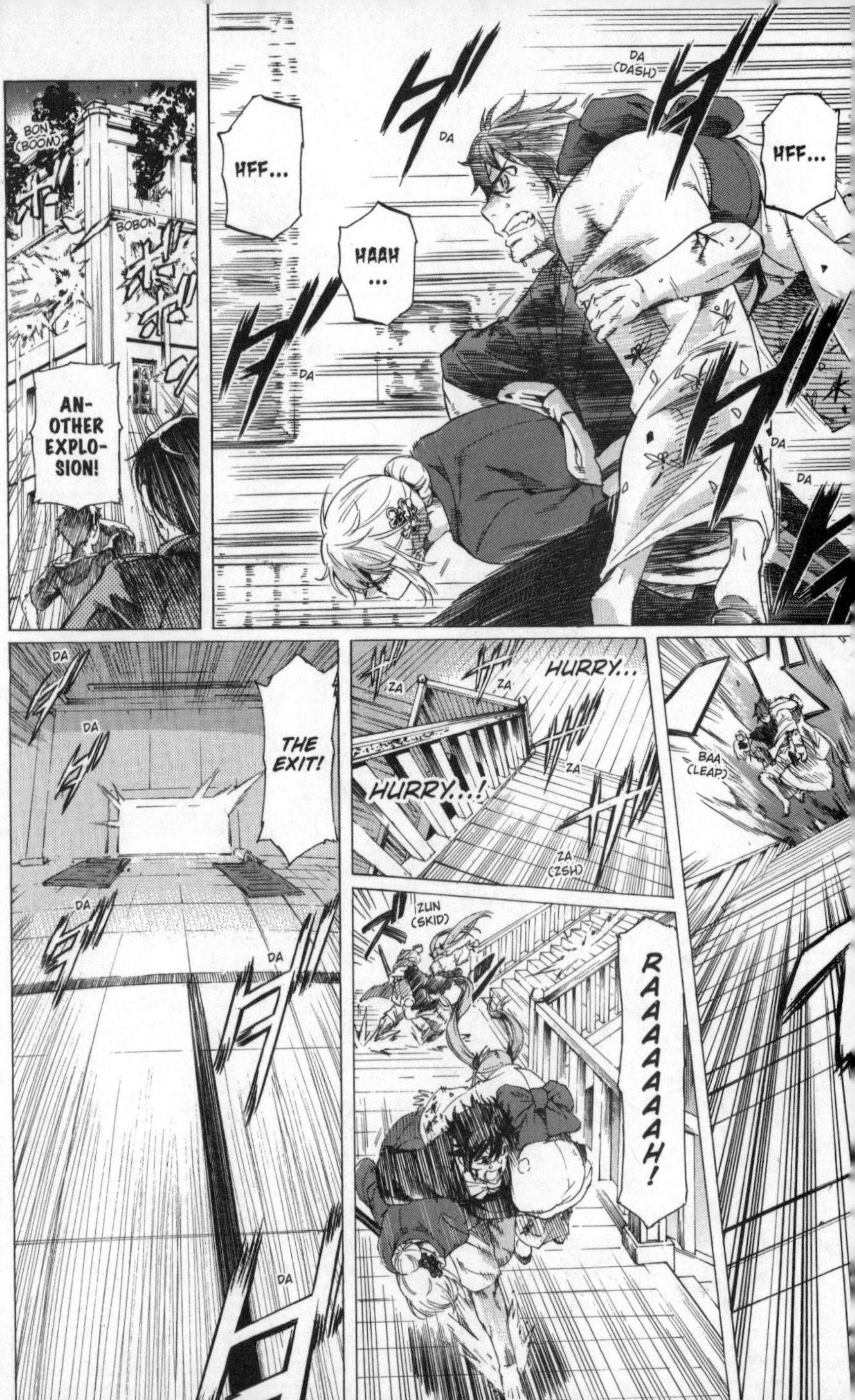
HFF...
DA (DASH)
DA
HFF...
HAAH ...
DA
DA
DA
DA
BON (BOOM)
BOBON
AN-OTHER EXPLOSION!
BAA (LEAP)
HURRY...
ZA
ZA
ZA
HURRY...!
ZA (ZSH)
ZUN (SKID)
RAAAAAAAH!
DA
DA
THE EXIT!
DA
DA
DA

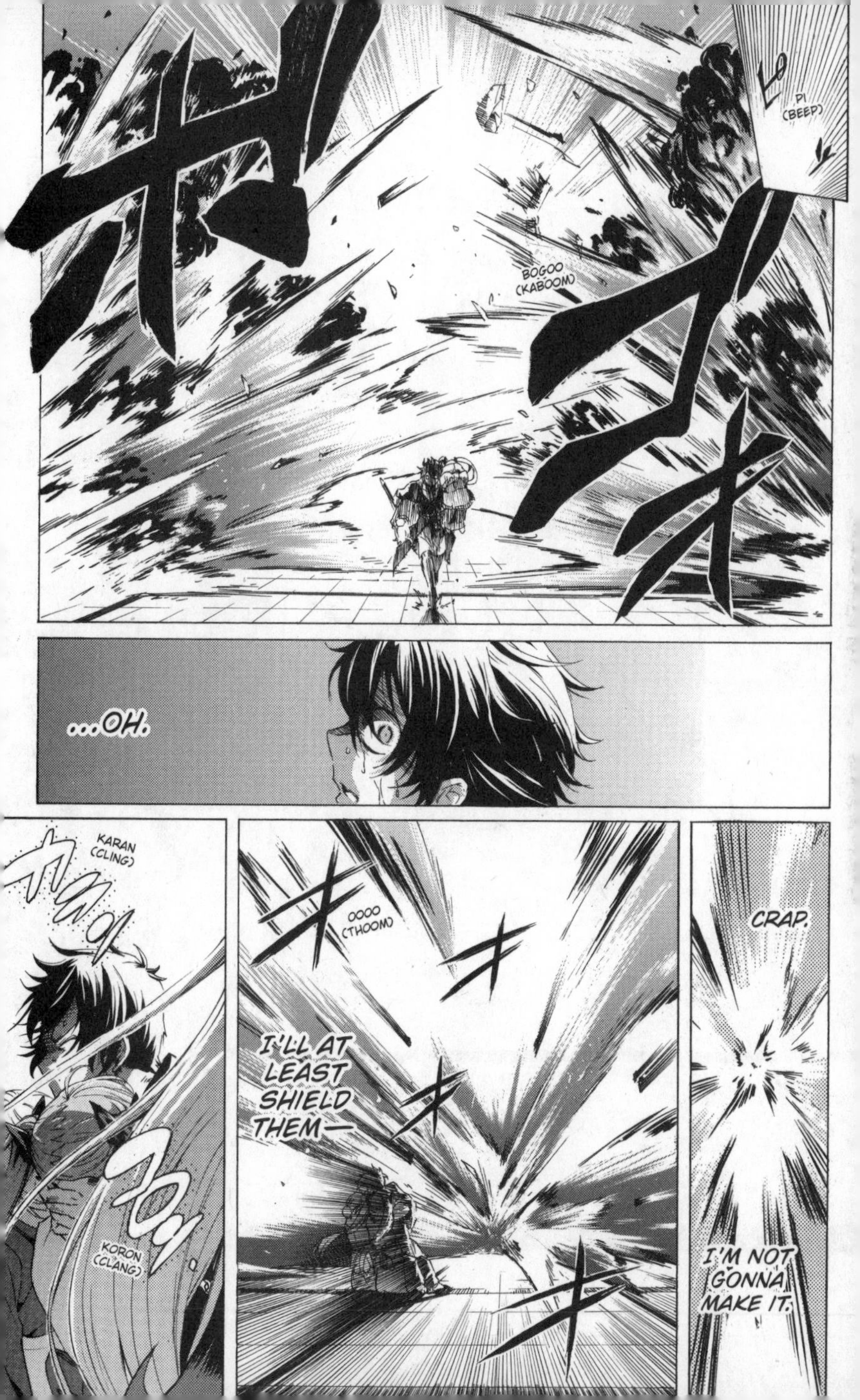
PI (BEEP)
BOGOO (KABOOM)
...OH.
CRAP.
I'M NOT GONNA MAKE IT.
OOOO (THOOM)
I'LL AT LEAST SHIELD THEM—
KARAN (CLING)
KORON (CLANG)

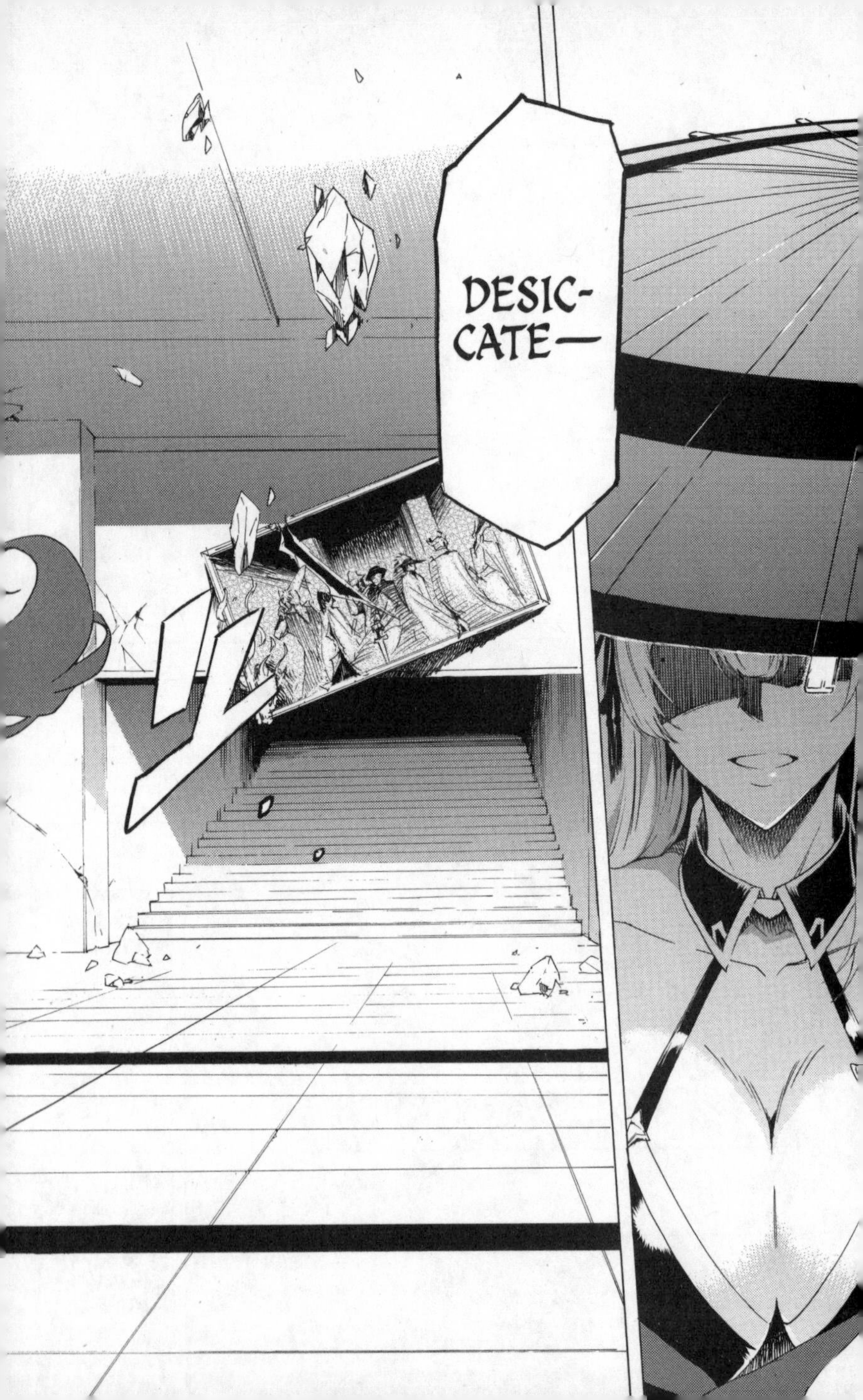
DESIC-
CATE—

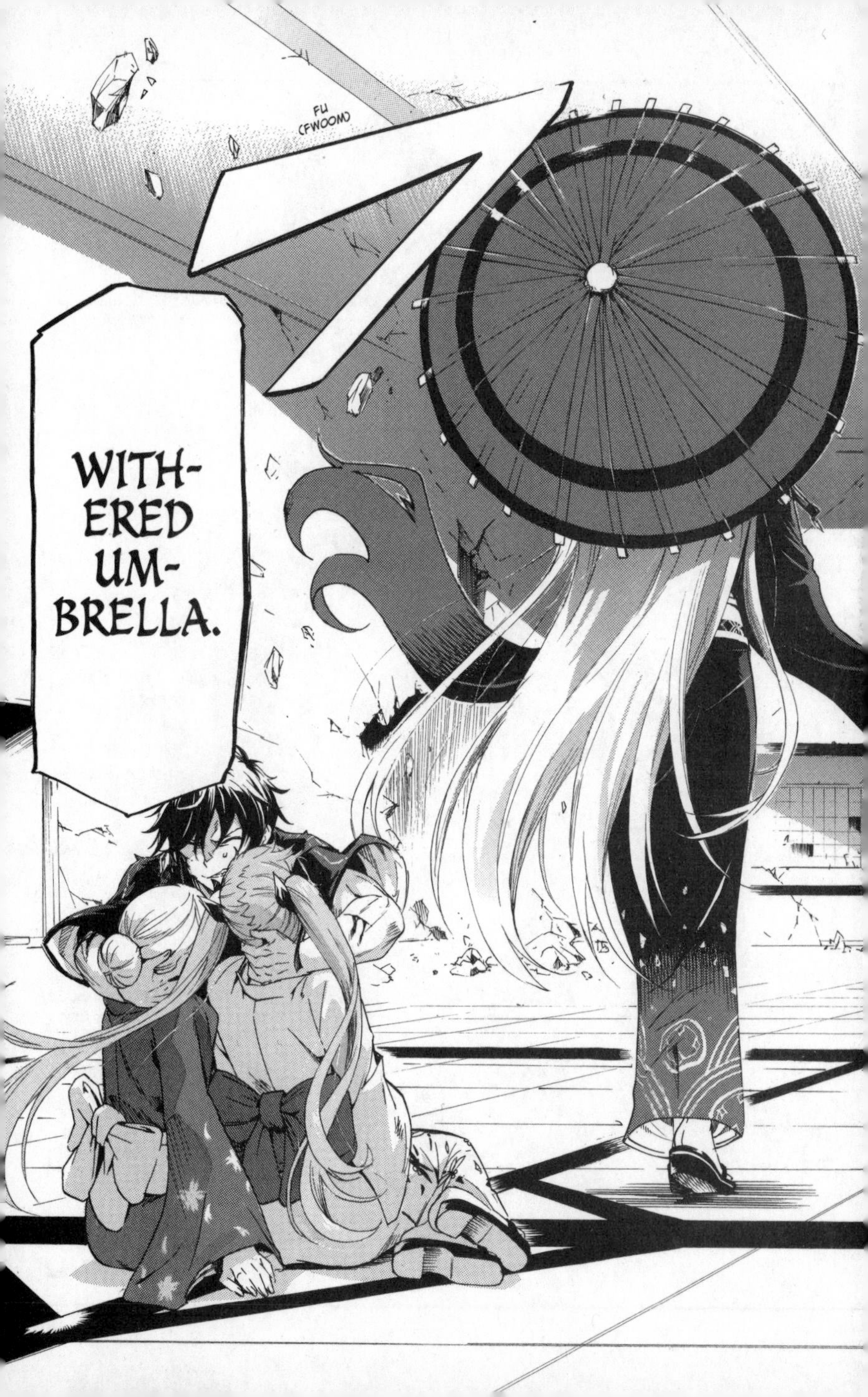
FU
(FWOOM)
WITH-ERED UM-BRELLA.

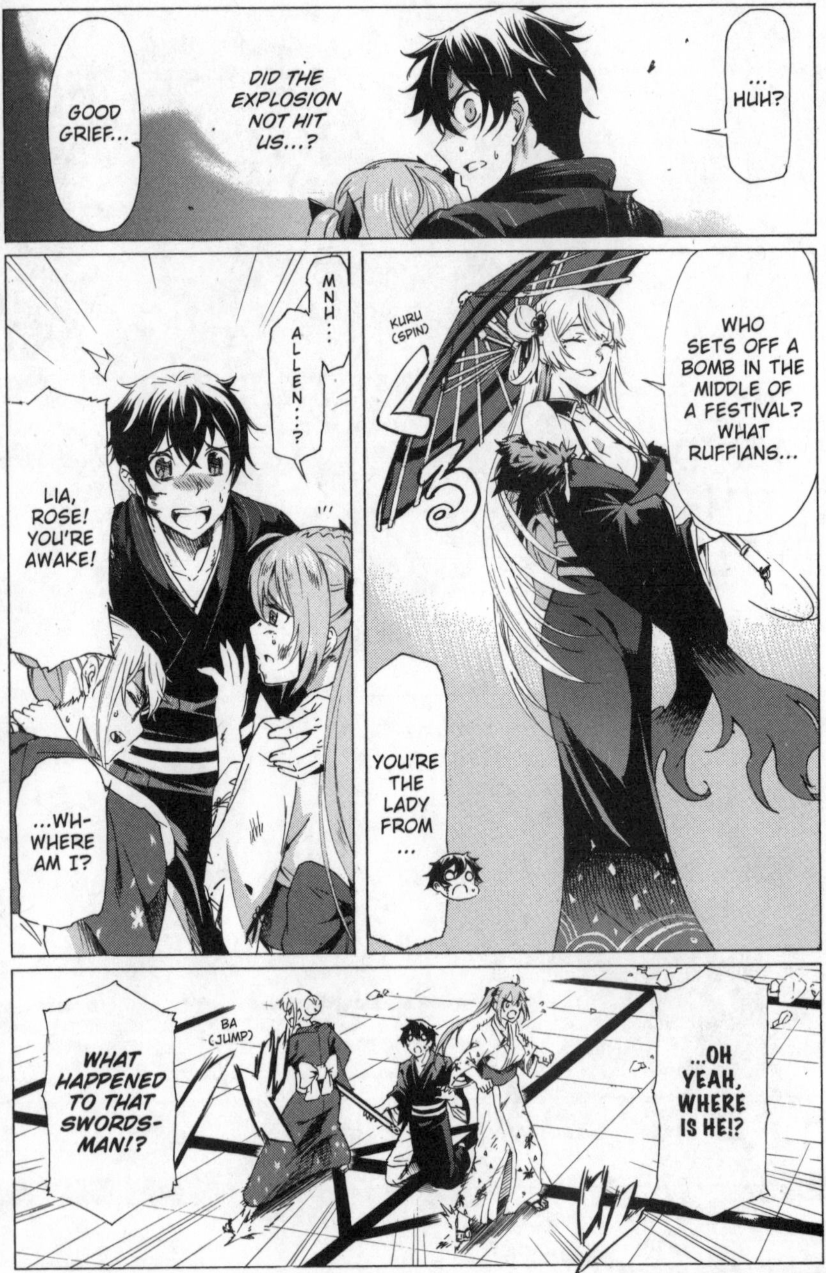

...HUH?
DID THE EXPLOSION NOT HIT US...?
GOOD GRIEF...
WHO SETS OFF A BOMB IN THE MIDDLE OF A FESTIVAL? WHAT RUFFIANS...
KURU (SPIN)
YOU'RE THE LADY FROM ...
MNH... ALLEN...?
LIA, ROSE! YOU'RE AWAKE!
...WH-WHERE AM I?
...OH YEAH, WHERE IS HE!?
BA (JUMP)
WHAT HAPPENED TO THAT SWORDSMAN!?

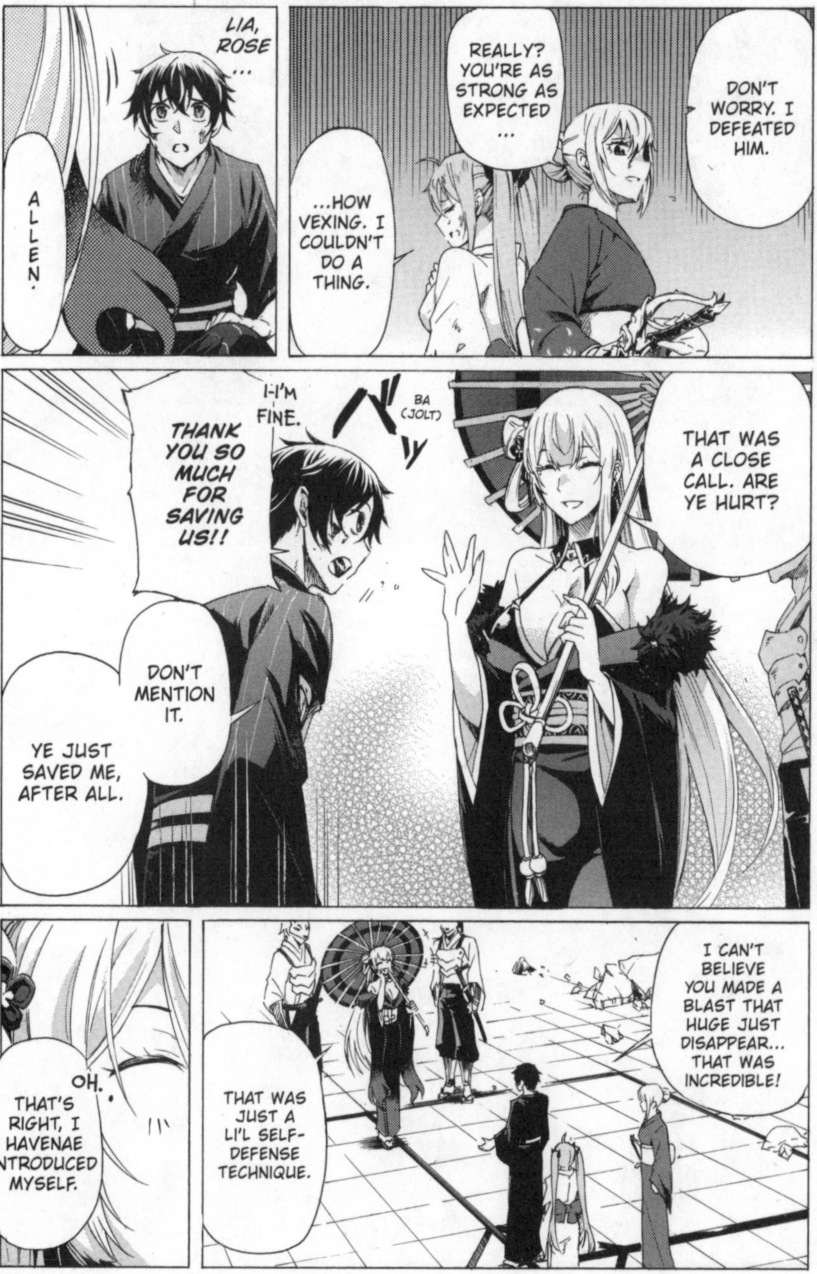
DON'T WORRY. I DEFEATED HIM.
REALLY? YOU'RE AS STRONG AS EXPECTED ...
...HOW VEXING. I COULDN'T DO A THING.
LIA, ROSE ...
ALLEN.
THAT WAS A CLOSE CALL. ARE YE HURT?
BA (JOLT)
I-I'M FINE.
THANK YOU SO MUCH FOR SAVING US!!
DON'T MENTION IT.
YE JUST SAVED ME, AFTER ALL.
I CAN'T BELIEVE YOU MADE A BLAST THAT HUGE JUST DISAPPEAR... THAT WAS INCREDIBLE!
THAT WAS JUST A LI'L SELF-DEFENSE TECHNIQUE.
OH.
THAT'S RIGHT, I HAVENAE INTRODUCED MYSELF.

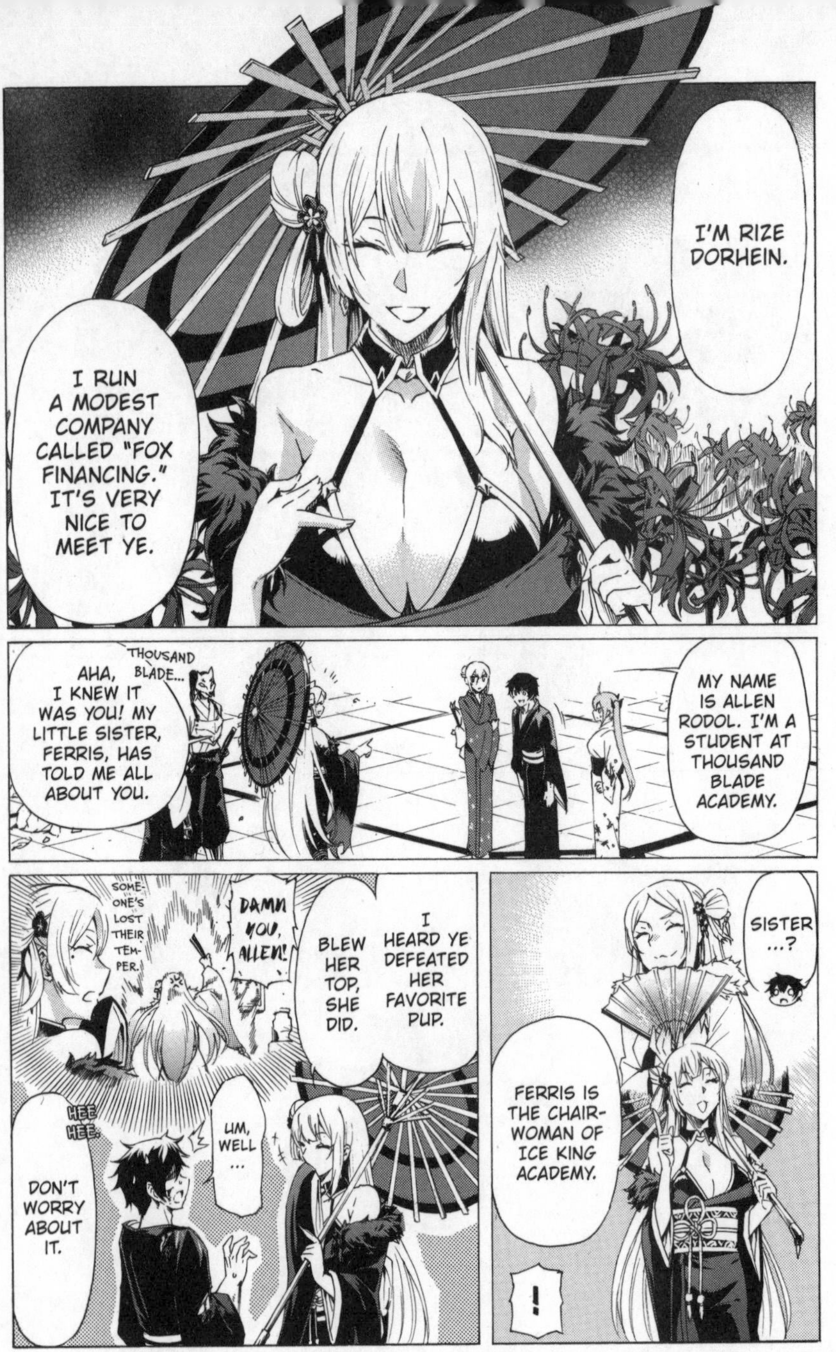
I'M RIZE DORHEIN.
I RUN A MODEST COMPANY CALLED "FOX FINANCING." IT'S VERY NICE TO MEET YE.
MY NAME IS ALLEN RODOL. I'M A STUDENT AT THOUSAND BLADE ACADEMY.
THOUSAND BLADE...
AHA, I KNEW IT WAS YOU! MY LITTLE SISTER, FERRIS, HAS TOLD ME ALL ABOUT YOU.
SISTER...?
FERRIS IS THE CHAIRWOMAN OF ICE KING ACADEMY.
!
I HEARD YE DEFEATED HER FAVORITE PUP.
BLEW HER TOP, SHE DID.
DAMN YOU, ALLEN!
SOMEONE'S LOST THEIR TEMPER.
UM, WELL...
HEE HEE.
DON'T WORRY ABOUT IT.

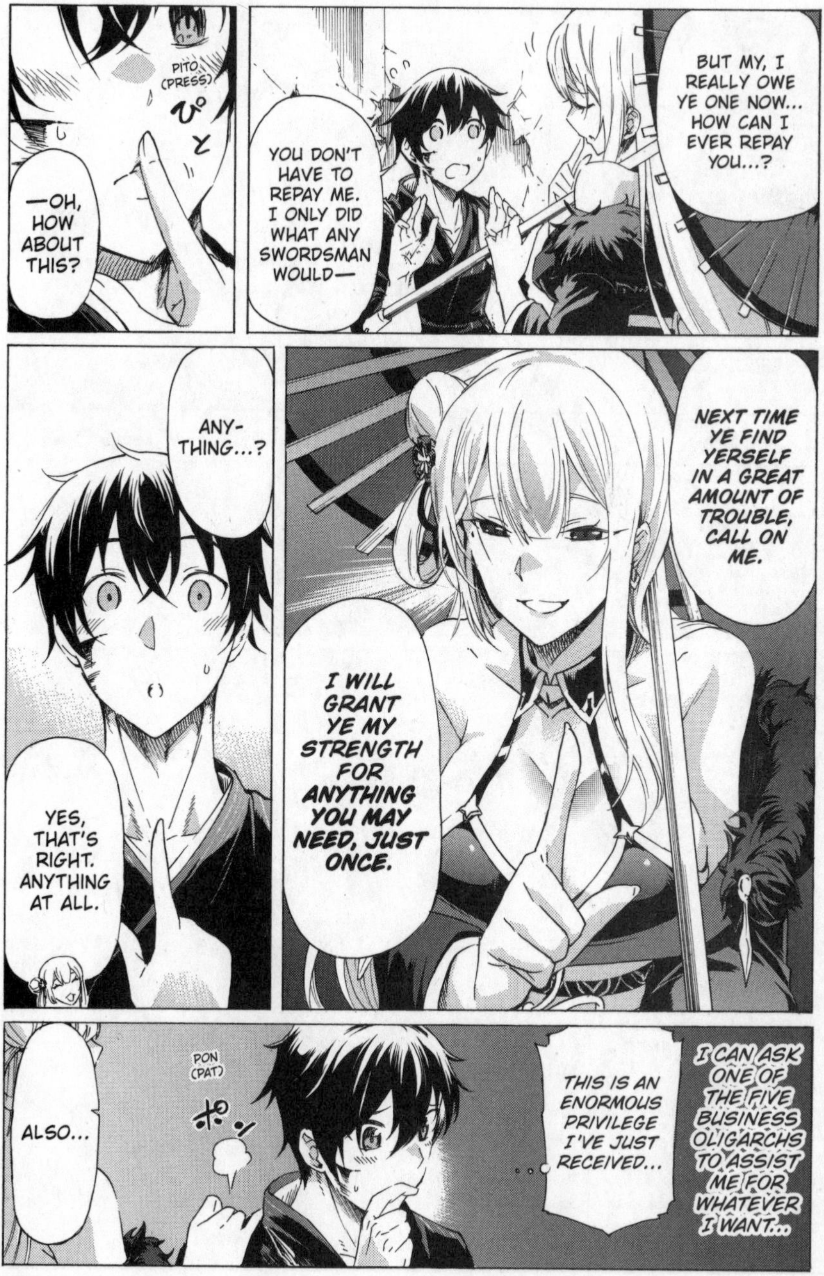
BUT MY, I REALLY OWE YE ONE NOW... HOW CAN I EVER REPAY YOU...?
YOU DON'T HAVE TO REPAY ME. I ONLY DID WHAT ANY SWORDSMAN WOULD—
PITO (PRESS)
ぴと
—OH, HOW ABOUT THIS?
NEXT TIME YE FIND YERSELF IN A GREAT AMOUNT OF TROUBLE, CALL ON ME.
I WILL GRANT YE MY STRENGTH FOR ANYTHING YOU MAY NEED, JUST ONCE.
ANY-THING...?
YES, THAT'S RIGHT. ANYTHING AT ALL.
I CAN ASK ONE OF THE FIVE BUSINESS OLIGARCHS TO ASSIST ME FOR WHATEVER I WANT...
THIS IS AN ENORMOUS PRIVILEGE I'VE JUST RECEIVED...
PON (PAT)
ALSO...

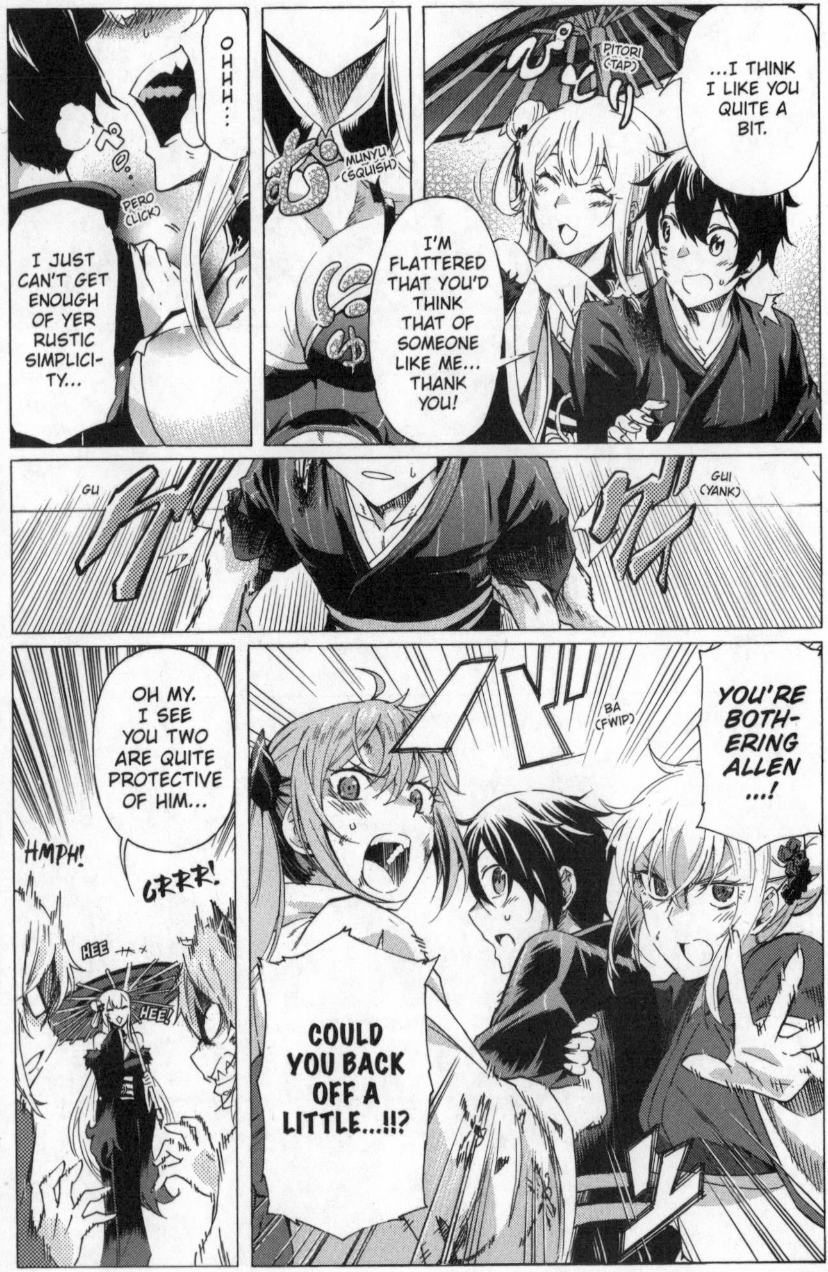
...I THINK I LIKE YOU QUITE A BIT.
PITORI (TAP)
I'M FLATTERED THAT YOU'D THINK THAT OF SOMEONE LIKE ME... THANK YOU!
MUNYU (SQUISH)
OHHH...
PERO (LICK)
I JUST CAN'T GET ENOUGH OF YER RUSTIC SIMPLICITY...
GUI (YANK)
GU
YOU'RE BOTH-ERING ALLEN ...!
BA (FWIP)
COULD YOU BACK OFF A LITTLE...!!?
OH MY. I SEE YOU TWO ARE QUITE PROTECTIVE OF HIM...
HMPH!
GRRR!
HEE
HEE!

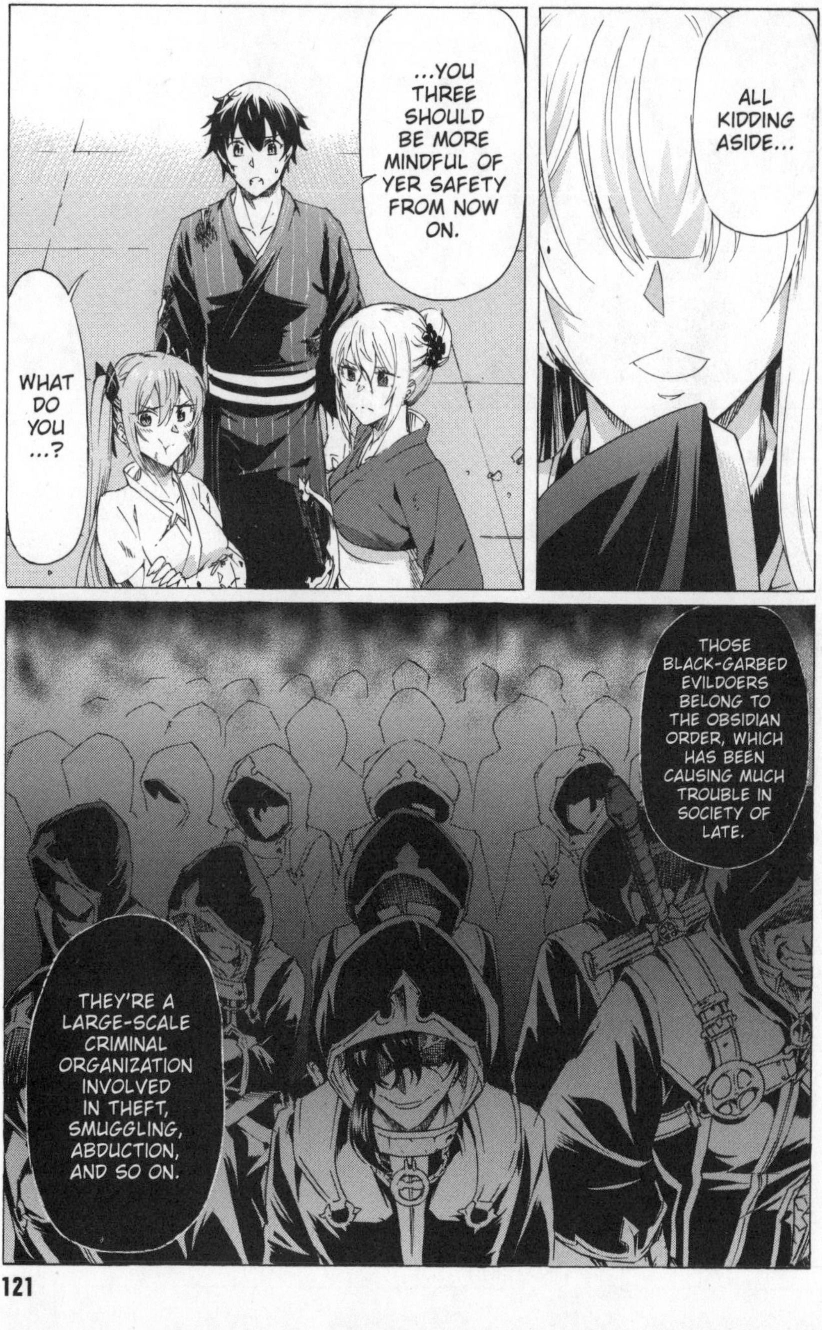
ALL KIDDING ASIDE...
...YOU THREE SHOULD BE MORE MINDFUL OF YER SAFETY FROM NOW ON.
WHAT DO YOU ...?
THOSE BLACK-GARBED EVILDOERS BELONG TO THE OBSIDIAN ORDER, WHICH HAS BEEN CAUSING MUCH TROUBLE IN SOCIETY OF LATE.
THEY'RE A LARGE-SCALE CRIMINAL ORGANIZATION INVOLVED IN THEFT, SMUGGLING, ABDUCTION, AND SO ON.

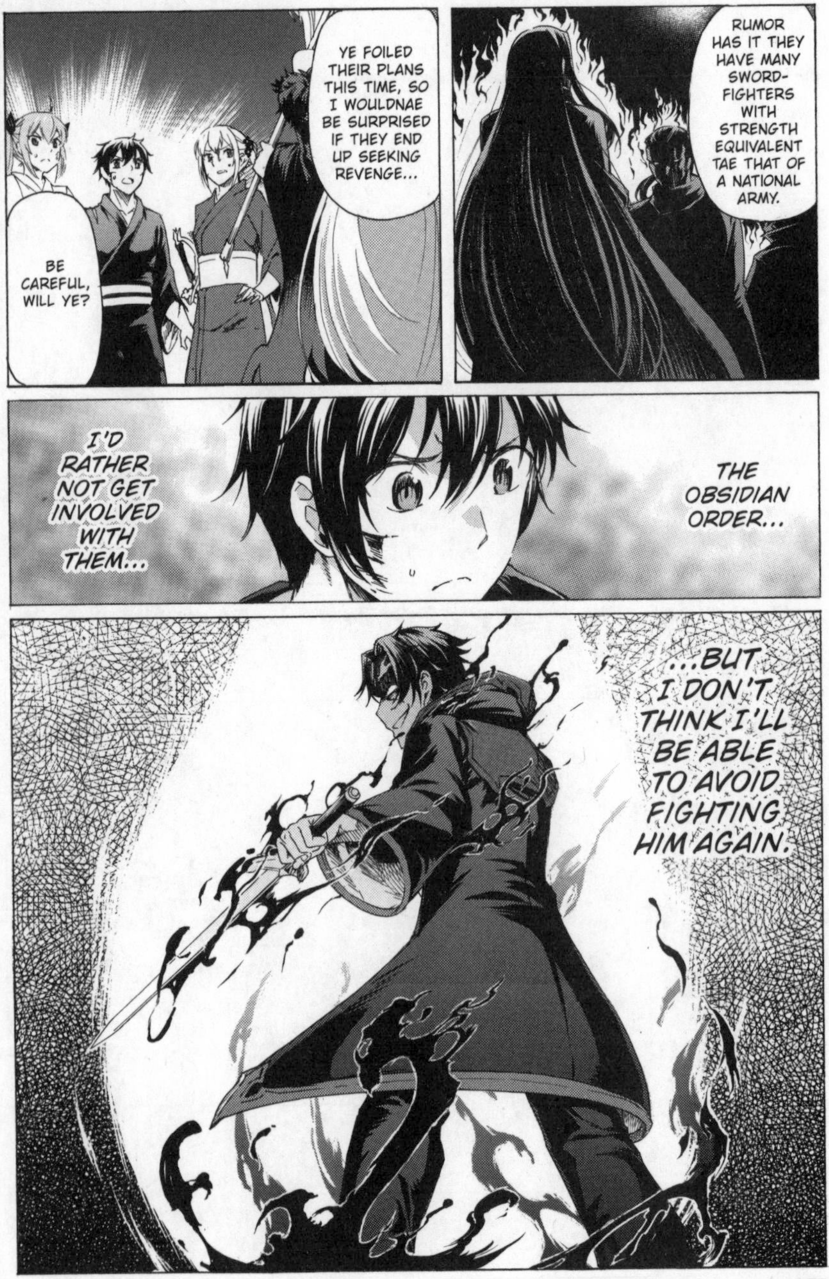
RUMOR HAS IT THEY HAVE MANY SWORD-FIGHTERS WITH STRENGTH EQUIVALENT TAE THAT OF A NATIONAL ARMY.
YE FOILED THEIR PLANS THIS TIME, SO I WOULDNAE BE SURPRISED IF THEY END UP SEEKING REVENGE...
BE CAREFUL, WILL YE?
THE OBSIDIAN ORDER...
I'D RATHER NOT GET INVOLVED WITH THEM...
...BUT I DON'T THINK I'LL BE ABLE TO AVOID FIGHTING HIM AGAIN.

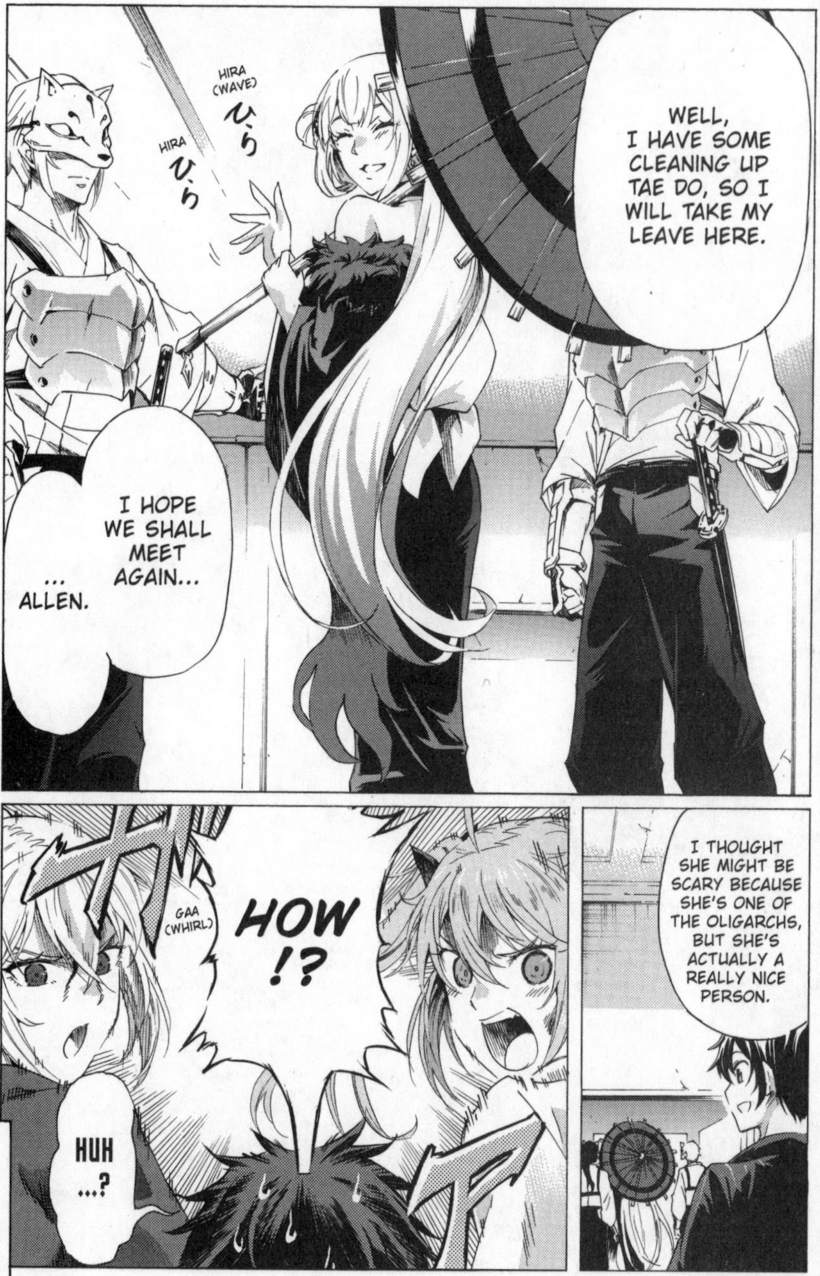
WELL, I HAVE SOME CLEANING UP TAE DO, SO I WILL TAKE MY LEAVE HERE.
HIRA (WAVE) ひら
HIRA ひら
I HOPE WE SHALL MEET AGAIN...
... ALLEN.
I THOUGHT SHE MIGHT BE SCARY BECAUSE SHE'S ONE OF THE OLIGARCHS, BUT SHE'S ACTUALLY A REALLY NICE PERSON.
GAA (WHIRL)
HOW !?
HUH ...?

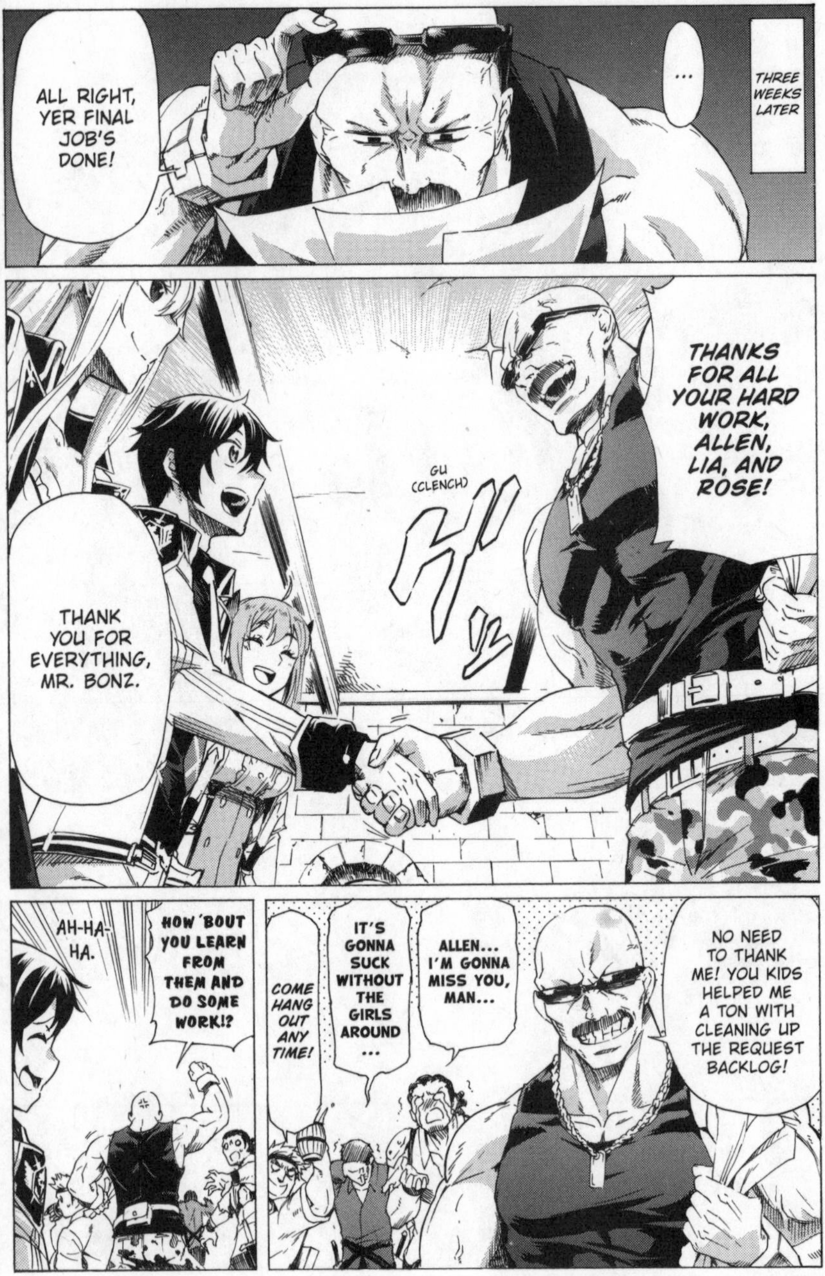
THREE WEEKS LATER
...
ALL RIGHT, YER FINAL JOB'S DONE!
THANKS FOR ALL YOUR HARD WORK, ALLEN, LIA, AND ROSE!
GU (CLENCH)
THANK YOU FOR EVERYTHING, MR. BONZ.
NO NEED TO THANK ME! YOU KIDS HELPED ME A TON WITH CLEANING UP THE REQUEST BACKLOG!
ALLEN... I'M GONNA MISS YOU, MAN...
IT'S GONNA SUCK WITHOUT THE GIRLS AROUND...
COME HANG OUT ANY TIME!
HOW 'BOUT YOU LEARN FROM THEM AND DO SOME WORK!?
AH-HA-HA.

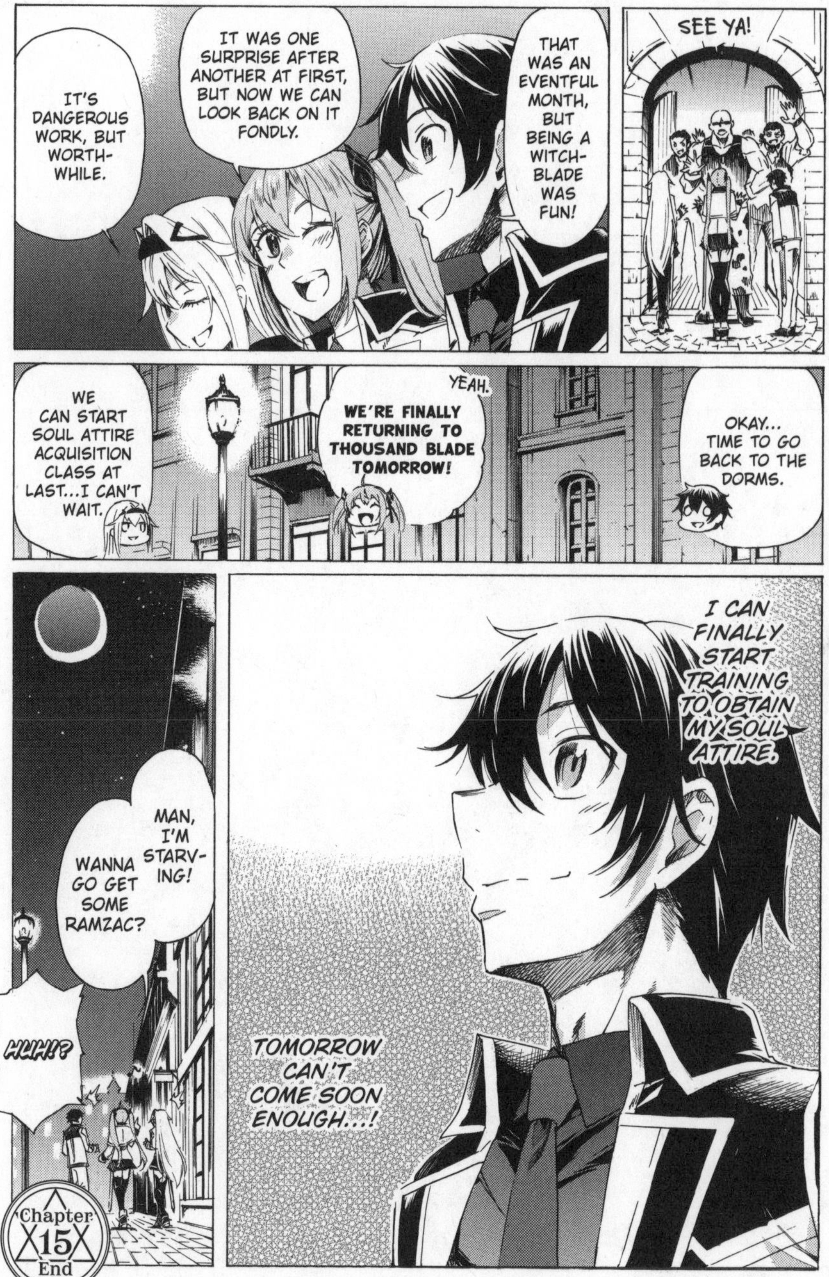
SEE YA!
THAT WAS AN EVENTFUL MONTH, BUT BEING A WITCH-BLADE WAS FUN!
IT WAS ONE SURPRISE AFTER ANOTHER AT FIRST, BUT NOW WE CAN LOOK BACK ON IT FONDLY.
IT'S DANGEROUS WORK, BUT WORTH-WHILE.
OKAY... TIME TO GO BACK TO THE DORMS.
YEAH.
WE'RE FINALLY RETURNING TO THOUSAND BLADE TOMORROW!
WE CAN START SOUL ATTIRE ACQUISITION CLASS AT LAST...I CAN'T WAIT.
I CAN FINALLY START TRAINING TO OBTAIN MY SOUL ATTIRE.
TOMORROW CAN'T COME SOON ENOUGH...!
MAN, I'M STARV-ING!
WANNA GO GET SOME RAMZAC?
HUH!?
Chapter 15 End

I KEPT PRESSING THE 100-MILLION-YEAR BUTTON AND CAME OUT ON TOP

~THE UNBEATABLE REJECT SWORDSMAN~

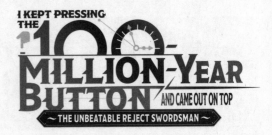

Chapter 16

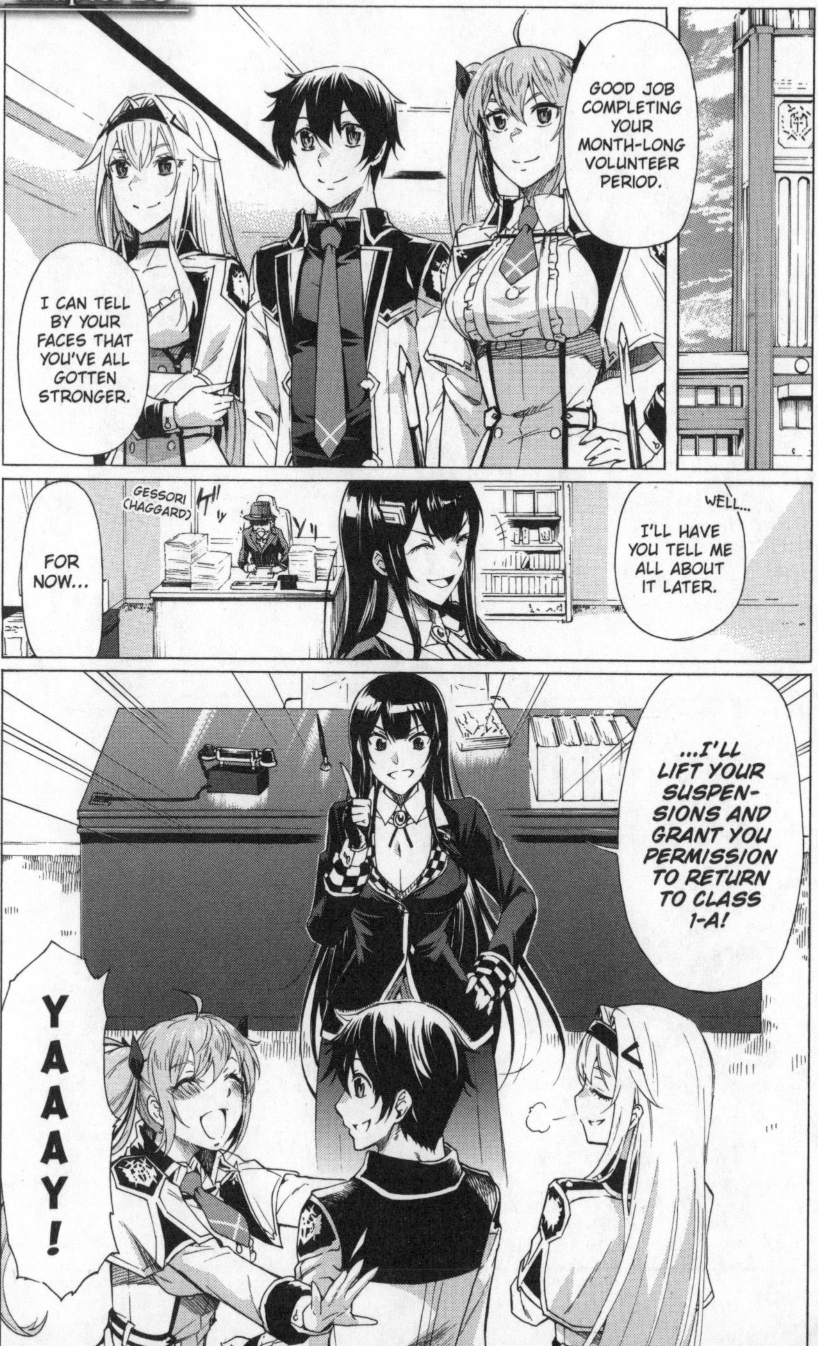
GOOD JOB COMPLETING YOUR MONTH-LONG VOLUNTEER PERIOD.
I CAN TELL BY YOUR FACES THAT YOU'VE ALL GOTTEN STRONGER.
WELL... I'LL HAVE YOU TELL ME ALL ABOUT IT LATER.
GESSORI (HAGGARD)
FOR NOW...
...I'LL LIFT YOUR SUSPENSIONS AND GRANT YOU PERMISSION TO RETURN TO CLASS 1-A!
YAAAAY!

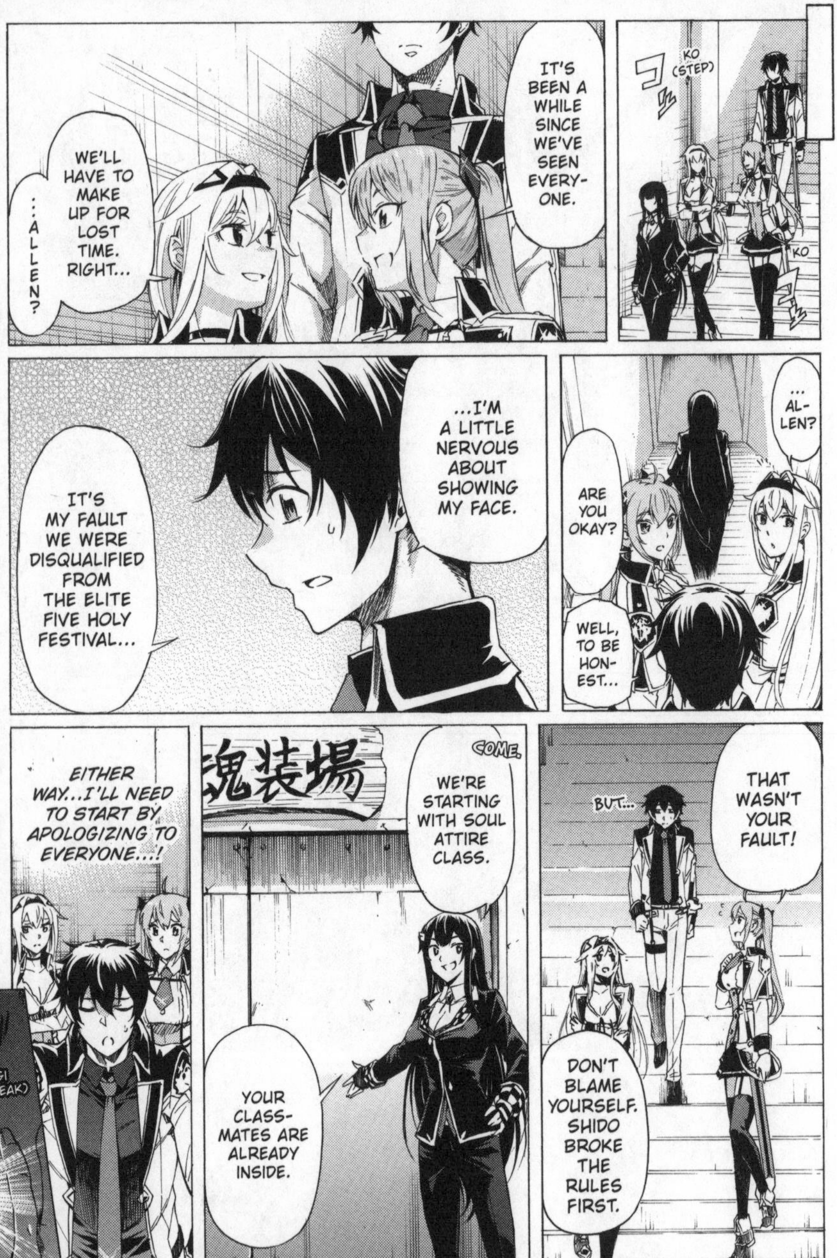
KO (STEP)
KO
IT'S BEEN A WHILE SINCE WE'VE SEEN EVERYONE.
WE'LL HAVE TO MAKE UP FOR LOST TIME. RIGHT...
...ALLEN?
...ALLEN?
ARE YOU OKAY?
WELL, TO BE HONEST...
...I'M A LITTLE NERVOUS ABOUT SHOWING MY FACE.
IT'S MY FAULT WE WERE DISQUALIFIED FROM THE ELITE FIVE HOLY FESTIVAL...
THAT WASN'T YOUR FAULT!
BUT...
DON'T BLAME YOURSELF. SHIDO BROKE THE RULES FIRST.
COME.
WE'RE STARTING WITH SOUL ATTIRE CLASS.
YOUR CLASSMATES ARE ALREADY INSIDE.
魂装場
EITHER WAY...I'LL NEED TO START BY APOLOGIZING TO EVERYONE...!
GI
CREAK)
SIGN: SOUL ATTIRE ROOM

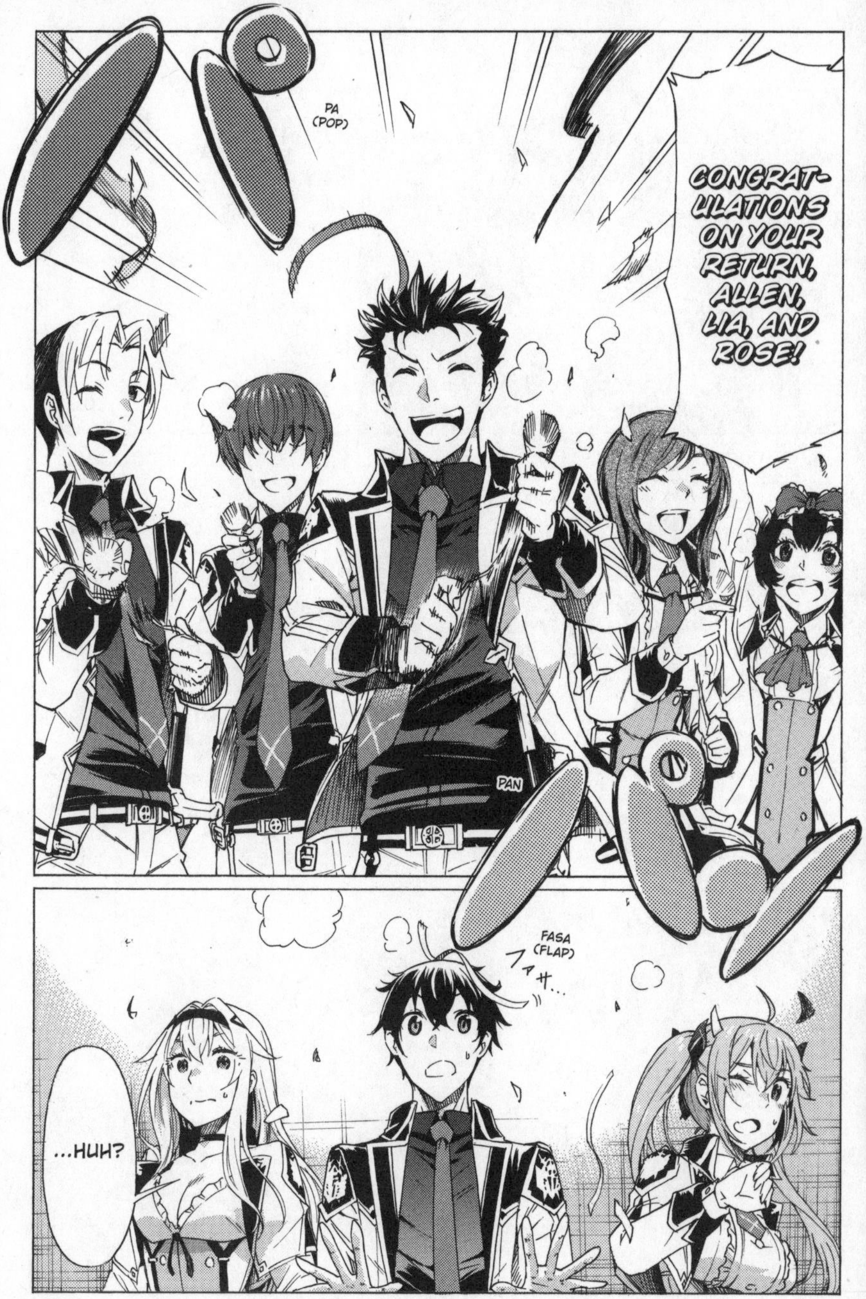
CONGRATULATIONS ON YOUR RETURN, ALLEN, LIA, AND ROSE!
PA (POP)
PAN
FASA (FLAP)
...HUH?

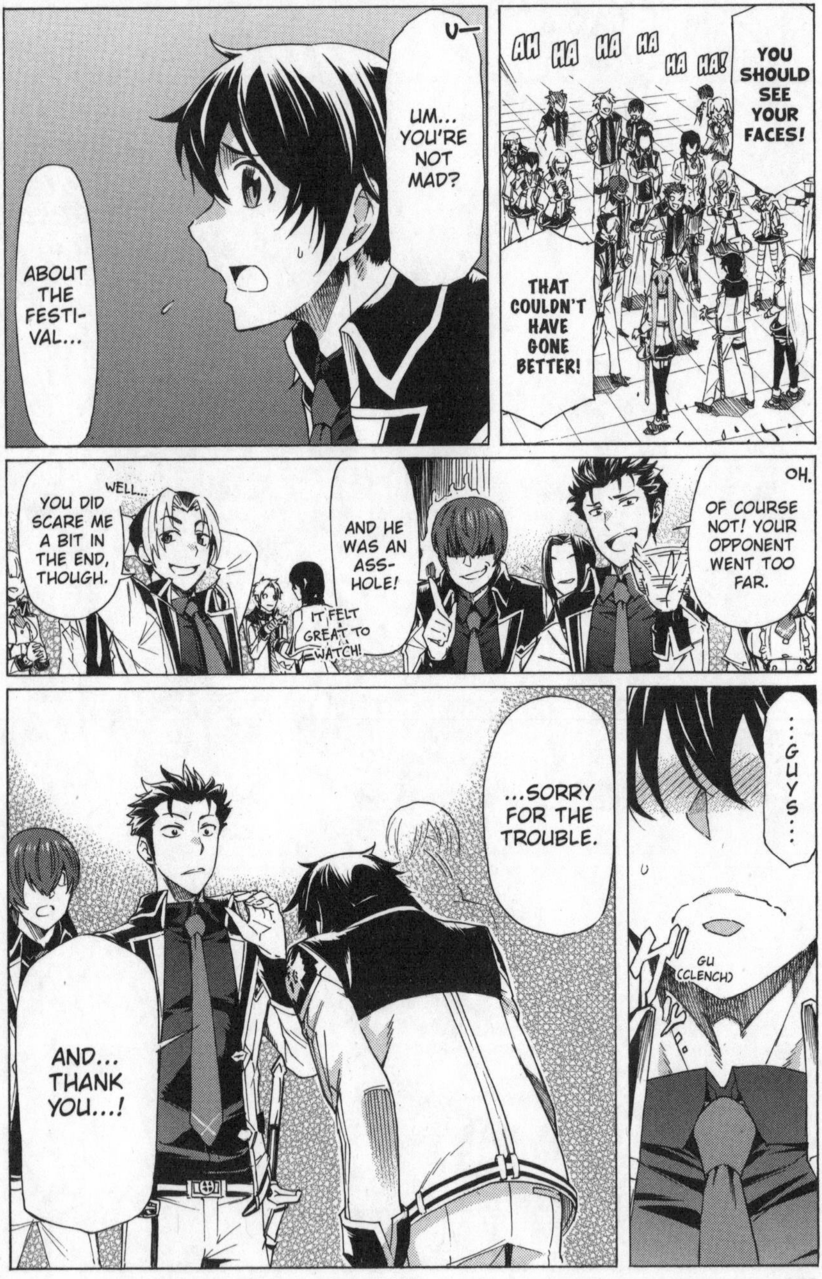
AH HA HA HA HA HA!
YOU SHOULD SEE YOUR FACES!
THAT COULDN'T HAVE GONE BETTER!
U—
UM... YOU'RE NOT MAD?
ABOUT THE FESTI-VAL...
OH.
OF COURSE NOT! YOUR OPPONENT WENT TOO FAR.
AND HE WAS AN ASS-HOLE!
IT FELT GREAT TO WATCH!
WELL...
YOU DID SCARE ME A BIT IN THE END, THOUGH.
...GUYS...
GU (CLENCH)
...SORRY FOR THE TROUBLE.
AND... THANK YOU...!

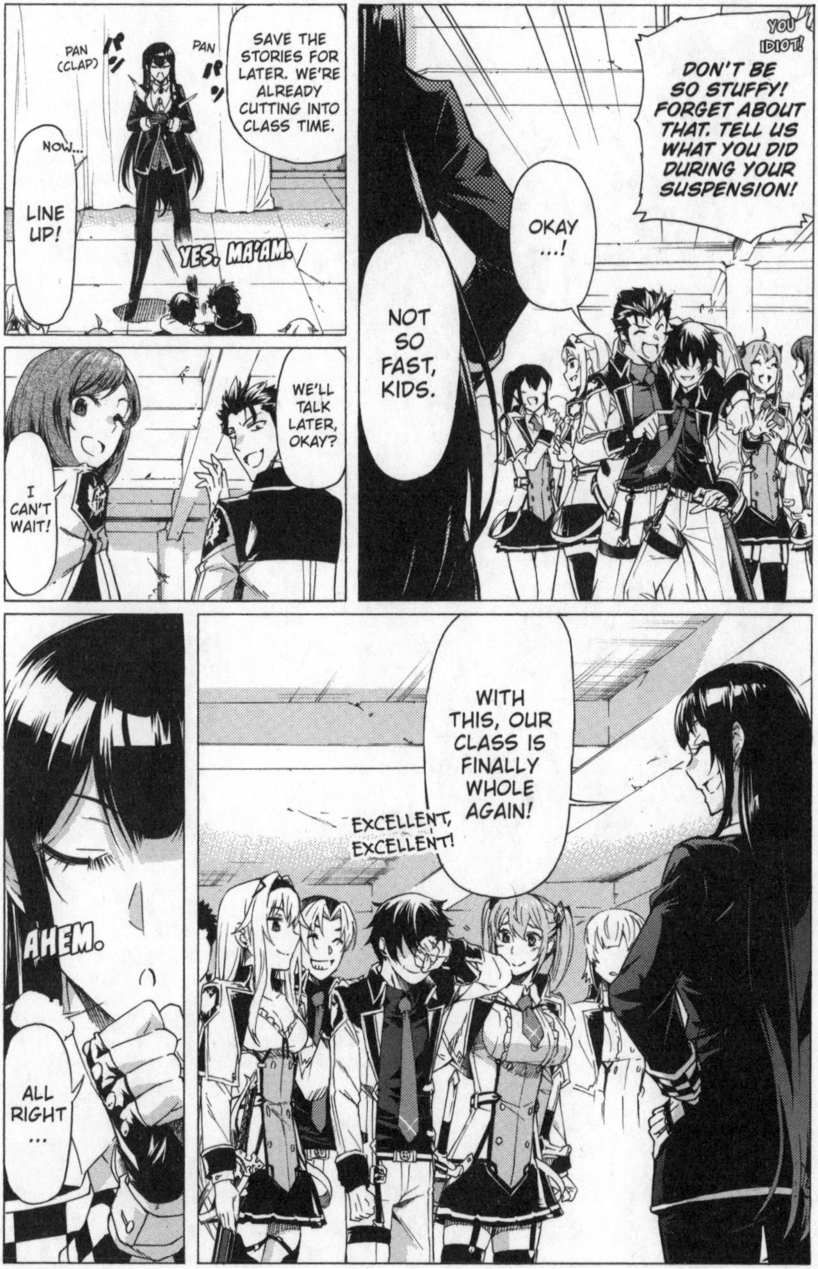
YOU IDIOT!
DON'T BE SO STUFFY! FORGET ABOUT THAT. TELL US WHAT YOU DID DURING YOUR SUSPENSION!
OKAY ...!
NOT SO FAST, KIDS.
SAVE THE STORIES FOR LATER. WE'RE ALREADY CUTTING INTO CLASS TIME.
PAN
PAN (CLAP)
NOW...
LINE UP!
YES, MA'AM.
WE'LL TALK LATER, OKAY?
I CAN'T WAIT!
WITH THIS, OUR CLASS IS FINALLY WHOLE AGAIN!
EXCELLENT, EXCELLENT!
AHEM.
ALL RIGHT ...

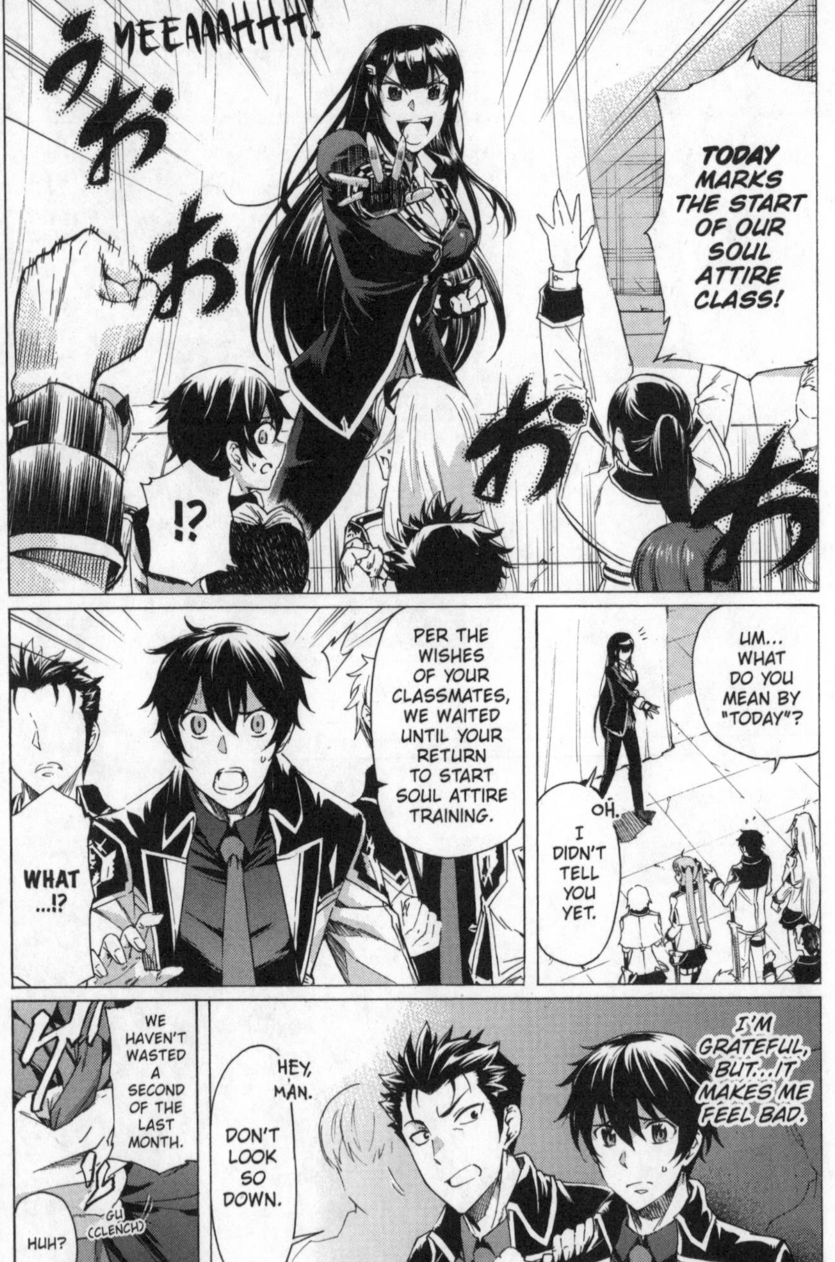
うおおおお
YEEAAAHHH!
TODAY MARKS THE START OF OUR SOUL ATTIRE CLASS!
!?
UM... WHAT DO YOU MEAN BY "TODAY"?
OH. I DIDN'T TELL YOU YET.
PER THE WISHES OF YOUR CLASSMATES, WE WAITED UNTIL YOUR RETURN TO START SOUL ATTIRE TRAINING.
WHAT ...!?
I'M GRATEFUL, BUT...IT MAKES ME FEEL BAD.
HEY, MAN.
DON'T LOOK SO DOWN.
WE HAVEN'T WASTED A SECOND OF THE LAST MONTH.
GU (CLENCH)
HUH?

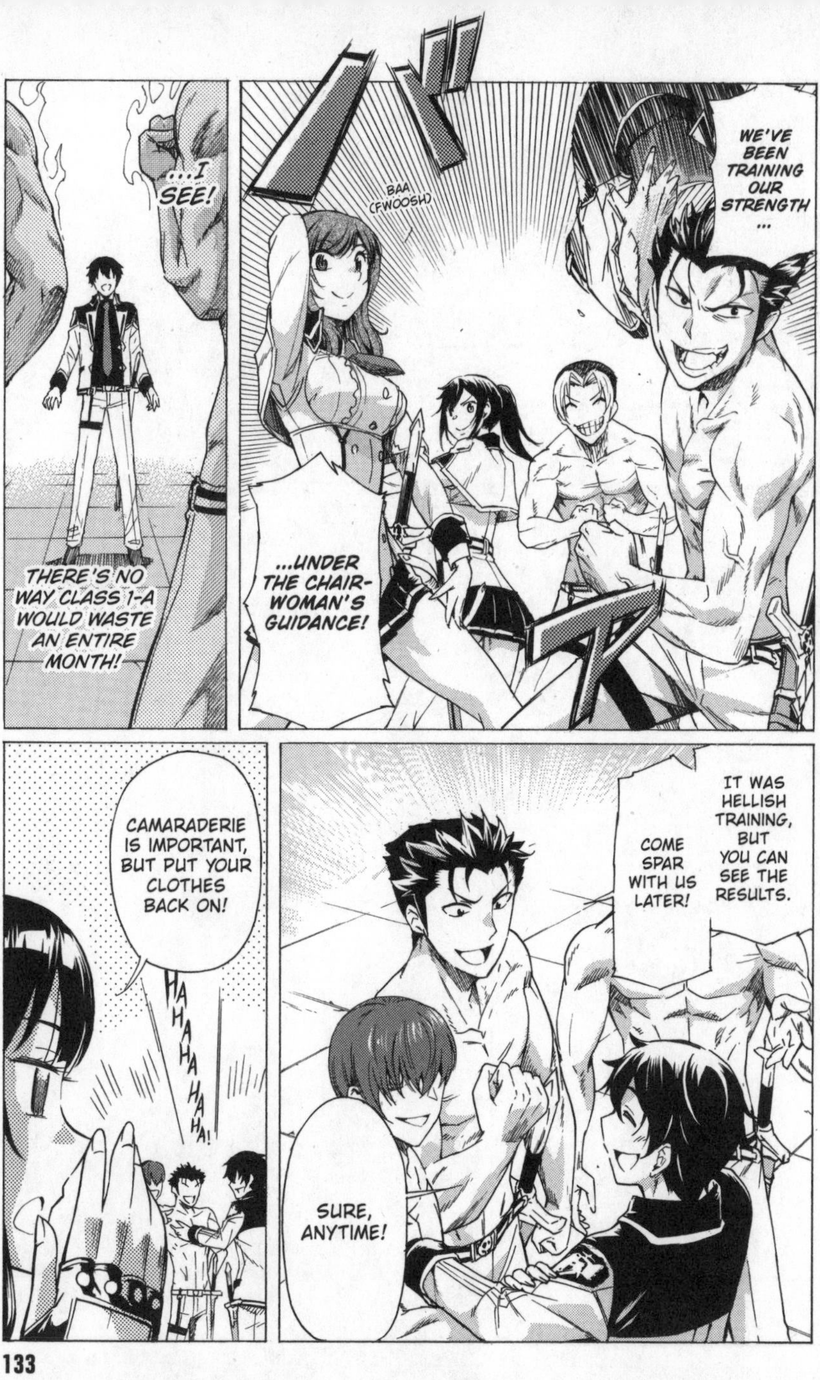
WE'VE BEEN TRAINING OUR STRENGTH...
BAA (FWOOSH)
...UNDER THE CHAIR-WOMAN'S GUIDANCE!
...I SEE!
THERE'S NO WAY CLASS 1-A WOULD WASTE AN ENTIRE MONTH!
IT WAS HELLISH TRAINING, BUT YOU CAN SEE THE RESULTS.
COME SPAR WITH US LATER!
SURE, ANYTIME!
CAMARADERIE IS IMPORTANT, BUT PUT YOUR CLOTHES BACK ON!
HAHAHAHAHAHA!

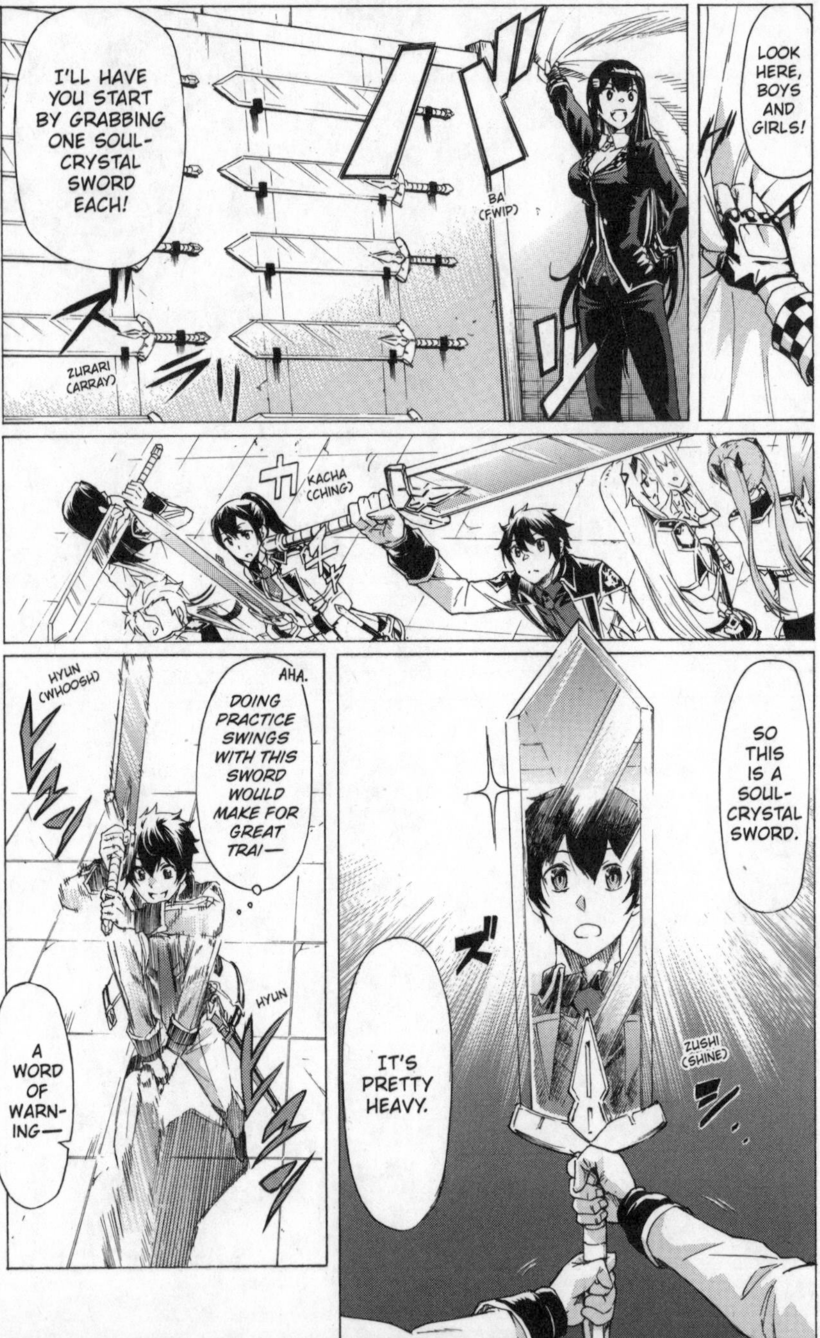
LOOK HERE, BOYS AND GIRLS!
I'LL HAVE YOU START BY GRABBING ONE SOUL-CRYSTAL SWORD EACH!
BA (FWIP)
ZURARI (ARRAY)
KACHA (CHING)
SO THIS IS A SOUL-CRYSTAL SWORD.
ZUSHI (SHINE)
IT'S PRETTY HEAVY.
AHA. DOING PRACTICE SWINGS WITH THIS SWORD WOULD MAKE FOR GREAT TRAI—
HYUN (WHOOSH)
HYUN
A WORD OF WARNING—

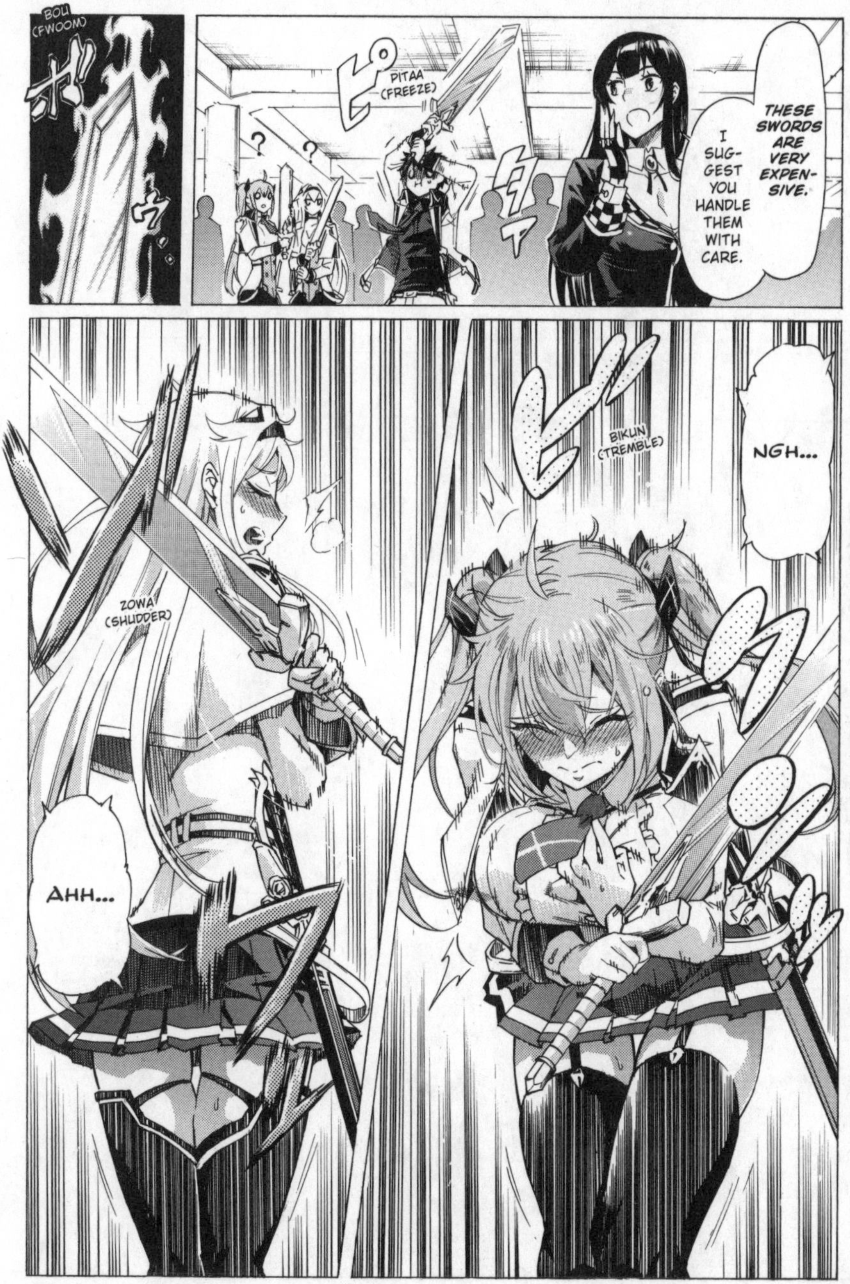
THESE SWORDS ARE VERY EXPENSIVE.
I SUGGEST YOU HANDLE THEM WITH CARE.
PITAA (FREEZE)
BOU (FWOOM)
NGH...
BIKUN (TREMBLE)
ZOWA (SHUDDER)
AHH...

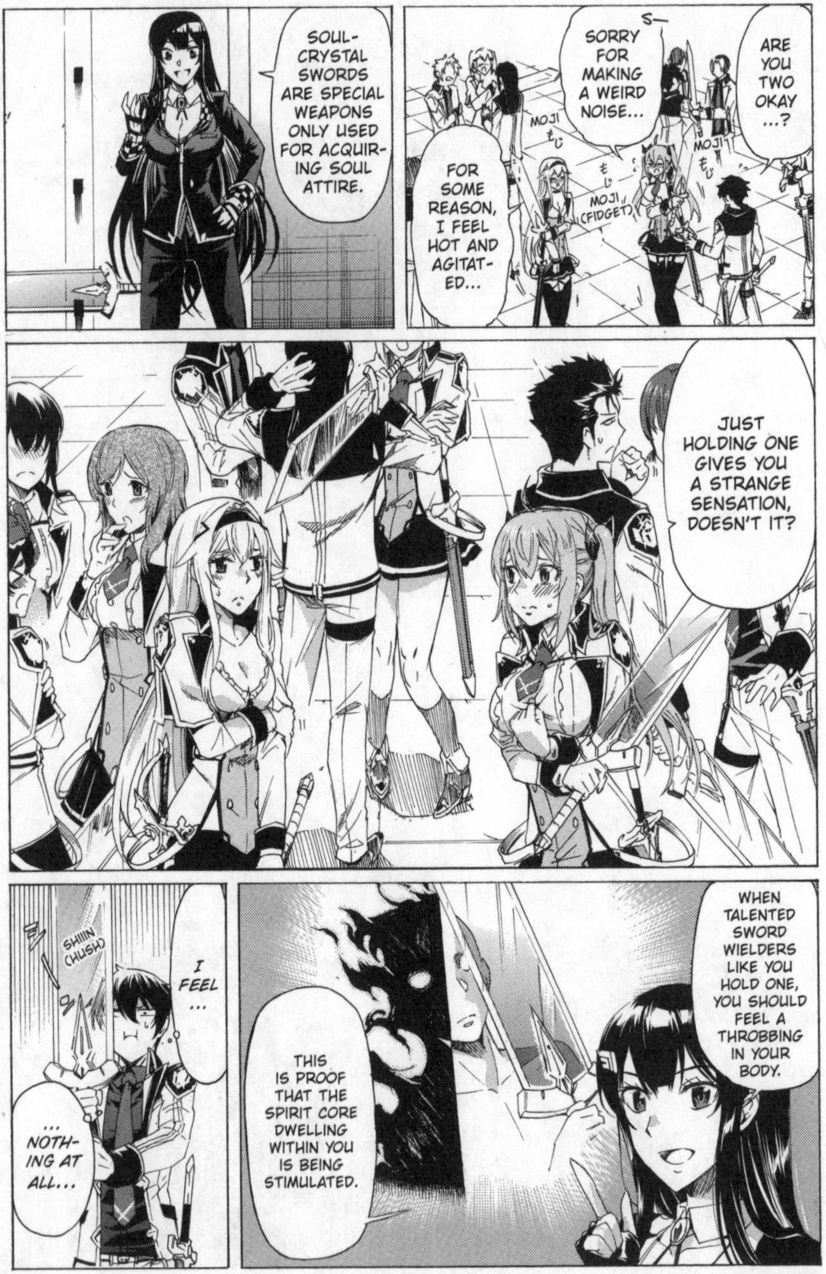
ARE YOU TWO OKAY ...?
S—
SORRY FOR MAKING A WEIRD NOISE...
MOJI もじ
MOJI もじ
FOR SOME REASON, I FEEL HOT AND AGITATED...
もじ MOJI (FIDGET)
SOUL-CRYSTAL SWORDS ARE SPECIAL WEAPONS ONLY USED FOR ACQUIRING SOUL ATTIRE.
JUST HOLDING ONE GIVES YOU A STRANGE SENSATION, DOESN'T IT?
WHEN TALENTED SWORD WIELDERS LIKE YOU HOLD ONE, YOU SHOULD FEEL A THROBBING IN YOUR BODY.
THIS IS PROOF THAT THE SPIRIT CORE DWELLING WITHIN YOU IS BEING STIMULATED.
SHIIIN (HUSH)
I FEEL ...
... NOTHING AT ALL...

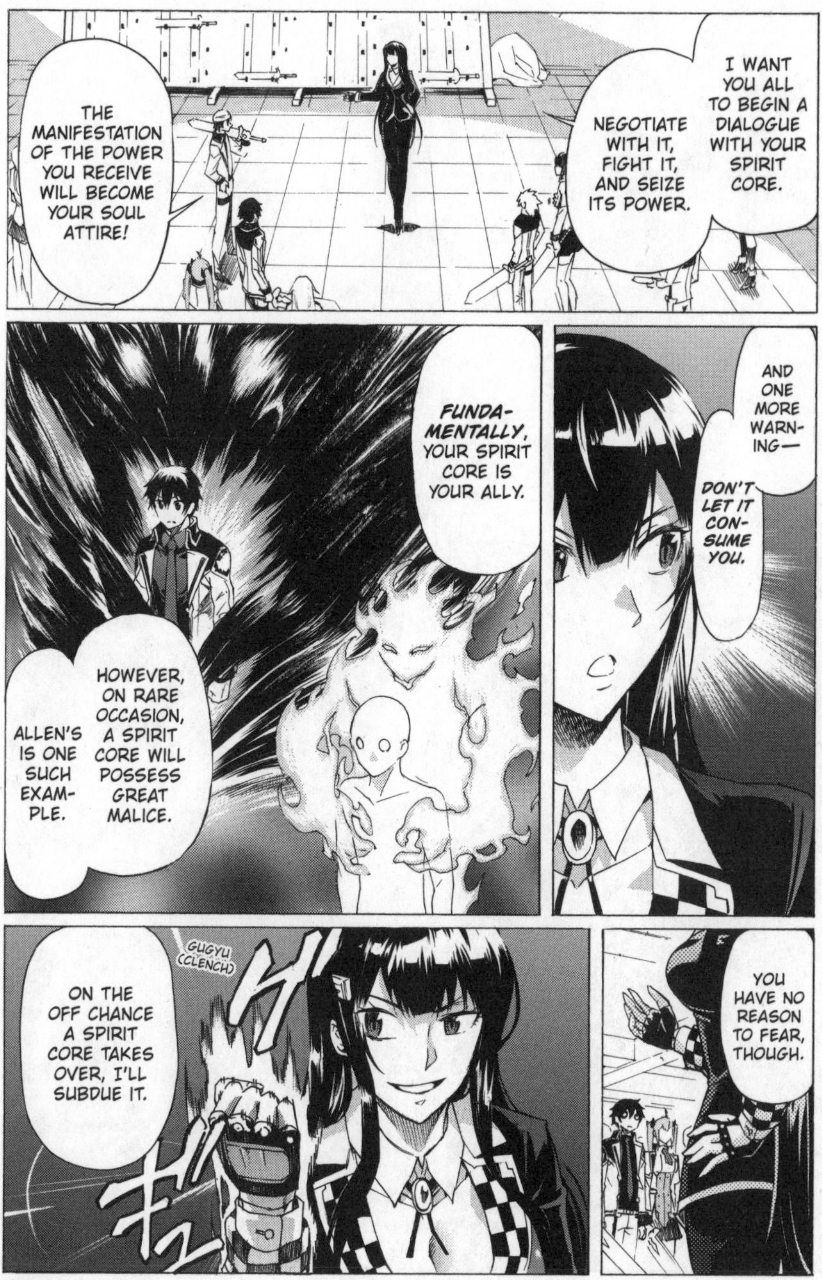
I WANT YOU ALL TO BEGIN A DIALOGUE WITH YOUR SPIRIT CORE.
NEGOTIATE WITH IT, FIGHT IT, AND SEIZE ITS POWER.
THE MANIFESTATION OF THE POWER YOU RECEIVE WILL BECOME YOUR SOUL ATTIRE!
AND ONE MORE WARNING—
DON'T LET IT CONSUME YOU.
FUNDAMENTALLY, YOUR SPIRIT CORE IS YOUR ALLY.
HOWEVER, ON RARE OCCASION, A SPIRIT CORE WILL POSSESS GREAT MALICE.
ALLEN'S IS ONE SUCH EXAMPLE.
YOU HAVE NO REASON TO FEAR, THOUGH.
GUGYU (CLENCH)
ON THE OFF CHANCE A SPIRIT CORE TAKES OVER, I'LL SUBDUE IT.

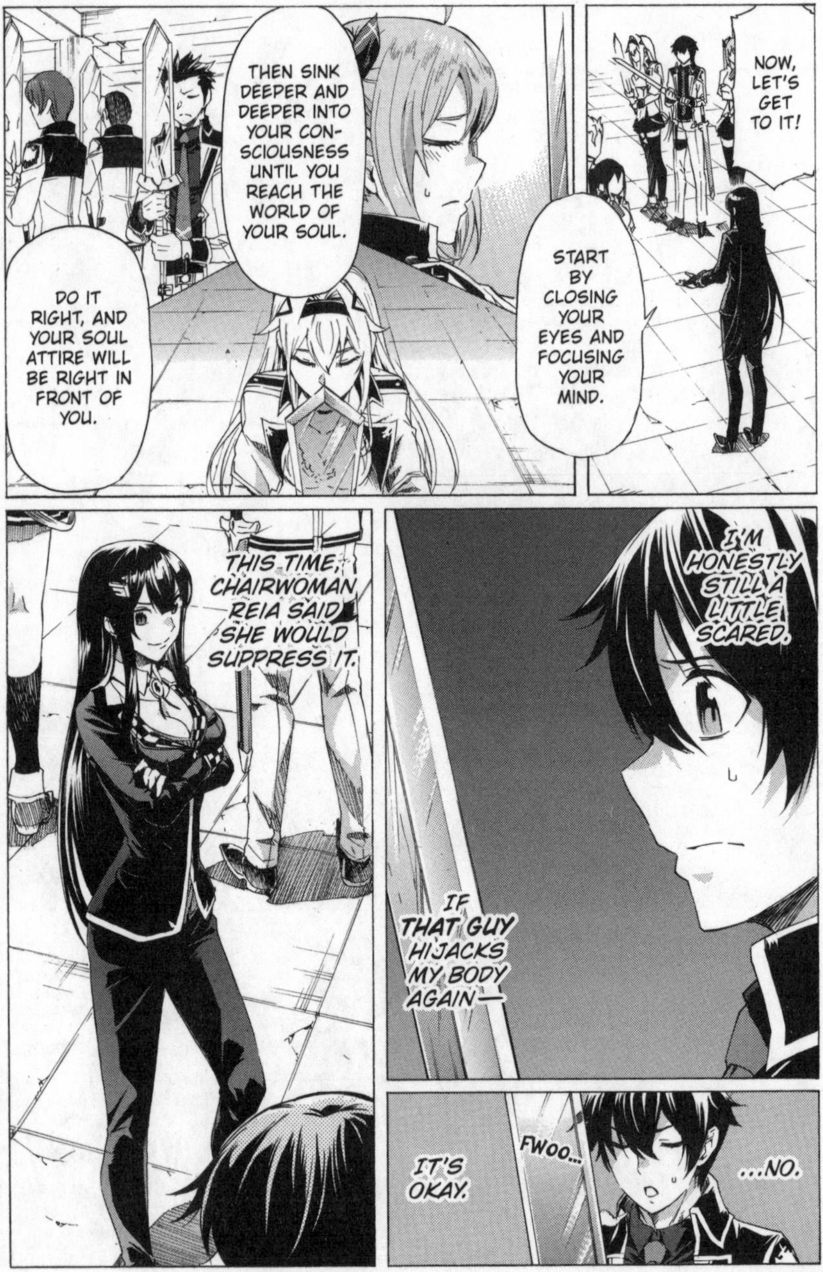
NOW, LET'S GET TO IT!
START BY CLOSING YOUR EYES AND FOCUSING YOUR MIND.
THEN SINK DEEPER AND DEEPER INTO YOUR CON-SCIOUSNESS UNTIL YOU REACH THE WORLD OF YOUR SOUL.
DO IT RIGHT, AND YOUR SOUL ATTIRE WILL BE RIGHT IN FRONT OF YOU.
I'M HONESTLY STILL A LITTLE SCARED.
IF THAT GUY HIJACKS MY BODY AGAIN—
...NO.
FWOO...
IT'S OKAY.
THIS TIME, CHAIRWOMAN REIA SAID SHE WOULD SUPPRESS IT.

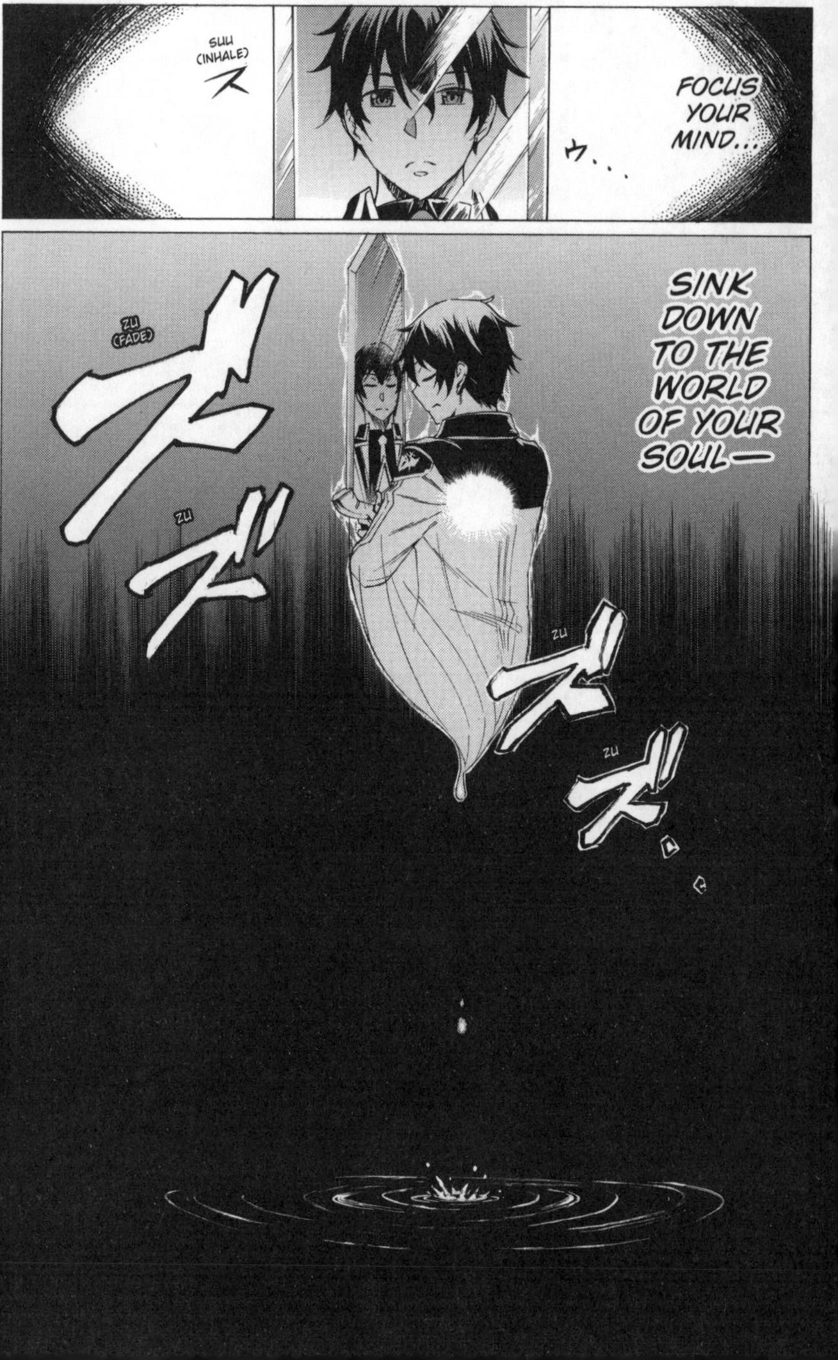
FOCUS YOUR MIND...
SUU (INHALE)
SINK DOWN TO THE WORLD OF YOUR SOUL—
ZU (FADE)
ZU
ZU
ZU

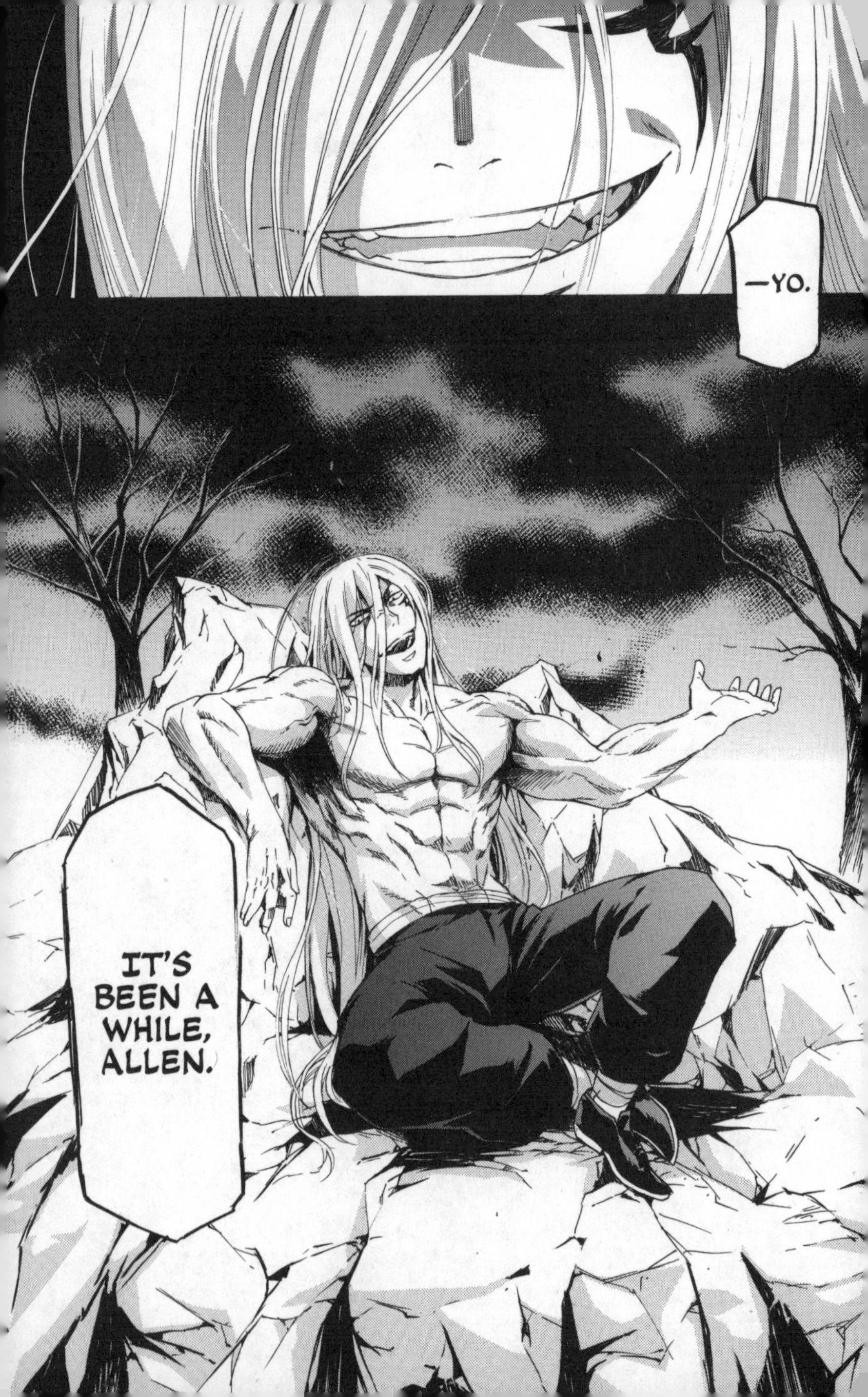
—YO.
IT'S BEEN A WHILE, ALLEN.

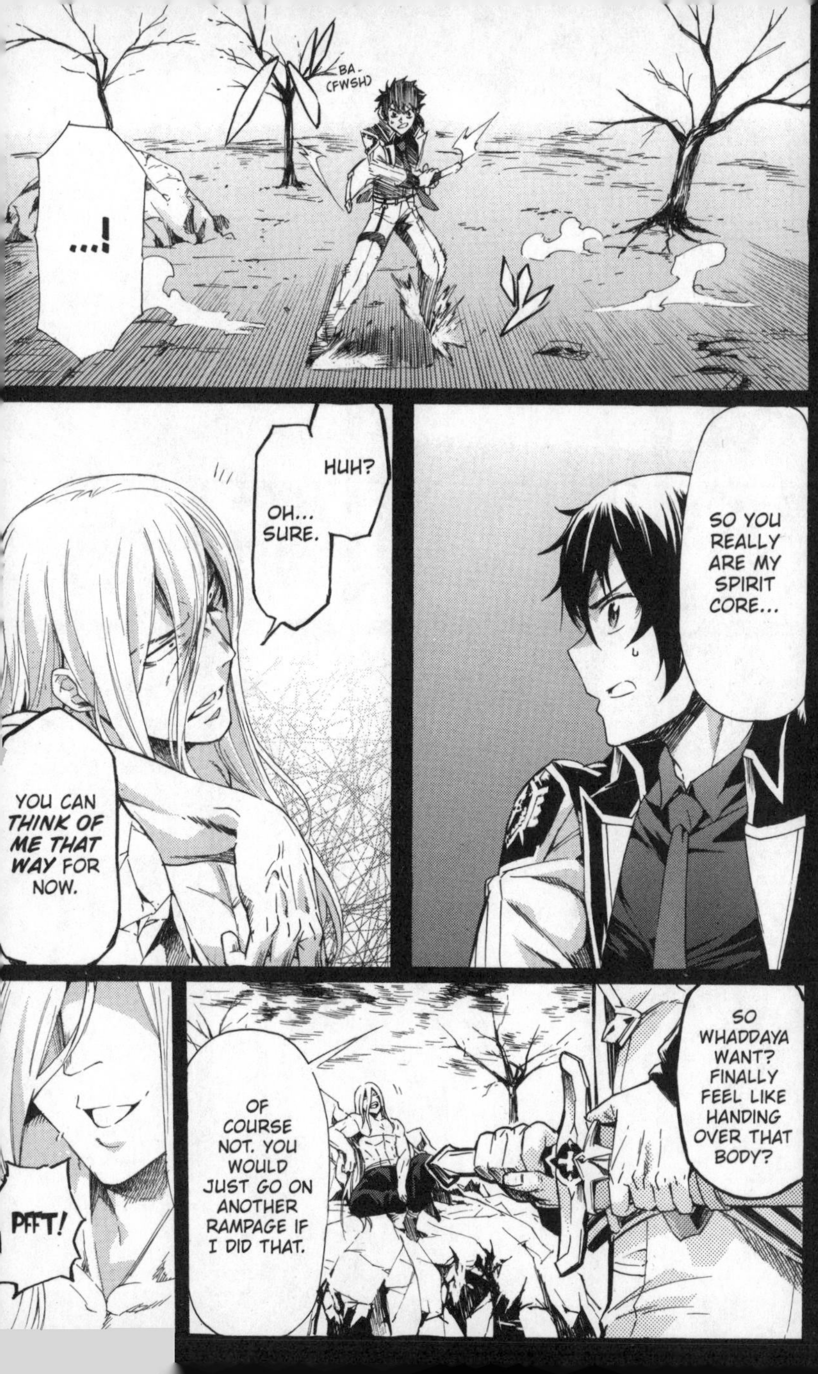
BA- (FWSH)
...!
SO YOU REALLY ARE MY SPIRIT CORE...
HUH?
OH... SURE.
YOU CAN *THINK OF ME THAT WAY* FOR NOW.
SO WHADDAYA WANT? FINALLY FEEL LIKE HANDING OVER THAT BODY?
OF COURSE NOT. YOU WOULD JUST GO ON ANOTHER RAMPAGE IF I DID THAT.
PFFT!

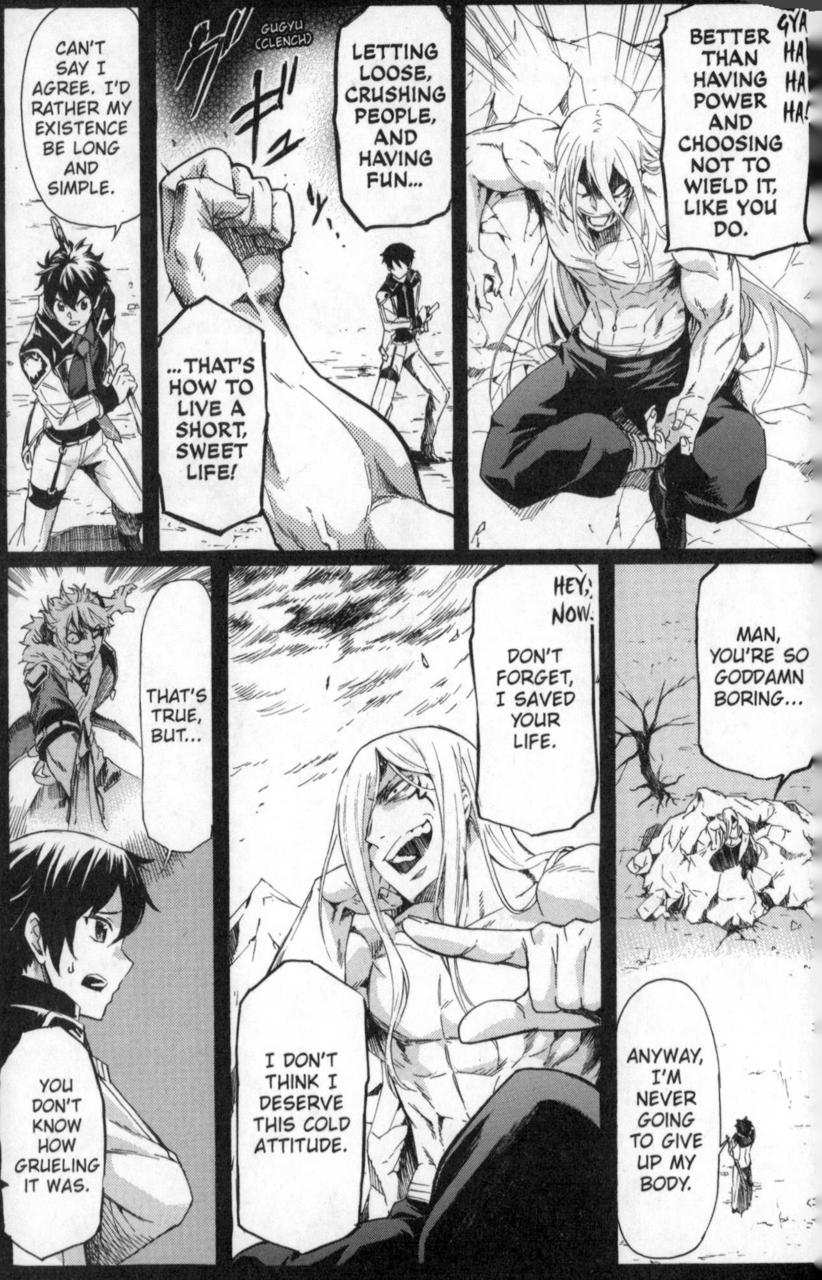
GYA HA HA HA!
BETTER THAN HAVING POWER AND CHOOSING NOT TO WIELD IT, LIKE YOU DO.
LETTING LOOSE, CRUSHING PEOPLE, AND HAVING FUN...
GUGYU (CLENCH)
...THAT'S HOW TO LIVE A SHORT, SWEET LIFE!
CAN'T SAY I AGREE. I'D RATHER MY EXISTENCE BE LONG AND SIMPLE.
MAN, YOU'RE SO GODDAMN BORING...
ANYWAY, I'M NEVER GOING TO GIVE UP MY BODY.
HEY, NOW.
DON'T FORGET, I SAVED YOUR LIFE.
I DON'T THINK I DESERVE THIS COLD ATTITUDE.
THAT'S TRUE, BUT...
YOU DON'T KNOW HOW GRUELING IT WAS.

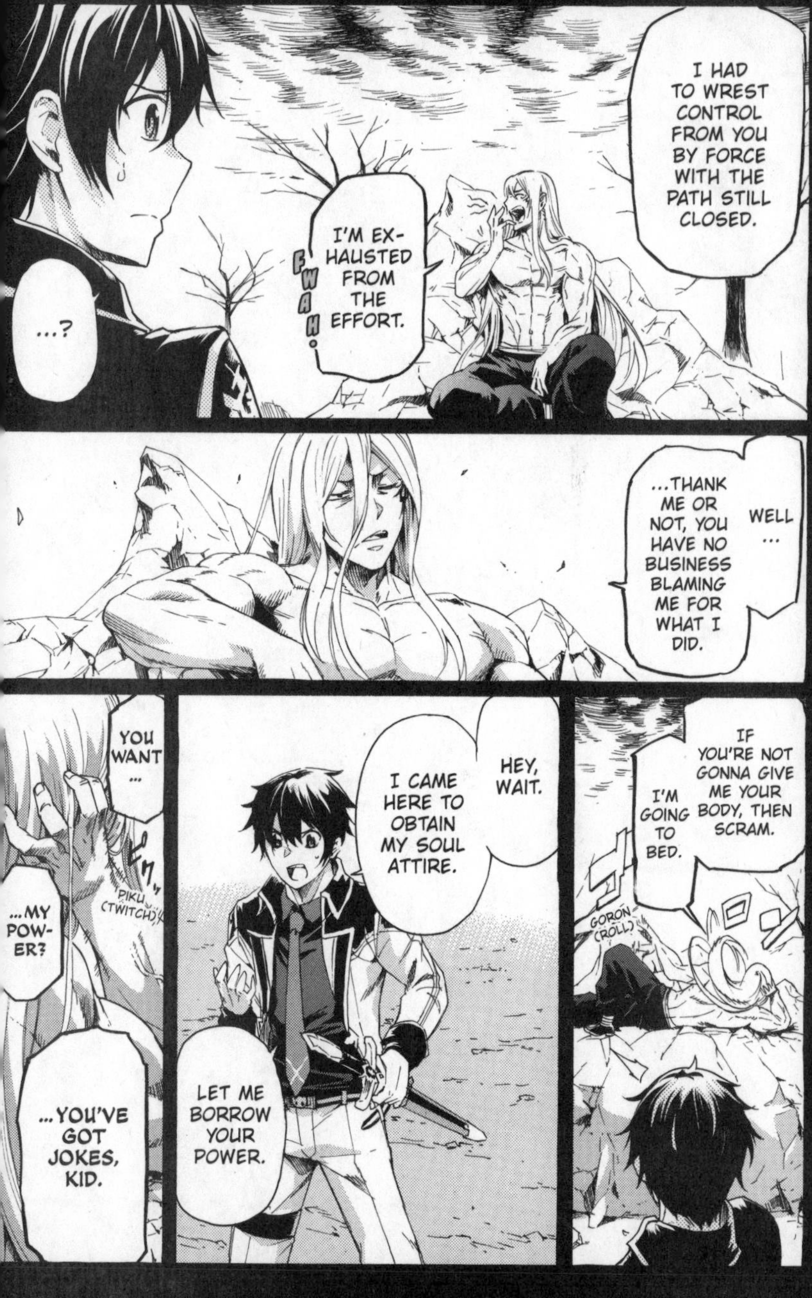
I HAD TO WREST CONTROL FROM YOU BY FORCE WITH THE PATH STILL CLOSED.
FWAH!
I'M EX-HAUSTED FROM THE EFFORT.
...?
WELL ...
...THANK ME OR NOT, YOU HAVE NO BUSINESS BLAMING ME FOR WHAT I DID.
IF YOU'RE NOT GONNA GIVE ME YOUR BODY, THEN SCRAM.
I'M GOING TO BED.
GORON (ROLL)
HEY, WAIT.
I CAME HERE TO OBTAIN MY SOUL ATTIRE.
LET ME BORROW YOUR POWER.
YOU WANT ...
PIKU (TWITCH)
...MY POWER?
...YOU'VE GOT JOKES, KID.

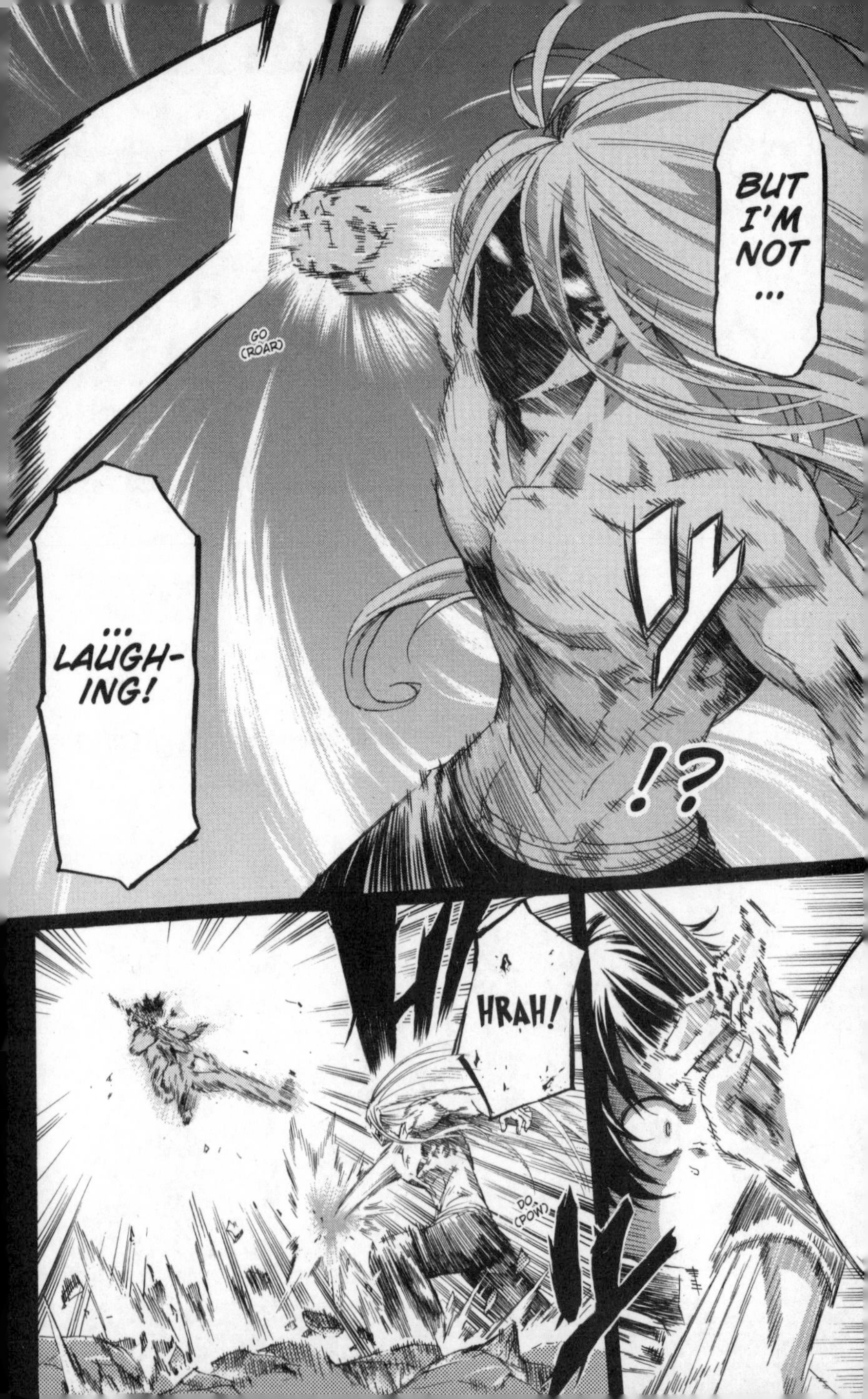
BUT I'M NOT ...
GO (ROAR)
... LAUGH-ING!
!?
HRAH!
DO- (POW)

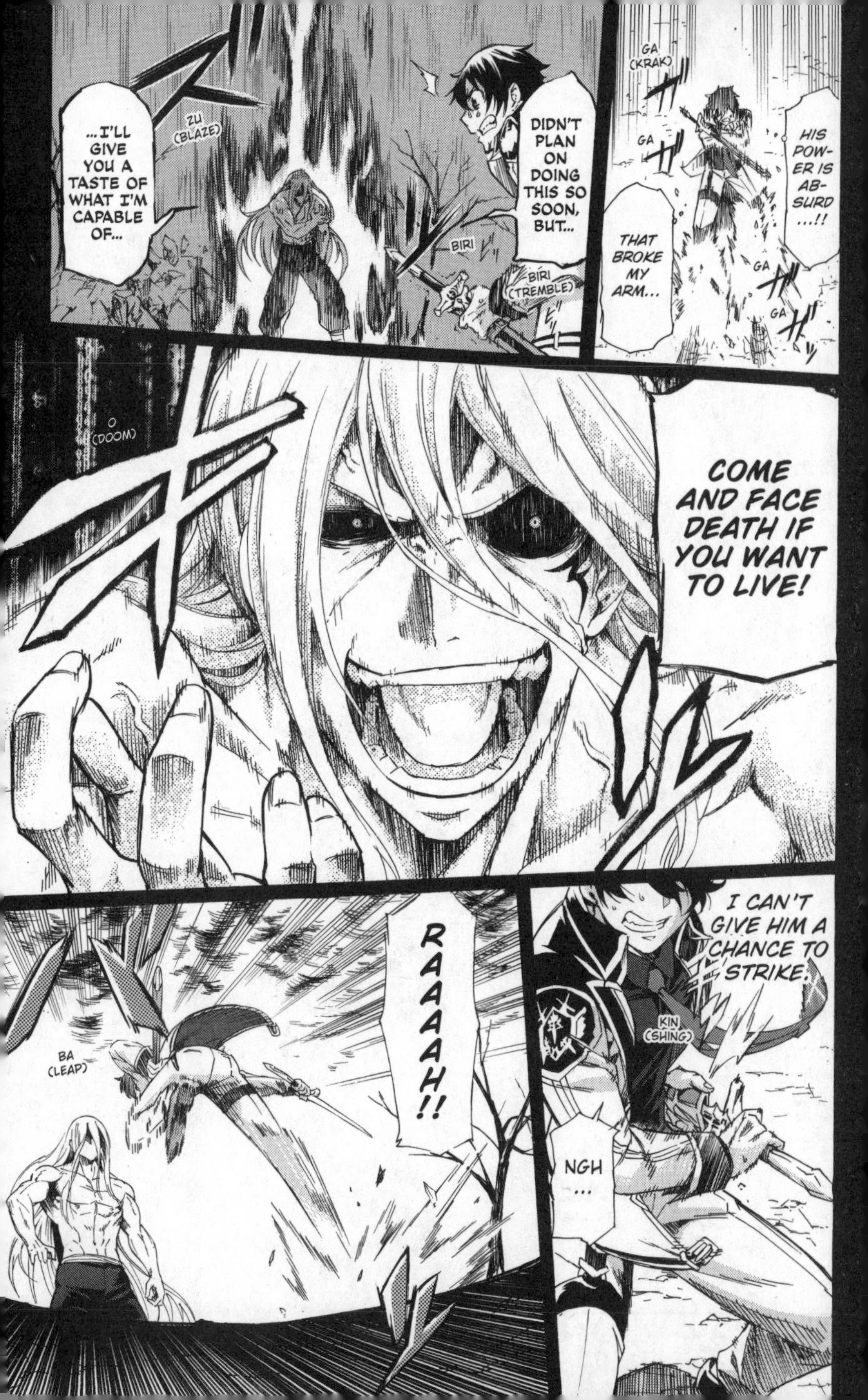
GA (KRAK)
GA
HIS POWER IS ABSURD...!!
THAT BROKE MY ARM...
GA
GA
DIDN'T PLAN ON DOING THIS SO SOON, BUT...
...I'LL GIVE YOU A TASTE OF WHAT I'M CAPABLE OF...
ZU (BLAZE)
BIRI
BIRI (TREMBLE)
COME AND FACE DEATH IF YOU WANT TO LIVE!
O (DOOM)
I CAN'T GIVE HIM A CHANCE TO STRIKE.
KIN (SHING)
NGH...
RAAAAAH!!
BA (LEAP)

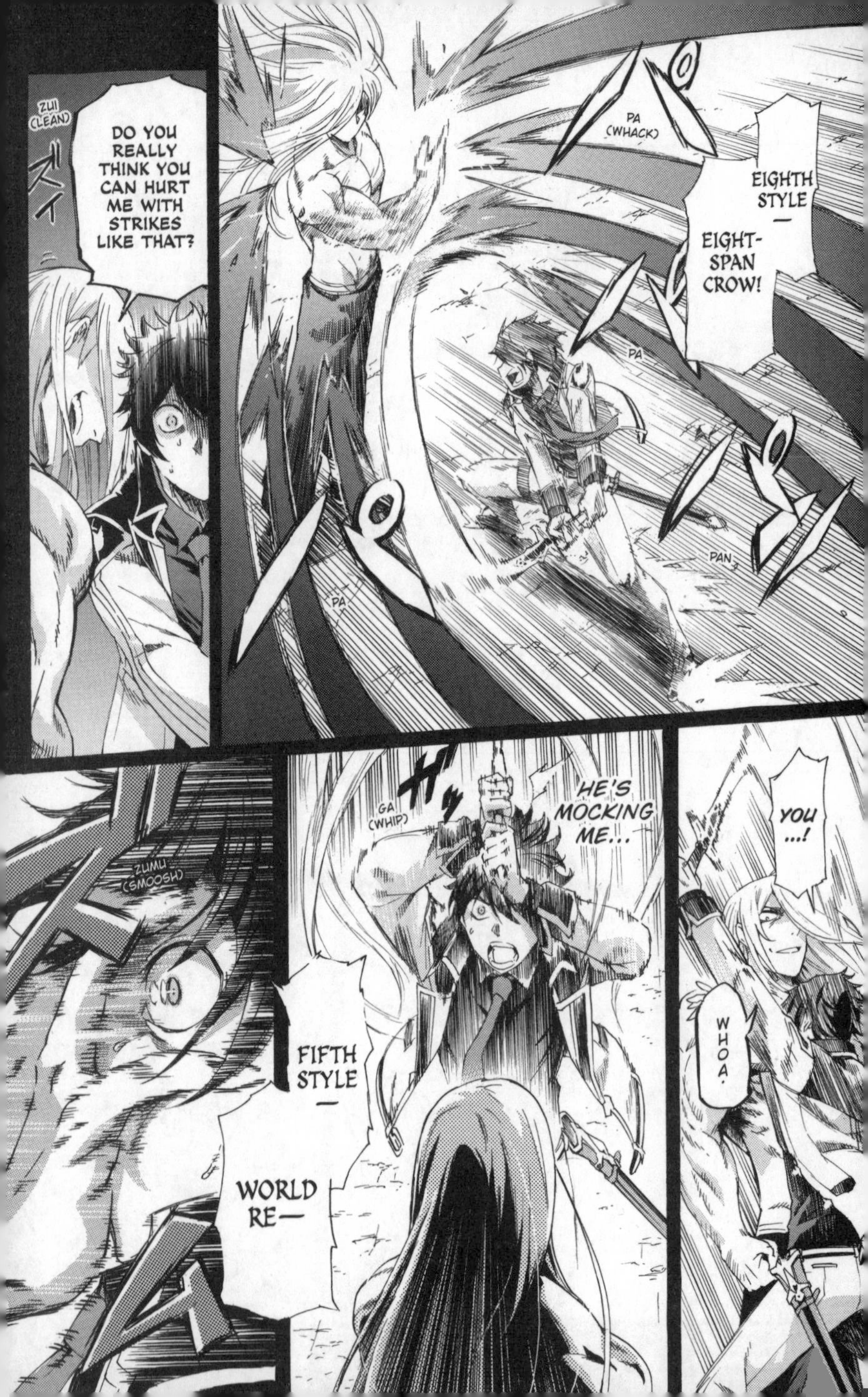
EIGHTH STYLE
—
EIGHT-SPAN CROW!
PA (WHACK)
PA
PAN
PA
ZUI (CLEAN)
DO YOU REALLY THINK YOU CAN HURT ME WITH STRIKES LIKE THAT?
YOU ...!
WHOA.
HE'S MOCKING ME...
GA (WHIP)
FIFTH STYLE
—
WORLD RE—
ZUMU (SMOOSH)

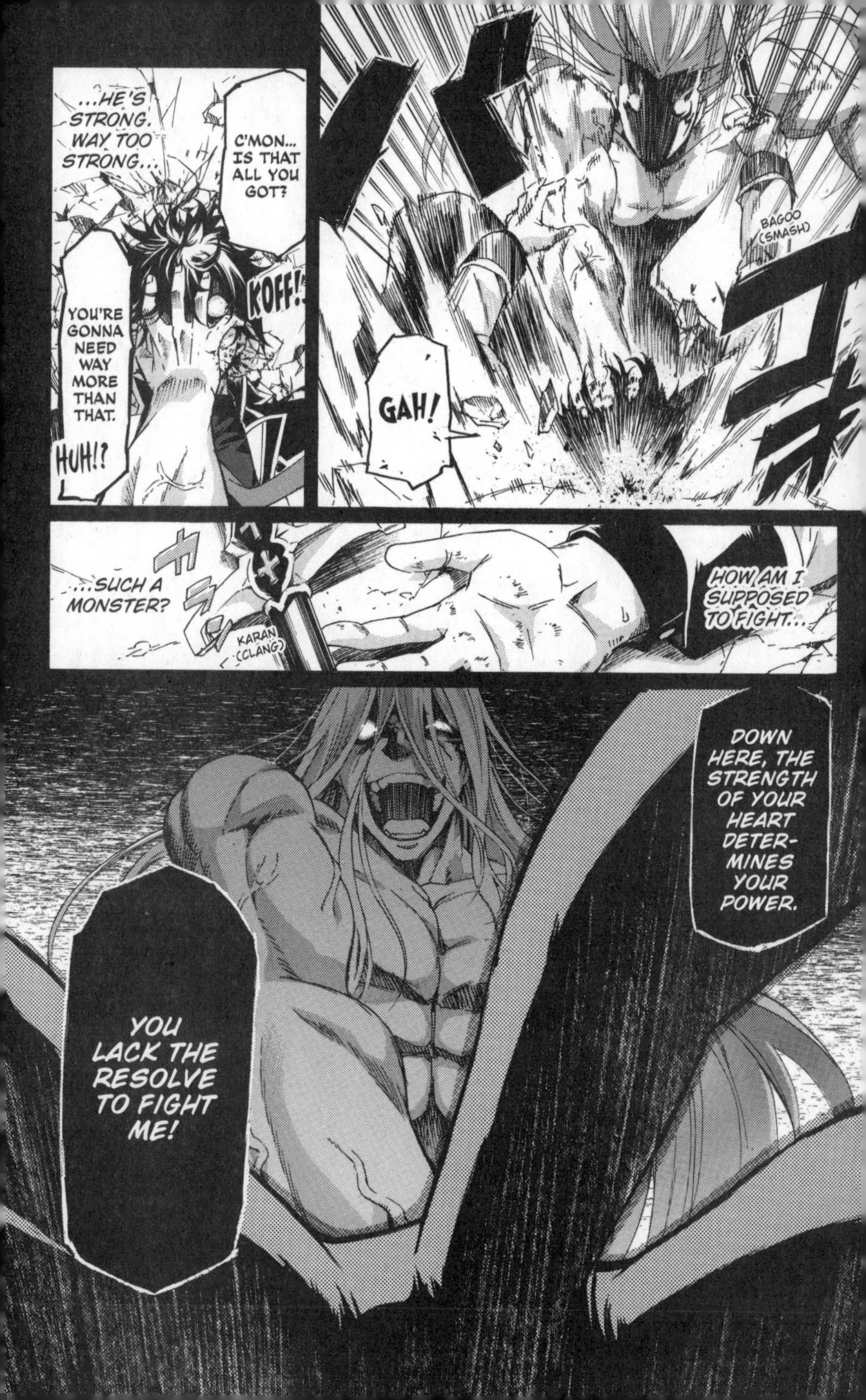
BAGOO (SMASH)
GAH!
C'MON... IS THAT ALL YOU GOT?
...HE'S STRONG. WAY TOO STRONG...
KOFF!
YOU'RE GONNA NEED WAY MORE THAN THAT.
HUH!?
HOW AM I SUPPOSED TO FIGHT...
KARAN (CLANG)
...SUCH A MONSTER?
DOWN HERE, THE STRENGTH OF YOUR HEART DETERMINES YOUR POWER.
YOU LACK THE RESOLVE TO FIGHT ME!

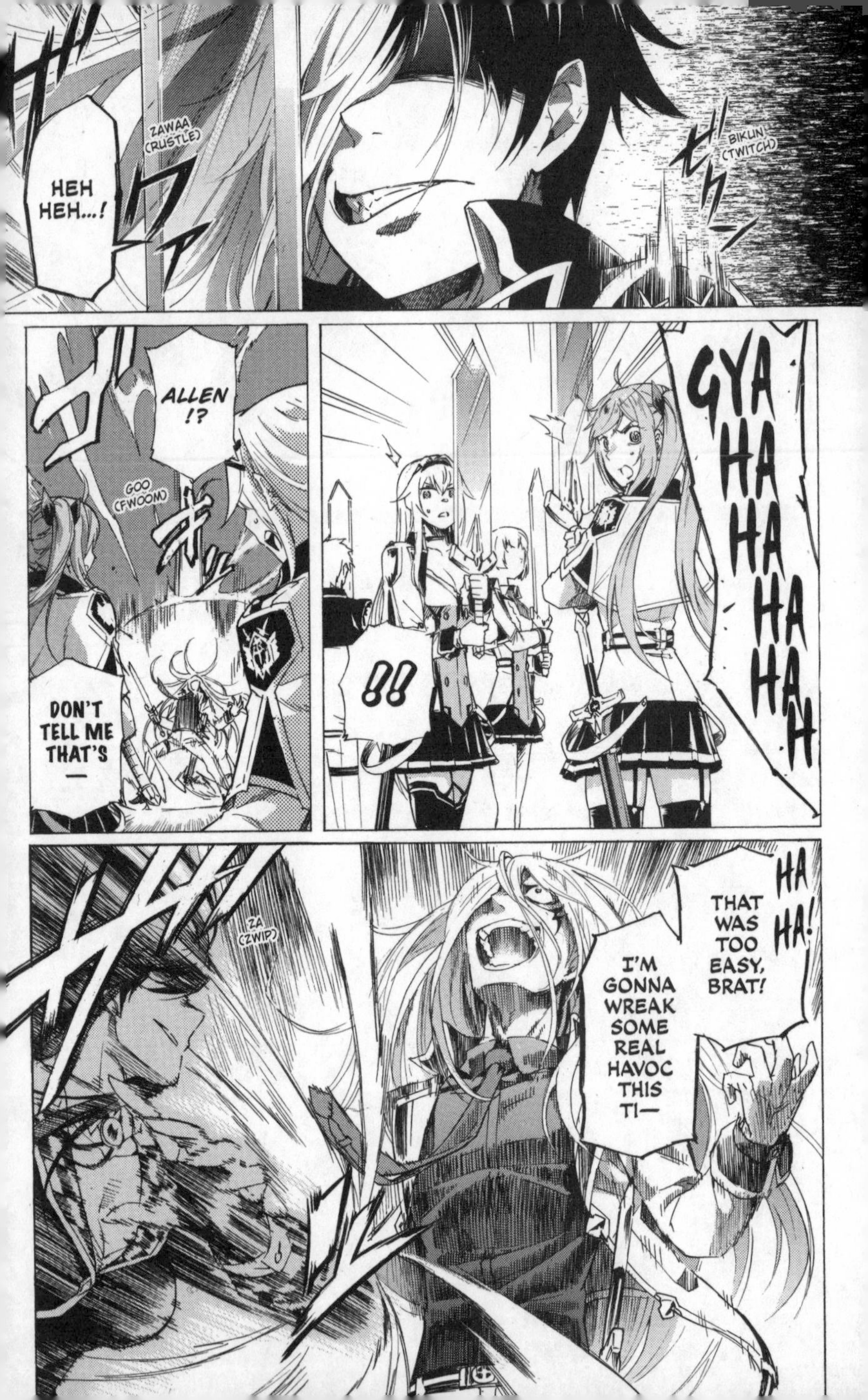
BIKUN (TWITCH)
ZAWAA (RUSTLE)
HEH HEH...!
GYAHAHAHAHAHAHAHAH
!!
ALLEN!?
GOO (FWOOM)
DON'T TELL ME THAT'S—
HA HA!
THAT WAS TOO EASY, BRAT!
I'M GONNA WREAK SOME REAL HAVOC THIS TI—
ZA (ZWIP)

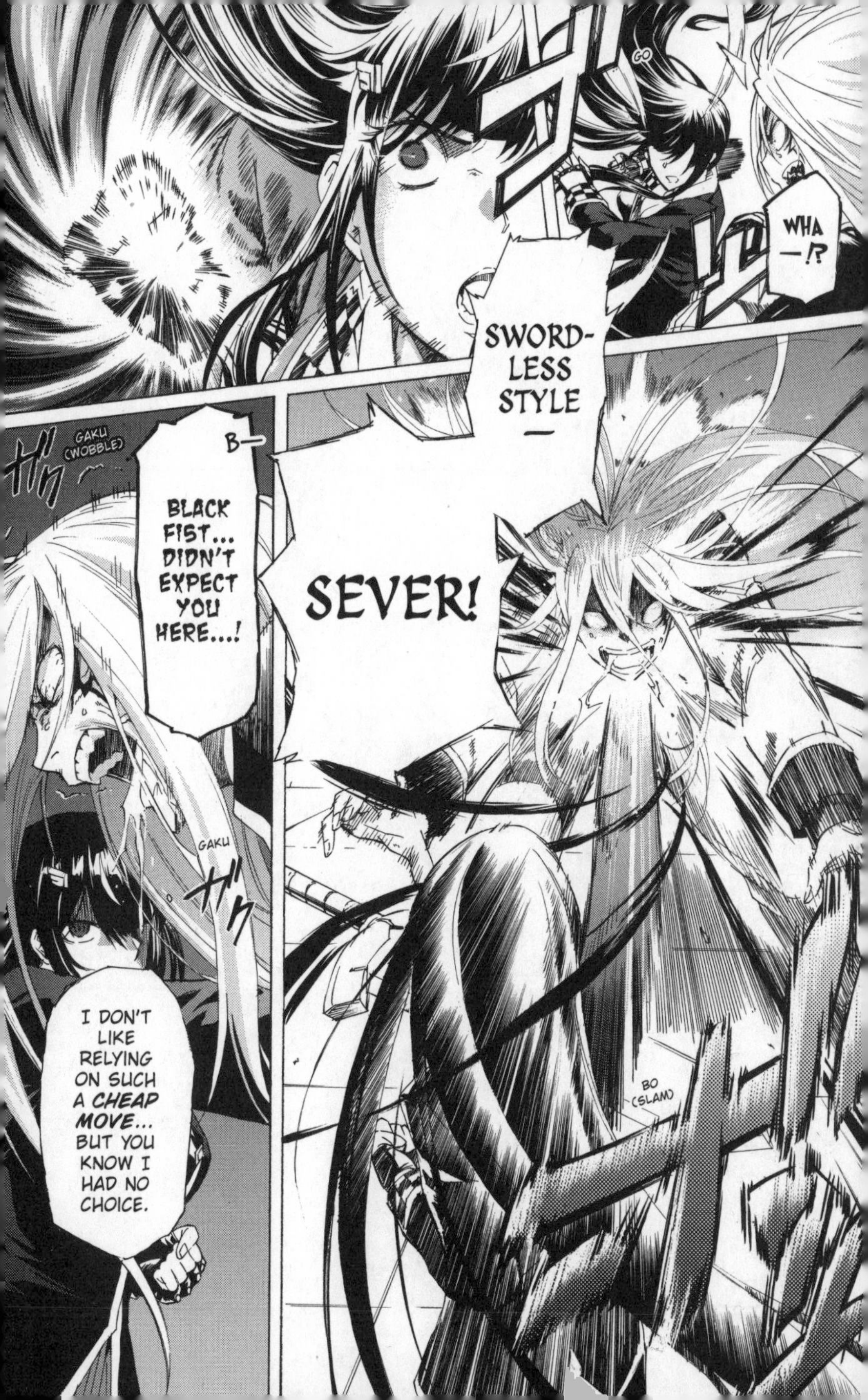
GO
WHA—!?
SWORD-LESS STYLE—
SEVER!
BO (SLAM)
GAKU (WOBBLE)
B— BLACK FIST... DIDN'T EXPECT YOU HERE...!
GAKU
I DON'T LIKE RELYING ON SUCH A ***CHEAP MOVE***... BUT YOU KNOW I HAD NO CHOICE.

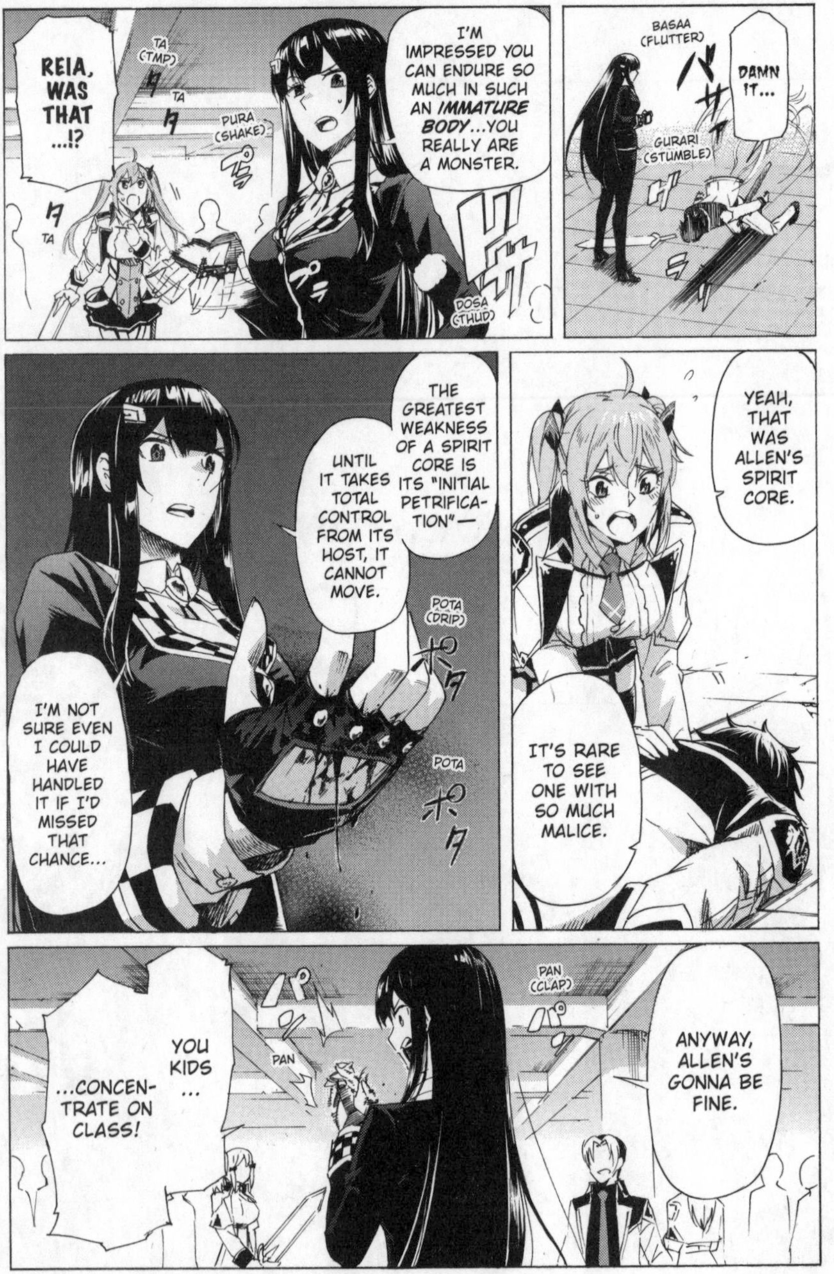

BASAA (FLUTTER)
DAMN IT...
GURARI (STUMBLE)
I'M IMPRESSED YOU CAN ENDURE SO MUCH IN SUCH AN *IMMATURE BODY*...YOU REALLY ARE A MONSTER.
TA (TMP)
TA
PURA (SHAKE)
REIA, WAS THAT ...!?
TA
DOSA (THUD)
YEAH, THAT WAS ALLEN'S SPIRIT CORE.
IT'S RARE TO SEE ONE WITH SO MUCH MALICE.
THE GREATEST WEAKNESS OF A SPIRIT CORE IS ITS "INITIAL PETRIFICATION"—
UNTIL IT TAKES TOTAL CONTROL FROM ITS HOST, IT CANNOT MOVE.
POTA (DRIP)
POTA
I'M NOT SURE EVEN I COULD HAVE HANDLED IT IF I'D MISSED THAT CHANCE...
ANYWAY, ALLEN'S GONNA BE FINE.
PAN (CLAP)
YOU KIDS ...
PAN
...CONCENTRATE ON CLASS!

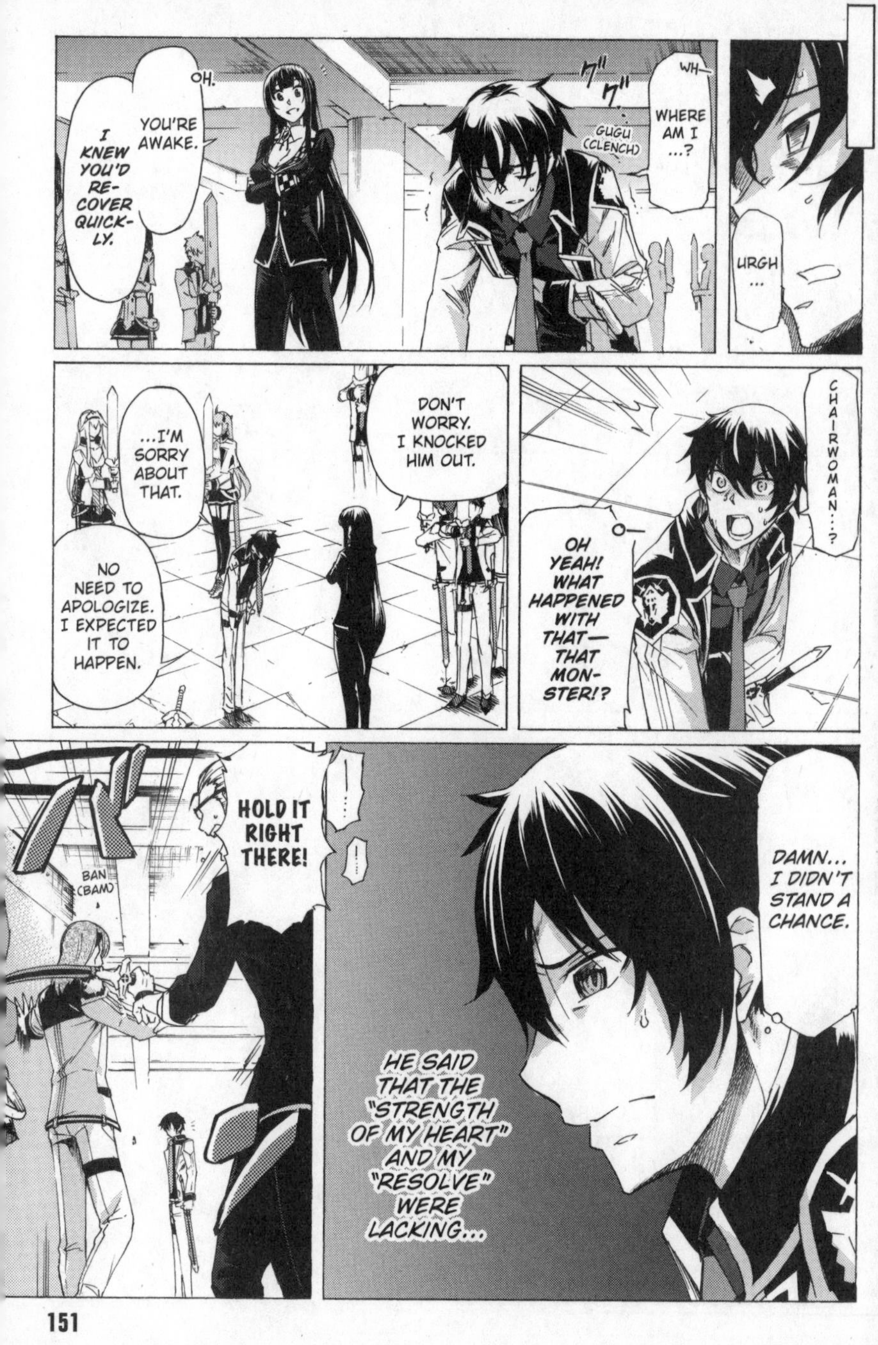
URGH...
WH—
WHERE AM I ...?
GUGU (CLENCH)
OH.
YOU'RE AWAKE.
I KNEW YOU'D RE-COVER QUICK-LY.
CHAIRWOMAN...?
O—
OH YEAH! WHAT HAPPENED WITH THAT—THAT MON-STER!?
DON'T WORRY. I KNOCKED HIM OUT.
...I'M SORRY ABOUT THAT.
NO NEED TO APOLOGIZE. I EXPECTED IT TO HAPPEN.
DAMN... I DIDN'T STAND A CHANCE.
HE SAID THAT THE "STRENGTH OF MY HEART" AND MY "RESOLVE" WERE LACKING...
!...
!...
HOLD IT RIGHT THERE!
BAN (BAM)

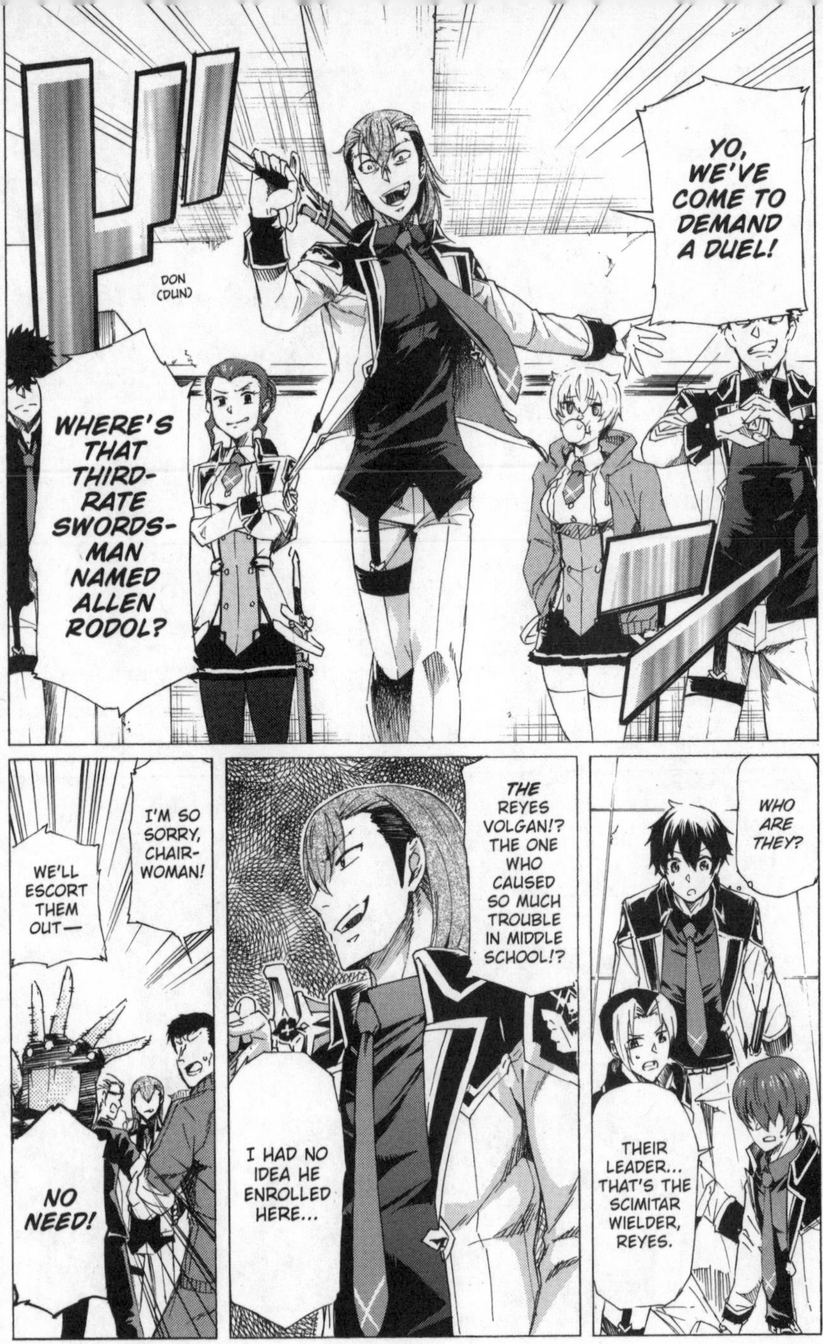
YO, WE'VE COME TO DEMAND A DUEL!
DON (DUN)
WHERE'S THAT THIRD-RATE SWORDSMAN NAMED ALLEN RODOL?
WHO ARE THEY?
THEIR LEADER... THAT'S THE SCIMITAR WIELDER, REYES.
THE REYES VOLGAN!? THE ONE WHO CAUSED SO MUCH TROUBLE IN MIDDLE SCHOOL!?
I HAD NO IDEA HE ENROLLED HERE...
I'M SO SORRY, CHAIRWOMAN!
WE'LL ESCORT THEM OUT—
NO NEED!

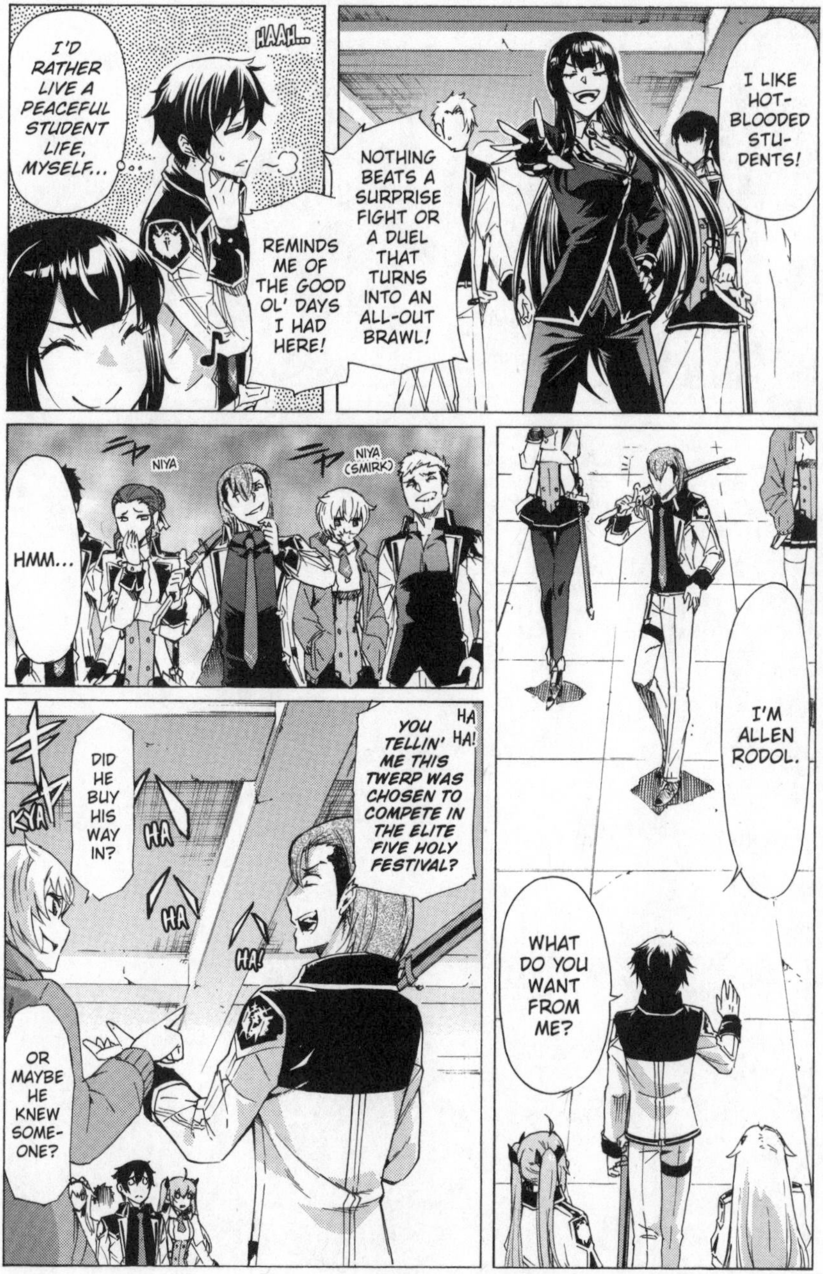
I LIKE HOT-BLOODED STU-DENTS!
NOTHING BEATS A SURPRISE FIGHT OR A DUEL THAT TURNS INTO AN ALL-OUT BRAWL!
REMINDS ME OF THE GOOD OL' DAYS I HAD HERE!
HAAH...
I'D RATHER LIVE A PEACEFUL STUDENT LIFE, MYSELF...
I'M ALLEN RODOL.
WHAT DO YOU WANT FROM ME?
NIYA (SMIRK)
NIYA
HMM...
HA HA!
YOU TELLIN' ME THIS TWERP WAS CHOSEN TO COMPETE IN THE ELITE FIVE HOLY FESTIVAL?
HA
HA
HA!
DID HE BUY HIS WAY IN?
KYA
OR MAYBE HE KNEW SOME-ONE?

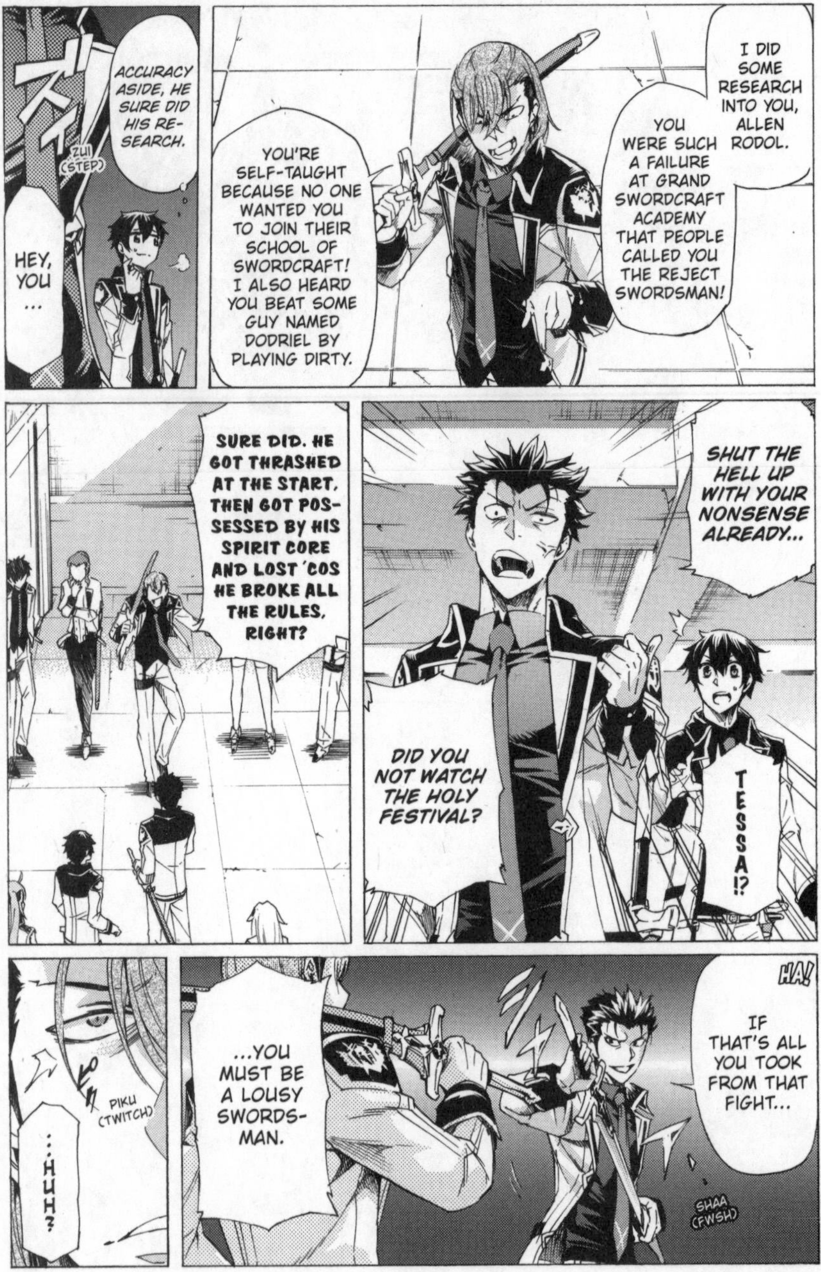
I DID SOME RESEARCH INTO YOU, ALLEN RODOL.
YOU WERE SUCH A FAILURE AT GRAND SWORDCRAFT ACADEMY THAT PEOPLE CALLED YOU THE REJECT SWORDSMAN!
YOU'RE SELF-TAUGHT BECAUSE NO ONE WANTED YOU TO JOIN THEIR SCHOOL OF SWORDCRAFT! I ALSO HEARD YOU BEAT SOME GUY NAMED DODRIEL BY PLAYING DIRTY.
ACCURACY ASIDE, HE SURE DID HIS RE-SEARCH.
ZUI (STEP)
HEY, YOU ...
SHUT THE HELL UP WITH YOUR NONSENSE ALREADY...
TESSA!?
DID YOU NOT WATCH THE HOLY FESTIVAL?
SURE DID. HE GOT THRASHED AT THE START, THEN GOT POS-SESSED BY HIS SPIRIT CORE AND LOST 'COS HE BROKE ALL THE RULES, RIGHT?
HA!
IF THAT'S ALL YOU TOOK FROM THAT FIGHT...
...YOU MUST BE A LOUSY SWORDS-MAN.
SHAA (FWSH)
PIKU (TWITCH)
...HUH?

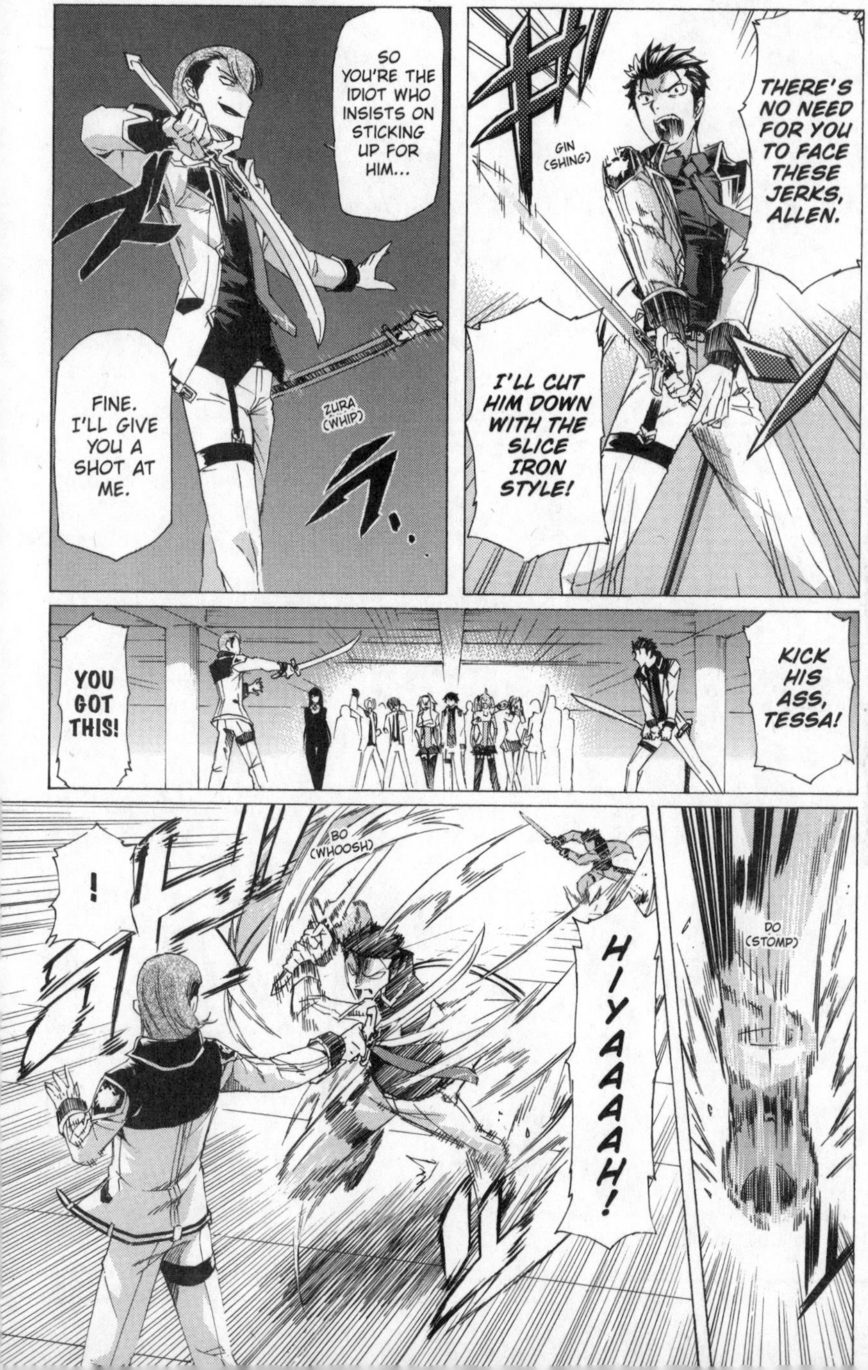
THERE'S NO NEED FOR YOU TO FACE THESE JERKS, ALLEN.
GIN (SHING)
I'LL CUT HIM DOWN WITH THE SLICE IRON STYLE!
SO YOU'RE THE IDIOT WHO INSISTS ON STICKING UP FOR HIM...
FINE. I'LL GIVE YOU A SHOT AT ME.
ZURA (WHIP)
KICK HIS ASS, TESSA!
YOU GOT THIS!
DO (STOMP)
BO (WHOOSH)
HIYAAAAAH!
!

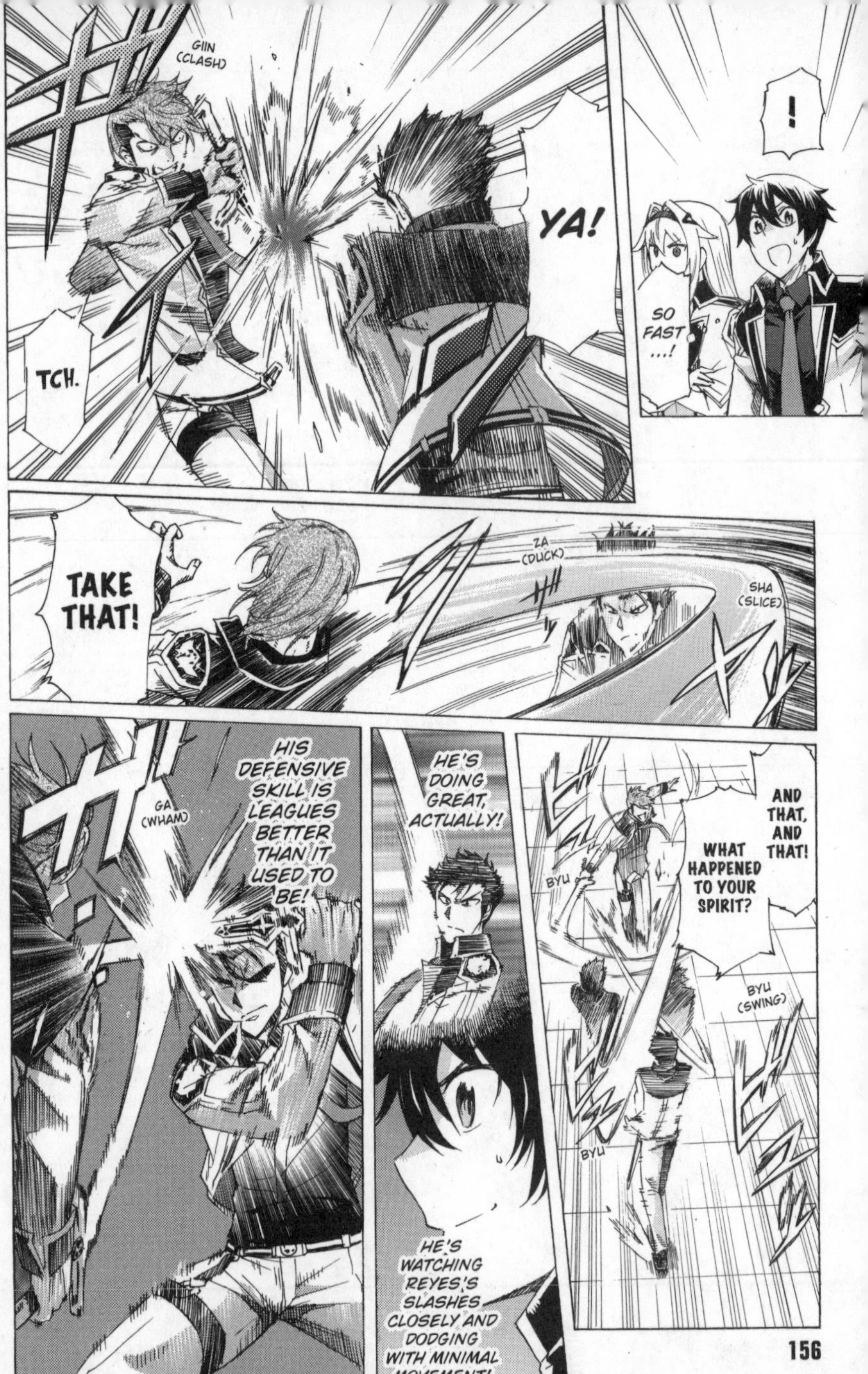
!
SO FAST ...!
YA!
GIIN (CLASH)
TCH.
SHA (SLICE)
ZA (DUCK)
TAKE THAT!
AND THAT, AND THAT!
WHAT HAPPENED TO YOUR SPIRIT?
BYU
BYU (SWING)
BYU
HE'S DOING GREAT, ACTUALLY!
HE'S WATCHING REYES'S SLASHES CLOSELY AND DODGING WITH MINIMAL MOVEMENT!
HIS DEFENSIVE SKILL IS LEAGUES BETTER THAN IT USED TO BE!
GA (WHAM)

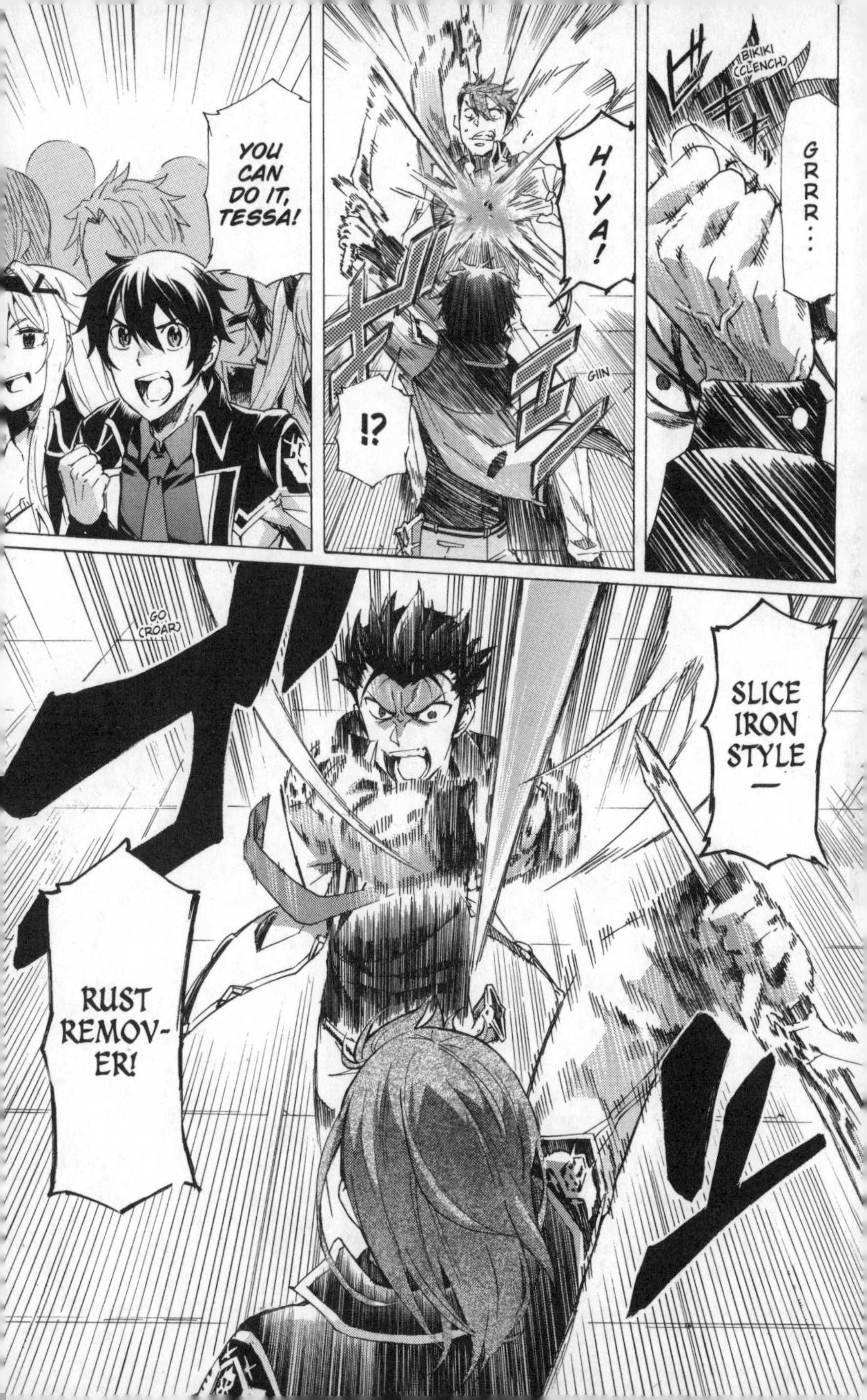
BIKIKI (CLENCH)
GRRR...
HIYA!
GIN
!?
YOU CAN DO IT, TESSA!
SLICE IRON STYLE—
GO (ROAR)
RUST REMOV-ER!

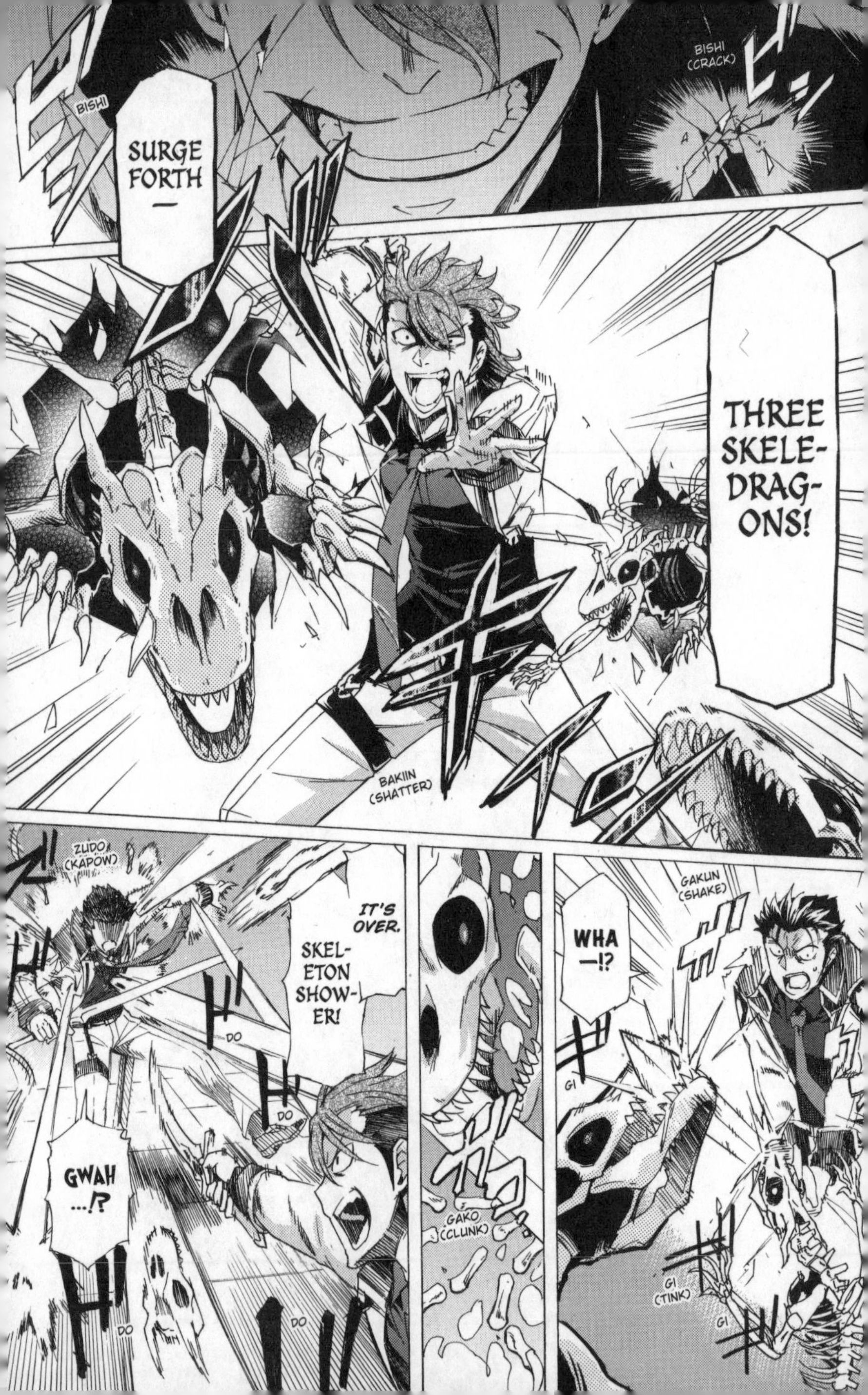
BISHI (CRACK)
BISHI
SURGE FORTH —
THREE SKELE-DRAGONS!
BAKIIN (SHATTER)
GAKUN (SHAKE)
WHA —!?
GI
GI (TINK)
GI
IT'S OVER.
SKEL-ETON SHOW-ER!
GAKO (CLUNK)
ZUDO (KAPOW)
DO
DO
GWAH ...!?
DO
DO

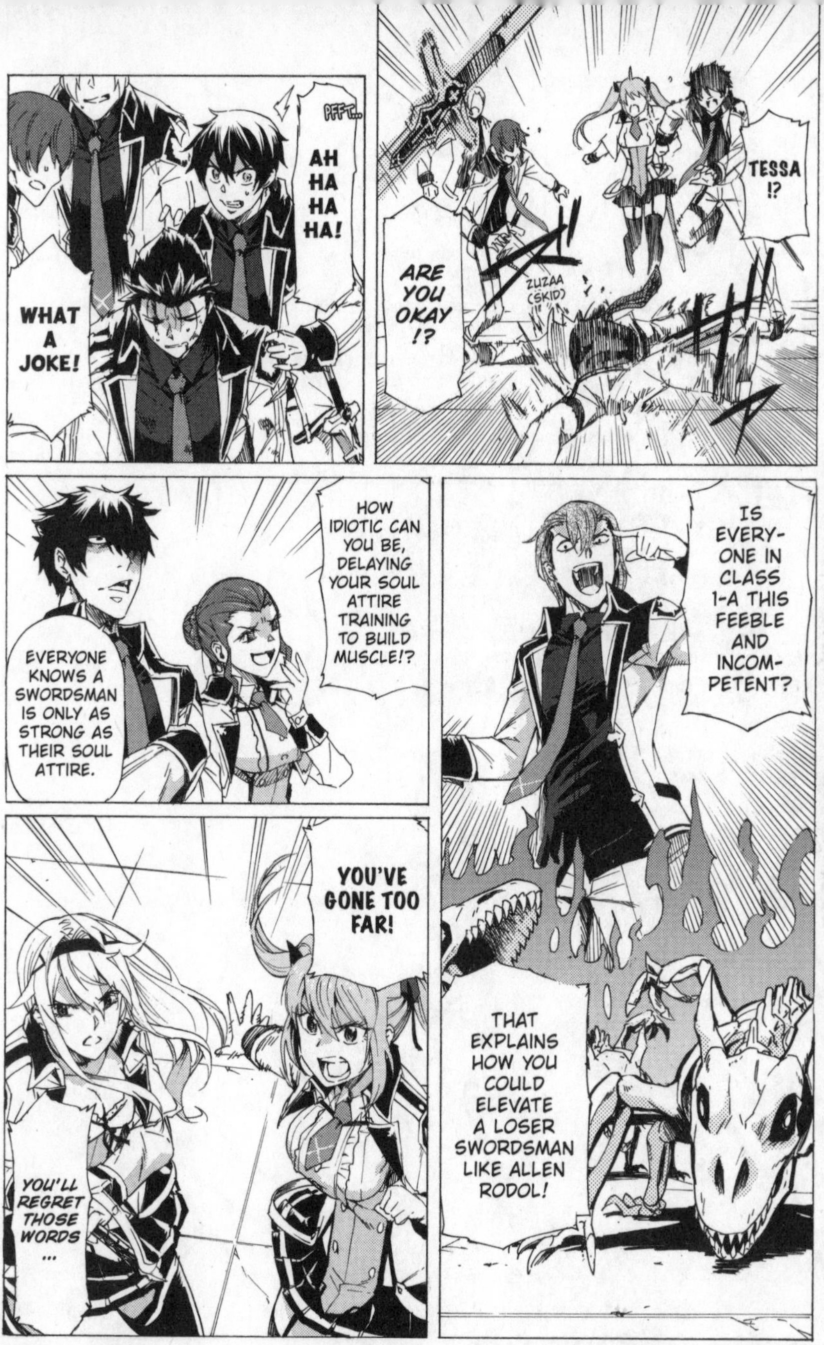
TESSA !?
ZUZAA (SKID)
ARE YOU OKAY !?
PFFT...
AH HA HA HA!
WHAT A JOKE!
IS EVERY-ONE IN CLASS 1-A THIS FEEBLE AND INCOM-PETENT?
THAT EXPLAINS HOW YOU COULD ELEVATE A LOSER SWORDSMAN LIKE ALLEN RODOL!
HOW IDIOTIC CAN YOU BE, DELAYING YOUR SOUL ATTIRE TRAINING TO BUILD MUSCLE!?
EVERYONE KNOWS A SWORDSMAN IS ONLY AS STRONG AS THEIR SOUL ATTIRE.
YOU'VE GONE TOO FAR!
YOU'LL REGRET THOSE WORDS ...

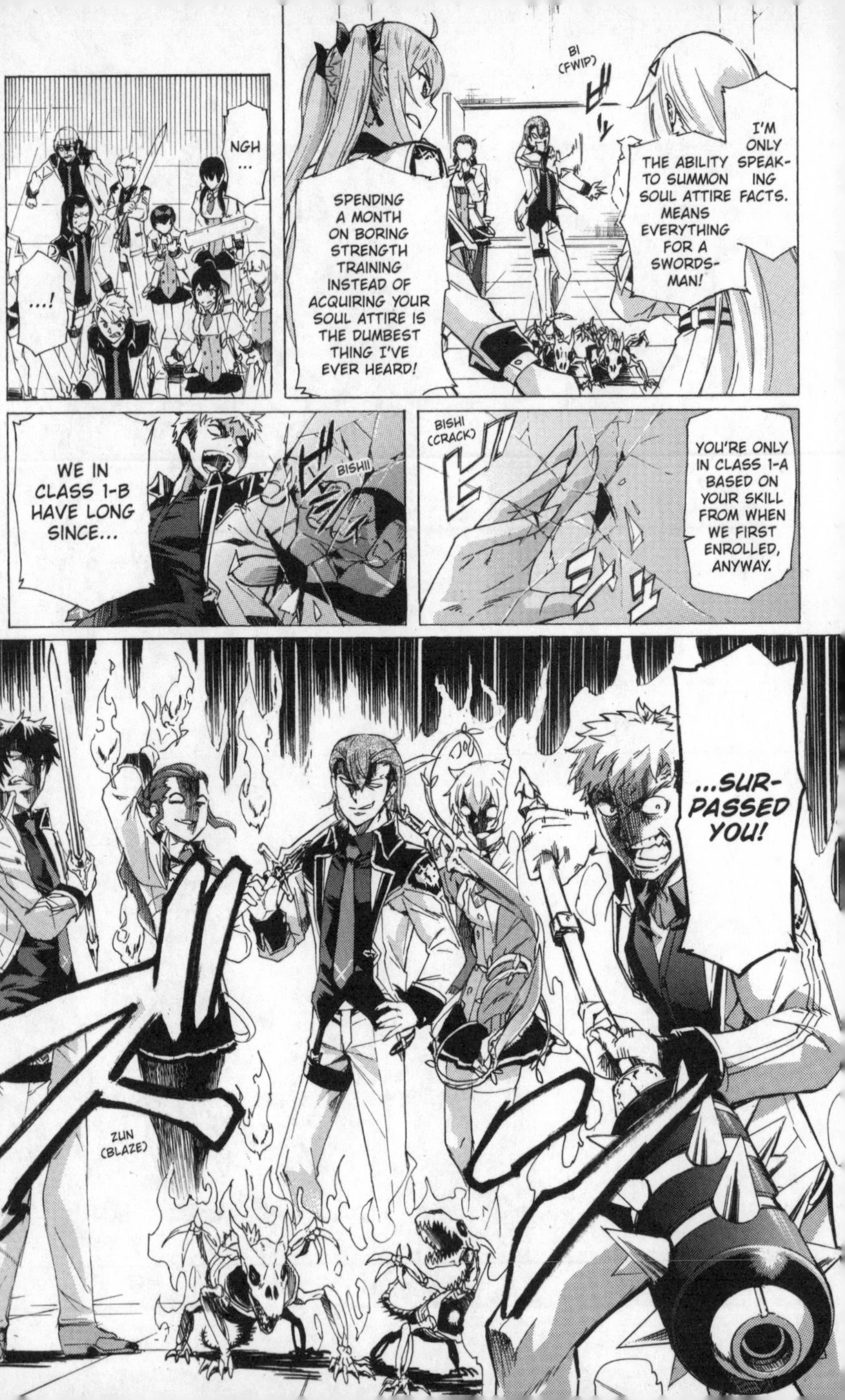
BI (FWIP)
THE ABILITY TO SUMMON SOUL ATTIRE MEANS EVERYTHING FOR A SWORDSMAN!
I'M ONLY SPEAKING FACTS.
SPENDING A MONTH ON BORING STRENGTH TRAINING INSTEAD OF ACQUIRING YOUR SOUL ATTIRE IS THE DUMBEST THING I'VE EVER HEARD!
NGH ...
...!
BISHI (CRACK)
YOU'RE ONLY IN CLASS 1-A BASED ON YOUR SKILL FROM WHEN WE FIRST ENROLLED, ANYWAY.
BISHI!
WE IN CLASS 1-B HAVE LONG SINCE...
...SUR-PASSED YOU!
ZUN (BLAZE)

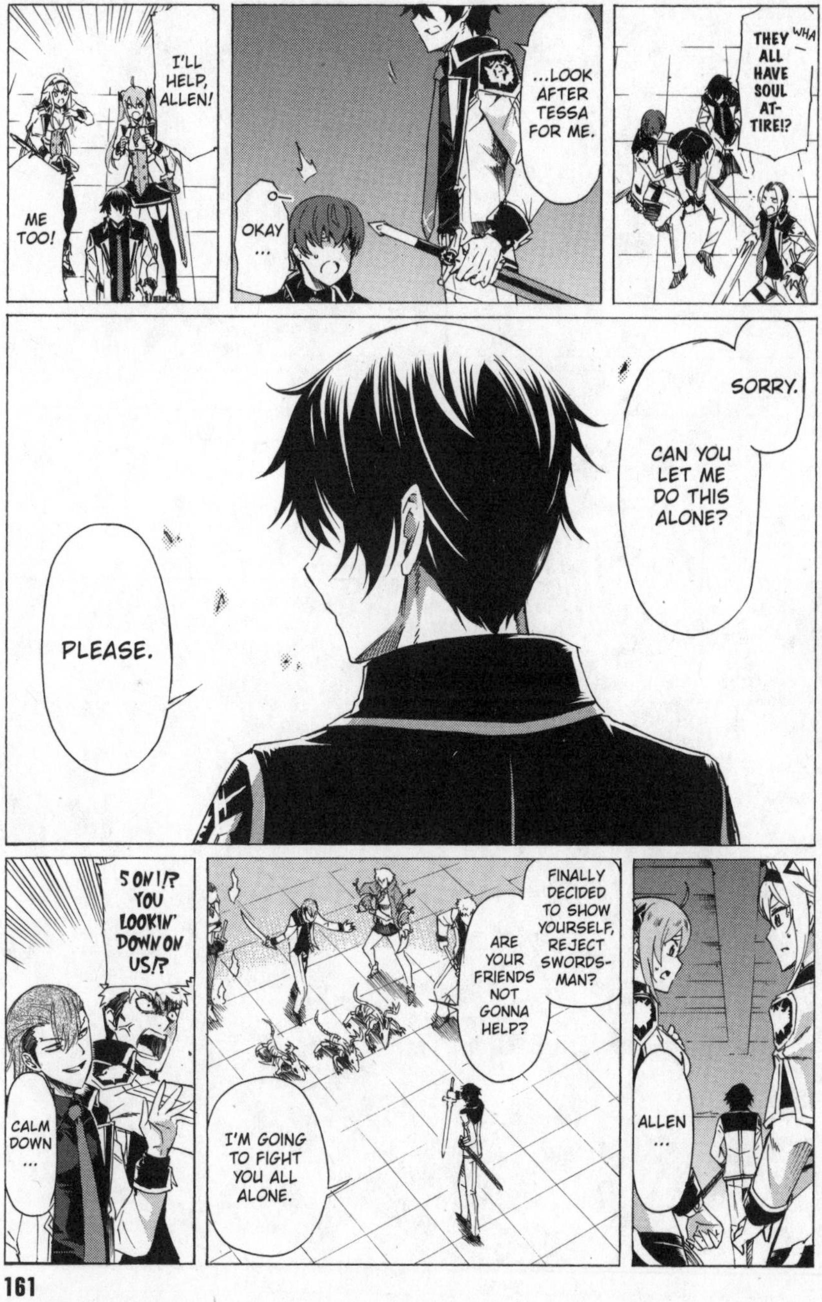
THEY ALL HAVE SOUL AT-TIRE!?
WHA—
...LOOK AFTER TESSA FOR ME.
O- OKAY...
I'LL HELP, ALLEN!
ME TOO!
SORRY.
CAN YOU LET ME DO THIS ALONE?
PLEASE.
ALLEN...
FINALLY DECIDED TO SHOW YOURSELF, REJECT SWORDS-MAN?
ARE YOUR FRIENDS NOT GONNA HELP?
I'M GOING TO FIGHT YOU ALL ALONE.
5 ON 1!? YOU LOOKIN' DOWN ON US!?
CALM DOWN...

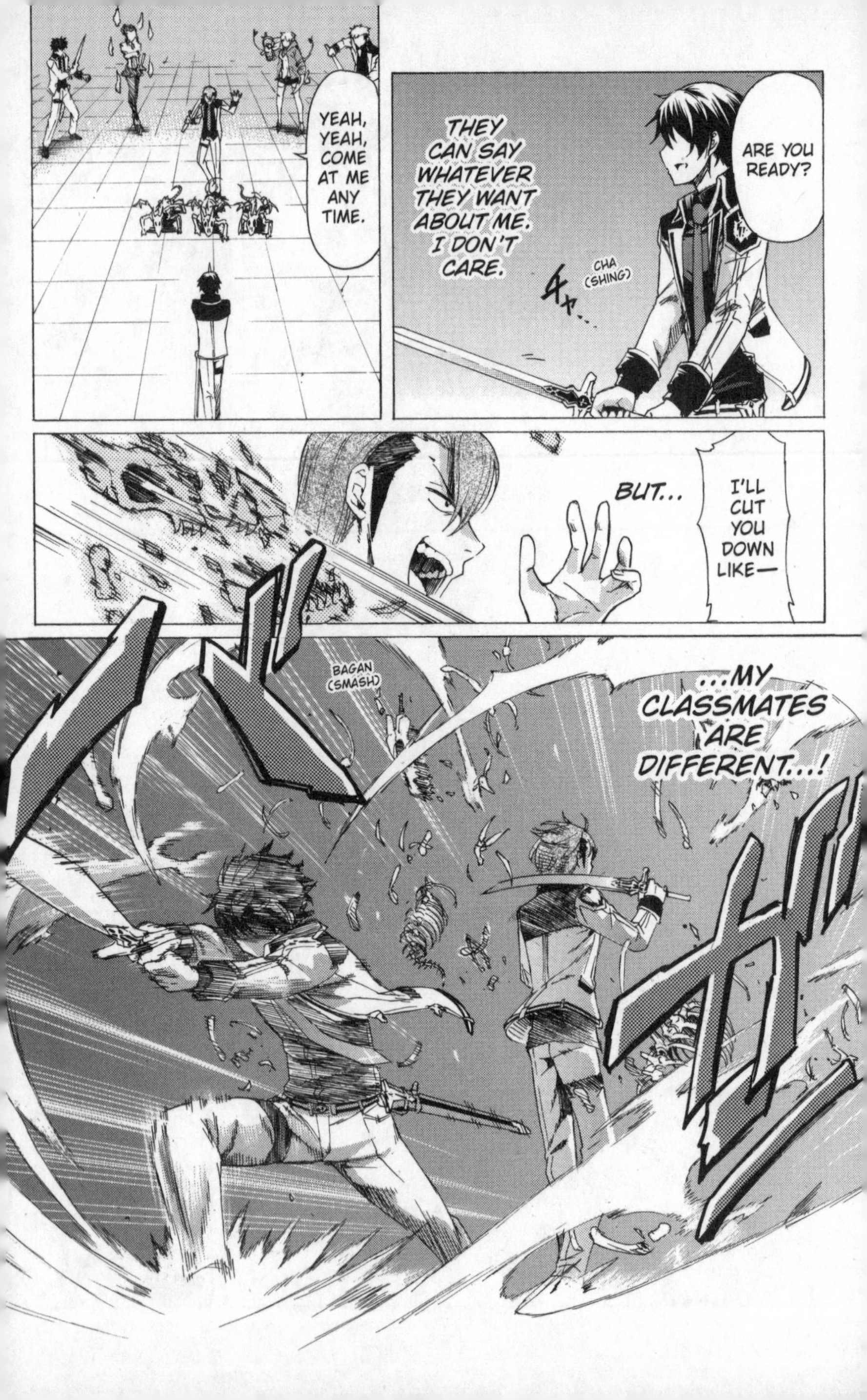
ARE YOU READY?
THEY CAN SAY WHATEVER THEY WANT ABOUT ME. I DON'T CARE.
CHA (SHING)
YEAH, YEAH, COME AT ME ANY TIME.
I'LL CUT YOU DOWN LIKE—
BUT...
...MY CLASSMATES ARE DIFFERENT...!
BAGAN (SMASH)

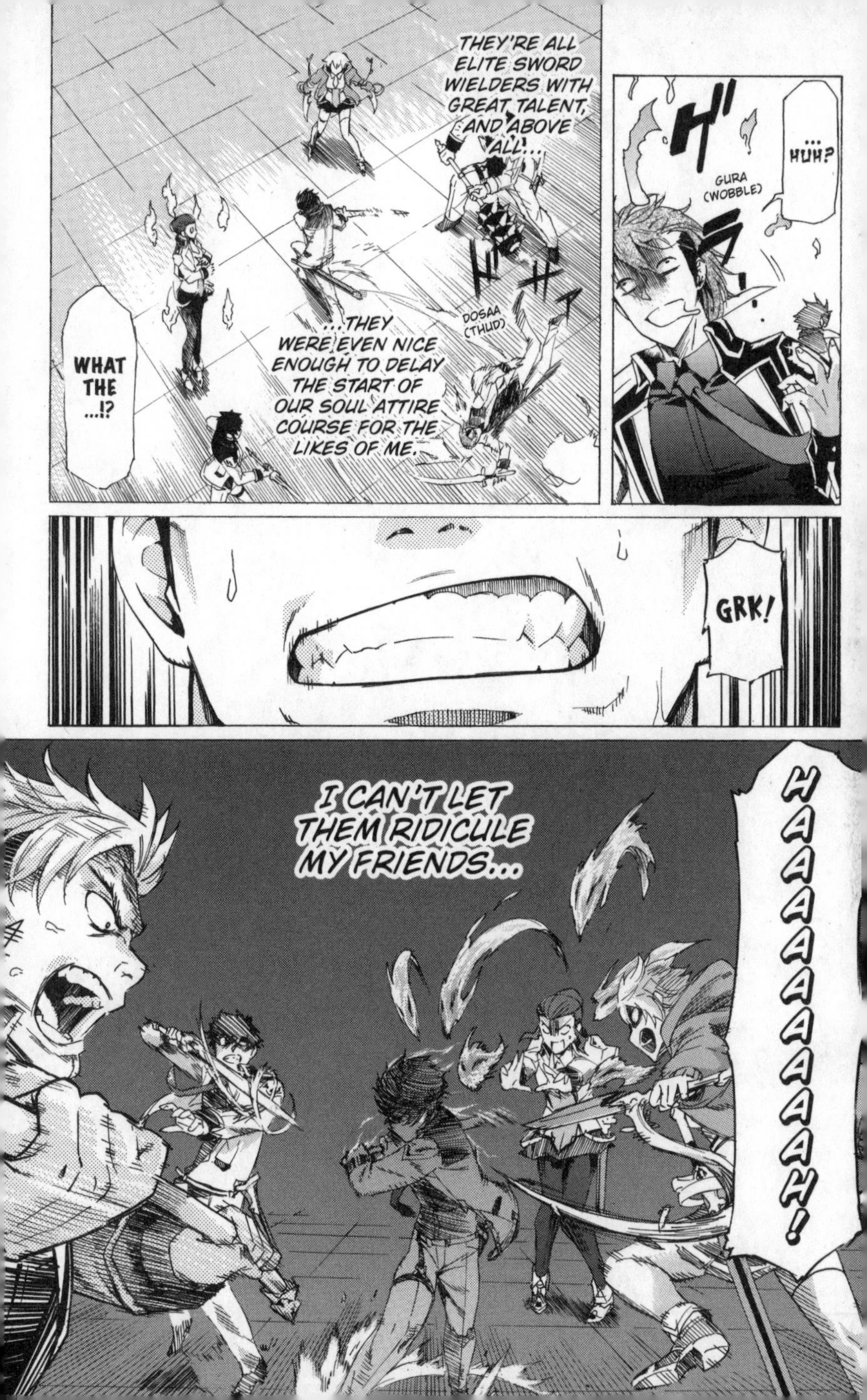

...HUH?
GURA (WOBBLE)
THEY'RE ALL ELITE SWORD WIELDERS WITH GREAT TALENT, AND ABOVE ALL...
DOSAA (THUD)
...THEY WERE EVEN NICE ENOUGH TO DELAY THE START OF OUR SOUL ATTIRE COURSE FOR THE LIKES OF ME.
WHAT THE ...!?
GRK!
HAAAAAAAAAAAAAH!
I CAN'T LET THEM RIDICULE MY FRIENDS...

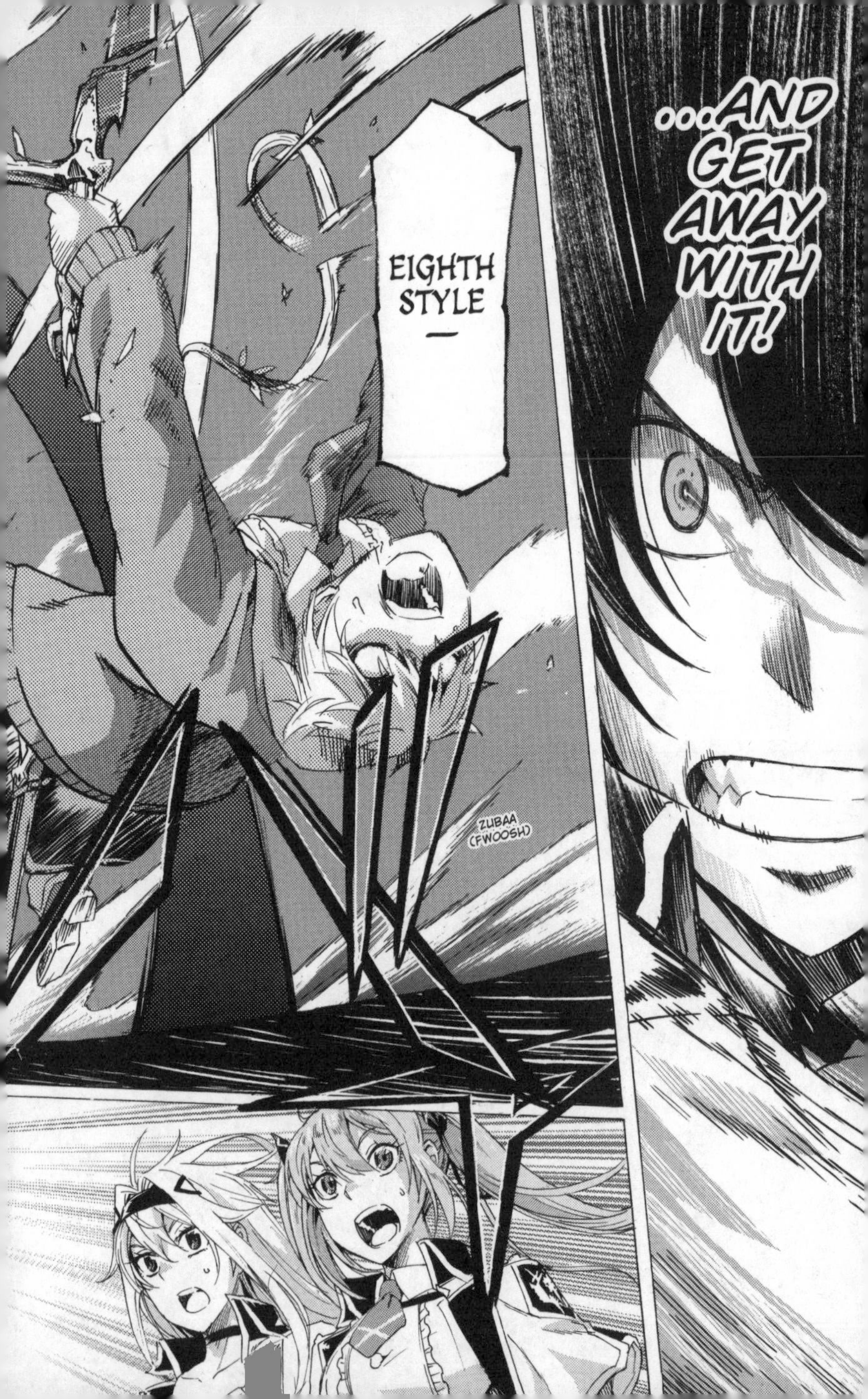
...AND GET AWAY WITH IT!
EIGHTH STYLE —
ZUBAA (FWOOSH)

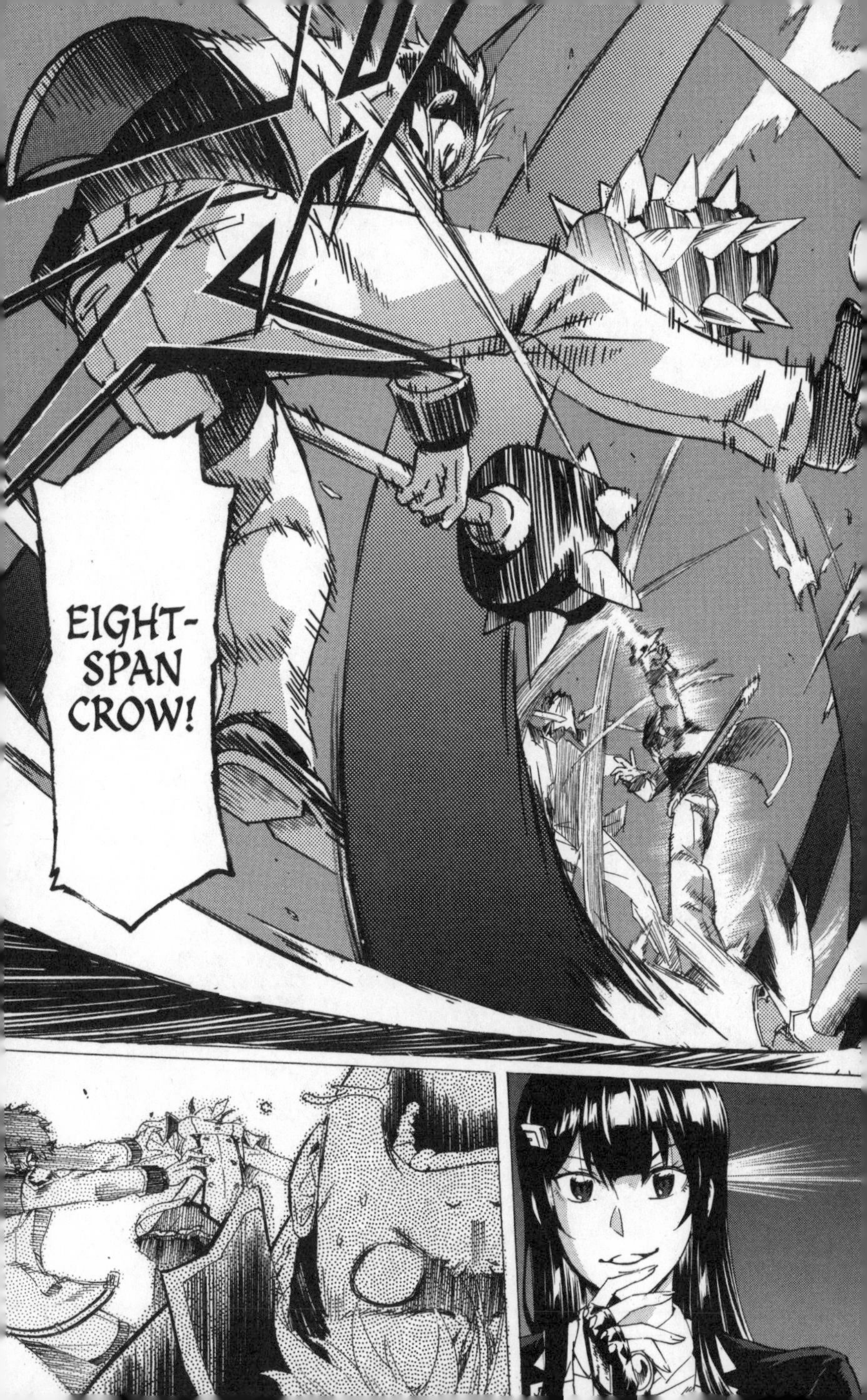
EIGHT-SPAN CROW!

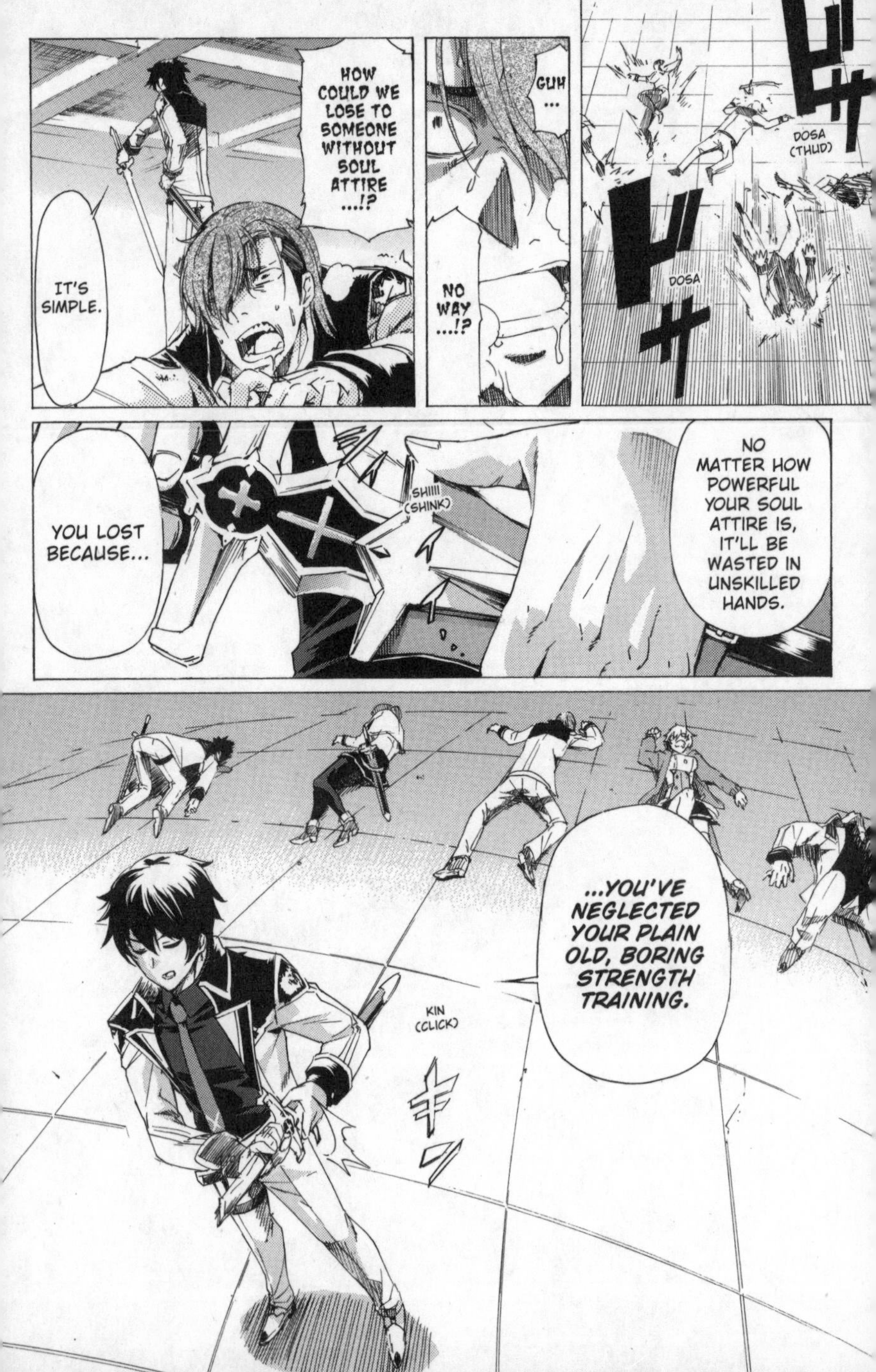
DOSA (THUD)
DOSA
GUH ...
NO WAY ...!?
HOW COULD WE LOSE TO SOMEONE WITHOUT SOUL ATTIRE ...!?
IT'S SIMPLE.
NO MATTER HOW POWERFUL YOUR SOUL ATTIRE IS, IT'LL BE WASTED IN UNSKILLED HANDS.
SHIIII (SHINK)
YOU LOST BECAUSE...
...YOU'VE NEGLECTED YOUR PLAIN OLD, BORING STRENGTH TRAINING.
KIN (CLICK)

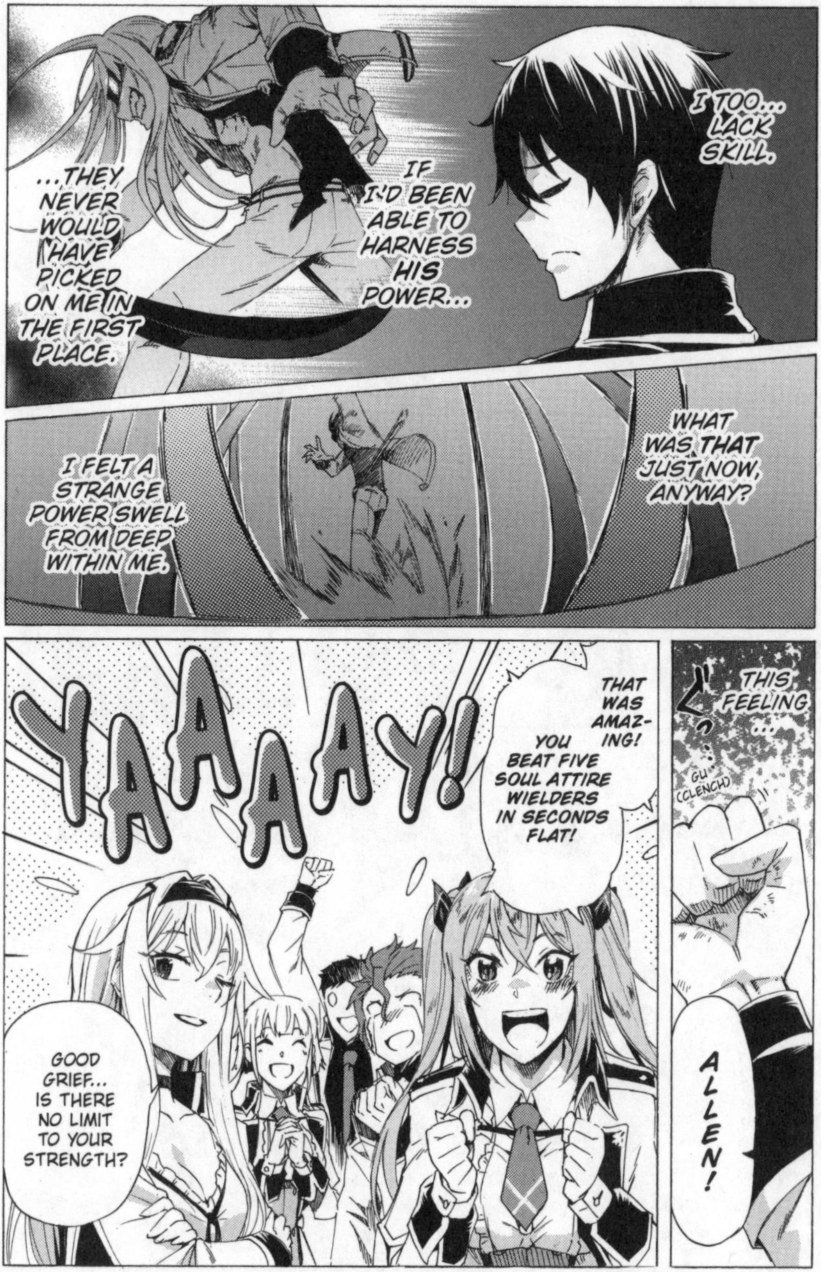
I TOO... LACK SKILL.
IF I'D BEEN ABLE TO HARNESS HIS POWER...
...THEY NEVER WOULD HAVE PICKED ON ME IN THE FIRST PLACE.
WHAT WAS THAT JUST NOW, ANYWAY?
I FELT A STRANGE POWER SWELL FROM DEEP WITHIN ME.
THIS FEELING...
GU (CLENCH)
ALLEN!
YAAAAY!
THAT WAS AMAZING! YOU BEAT FIVE SOUL ATTIRE WIELDERS IN SECONDS FLAT!
GOOD GRIEF... IS THERE NO LIMIT TO YOUR STRENGTH?

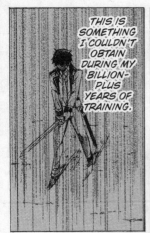

YOU GUYS ...!
THAT'S OUR ALLEN!
WE'VE GOTTA STEP IT UP!
OH...I THINK I'M STARTING TO GET IT.
THIS IS SOMETHING I COULDN'T OBTAIN DURING MY BILLION-PLUS YEARS OF TRAINING.
THE SPIRIT AND DETERMINATION TO FIGHT FOR MY CLASSMATES. THE RESOLVE TO WIN NO MATTER WHAT.
IF THIS IS THE "STRENGTH OF MY HEART" HE WAS TALKING ABOUT...
THEN I KNOW...
MY BAD.
...I CAN KEEP GETTING STRONGER!
BUT DON'T BE SO RECK-LESS!

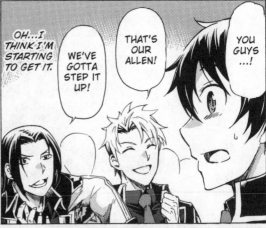

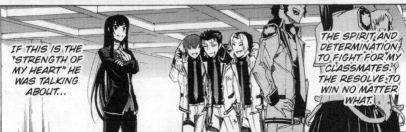

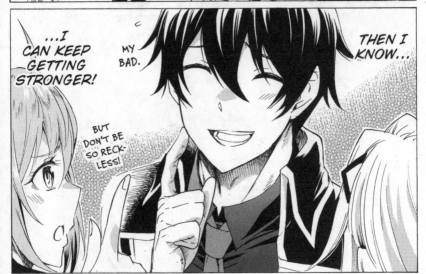

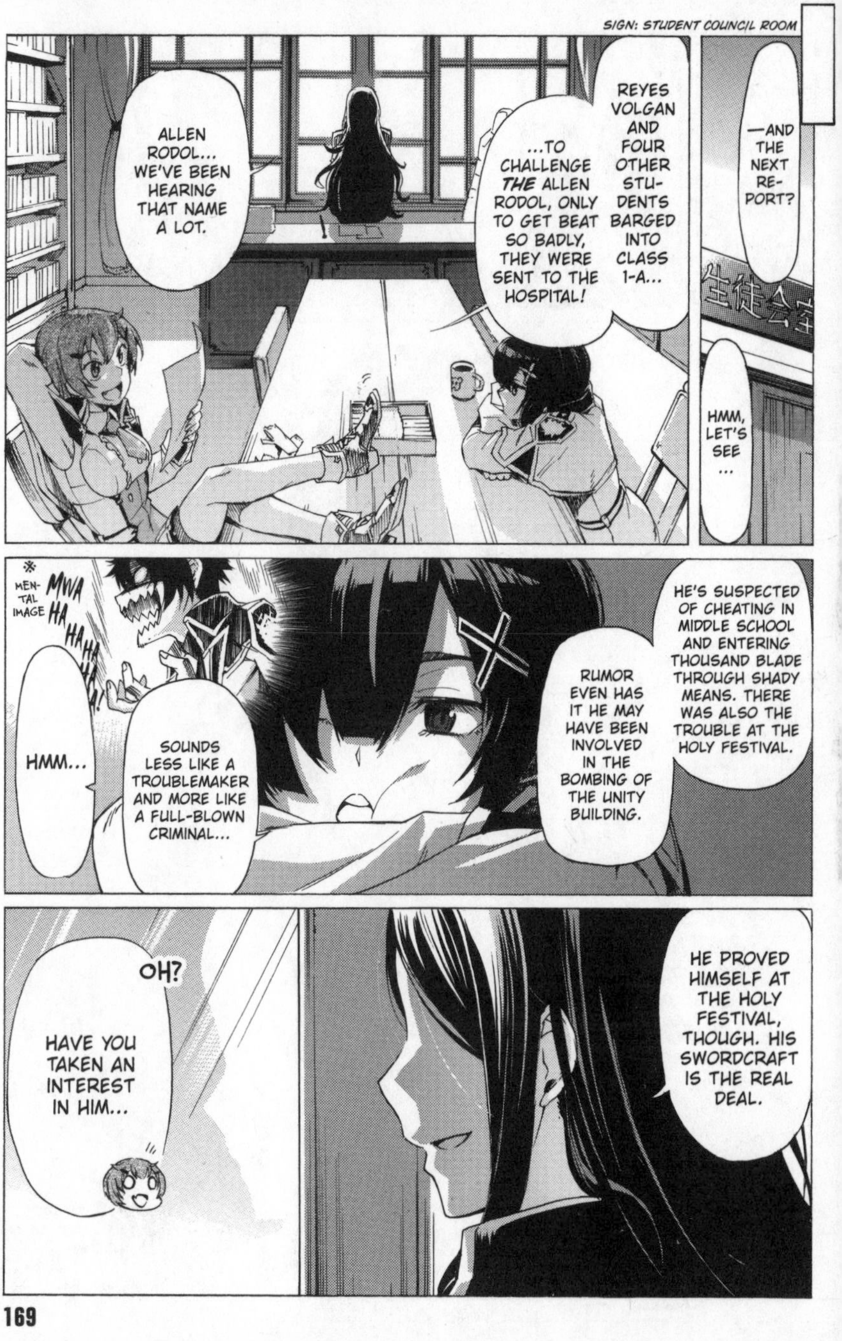
SIGN: STUDENT COUNCIL ROOM
—AND THE NEXT REPORT?
HMM, LET'S SEE...
REYES VOLGAN AND FOUR OTHER STUDENTS BARGED INTO CLASS 1-A...
...TO CHALLENGE *THE* ALLEN RODOL, ONLY TO GET BEAT SO BADLY, THEY WERE SENT TO THE HOSPITAL!
ALLEN RODOL... WE'VE BEEN HEARING THAT NAME A LOT.
HE'S SUSPECTED OF CHEATING IN MIDDLE SCHOOL AND ENTERING THOUSAND BLADE THROUGH SHADY MEANS. THERE WAS ALSO THE TROUBLE AT THE HOLY FESTIVAL.
RUMOR EVEN HAS IT HE MAY HAVE BEEN INVOLVED IN THE BOMBING OF THE UNITY BUILDING.
SOUNDS LESS LIKE A TROUBLEMAKER AND MORE LIKE A FULL-BLOWN CRIMINAL...
※ MENTAL IMAGE
MWA HA HA HA HA HA!
HMM...
HE PROVED HIMSELF AT THE HOLY FESTIVAL, THOUGH. HIS SWORDCRAFT IS THE REAL DEAL.
OH?
HAVE YOU TAKEN AN INTEREST IN HIM...

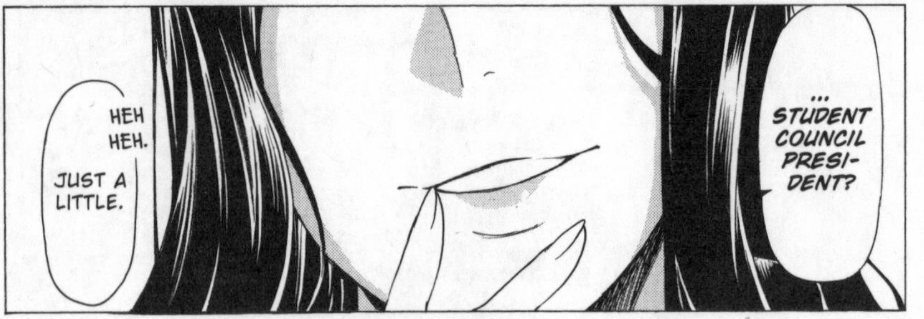
...STUDENT COUNCIL PRESI- DENT?
HEH HEH.
JUST A LITTLE.
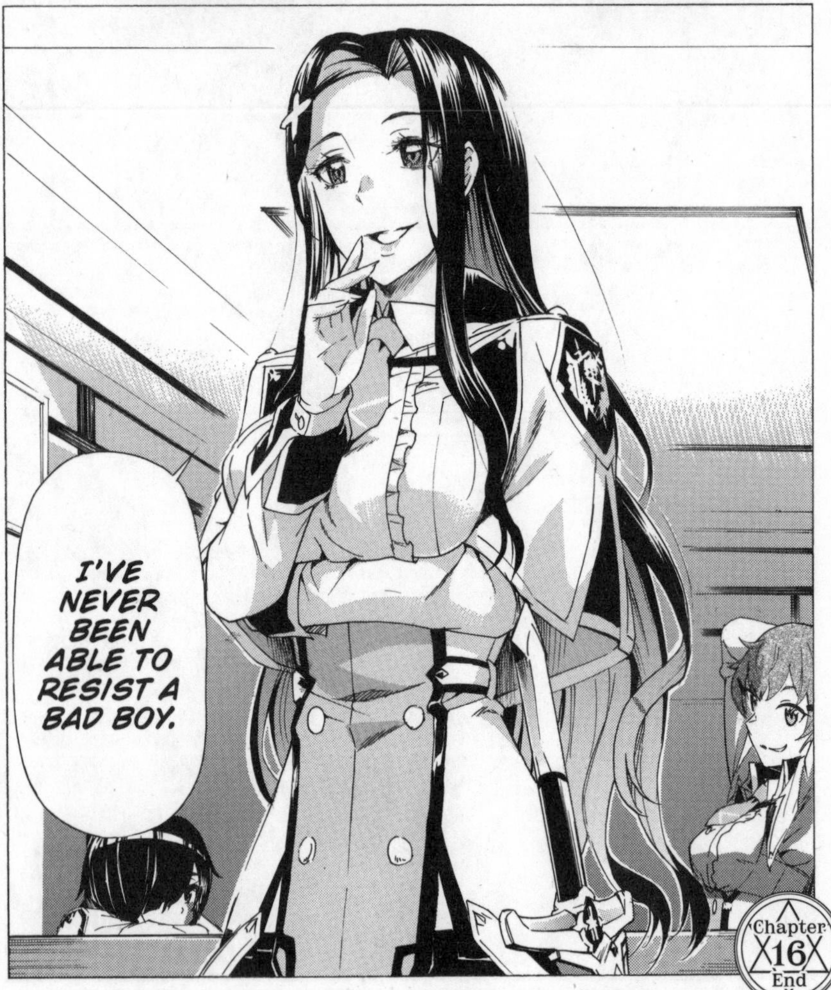
I'VE NEVER BEEN ABLE TO RESIST A BAD BOY.
Chapter 16 End

AFTERWORD

HUH!?

THANK YOU VERY MUCH FOR PURCHASING VOLUME 3 OF THE *100-MILLION-YEAR BUTTON* MANGA! THIS WAS ANOTHER REWARDING ISSUE TO DRAW. IT STARTED WITH A BALD-HEADED BEEFCAKE AND ENDED WITH A LONG SILVER-HAIRED BEEFCAKE...IS THIS A MUSCLE MANGA...? ALL KIDDING ASIDE, I HOPE YOU ENJOYED IT. NOW THAT I THINK ABOUT IT, THIS IS MY FIRST-EVER THIRD VOLUME. I'LL KEEP WORKING HARD TO PUT OUT MORE. MAY WE MEET AGAIN IN VOLUME 4.

YUTARO SHIDO

THE 8 BOOB MUSKETEERS OF VOLUME 8

YUTARO SHIDO
Original Story
SYUICHI TSUKISHIMA
Character Design
MOKYU

I KEPT PRESSING THE 100-MILLION-YEAR BUTTON AND CAME OUT ON TOP
~THE UNBEATABLE REJECT SWORDSMAN~
3

Translation **DANIEL LUKE HUTTON**   Lettering **ARBASH MUGHAL**

ICHIOKUNEN BUTTON WO RENDA SHITA ORE WA, KIZUITARA SAIKYO NI NATTE ITA ~RAKUDAI KENSHI NO GAKUIN MUSO~ Volume 3
©Syuichi Tsukishima, Mokyu 2022
©Yutaro Shido 2022
First published in Japan in 2022 by KADOKAWA CORPORATION, Tokyo. English translation rights arranged with KADOKAWA CORPORATION, Tokyo through TUTTLE-MORI AGENCY, INC., Tokyo.

English translation © 2023 by Yen Press, LLC

Yen Press
150 West 30th Street, 19th Floor
New York, NY 10001

Visit us!
yenpress.com • facebook.com/yenpress • twitter.com/yenpress
yenpress.tumblr.com • instagram.com/yenpress

First Yen Press Edition: July 2023
Edited by Yen Press Editorial: Jacquelyn Li, Carl Li
Designed by Yen Press Design: Andy Swist

Yen Press is an imprint of Yen Press, LLC.
The Yen Press name and logo are trademarks of Yen Press, LLC.

Library of Congress Control Number: 2022940150
ISBNs: 978-1-9753-6293-5 (paperback)
978-1-9753-6294-2 (ebook)

10 9 8 7 6 5 4 3 2 1

WOR

Printed in the United States of America